Introduction to
EDUCATION

Introduction to EDUCATION

Robert F. Hessong
Thomas H. Weeks

Butler University

MACMILLAN PUBLISHING COMPANY
NEW YORK

Collier Macmillan Publishers
London

Macmillan Publishing Company
866 Third Avenue, New York, New York 10022

Collier Macmillan Canada, Inc.

Library of Congress Cataloging-in-Publication Data

Hessong, Robert F.
  Introduction to education.

  Bibliography: p.
  Includes index.
  1. Education—United States—History.   2. Educational
sociology—United States.   3. Education—Philosophy.
4. Educational law and legislation—United States.
5. Education and state—United States.   6. School
management and organization—United States.   I. Weeks,
Thomas H. (Thomas Harold).   II. Title.
LA205.H47   1978   370'.973   86–2918
ISBN 0–02–354380–9

Printing: 1 2 3 4 5 6 7   Year: 7 8 9 0 1 2 3

Acknowledgments

Permission has been granted to quote from the following publications:

Edward Magnuson, ''Child Abuse: The Ultimate Betrayal,'' *Time*, 122 (Sept. 5, 1983). Copyright ©
     1983 Time Inc. All rights reserved. Reprinted by permission from TIME.
Alice Rossi, ''Equality of the Sexes: An Immodest Proposal,'' *Daedalus*, ''Women in America,''
     93(2), 1964, pp. 647–649. Reprinted by permission of the author, and *Daedalus*, Journal of
     the American Academy of Arts and Sciences, Boston, MA.
James A. Banks, *Teaching Strategies for Ethnic Studies*, Third Edition. Newton, MA: Allyn and
     Bacon, 1984. Reprinted by permission.
Allen C. Ornstein, ''Teacher Salaries, Past, Present, Future,'' *Phi Delta Kappan*, June 1980. Re-
     printed by permission of the publisher and the author.
Chris Pipho, ''Rich States, Poor States,'' *Phi Delta Kappan*, June 1981. Reprinted by permission of
     the publisher and the author.
Edward F. DeRoche et al., ''A Survey of Teacher Supply and Demand in the West,'' *Phi Delta
     Kappan*, April 1982. Reprinted by permission of the publisher and the author.

ISBN   0-02-354380-9

Thomas R. McDaniel, "Exploring Alternatives to Punishment: The Keys to Effective Discipline," *Phi Delta Kappan*, March 1980. Reprinted by permission of the publisher and the author.

Charles S. Benson, *Educational Finance in the Coming Decade*. Bloomington, IN: Phi Delta Kappa, 1975. Reprinted by permission of the publisher.

William B. Lauderdale, *Progressive Education: Lessons from Three Schools*. Bloomington, IN: Phi Delta Kappa, 1981. Reprinted by permission of the publisher.

Gerald L. Gutek, *Basic Education: A Historical Perspective*. Bloomington, IN: Phi Delta Kappa, 1981. Reprinted by permission of the publisher.

Merrill Harmin, "What I've Learned About Values Education," *Fastback #91*. Bloomington, IN: Phi Delta Kappa, 1981. Reprinted by permission of the publisher.

Cecilia H. Foxley, *Nonsexist Counseling: Helping Women and Men Re-define Their Roles*. Copyright © 1979 by Kendall/Hunt Publishing Company. Reprinted by permission.

Clifton Johnson, *Old-Time Schools and School Books*. New York: Dover Publications, Inc., 1963. Reprinted by permission.

Jon Wiles and Joseph C. Bondi, *Curriculum Development: A Guide to Practice*. Columbus, OH: Charles E. Merrill Publishing Company, 1984. Reprinted by permission.

Benjamin S. Bloom et al. (Eds.), *Taxonomy of Educational Objectives: Handbook I: Congnitive Domain*. Copyright © 1956 by Longman Inc. Reprinted by permission of Longman Inc., New York.

Roald F. Campbell, *The Organization and Control of American Schools*, Fourth Edition. Columbus, OH: Charles E. Merrill Publishing Company, 1980. Reprinted by permission.

"How Should Schools Be Ruled?" Reprinted by permission of the Association for Supervision and Cirriculum Development. Copyright © 1980 by the Association for Supervision and Cirriculum Development. All rights reserved.

Marshall O. Donley, *Power to the Teacher*. Bloomington, IN: Indiana University Press. Reprinted by permission.

William Edward Eaton, *The American Federation of Teachers, 1916–1961: A History of the Movement*. Carbondale, IL: Southern Illinois University Press, 1975. Reprinted by permission.

Thomas J. Flygare, "Collective Bargaining in the Public Schools," *Fastback #99*. Bloomington, IN: Phi Delta Kappa, 1977. Reprinted by permission of the publisher.

Ruth L. Ault, *Children's Cognitive Development*, Second Edition. Copyright © 1977, 1983 by Oxford University Press, Inc. Reprinted by permission.

Darlene B. Bordeaux, "How to Get Kids to Do What is Expected of Them." *Clearing House*, 55, 1982, pp. 273–278, a publication of the Helen Dwight Reid Educational Foundation.

Denis P. Doyle, "Your Meager Slice of New Federalism Could Contain Delicious Options for Schools." Reprinted by permission, from *The American School Board Journal*, April 1982. Copyright © 1982 by the National School Boards Association. All rights reserved.

S. Strong, "It's Time to Get Tough on Alcohol and Drug Abuse in Schools." Reprinted by permission, from *The American School Board Journal*, February 1983. Copyright © 1983 by the National School Boards Association. All rights reserved.

Brian G. Fraser, *The Educator and Child Abuse*. Chicago, IL: National Committee for Prevention of Child Abuse, 1977. Reprinted by permission.

Terrel H. Bell, *A Philosophy of Education for the Space Age*. Pompano Beach, FL: Exposition Press, 1962. Reprinted by permission.

Allan M. West, *The National Education Association: The Power Base for Education*. Copyright © 1980 by The Free Press, a Division of Macmillan, Inc. Reprinted by permission of the publisher.

Edgar B. Wesley, *NEA: The First Hundred Years*. Copyright © 1957 by Edgar B. Wesley. Reprinted by permission of Harper & Row, Publishers, Inc.

Frederick C. Gruber, *Historical and Contemporary Philosophies of Education*. Copyright © 1973 by Harper & Row, Publishers, Inc. Reprinted by permission of Harper & Row, Publishers, Inc.

Jerry J. Herman, *Administrator's Practical Guide to School Finance*. Copyright © 1977 by Parker Publishing Company, Inc., West Nyack, New York. Reprinted by permission of the publisher.

Roe L. Johns and Edgar L. Morphet, *The Economics and Financing of Education: A Systems Approach*, Third Edition. Copyright © 1975 by Prentice-Hall, Inc., Englewood Cliffs, NJ. Reprinted by permission of the publisher.

Walter I. Garms, James W. Guthrie, and Lawrence C. Pierce, *School Finance: The Economics and Politics of Public Education.* Copyright © 1978 by Prentice-Hall, Inc., Englewood Cliffs, NJ. Reprinted by permission of the publisher.

NEA Handbook, 1985–86. Reprinted by permission of the National Education Association, Washington, DC.

Dickson J. Preston, *Young Frederick Douglass, The Maryland Years.* Baltimore: The Johns Hopkins University Press, 1980. Reprinted by permission.

Adolphe E. Meyer, *Grandmasters of Educational Thought.* New York: McGraw-Hill, 1975. Reprinted by permission.

Lewis Flint Anderson, *Pestalozzi.* New York: McGraw-Hill, 1931. Reprinted by permission.

R. Freeman Butts, *A Cultural History of Western Education.* New York: McGraw-Hill, 1955. Reprinted by permission of the author.

F. Bruce Rosen, *Philosophic Systems and Education.* Columbus, OH: Charles E. Merrill Publishing Company, 1968. Reprinted by permission.

John J. Callahan and William H. Wilken (Eds.), *School Finance Reform: A Legislator's Handbook.* Denver, CO: National Conference of State Legislatures, 1976. Reprinted by permission.

Henry Campbell Black, *Black's Law Dictionary*, Fifth Edition. St. Paul, MN: West Publishing Company, 1979. Reprinted by permission.

The Random House College Dictionary, 1980 Revised Edition. New York: Random House, 1980. Reprinted by permission.

Lawrence A. Cremin, *The Transformation of the School.* New York: Random House, 1961. Reprinted by permission.

George F. Kneller, *Introduction to the Philosophy of Education.* New York, John Wiley & Sons, Inc., 1971. Reprinted by permission.

To our wives, Dotty and Kathy, whose patience and understanding made the completion of this work possible

Preface

This book is designed to present foundations of education material to the beginner in teacher education, the graduate student in education, and to the layperson interested in schools. Potential and current school board members will find this book helpful in gaining the perspectives on the primary issues that affect schools and education today.

At Butler we are recommending that our students obtain the textbook for their first course in foundations, currently known as "Concepts of Education," taken during their sophomore year; and keep the book for a course called "Exit Foundations," taken during their senior year. The book will serve as a handbook during this important learning and developmental period.

Organization

The chapters are ordered so that instruction and learning may logically begin with Chapter 1 and move sequentially through the text. The major and traditional units of foundations are placed at the beginning of the book; social, historical, and philosophical foundations are covered in the first seven chapters. The study of the curriculum from past, present, and future perspectives is the next content area, followed by the law and education, control and governance, finance, teacher organizations, and a unit on orientation to teaching.

The general organization of material moves from the general to the specific. However, as the units and chapters can stand on their own, the sequencing of topics can easily be left up to the individual instructor. For instance, Chapter 16 on "Planning for Teaching" could logically be taken out of the established sequence; and for those who place a heavy emphasis on teacher organizations, Chapter 15 could be an earlier selection. Instructors benefit when material can be ordered conveniently to fit their own special interest areas, their teaching styles, and the learning styles of their students.

Theoretical Base

In Chapter 1 of the sociology unit are identified most of the important social issues that have an impact on the schools. Chapter 2 follows up with discussions of how schools are responding to this impact. It is the authors' wish that students will thus have some practical solutions for problems that they can apply in their work as teachers. Graduate students in foundations should be able to relate well to this unit, gaining new insight and relating their own experiences and ideas to the issues.

In the history unit is presented a sequential history of education, built around significant headings and divided among three chapters; we feel that the logical headings highlight the accomplishments in each area. Chapter 3 explores the ancient foundations of education and European ideas, because it is important for students to know that American educational history did not begin with the colonial settlements but rather has much older roots. Chapter 4 presents the more traditional material about the three colonial areas and their educational contributions, which have been identified by many authors. The federal, private, and public sections in Chapters 4 and 5 will serve to provide the reader with an understanding of the contributions of these areas to the growth of education in America and of the logical relationships between them.

The philosophy unit, Chapters 6 and 7, is designed to help the student understand the traditional philosophies (as they apply to education), the educational philosophies, and their applications to current practices in education. The curriculum chapter, Chapter 8, is based on twelve significant questions that should give the student a broad understanding of curricular background. From Chapters 9 and 10, students will be able to gain an understanding of the sources of law, the court system, and the many ways in which the law is applied to schools and to teachers. In Chapters 11–14, the governance, control, and financing of education are discussed in detail, and the state, local, and federal aspects of each topic are explored. These same chapters could be used as a separate course. Chapter 15 reviews the background of educational organizations and outlines the collective bargaining process. The final chapter, Chapter 16, "Planning for Teaching," is intended to give the prospective teacher a realistic picture of the teaching profession, pointing out both its stresses and its benefits.

Learning Aids

Two of the most useful learning/reading aids are the introduction and summary of each chapter. Each unit of subject matter is followed by a list of *questions* for the reading; these questions can serve as a review, as a stimulus before reading, or as a point of departure for a class discussion. The *activities* are placed at the end of each unit to serve as hands-on or involvement projects; activities include interviews, debates, simulations, and research topics. A list of references is placed near the end of the book to facilitate the search for more information on a chapter topic. An appendix useful to the reader is placed in the back of the book. It contains key educational dates, the NEA Code of Ethics, the AFT Bill of Rights, and a list of professional organizations. Additional aids to learning are located in the instructor's manual, which includes suggestions for organizing the course with either a traditional or a progressive approach.

Acknowledgments

We gratefully acknowledge the assistance of many dedicated people in the writing of this book. First, we wish to express our appreciation to Butler University for the generous support and encouragement given to this lengthy project through the Butler Academic Grants Committee for funding and to the Butler Committee on Sabbatical Leaves and Faculty Fellowships, which provided the time for reflecting on, researching, and writing this textbook. In particular, we want to express our appreciation to Joseph F. Lamberti, Dean of the College of Education, and to Thomas J. Hegarty, Vice President for Academic Affairs, without whose encouragement and support this project would have been impossible. We are indebted to Dr. Joseph M. Nygaard, Professor of Education at Butler, for the preparation of the two concise chapters on the legal foundations of education. We appreciate the assistance of Larry DeWester, Janet Hudson, and Ann Riemer, whose work as our graduate assistants propelled the book toward completion. We extend thanks to Larry for his analysis of data on market trends and for his work on revising the initial chapters, and to Janet for accepting the project as her own, revising the manuscript, proofreading, obtaining the necessary permissions, rewriting material, compiling photographs, drawing charts and illustrations, writing test questions for the teacher's manual, and generally assisting with the majority of the textbook manuscript. Her work was truly invaluable to us and to the project as a whole, and we are indebted to her for more than a year of diligent work on this book. We wish to thank Ann Reimer for helping us to complete preparation of the manuscript. We are also grateful to Nancy Leigh for typing the manuscript with ease and speed and to Karen Ellsworth for coming to our aid numerous times with secretarial help on short notice. We are also indebted to the Butler undergraduate and graduate students of educational foundations who have field-tested the material in this text and have offered helpful suggestions over the past several years.

For their assistance in providing photographs for this book, we are indebted to the Indianapolis Public Schools; the Metropolitan School District of Lawrence Township in Marion County, Indiana; the Indiana State Teachers Association; the Indiana Federation of Teachers; the Indiana State Department of Education; the Library of Congress; the Sudbury Valley School in Framingham, Massachusetts; and photographer Dan Axler. We also want to thank all of the parents and young people who graciously consented to having their photographs in this book. In addition, we wish to acknowledge the professional help given by librarians at the Library of Congress, the Indiana State Library, the library of the Indiana Department of Education, the Karl Kalp Library of the Indianapolis Public Schools, Indiana University Library, and the Irwin Library at Butler University. We are also indebted to the Indiana Farm Bureau for information on school finance and to Dr. Paul Krohne for material on the early history of education in Indiana.

We gratefully acknowledge the encouragement and assistance of those at Macmillan: Lloyd Chilton, without whose help this project would not have come to fruition; Wendy Polhemus, production editor; Lynne Greenberg, education editor; and Eileen Burke, designer. We are also grateful for the counsel of Dr. John Best, Professor of Education Emeritus at Butler University, whose book *Research in Education* served as an inspiration for this project. We also wish to express our appreciation for the extremely helpful comments of the professionals who were chosen by Macmillan to critique this text, especially to Dr. Tony L. Williams, Professor of Education at Marshall University in Huntington, West Virginia.

Finally, thanks are due to our wives, Kathy and Dotty; our families, who encouraged us in this long project; and to Dotty for her aid in revising and editing several early chapters of this manuscript. Without their forbearance and support, the writing of this text would have been impossible.

R. F. H.
T. H. W.

Contents

UNIT II

The History of Education

UNIT **III**

The Philosophy of Education

UNIT **IV**

The School Curriculum

UNIT **V**

Legal Elements of Education

UNIT **VI**

Control and Governance of Education

UNIT VII

Financing Education

UNIT VIII

Educational Organizations

UNIT IX

Orientation to Teaching

Introduction to
EDUCATION

SOCIOLOGY AND EDUCATION

1

Society's Impact on the Public Schools

OBJECTIVES

After reading Chapter 1, the student will be able to:

- Identify key sociological issues that affect our schools.
- Become sensitized to the real impact that these social forces have on individuals and the schools.
- Start to think about possible solutions to these problems.
- Assess where his or her values are in relation to the rest of the society.
- Develop some depth of understanding of the key sociological issues.

The Impact of the Economic System

The system of capitalism and free enterprise brings with it some pluses and minuses. On the plus side, capitalism allows Americans to invest money in an endless variety of enterprises to meet the needs of society. If the entrepreneurs have been careful in their investments, they make a profit, and they may decide to expand their businesses. As long as the economy is in a developing cycle, the GNP (gross national product) will increase, and most citizens will be employed. On the negative side, or minus side, there will be down cycles in the economy when a certain percentage of the population will not be able to work. People in lower socioeconomic strata find it difficult to make a living during a developing cycle and find life grim in a down cycle of our economy.

America is a land of opportunity where one can rise in social and economic status; the system will also allow one to fail in all aspects. Many Americans feel good about their country because in the United States there are not as many serious economic problems and because there are fewer poor people than in most countries of the world. Some well-meaning people say that the poor will always be with us; having said this, they seem to feel released from caring about the poor in our country. The material goods or rewards that one can attain in America are tremendous, and these, too, tend to insulate us from dealing with the poor and the social problems that are part of poverty. Since they have become widespread, crime and drug problems have tended to excite the average citizen more than in the past. Keeshan (1983), known popularly as Captain Kangaroo, placed our society's problems in perspective, when he wrote:

> Forty percent of our preschoolers are not immunized against polio. How quickly we forget. Incredible. Twenty percent of our children live in poverty. Many of our children go to bed hungry, many more go to bed ill-nourished. Many go to bed in detention centers and jails. Incredible. Why do we allow this to happen in the wealthiest, most technologically advanced nation in the world? Incredible. (p. 55)

The majority of us who are a part of the mainstream of American life act as a protection to our economic system. Most of us save money, perhaps give a little to charity, and fight to keep all the money we can from going into unnecessary taxes. Some change agents in our society are constantly searching for new and better ways to serve the poor. A few people are conceiving programs that would lead to solutions, but many, mostly through ignorance, are content to treat the symptoms of poverty. This treatment of symptoms does make a few people feel better, but no solution is ever reached.

Our welfare system, with its food stamps and unemployment payments, does not appear to give people a sense of dignity; instead, it may lead to

4

Many Societal Problems Affect Our Schools

THE SOCIETY AT LARGE

Poverty and the economic system · Delinquency and crime · Teenage suicides · Family life · Teenage pregnancy · Communications media · Prejudice, racism, and segregation · Child abuse · Ethnic diversity · Women's rights · Other societal problems · Drugs and alcohol

School

idleness and purposeless behavior. The welfare system operates on the premise that feeding a hungry stomach will solve the poverty problem, but it may only be treating the symptoms. Parents who are operating under this welfare system are influencing children who are attending our schools. The solution-type thinkers would say that whatever the cost to our economy, we must do something to give all people a sense of dignity in our economic system. It appears that a solution must be found that involves putting more people in the work force—ultimately, all people who want to work. Including most Americans in the regular work force would possibly do more to solve educational problems than would most proposed and current in-service educational solutions.

The authors are not suggesting that if the United States abandoned capitalism and substituted socialism in its place, society would be any better. We in the United States must maintain our free enterprise system, but we also need to put limits on the system so that more and more of the wealth does not end up in fewer and fewer hands. In some ways, larger enterprises are more efficient than smaller family-run operations, but the problems of large businesses also create some major social problems.

Teachers need to be aware of the economics of our society so that they

Some of the stark economic realities faced by this family of migrants in the 1930s were repeated in the late 1970s, as automobile and tent communities of homeless, jobless families sprang up wherever rumors of employment existed. *(Photo courtesy of the Library of Congress.)*

can better understand its educational implications. Teachers are public servants who are trying their best to help students become productive citizens, but teachers are also citizens who have a stake in ensuring the continued existence of our country. Informed citizens and teachers may need to recognize that a completely free enterprise system or a nonproductive welfare system will not work. Perhaps all concerned citizens will need to work together to change the system before it is too late. Some have said that neither the idle rich nor the idle poor are good for our public schools or America's future. (For the schools' response to the economics of American society see Chapter 2.)

The Impact of Delinquency and Crime

The negative effect of crime in our country is overwhelming even when we consider only the tax dollar loss for fighting crime. In 1979, local, state, and federal branches of government spent a total of $26 billion fighting and preventing crime. The $26 billion cost takes into consideration police, judicial, legal service, public defense, and correction agencies (U.S. Department of

Commerce [USDC], 1984). In 1983, there were 10,287,000 arrests, 2,151,000 of these for serious crimes. About 80 percent of the serious crimes were committed by males, 12.1 percent of them under fifteen years old, and 30.4 percent of them under eighteen years old (USDC, 1985). In 1981, the juvenile courts, which handle the cases of children aged ten to seventeen, were deluged with 1,350,000 cases (USDC, 1985).

Sociologists and criminologists are trying to find the critical point in the crime cycle of the juvenile offender, so as to intervene with a program to remove them from the cycle. Society wants an answer to the crime problem, and logically, the earlier we can identify a potential juvenile offender, the better are our chances of helping him or her to lead a life free of crime. At the highest levels of government, including the U.S. Senate, work is under way to address this major issue. David P. Farrington of the Institute of Criminology, Cambridge University, England, testified before the Senate Subcommittee on Juvenile Justice in October 1981. According to Dr. Farrington, some of the requirements for delinquency prevention were the following:

1. Emphasis should be placed on early environment and upbringing. The earlier the intervention, the better.
2. Educationally retarded children from large, poor, and criminal families are especially at risk of committing criminal and delinquent acts. Scarce welfare resources should be concentrated on this high-risk group.
3. All the evidence indicates that first convictions are followed by a worsening of delinquent behavior. (Subcommittee on Juvenile Justice [SJJ], 1981, pp. 50–54)

Also testifying before the Senate Subcommittee on Juvenile Justice was Gerald R. Patterson, a research scientist at the Oregon Social Learning Center. Patterson's group studied 200 families of antisocial children and then 200 normal families for a fifteen-year period. The parents of the antisocial children were taught how to monitor their children, and they were paid $10 per week to do the monitoring. Parents were taught to find out where their children were when they did not come home, who they were with, what they were doing, and when they were coming back. All of these children were practicing predelinquent behavior (described as stealing at least twice a month). Most of these parents did not know very much about what their children were doing, and even when they saw the child perform an antisocial act, such as assaulting another family member, they did not punish the child. The parents were also taught how to administer sane punishment, which means a confrontation with the child that results in a work detail, the withdrawal of a privilege, or a time-out period for smaller children. The result of the experiment was that the stealing stopped for six months while the monitoring and sane punishment went on. The experiment ended, when the children were six, seven, or eight years old. By the time they had reached the age of fourteen the parents had removed all controls, and 57 percent of this group of children had become chronic juvenile offenders (SJJ, 1981, pp. 55–59). The experiment gives us some hope that early intervention may work, but more research is needed to detect whether a longer term of supervised parent monitoring and sane punishment would yield a higher success rate.

According to John Monahan, professor of law, psychology, and legal medicine at the University of Virginia School of Law, who also testified before the Subcommittee on Juvenile Justice, three clusters of factors relate to future violent behavior:

A. Parent factors.
   1. Parents themselves criminal.
   2. Lack of supervision of child.
   3. Conflict between parents.
   4. Harsh physical discipline.
B. Child factors.
   1. Gender.
   2. Race.
   3. I.Q.
   4. Temperament.
   5. Age of onset of delinquency.
C. School factors.
   1. Interpersonal difficulties.
   2. Academic difficulties. (SJJ, 1981, p. 9)

As teachers, we would be more concerned with the final cluster, but as we look at all three clusters, we can detect how complex the solution to the whole problem would be. The idea of working with the parents, the child, and the school at the earliest possible time appears to be the best plan. The school problems a child may be having are tied to several other factors that teachers have no control over, but the results of this complex problem have a negative impact on the public schools. How many hours per semester do teachers have to stop what they are teaching to deal with a predelinquent or a delinquent student, thus spending a large portion of their time trying to discipline and counsel young people while academic learning must be set aside?

A study by Blau and Blau (1983) that examined the influence of social inequality on the violent crime rate came to some interesting conclusions and inferences. The Blaus collected data from 125 of the largest American metropolitan areas, and they concluded that socioeconomic inequality engenders alienation, despair, and pent-up aggression, which find expression in frequent conflicts, including a high incidence of criminal violence. These facts are important for teachers to understand because so many opportunities come up in the daily operation of schools to verbalize or demonstrate principles of human equality. Blau and Blau (1983) also found that economic in-

Possible Causes and Results of Delinquent Behavior

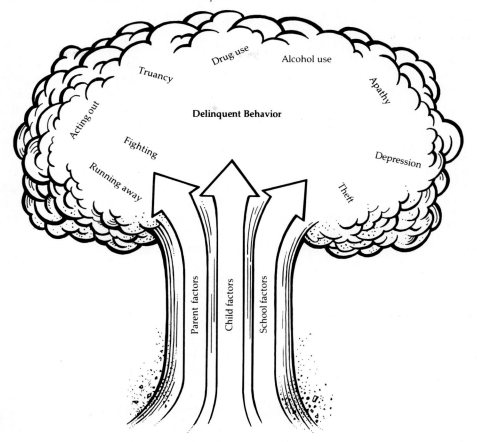

equality itself may be an alienating experience that engenders conflict and violent crimes in a democracy; but when overall inequality and its mediating influences are controlled, racial inequality still exerts an independent influence on criminal violence. Obviously, all inequality has a negative effect, but racial inequality has a far worse negative effect.

The answer to the problem of crime and delinquency can be found through research and a much greater public commitment. When we decided, as a country, that we wanted to land on the moon before 1970, we achieved that goal; and we can set a goal to eradicate juvenile crime by the year 2000 and accomplish that, too. Any country like the United States, with a $3-trillion GNP, can afford what it takes monetarily to solve this problem. (For the schools' response to the impact of delinquency and crime in our society, see Chapter 2.)

The Impact of Adolescent Suicides

Adolescent suicides are another problem in our society. Between 1968 and 1978 the suicide rate for teenagers nearly doubled, and in 1978, about five thousand children and adolescents committed suicide, or nearly three times the number that had done so twenty years earlier (Smith, 1981).

Emile Durkheim, an authority on suicide, believed that a rising suicide rate was a reflection of the state of the society. Durkheim (1981) viewed the rising suicide rate in the civilized world as a function of the failure of state, church, and family to act as the forces of social integration that they had been before the Industrial Revolution. If the Industrial Revolution caused such trouble, what do we have to look forward to from the high-tech revolution? On the positive side, high-tech may free us to explore and deal with the causes of suicide, but it could also put a lot more stress on people and thus cause more suicides.

Alcohol and drug abuse among teenagers appear to be related to teen suicides. According to Greuling and DeBlassie (1980), "based on statistics in several large cities, it is not unreasonable to assume that at least 50% of the teenagers who committed suicide were involved in moderate to heavy drinking and abusive use of dangerous drugs prior to their death" (p. 589). These authors were not suggesting, however, that drinking and drug abuse are the cause of suicides. The key here is to find out what led to the drinking and drug abuse in the first place.

Alienation of youth comes up in most of the literature as a contributing

Most teenagers will grow to be strong, healthy adults, but some will become victims of drugs, alcohol, or even suicide. (Photo by Axler.)

factor to teen suicides. Being cut off from parents, friends, and relatives causes loneliness and depression. Many studies have indicated that isolated youngsters, particularly boys, are most likely to commit suicide (Greuling and DeBlassie, 1980).

No matter what experts think the specific causes of suicide may be, many feel that individuals in society have withdrawn their commitment to children and substituted "self" as the most important priority. Spencer (1979) wrote that adults were once willing to suffer genuine material hardships in order to have and raise children, but that now the greatest priority appears to be a country house, a larger air conditioner, a microwave oven, or a better retirement. Blame for the increase in teen suicides cannot be attributed to any one factor when all of society is somewhat the cause. (For the schools' response to the impact of adolescent suicides on our society, see Chapter 2.)

The Impact of Family Life in America

Because of how the family structure is changing in the United States, one might wonder what type of family organization or pattern is really the best. Not surprisingly, Nunn and Parish (1982) found that children who fared the best in their personal, family, and school adjustment came from intact families; the next best were children from families in which the fathers had died; and the least adjusted were children from homes broken by divorce. All options were not measured by the Nunn and Parish study, but the results were based heavily on the children's self-concept, their anxiety level, and their adjustment to home and school.

In this section, we are obviously more concerned about families with children, as they are the ones that the schools must work with in the educational process. The family with children has a tremendous direct influence on educational practice in the form of the attitudes and values the family instills in its children toward education, teachers, and life in general.

The egalitarian marriage, where all roles in the family are shared equally by the husband and the wife, is here for a few, but may increase in future years. The changing patterns in the family, where the wife works outside the home as much as the husband, is common today for more than half of the married women in the United States (Smith and Reid, 1982). By *egalitarian marriage*, we refer not to the wife who has a part-time job or a job that supplements the husband's income, but to one who is an equal partner in the breadwinning role. Sharing of duties around the home tends to be along the lines of traditional roles for men and women, but it is predicted that this pattern will change. Studies have indicated that fathers have shown just as much competence in taking care of newborn infants as mothers. Implications for schools include the development of courses in family life that teach examples for living in family patterns other than the traditional nuclear family.

Changing patterns of family
life are reflected in increased
out-of-home child care.
(Photo by Axler.)

The poor and disadvantaged families living in the crowded urban areas of our country may need much assistance from the public schools. The government must find ways to help the poor, economically and educationally, or eventually this country may face some of the same problems as other countries that have no organized system to help the disadvantaged improve their lot in society. The poor in India and other Third World countries travel the streets begging for money and sleeping or living wherever they can. If the children of the economically and socially disadvantaged are to move up the socioeconomic ladder, they must get vocational assistance along with basic assistance for food, housing, and medical care; and these children must absolutely get the opportunity for a good education.

One dramatic victory in aid to the poor was a bill passed in the U.S. Congress to improve access to health care for fifteen million poor pregnant mothers and children. One program, Head Start, which has meant much to poor families, is still intact, but a real effort by advocates is required to keep it alive. Early stimulation of the mind toward learning is just as important for poor children as it is for mainstream Americans. Unfortunately, 80 percent of the American children eligible for Head Start will never see a Head Start center (Edelman, 1983). If the nation's poor children are better fed, better cared for, and better educated, we can save money. Edelman (1983) of the Children's Defense Fund wrote, "Child care is an antiwelfare and antidependency measure, because it will help reduce federal spending on income transfers more than any other program" (p. 26). People who have the good life in America want the best for their own children, yet when asked to give more in taxes for the poor and oppressed, they often do not see these people as being their problem. Where are we in America in reaching the goal of dignity for all people?

Teenage Pregnancy

Another problem with huge educational implications is the growing number of teenage pregnancies, which is related to two phenomena: the first is a dramatic shift in the age of menarche in young girls from a mean age of 14.2 in 1900 to a mean age of 11.8 today; the second is the steady increase in the number of sexually active young people (Bell, Casto, and Daniels, 1983). Some experts are saying that the number of teen pregnancies may now be around one million per year.

Because most of these births occur at lower socioeconomic strata, where there is no proper nutrition or medical care, these children start life in a handicapped position. The mothers themselves are still going through adolescence and have not completed their own education. More often than not, unmarried teen mothers find themselves alienated from the mainstream of society, so they do not get all the help they need, especially when they also have very little or no help from their families.

Utah has started a program of intervention that is helping a few young mothers and that could serve as a model for other states. This program helps both the mothers and the children, taking advantage of materials from Parent Effectiveness Training and Head Start. So far, the results from the program indicate that its graduates have had significantly higher employment rates, less dependence on AFDC (Aid to Families with Dependent Children), and fewer referrals for child abuse (Bell et al., 1983, p. 172). As the tend toward increased teen pregnancies continues, programs of this type will be needed to improve opportunities for the next generation of children. (For the schools' response to the impact of family life in America, see Chapter 2.)

The Impact of Racial Prejudice, Racism, and Segregation

The topic of prejudice, racism, and segregation is not a pleasant one. Some might say that these problems do not exist in their hometowns and that the rest of the country took care of these problems back in the turbulent 1960s and 1970s. It is true that we, as a country, have made progress in solving them, but as they all still exist, they do have adverse effects on education.

Prejudice and Racism

The *Random House College Dictionary* (1980, revised edition) defines prejudice as "an unfavorable opinion or feeling formed beforehand without knowledge, thought or reason (p. 1046). One example of prejudice concerns a black professional worker in a northern city in 1983. This man told of having to change his bike path frequently on his way to work because he was stopped by the police and asked all types of questions about his bike license when he passed from one area of the city to another.

Racism is even stronger than prejudice; it is the doctrine that "inherent differences among the various human races determine cultural or individual achievement, usually involving the idea that one's own race is superior" (p. 1088). Racism may take the form of an action or an institutional structure that subordinates a person or a group because of race. Racism was a legal part of the southern lifestyle in the United States before the *Brown* v. *Board of Education of Topeka* U.S. Supreme Court case of 1954 and the Civil Rights Acts of the 1960s changed laws and their interpretation. Blacks were to use separate drinking fountains and restrooms, sit in the rear of buses, and attend separate schools. Racism remains a part of the lifestyle of many U.S. citizens, both northern and southern, although it is no longer legally sanctioned.

Institutional Racism

The denial of equal opportunities to all races in the various institutions in our society affects schools both directly and indirectly. Institutional racism

> that has obstructed and in some cases continues to impede realization of status equality is of three types: (1) *Prerequisites* or *preconditions* that cannot be justified on grounds of necessity and that disproportionately bar minorities; these prerequisites are frequently economic or have economic antecedents. (2) *Freezing,* which occurs when standards are rigorously imposed on all applicants, regardless of race, but only after most whites have qualified during a period of less stringent requirements. (3) *Mapping*—the drawing of district lines in a way that dilutes minority political strength and produces racial isolation in the public schools. (Bullock & Rogers, 1975, p. 54)

An example of the first type of institutional racism (prerequisites or preconditions) is housing. Because minority Americans are found in disproportionate numbers among our nation's poor, minorities are hurt most when there is a housing configuration based on economic considerations. Consequently, suburban areas are mostly white, whereas urban areas contain three times as many blacks as whites. Blacks often share overcrowded housing because of their low income. The government has tried to help solve the housing problem by either building low-income housing or making available older housing units at reduced rents. Low-income housing is only a partial interim solution for the poor, particularly blacks and other minority groups; the real solution is equal opportunity in the job market. Schools feel the pressure from blighted neighborhoods and communities that suffer from inadequate opportunities.

An example of the second type of institutional racism (freezing) is found in employment. New criteria for jobs may be equally applied to all racial groups now, but whites were able to gain those same types of jobs when there were less stringent requirements. The consequence is that minorities now find themselves discriminated against in applying for certain jobs because of institutional requirements, but not overtly. Minorities suffer from economic immobility, and schools receive the fallout of this type of alienation.

Mapping is a type of institutional racism that directly affects the schools and education. Since the *Brown* decision in 1954, school districts have been realigned because of their *de jure* (deliberate) placement or *de facto* (not deliberate, but as a result of circumstances) placement of students. The goal, of course, has been to distribute minority groups equally within a district or across districts to achieve the best balance possible among all groups. In the South, this has meant abolishing exclusively white and exclusively black public schools. Busing for racial reasons is in process all across America at the present time.

Segregation

No doubt segregation of one form or another has been in effect from the beginning of human history, but in the United States, it is more pronounced between white and black people. Basically, racial segregation means restricting the actions of one or more groups on the basis of racial or ethnic membership. Because of the civil rights legislation in the United States in the 1960s and 1970s, legal segregation came to an end. Segregation in the South had been legal since the *Plessy* v. *Ferguson* case was decided by the Supreme Court in 1896. In this case, the Court ruled that it was legal to segregate white people from black people on railroad cars as long as equal facilities were provided. Eventually the practice spread to schools, waiting rooms, buses, and drinking fountains. Northerners practiced segregation in different ways, and the effect was that black people were denied equal access to jobs, housing, schools, and private clubs.

December 1, 1955, marked a day in our nation's history when old segregational tactics began to change. It was on this day that Rosa Parks boarded a bus in Montgomery, Alabama, and sat in a seat normally reserved for white people. Because she refused to move from her seat, she was arrested and convicted of breaking the law. This one act really signaled the start of the civil rights movement just as Sputnik signaled the beginning of space exploration and placing humans on the moon twelve years later. Rosa Parks, in the words of Martin Luther King, Jr., was

anchored to that seat by the accumulated indignities of days gone by and the boundless aspirations of generations yet unborn. She was the victim of both the forces of history and the forces of destiny. She had been tracked down by the *Zeitgeist*—the spirit of the time. (Lindsey & Lindsey, 1974, p. 60)

Among the violent acts that occurred in the 1960s were the bombing of a Sunday-school room in a black Baptist church in Alabama, killing four little girls, and the slaying of three civil rights workers in Mississippi. The three civil rights workers, James Chaney, Andrew Goodman, and Michael Schwerner, were in Mississippi to encourage blacks to register to vote and to take advantage of their civil rights. Minorities have had a long struggle for the rights guaranteed by the U.S. Constitution.

The United States has not had a monopoly on segregation in the world. As one illustration, South Africa today has one of the most racist school systems in the world. Under apartheid in South Africa, different racial groups are educated separately for entirely separate career goals; for example, most blacks are trained for blue-collar work and whites for professional positions. It would be very difficult to estimate the losses in the United States alone in dollars to our gross national product because of prejudice and racism, but it is, no doubt, in the billions of dollars.

After the *Brown* case in 1954, separation by race in American schools was declared inherently unequal. This one court case has changed the way Americans relate to one another more than any one act since before the turn of the century. The Supreme Court mandated the desegregation of American public schools, whether segregation was purposeful (*de jure*) or the result of neighborhood placement (*de facto*). Desegregation did not move rapidly after *Brown;* but inch by inch, court decision after court decision, headway has been made. As lawsuits have been brought against various school districts across the country and court decisions have been made, various solutions have been proposed; most of these solutions have involved busing or changing school-district boundaries.

Many white parents have been angered by the court orders and have moved their families to the suburbs. Other white families have stayed in their old districts and participated in the great experiment. Frequently white children have met black children, have found new friends, and have become learning and social partners. As integration has proceeded, it has become easier for all groups in our society to meet and communicate better. Greater opportunities for minority groups have opened up, and a good many of them have climbed and are climbing the ladder of economic success. Many suburban housing developments are no longer all white, and a number of school districts have integrated themselves naturally.

Today, legal segregation is in the past, and the attitude in the nation is much better than it was in 1955, when Rosa Parks made her initial protest. However, some workers in skilled trades are opposed to accepting black workers in their ranks; in many places, fair housing laws have not been passed; blacks are still harassed when they move into neighborhoods or communities where they are not wanted; and minority businesses still must fight for their existence. There is still work to be done in order to fulfill Martin Luther King's dream for America. (For the schools' response to the impact of desegregation, see Chapter 2.)

The Impact of Alcohol and Drug Abuse

Alcohol

Alcoholism is a growing health problem in the United States, claiming more victims than any disease with the exception of cancer and heart disease (Coorsch, 1982). The problem is causing our country so many difficulties that it is hard to estimate the magnitude of the losses both in dollars and in human agony. Some estimate the financial loss due to alcoholism and alcohol abuse to be nearly $50 billion a year. Employers lose as a result of an employee's lack of productivity on the job, poor morale, high medical costs, absenteeism, and replacement costs. Workers with alcoholism are at least 25 percent less productive than their coworkers (Coorsch, 1982). A family suffers whenever a family member deteriorates because of alcoholism, particularly if that person is a main source of income. The victim of alcoholism is one who faces great adversity. Other than the money factor, distorted attitudes and values affect families because of alcoholism. These problems can cause psychological problems in the children and affect their school performance.

A driver's being under the influence of alcohol may be the cause of as many as 50 percent of all fatal accidents. Kevin Tunell was arrested and convicted of manslaughter for the death of an eighteen-year-old girl while driving under the influence of alcohol. Kevin had been drinking with his friends, who had warned him not to drive home; they had even tried to take his car keys. The unique thing about Kevin's case is that he was sentenced to spend the next year reliving that New Year's Eve before groups of high-school students in Virginia. The judge wanted him to lecture to peers and their parents on the evils of drunk driving several hours each week for a year. At first, many people thought that his sentence was too light, but he felt that it was harder reliving the incident each time he told the story than if he had been in jail. Generally, at the conclusion of his talks, he would say, "I wouldn't want anybody here to go through what I've had to go through. If it just helps one person, though, it will make me feel better" (Moore, 1982, p. 10).

Another teenage death, that of Cari Lightner, age thirteen, took place in California. Cari was struck by a drunk driver who had already been convicted twice for drunk driving. Cari's mother wanted to do something to get drunk drivers off the road. Ms. Lightner and several other mothers who had lost relatives in automobile accidents caused by drunk drivers formed MADD (Mothers Against Drunk Drivers) to campaign for tougher laws against drunk driving (Gorman, 1982). The federal government, through the Office of the President, has set up a thirty-member commission to help state and local governments attack the drunk driver problem. Also, both houses of Congress are considering bills to set up programs to deter drunk driving.

The magnitude of the alcohol problem is not so surprising when we consider that Americans drink 180 million barrels of beer a year. That is 42 gallons for each person in the United States aged fourteen or older, and that statistic does not include wine or hard liquor (Strong, 1983). The fact is that drinking is a part of many or most people's lifestyles in the United States. Problems related to the use of alcohol impact heavily on education.

Dr. George Vaillant, a noted researcher on alcoholism, believes that we should teach children how to make intelligent drinking decisions (cited by O'Reilly, 1983). He himself is a social drinker, and he serves wine on special occasions to his two teenage children. In this case, the model he sets for his children is that moderate drinking is all right; it makes sense that teaching them about his lifestyle is a good idea because children tend to follow adults whom they love and respect. Some children are not so fortunate as to have parents who drink moderately, and the example they see is excessive drinking. Other children come from homes where alcohol has never been a part of the family's lifestyle. No doubt Dr. Vaillant's idea is a good one for some families, but a number of approaches will have to be used in the home and in the school in order to educate most schoolchildren.

Drug Abuse

More evidence is accumulating daily to indicate that damage is done to the body by the continued use of drugs such as marijuana. Although this problem was once primarily confined to the ghettos of larger American cities, today it can be found in any neighborhood. Sometimes the more money children have to spend, the more likely they are to be involved in taking drugs.

The U.S. Bureau of the Census listed the statistics on drug use from 1972 to 1982. Table 1–1 lists marijuana as the third most used drug by young people and adults, after alcohol and cigarettes. Note that these statistics are percentages, so the total numbers of youths involved in drugs is enormous.

The real question is why people want to alter their minds with drugs in the first place. People have many reasons for using drugs, and society needs to seriously consider the underlying causes of drug use. Treatment programs often overlook the real causes of drug misuse. Treatment must often involve more than just the user if there are to be real results, and many treatment centers around the country address this concern by involving other family members.

The question is asked: Is society, as a whole, really concerned about the problem? There are signs that society does care and signs that it does not care enough. We try to arrest drug pushers and to discourage the use of harmful

TABLE 1–1   Drug Use, by Type of Drug and by Age Group: 1972–1982[a]

| Type of Drug | Percent of Youths | | | | Percent of Young Adults | | | | Percent of Adults | | | |
| | Ever Used | | Current User | | Ever Used | | Current User | | Ever Used | | Current User | |
	1972	1982	1972	1982	1974	1982	1974	1982	1974	1982	1974	1982
Marijuana	14.0	26.7	7.0	11.5	52.7	64.1	25.2	27.4	9.9	23.0	2.0	6.6
Inhalants	6.4	(NA)	1.0	(NA)	9.2	(NA)	(Z)	(NA)	1.2	(NA)	(Z)	(NA)
Hallucinogens	4.8	5.2	1.4	1.4	16.6	21.1	2.5	1.7	1.3	6.4	(Z)	1.2
Cocaine	1.5	6.5	0.6	1.6	12.7	28.3	3.1	6.8	0.9	8.5	(Z)	(NA)
Heroin	0.6	(Z)	(Z)	(Z)	4.5	1.2	(Z)	(Z)	0.5	1.1	(Z)	0.6
Analgesics	(NA)	4.2	(NA)	2.6	(NA)	12.1	(NA)	4.7	(NA)	3.2	(NA)	(NA)
Stimulants[b]	4.0	6.7	(NA)	1.3	17.0	18.0	3.7	2.6	3.0	6.2	(Z)	(NA)
Sedatives[b]	3.0	5.8	(NA)	0.9	15.0	18.7	1.6	1.6	2.0	4.8	(Z)	(NA)
Tranquilizers[b]	3.0	4.9	(NA)	0.7	10.0	15.1	1.2	1.0	2.0	3.6	(Z)	1.2
Alcohol	(NA)	65.2	24.0	26.9	81.6	94.6	69.3	67.9	73.2	88.2	54.5	56.7
Cigarettes	(NA)	49.5	17.5	17.0	14.7	68.8	48.8	39.5	65.4	78.7	39.1	34.6

[a]Current users are those who used drugs at least once within the month prior to this study. For 1982, based on national samples of 1,581 youths (12–17 yrs. old), 1,283 young adults (18–25 yrs. old), and 2,760 older adults (26 yrs. old and over). Subject to sampling variability; see source.

[b]Prescription drugs.

NA: Not available; Z: Less than 0.5 percent.

Source: U.S. Department of Commerce, Bureau of the Census. (1984). *Statistical abstract of the United States.* Washington, DC: U.S. Government Printing Office, p. 126.

drugs. At present, the federal government—and the U.S. Coast Guard, in particular—is arresting illegal importers of marijuana and other drugs, but most importers are not caught. Because enormous profits are to be made on drugs, even established businesspeople sometimes find it difficult to resist the profits. Rock stars are admired by teenagers, but some are known users of drugs, and they are allowed to perform in arenas where the use of drugs is very public. Respected businesspeople, who control the keys to these arenas, are tacitly accepting the use of drugs in this way—and often these same people wonder what is happening to our young people in the schools. Does society really care? (For the schools' response to the impact of alcohol and drug abuse, see Chapter 2.)

The Impact of Child Abuse

The number of child abuse cases reported in the United States is rising each year. In 1976, the American Humane Association reported 413,000 cases of child abuse; by 1981, the count had doubled to 851,000, and in 1982, the count had risen another 12 percent (Magnuson, 1983). Child abuse strikes at all socioeconomic levels and in all racial groups, and for every case reported, four go unreported. The exact causes of child abuse are not known, but several theories have been proposed. The most disturbing finding about child abusers is that they themselves grew up being abused and that their children will very likely become abusers also. The cyclical pattern of child abuse must be broken, and teachers can be of much assistance in the identity of victims.

In 1974, Congress passed the Child Abuse Prevention and Treatment Act, which defines child abuse and neglect as "the physical or mental injury, sexual abuse, negligent treatment, or maltreatment of a child under the age of eighteen by a person who is responsible for the child's welfare under circumstances which indicate that the child's health or welfare is harmed or threatened thereby (U.S. Department of Health, Education, and Welfare [USDHEW], 1976)." There are thus four basic types of child abuse: physical abuse, neglect, emotional abuse, and sexual abuse.

A child is *physically abused* when any physical injury is inflicted on him or her by other than accidental means. Typical injuries are unusual bruises, welts, burns, fractures, or bite marks.

Abuse in the form of *neglect* is failure to provide a child with the basic necessities of life such as food, clothing, shelter, medical care, and education. Typically, neglected children appear dirty, tired, and lethargic; they come to school with no breakfast; they are alone for long periods of time; they may need glasses, dental care, or other medical attention.

The *emotionally abused* child has parents with excessive, aggressive, or unreasonable behavior that places demands on the child to perform above her or his capabilities. Typically, the emotionally abused child's parent blames or belittles the child; is cold and rejecting; withholds love; or treats the children in the family unequally.

The *sexually abused* child is exploited for an adult's own sexual gratification; sexual abuse takes the form of rape, incest, fondling of genitals, or exhibitionism. Typically, children who have been sexually abused appear withdrawn or engage in fantasies or babylike behavior, have poor relations with other children, are unwilling to participate in physical activities, and may state that they have been assaulted by a parent or caretaker.

Most people have a stereotypical image of parenthood that is always caring and is overly patient; therefore, it is hard for most people to believe that parents may act otherwise. As a result, most cases of child abuse remain unreported. A greater percentage of child abuse cases are reported among the poor and the nonwhite population, mainly because of the access that public agencies, such as welfare agencies, hospitals, and outpatient clinics, have to these groups.

No one knows the exact breakdown of the percentage of child abusers by socioeconomic level, but poverty, drugs and alcohol, poor housing, unemployment, and racial discrimination produce stress that aggrevates any problem. Gil (1969) sees child abuse as a multidimensional problem, but he is a leading exponent of the theory that environmental stress is a major cause.

No matter what the environmental problems may be that contribute to child abuse, the fact is that child abuse is a form of character disorder in some adults and needs to be treated. Organizations such as Parents Anonymous and family support centers, as well as a government agency called Child Protective Services, have been set up to help those involved in child abuse, both the abusers and the victims, providing they can be identified.

Violent crimes like murder are nearly always reported and recorded, but child abuse is often covered up and unreported. Victims of child abuse exist in larger numbers than most of us realize, and inside themselves they are crying out for assistance. The cover article in *Time* magazine of September 5, 1983, attests to the importance of recognizing child abuse in our society so that we can begin to solve the problem for larger numbers of offenders and victims.

The number of cases of child abuse reported is rising rapidly, indicating a greater public awareness of the problem. There is better detection of child abuse in schools, hospitals, and social agencies. Some studies (Magnuson, 1983) indicate that as many as 90 percent of inmates in prison claim to have been abused as children. There is no doubt that helping children and adult abusers to overcome their emotional and/or psychological problems would have some effect on reducing the prison population. One cannot estimate the number of child abuse victims who cause problems for business and industry, as well as for themselves and others. How much more productive these citizens might be if they could be relieved of the legacy of their childhood trauma.

An article in *Time* magazine (Magnuson, 1983) contained a case study of a girl named Mary, which illustrates a very extreme case of child abuse. It serves to point out the cyclical effect of child abuse from one generation to another:

> Her name is Mary. She is 34 years old and lives in a suburb of New York City. With her neatly tailored beige suit, pink designer blouse and necklace of seed pearls, she has the well-scrubbed preppie look of someone who has had a safe, comfortable life. When she begins to speak, the words seem strange, as if they belong to some other person.

> What I remember most about my mother was that she was always beating me. She'd beat me with her high-heeled shoes, with my father's belt, with a potato masher. When I was eight, she black-and-blued my legs so badly, I told her I'd go tell the police. She said, "Go, they'll just put you into the darkest prison." So I stayed. When my breasts started growing at 13, she beat me across the chest until I fainted. Then she'd hug me and ask forgiveness. When I turned 16, a day didn't pass without my mother calling me a whore, and saying that I'd end up in Potter's Field, dead, forgotten and damned for all eternity. Most kids have nightmares about being taken away from their parents. I would sit on our front stoop, crooning softly of going far, far away to find another mother.

What she did to my young brother was worse. When he was two years old, she tried to hang him from the shower curtain and drown him in the toilet. He still has tic-tac-toe marks across his chest from being held down across a red-hot heating grate. From the time he was born, my mother groomed my brother to kill my father. When Daddy came home, she made us tell him how much we hated him. I went to bed and prayed he didn't believe me. It was after I'd been married two years that my mother and brother bludgeoned my father to death in the cellar with his own pool cue. They stuffed his body in the car trunk and drove him to the middle of town and left him there.

I started abusing my boy because his birth was an accident and a screamer. When he was four months old, I hit him so hard my engage-ment ring carved a deep bloody furrow across his soft face. His screams shattered my heart. I sank to the floor with self-loathing. Then I held him tightly in my arms, so tight he turned blue. I told him he had to do his share. Why didn't he help out? Why didn't he stop screaming. Deep down, I knew he couldn't understand. But I also thought he was doing it on purpose. He'd start crying again and I'd hit him again, and I felt so helpless when this happened.

When he was ten, I got so angry with him, I panicked. I was rush-ing to kill him. But I managed to tell him to go to his room and lock himself in and not to open the door no matter what I said. He fled. He was really afraid. I could hear him breathing like a frightened rabbit be-hind the door. I was fulfilling my predictions. I was no good and I'd never be any good. I went to Mass every Sunday, and every Sunday I'd say, "I'll confess." I couldn't. I'd go into the confession box and choke on the words. When you abuse your child, it seems like you're watching someone else do it. There is guilt, horror, pain. Society need not hate us. We hate ourselves. No one hates an abusing parent more than the abus-ing parent.

Most abused children, of course, do not murder their fathers. A parent who tries to kill or succeeds in killing a child is also relatively rare. Unfortu-nately, Mary's account of the physical and emotional humiliation inflicted on her by an out-of-control parent and the recycling of the same kind of abuse when she became a mother is all too typical. What is hopeful, although un-usual, about Mary's story is that she realized she needed help, found a group, Parents Anonymous, that knew how to help her, and made peace with her son. In high school now, he is a straight-A student and a starter on the baseball team. Mary says, "He is always telling me that when he is very rich, he'll build a beautiful house and put me and his father on the second floor with a sauna bath, a fireplace and a Jacuzzi. Now we are a warm, happy fam-ily." (p. 20)

As you can see, there are real possibilities for people to heal and live a normal life, thus breaking the abuse cycle. (For the schools' response to the impact of child abuse, see Chapter 2.)

The Impact of Our Culturally and Ethnically Diverse Society

We Americans live in a society composed of many diverse ethnic groups. Some estimate of the degree of racial diversity in America can be obtained from a look at the listings in the U.S. Census. Racial groups listed do not include those of various Spanish origins, such as Mexicans, Puerto Ricans, and Cubans, which were included in the Census under other headings. In 1984, there were approximately 227 million people living in the United States, and Table 1–2 lists the racial groups and their population in millions. White ethnic groups, such as Polish, Italians, and Irish Americans, add to the diversity in the population.

American Indians are the only ethnic group native to America; therefore, all other group members came to this country as immigrants. Immigrants could have chosen to blend in with other Americans when they arrived, and some of them did; but others decided that they felt more comfortable staying in ethnic enclaves. Most people would agree that a certain amount of "melting" is necessary for the survival of our society, that is, for our national security, for the maintenance of our republic, and for the promotion of our economic system. Historically, many Americans have been forced to melt into the system either more than they wanted to or more than was necessary for the common good. Still other groups have had to come up from slavery or

TABLE 1–2   Racial Groups Found in America

Race	Total Persons (in millions)
Total	226.55
White	188.37
Black	26.50
American Indian	1.42
Chinese	0.80
Filipino	0.77
Japanese	0.70
Asian Indian	0.36
Korean	0.35
Vietnamese	0.26
All other races	7.00

Source: U.S. Department of Commerce, Bureau of the Census. (1985). *Statistical abstract of the United States.* Washington, DC: U.S. Government Printing Office, p. 31.

have suffered the indignity of being placed on a reservation, as blacks and American Indians have had to do. Also, many Japanese-Americans were placed in internment camps during World War II.

Since World War II, more Americans have come to see their ethnic background as a real source of identity in this complex world. In addition, educators and intellectuals think it important to know more about other cultures and ethnic groups. During World Wars I and II, we did not trust German-Americans and Japanese-Americans, but time has brought a change. As we build more trust in each other, our ethnically and culturally pluralistic society seems to be an asset instead of a liability. (For the schools' response to the impact of this diversity, see Chapter 2.)

The Impact of the Women's Rights Movement

Many established societal practices in the United States from the mid-1960s until the early 1970s were in the process of social revolution. Among them were the practices related to women's rights and place in society. The attempted passage of the Equal Rights Amendment (ERA), the National Or-

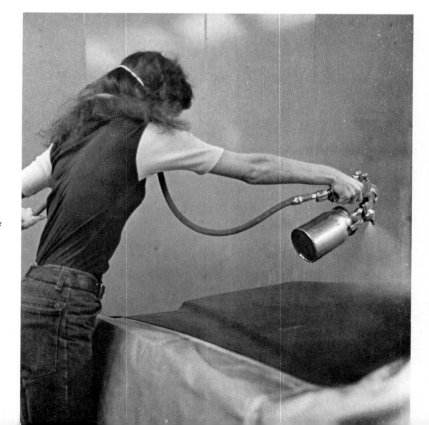

The women's rights movement has opened doors to new areas of endeavor. (Photo courtesy of the Indiana State Department of Education.)

ganization for Women, Bella Abzug, Gloria Steinem, and other events, organizations, and leaders emerged from that turbulent era in American politics. Although the initial thrust behind the women's movement may have dissipated, the message continues to be evident in our daily lives. The question we might all ask ourselves is "What is at the bottom of the women's movement now and in the past, and why should women be disturbed about the role they play in American society?" This question will not be answered entirely in this textbook, but the authors hope to arouse their readers' curiosity about this important source of impact on the schools.

When did the unfairness in the treatment of women begin? Some feminists (Dixon, 1978) have argued that the ability women have to give birth is the limiting factor in women's work activities. They say that when the communal kin group was broken up and individual families became isolated units, the female was relegated to doing domestic work for her husband, which subjugated her into virtual slavery.

Actually, women in the tribal state have been known to have leading political and economic responsibilities despite their child birth role; therefore, the argument that women are limited in work activities does not hold up. The other argument concerning the break up of communal kin groups is a more logical reason for the historical unfair treatment of women when you think about the communal decisions and the group problem-solving that must have taken place; no doubt, women had not been left out of communal decisions and group problem-solving while the kin groups were intact.

As capitalism and the Industrial Revolution became a part of Europe and America, families increasingly became consumers rather than producers. Families before the industrial period lived in communal kin groups, and they were a production unit as well as a consumer unit. Families in the industrial period became a dependent unit, and the husband sold himself as labor while the wife worked in the home. Now the big decisions in life were made away from the family; thus, the family was shifted from the central unit of social organization. Because of the reduction in the importance of the family unit, the wageless nature of female domestic labor, and women's dependence on their husband's wages, women found themselves in a low power position both economically and politically (Dixon, 1978). This scenario may not be entirely correct, but it offers some explanation of the beginnings of the unfair position in which women have found themselves in an industrialized society such as our own.

Today, the woman's role is changing, and for some, it has already changed; but most activists would say there is a long way to go. Alice Rossi (1971) wrote a proposal for changing the whole status of women from birth through later life experiences. At the conclusion of her essay, Rossi described a hypothetical case of a woman who is reared and lives out her life under the changed social conditions Rossi proposed in her essay. The Rossi proposal for change seems to offer a commonsense solution to the powerless and unrewarding dilemmas that women find themselves in because of their established role in the family in an industrialized society.

Today's young women must prepare to meet the opportunities and challenges of their changing roles. (Photo used by permission of the Indianapolis Public Schools.)

I shall describe a hypothetical case of a woman who is reared and lives out her life under the changed social conditions proposed in this essay.

She will be reared, as her brother will be reared, with a combination of loving warmth, firm discipline, household responsibility and encouragement of independence and self-reliance. She will not be pampered and indulged, subtly taught to achieve her ends through coquetry and tears, as so many girls are taught today. She will view domestic skills as useful tools to acquire, some of which, like fine cooking or needlework, having their own intrinsic pleasures but most of which are necessary repetitive work best gotten done as quickly and efficiently as possible. She will be able to handle minor mechanical breakdowns in the home as well as her brother can, and he will be able to tend a child, press, sew, and cook with the same easy skills and comfortable feeling his sister has.

During their school years, both sister and brother will increasingly assume responsibility for their own decisions, freely experiment with numerous possible fields of study, gradually narrowing to a choice that best suits their interests and abilities rather than what is considered appropriate or prestigeful work for men and women. They will be encouraged by parents and teachers alike to think ahead to a whole life span, viewing marriage and parenthood as one strand among many which will constitute their lives. The girl will not feel the pressure to belittle her accomplishments, lower her aspirations, learn to be a receptive listener in her relations with boys, but will be as true to her growing sense of self as her brother and male friends are. She will not marry before her adolescence and schooling are completed, but will be willing and able to view college years as a "moratorium" from deeply intense cross-sex commitments, a period of life during which her identity can be "at large and open and various." Her intellectual aggressiveness as well as her brother's tender sentiments will be welcomed and accepted as *human* characteristics, without the self-questioning doubt of latent homosexuality that troubles many college-age men and women in our era when these qualities are sex-linked. She will not cling to her parents, nor they to her, but will establish an increasingly larger sphere of her own independent world in which she moves and works, loves and thinks, as a maturing young person. She will learn to take pleasure in her own body and to view sex as a good and wonderful experience, but not as an exclusive basis for an ultimate commitment to another person, and not as a test of her competence as a female or her partner's competence as a male. Because she will have a many-faceted conception of her self and its worth, she will be free to merge and lose herself in the sex act with a lover or a husband.

Marriage for our hypothetical woman will not mark a withdrawal from the life and work pattern that she has established, just as there will be no sharp discontinuity between her early childhood and youthful adult years. Marriage will be an enlargement of her life experiences, the addition of a new dimension to an already established pattern, rather than an abrupt withdrawal to the home and a turning in upon the marital relationship. Marriage will be a "looking outward in the same direction" for both the woman and her husband. She will marry and bear children only if she deeply desires a mate and children, and will not be judged a failure as a person if she decides against either. She will have few children if she does have them, and will view her pregnancies, childbirth and early months of motherhood as one among many equally important highlights in her life, experienced intensely and with joy but not as the exclusive basis for a sense of self-fulfillment and purpose in life. With planning and foresight, her early years of child bearing and rearing can fit a long-range view of all sides of herself. If her children are not to suffer from "paternal deprivation," her husband will also anticipate that the assumption of parenthood will involve a weeding out of nonessential activities either in work, civic or social participation. Both the woman and the man will feel that unless a man can make room in his life for parenthood, he should not become a father. The woman will make sure, even if she remains at home during her child's infancy, that he has ample experience of being with and cared for by other adults besides herself, so that her return to a full-time position in her field will not constitute a drastic change in the life of the child, but a gradual pattern of increasing supplementation by others of the mother. The children will have a less intense involvement with their mother, and she with them, and they will all be the better for it. When they are grown and establish adult lives of their own, our woman will face no retirement twenty years before her husband, for her own independent activities will continue and expand. She will be neither an embittered wife, an interfering mother-in-law nor an idle parasite, but together with her husband she will be able to live an independent, purposeful and satisfying third act in life. (pp. 162–164)

In the Rossi proposal, there are many implications for teachers; for example, how does a teacher help intelligent young women to recognize their accomplishments and raise their aspirations? (For the schools' response to the impact of women's rights, see Chapter 2.)

The Impact of the Communications Media

Mass media is a term commonly used to refer to communication by television, radio, newspapers, magazines, and the film industry. No doubt, television has the greatest influence of all the mass media. Television is used as a baby-sitter by parents who do not care to be bothered with their children. Captain Kangaroo (Keeshan, 1983) was often told that he was the parent's best friend, the very best baby-sitter. Because much of televison programming is aimed toward adult audiences, most of the programs that children watch are adult-oriented. The fact is that children do watch a lot of TV, and the influence of TV programming on their lives is tremendous. The authors do not suggest that the government completely regulate the television industry; our wish is that parents become more aware of what their role should be and that television production become more responsive to the child audience.

The National Institute of Mental Health (NIMH) produced a report in 1971 for the U.S. Surgeon General, entitled *Television and Growing Up: The Impact of Televised Violence*. Ten years later, the NIMH published an updated report called *Television and Behavior: Ten Years of Scientific Progress and Implications for the Eighties*. Some of the highlights of the findings in this latest report are as follows:

1. Much of television's content seems to foster poor nutrition, especially in commercials for sweets and snack foods. The fact is that children who watch a lot of television have poorer nutritional habits than children who do not watch as much.
2. Alcohol consumption is common on TV, and it is condoned as a regular social practice.
3. When people drive cars on television, they do not wear seat belts. Correlational studies suggest that people's attitudes are influenced by these portrayals.
4. After ten more years, the consensus among most of the research community is that violence on television does lead to aggressive behavior by children and teenagers who watch the programs. Not all children become aggressive, of course, but the correlations between violence and aggression are positive.
5. Television can be used to enhance children's imaginative play if an adult watches with the child and interprets what is happening.
6. Women on television are generally stereotyped more as passive and feminine and men as strong and masculine.
7. About 10 percent of the television characters are black, but few are Hispanics, Native Americans or Asian Americans.
8. Television characters usually have higher status jobs than average people in real life. Few characters are blue-collar workers.
9. In general, researchers seem to agree that television has become a major socializing agent of American children.
10. People who are heavy viewers of television are more apt to think the

world is violent than are light viewers. They also trust other people less and believe that the world is a "mean and scary" place.

11. Television, according to some observers, reinforces the status quo and contributes to a homogenization of society and a promotion of middle-class values.

12. Television broadcasts of religious services bring religion to those who cannot get out, but they also may reduce attendance at churches and, thus, opportunities for social interactions. (*Television and Behavior*, 1982, pp. 5–8)

Television has a tremendous impact on American society. It subtly controls a lot of our thinking and actions. The NIMH report conservatively estimated that a child, during an average day's viewing, would see 10 episodes involving drinking, adding up to about 3,000 episodes per year. The effect of this type of repeated modeling in front of young children is very powerful. No wonder we have a drinking problem among our teenagers! Also, if most characters are portrayed as middle class or above, no wonder many children and adults, who are not middle class, are disillusioned in life as a result of the media influences. Some racial groups are almost entirely left out, and this omission does not represent the pluralism that is truly America.

The advertisers as well as the television executives share the problems that society faces in relation to TV. One prominent cereal company president said (Mason, 1979)

this attitude on the part of broadcasters and advertisers is plainly and simply irresponsible—because it does not make social sense. U.S. broadcasters have operating control of one of the most economically and socially important assets—the U.S. broadcast spectrum—in the world today. The TV medium is clearly the most pervasive influence in our society. This is particularly true in the case of children, who, by the time they reach college age, will have spent more time in front of a TV set than they will have spent in school, church, or in conversation with their parents. (p. 14)

The inference from this statement is that if nonnutritious breakfast foods are being advertised, then the cereal industry is as much to blame as anyone. Auto manufacturers are irresponsible when they supply free or discounted automobiles for use on TV shows and allow them to be used improperly, without seat belts.

The print media can also be accused of diminished social responsibility in advertising, particularly as it applies to cigarettes. Despite the heavy evidence of the link of cigarette smoking to cancer, advertisements picture healthy, good-looking people smoking while at work or during leisure activities. Is it any wonder that our young people want to smoke in order to imitate these adult models pictured in these expensive advertisements? Again, the advertisers as well as the media share the responsibility.

In some countries in Asia, the media are used to promote positive changes to effect better health standards. For example, in a few Asian countries, the media are playing an important role in promoting breast feeding and in educating women away from infant formula (Banerjee, 1983). (In the undeveloped countries of the world, there have been problems with contamination of bottled milk for infants.) So here we see the media being used to effect a positive change for a country. Most of these countries have a state-controlled press, whereas in America we have a free press. The hope is that our free media will become more responsible and will turn many of these negative effects into positive ones. In fairness to the American media, they act very responsibly in many situations.

Summary

In Chapter 1, we have tried to list and expand on some of the weighty social issues in society at large. Although our society has always had social problems, these difficulties seem to have multiplied either through greater public awareness or through an increase in the number of incidents. Our public schools are integral parts of the community; therefore, whatever affects the larger society generally affects the schools. Schoolteachers need to understand these sociological problems as well as possible so that they can also understand better why some of their pupils act the way they do.

Chapter 2, ''The Responses of Schools to Social Forces,'' is presented to help future teachers to better understand their role.

Questions

1. Because of the impact of poverty on the schools, is it as easy for one born into a family at a low socioeconomic level to advance to higher socioeconomic status? Why, or why not?
2. Patterson's study revealed that parents can be taught how to monitor their child's behavior. How did this experiment work?
3. How is your community addressing the problem of a higher percentage of unemployment among minority groups?
4. What is the effect of TV viewing on incidents of violence among young people? Suggest some solutions.
5. How can a local school principal or teacher lessen the impact of social problems in his or her school? Can the school superintendent or school board do more? Use specific examples from your community.
6. Describe any changes in family or school life that you have observed or experienced, which you feel are a result of the women's movement. Do you view them as favorable or unfavorable changes?

2

The Responses of Schools to Social Forces

OBJECTIVES

After reading Chapter 2, the student will be able to:
- Identify several solutions to the impact of social forces on our schools.
- Recognize specific actions to take to minimize the effects of such problems as child abuse, suicide, and sexism.
- Become more conscious of community agencies that can assist the teacher.
- Make a more positive response to the desegregation of our schools.
- Implement some values in educational procedures in the classroom.
- Through multiethnic education, respond more accurately to the pluralistic culture we live in.

Responses to the Impact of Our Economic System

It is not our purpose to come up with an alternative to the American free-enterprise system as it exists today, but we do need to discuss how schools are responding to the varying aspects of our economy. Currently, school systems across the country are responding to a massive need to teach computer technology, and millions of dollars are being spent on these programs. This response is important because if this country is to remain strong and in the forefront of world progress, we will need a population that is computer-literate. As teachers, we also need to be aware that a modern, highly computerized society may produce outcomes that are not all for the betterment of our society. For example, a computer-operated robot may weld a car body and prevent a person from having to breathe toxic gases given off by the welder, but some jobs may be eliminated, too.

The Alternative School Movement: A Response to Dropping Out

Among the specific school changes that are taking place today must be included the alternative school movement. This movement was begun to try to meet the needs of more of our student population. One of the target groups receiving aid through an alternative school are children from low-income families who drop out of school. In an earlier day, it was easy for young people who dropped out of schools to be absorbed into the work force, either on the farms or in the factories. But as the industrial age became increasingly complex, and society became more troubled, students without a high-school diploma found it increasingly difficult to find work. In the 1960s, the existence of so many dropouts from the public schools and the increased demands of business and industry caused school systems to search for alternatives.

Many types of innovations were tried within traditional schools in the 1960s and the early 1970s, and when most were evaluated, the general conclusion was that none of the innovations made a significant difference (Raywid, 1981). Then, in 1974, David Tyack wrote an interpretive history of American education that led many to question whether there is one best way to conduct school, that is, a single best set of aims for all, an ideal curriculum, and one best way to organize and administer schools and to prepare teachers. Tyack helped to encourage the promotion of alternative schools. Harlem Prep came into being in 1967, and Philadelphia's Parkway Program started in 1968. These two alternative schools popularized the movement. Money from the Ford, Carnegie, and Rockefeller Foundations gave support to these experimental programs. The movement has grown to more than ten thousand alternative schools, which can be found in 80 percent of the nation's larger school districts.

Alternative schools originally set out to humanize education, to make schools more relevant, and thus to reduce the school dropout rate. Now, in the 1980s, alternative schools or programs are looked on as a way to effect reform in education and perhaps to humanize the entire system; thus, the alternative schools of the 1980s are far different from those that inspired the movement in the 1960s.

Many movements or innovations in education last a short time, but the alternative school movement appears to be a more lasting type of change.

Alternative Education

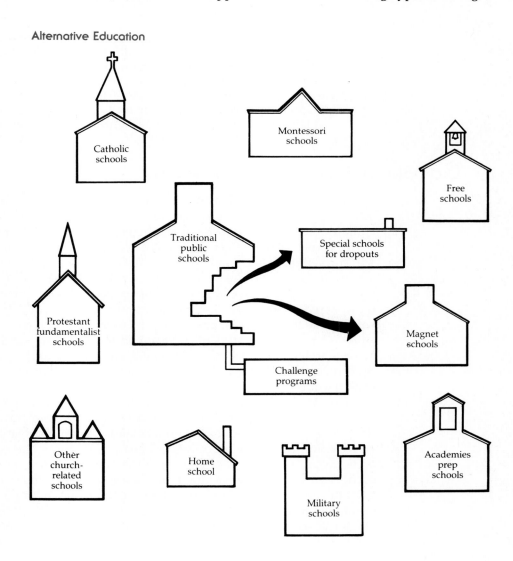

Educational movements of the past seem to have had an either/or outlook, but the 1980s are an era of variety, and alternative schools fit this variety. How long the alternative school movement will stay with us is not as important as the problems it may help to solve in the meantime and the legacy it will leave after its demise. Currently, evaluations show that alternative education is an extraordinarily effective solution to the problems of school vandalism and violence, high truancy, and high dropout rates (Raywid, 1981). The following quotation from Richard and Kammann (1972) is an analogy that illustrates how school systems have been doing business, and one can infer how the use of alternative schools may put selecting a school on the same basis as selecting the family doctor:

> Imagine a town where every family is assigned arbitrarily to one local doctor by a ruling of the board of health. Imagine that the board of health assigns families only on the basis of the shortest distance from the home to the doctor's office. Imagine, finally, that when a family complains that the assigned doctor is not helping one of its ailing members, the board of health replies: "Sorry, no exceptions to doctor assignments."
>
> If this sounds like a totalitarian nightmare, it also is a description of the way school boards assign children to schools and teachers. (p. 37)

Examples of Three Alternative Schools

In Denver, the Metropolitan Youth Education Center was created to educate school dropouts. Students are between the ages of sixteen and twenty-five, and they must have dropped out of school at least six months previously. The center's basic goal is to get students back into the mainstream of education. The curriculum focuses on basic skills, the academic requirements for a high-school diploma, and the preparation necessary to pass the General Educational Development (GED) test. The center issues no diplomas; instead, records of credits earned are sent to the schools that the students last attended, which issue the diplomas, preventing the permanent stigma of dropping out. Although most of the students who attend the center are much like students at regular high schools as far as intelligence and family backgrounds are concerned, they do have a higher than average incidence of personal problems (Jacques, 1982).

One alternative school program began as a result of innovative school programs in the Cupertino Union School District that were not accomplishing the task of education. According to its critics, Cupertino, near San Francisco, was "wishy-washy" in its educational goals. Cupertino, like many other districts during the late 1960s and the 1970s, changed to a more progressive curriculum with teachers acting more or less as facilitators in order to better meet the needs of a restless, sometimes militant student population. Parents eventually reacted negatively to the school program in Cupertino, especially when test scores went down, and they developed an alternative school pro-

Sudbury Valley School in Massachusetts is a modern, thriving private alternative school where students of all ages interact to pursue their own interests without grades or set curricula. (Photo used by permission of Sudbury Valley School, Framington, MA.)

gram. The change in the Cupertino district was engineered by the parents, not by professional educators. Unique aspects of this alternative type of school are that it is teacher-centered, it emphasizes field trips for seeing things directly related to class, and its homework is not "busy" work, and has a definite due date. These schools try to give the student the grades that she or he earns, and they stress true professionalism among their teachers. Cupertino (cited in Pursell, 1976, p. 30) called this return-to-basics program Academics-Plus, and the students in the program have scored at or above district norms in reading and math, although they have scored below district norms in language arts. What is interesting about this particular alternative school is that the "alternative" method is what many would perceive as old-fashioned, traditional, fundamental schooling.

Another alternative model, called the Zoo School, in Grand Rapids, Michigan, has been very successful in encouraging independent thinking. This school is adjacent to the zoo and is a one-year magnet school to attract motivated sixth-graders. The only criterion for acceptance into the school is that the students must be willing to work hard at learning. Eight specific independent learning skills are taught at the Zoo School: reading, writing, research, planning, problem solving, self-discipline, self-evaluation, and presentations. The basic idea during a single school year is to move the student from dependent learning to independent learning and, in the process, to concentrate on the eight skills listed. Teachers try to give each student as much freedom as he or she can handle in problem solving, but the school also recognizes that freedom, without an understanding of how to use it, can be harmful. The school uses facilities of the zoo as much as possible to build its academic curriculum. This very exciting alternative program, started in 1974, has been well received and highly evaluated. One hundred percent of both parents and children say that they would advise highly motivated students to attend the Zoo School. Most of the group evaluated agreed that the Zoo School allowed students to make greater use of their creative abilities.

These three examples of alternative schools indicate some of the variety that is available in alternative schools. Smith and others (cited in Schlemner, 1981, p. 564) made a study of alternative schools in four states and concluded that individuals are more likely to see merit in programs that they elect to attend than in those imposed on them; therefore, free choice was a most significant factor in this study. Alternative schools, most of which began by seeking to keep children in school, have expanded their focus. The idea that the options approach to education is a good one is borne out by the success of the alternative school movement.

The schools are responding in many ways to our economic system. We have mentioned just two examples: the computer education programs and alternative schools. However, good school systems, teachers, and administrators are changing constantly to meet needs that arise from our economic system. Still, the budgets of school corporations are not flexible enough to suit the needs of all people, and the needs of the poor are often not met at all.

Responses to Delinquency and Crime

The causes of students getting into trouble are many and varied, but the schools are making some rather general responses to this problem. Schools can do a great deal by having a fine academic program, by having teachers that make the curriculum exciting, and by having a sensitive and caring faculty with a good guidance program. Some schools are going even further to help students who are in trouble or those on the fringe of trouble: peer counseling is one such program.

Peer Counseling

All through junior and senior high school, students are trying to identify who they are in this complicated world. The value that schools and society put on academic achievement often causes them to overlook the development of the personality and the self-concept. It is fairly easy for children to develop intellectually and socially when they come from families that are free of trauma, but many of today's young people are exposed to alcoholism, child abuse, divorce, poverty, drugs, and a number of other negative influences. Some schools are trying to help students through peer counseling programs. In peer counseling, selected students counsel other students.

In a high school at Jericho, New York, the suicide of a promising senior provided the impetus for starting a peer counseling program. Peers began to lead rap sessions on such adolescent problems as personal freedom, dating,

Students are specially trained to be peer counselors or peer facilitators. *(Photo by Axler.)*

family difficulties, and interpersonal relationships. Counselors at Jericho found that students could discuss problems more freely with their peers. Peer leaders—students in senior high-school—were selected from groups that had been led by adults. They were given training and were assigned to small groups of ten to twelve junior-high students. After five years of peer counseling activities, a survey showed that 80 percent of the participants found the experience enjoyable and valuable enough to continue; 65 percent said that they were more aware and accepting of their own and other people's feelings. Only 26 percent of the participants said that they liked themselves better, but 54 percent of the parents felt that the peer counseling program had caused their youngsters to feel more positive about themselves. However, 90 percent of the student counselors felt an enhanced self-concept as a result of their participation (Hamberg, 1980). Jericho has refined its peer counseling procedure over the years, and it represents an exemplary effort to meet student needs.

At Laredo Middle School in Colorado, a successful program of peer counseling has been developed at the middle-school level. The school community backs the program, which is a real key to its success. The students are well trained and carefully selected to perform a number of counseling tasks. Peer counselors meet once a day in a regularly scheduled class. Their assignments include counseling at least one student regularly in a one-to-one relationship; working as aides in a preschool housed in the same building; peer tutoring; working as aides in a learning disabilities program; hosting visitors who come to the school; and introducing new students to their school, teachers, and classes. School officials conclude that the Laredo program of peer counseling works because it is educational and because it makes the school a place where students, teachers, and parents like to spend their time (Grady, 1980).

These two examples of the use of peer counselors at both the senior-high and middle-school levels show how students can become more involved through training and through developing leadership responsibility. Any such program takes much careful planning on the part of staff, at least one capable adult leader, community support, and, most of all, administrative support and encouragement. These programs are bound to increase school spirit and support of other aspects of the academic program.

Responses to Potential Suicide Victims

As a teacher, you may never have a student commit suicide while he or she is a student of yours, but learning how to treat potential victims will not be a waste of your time. Learning the methods of treatment used to help students with potential suicide problems will have a ripple effect on how you treat all members of your classes.

School officials, particularly guidance counselors, need to know how to evaluate potential victims. The schools need to help teachers and staff understand factors that are associated with childhood suicidal behavior. In addition, schools should develop effective intervention services within the school and between schools and community mental health facilities. It is also important for you as a teacher to know your own attitudes and skills in responding to a potentially suicidal child (Pfeffer, 1981).

As a teacher, it would help you to keep in mind some general characteristics of potential suicide victims. The majority of adolescents who have attempted suicide have evidenced some of the following changes (McKenry, Tishler, and Christman, 1980):

1. A drastic change in the student's personal appearance, generally from good to bad.
2. Inability to concentrate and exhibition of problems in judgment and memory.
3. A dramatic shift in quality of school work.
4. Changes in daily behavior and living patterns, such as extreme fatigue, boredom, stammering, and/or decreased appetite.
5. Changes in social behavior such as falling asleep in class or becoming a discipline problem in class.
6. Open signs of mental illness, such as delusions and hallucinations.
7. A sense of overwhelming guilt and shame.
8. Loss of friends. (p. 43)

Some of these changes occur from time to time in many students, but a composite of these behavioral changes may fit into the overall pattern of a potential suicide victim. In addition to the above-mentioned behavioral changes, dramatic changes in the family or school situation can precipitate a teen suicide. Two examples in the family would be a marriage breakup or a family member's death. Certainly, boy–girl relationships are very important, and a breakup in a relationship could create a crisis. Also, "Studies of adolescents who have attempted suicide indicate that school adjustment is often one of the major precipitating factors" (McKenry et al., 1980, p. 44).

After you have identified students who may be potential suicides, talk to them about what you have noticed in their behavior and ask them how they see themselves. Chances are, if you have developed trusting relationships with your students, that they will be willing to talk to you about their problems. Because your time is limited, find out from the students if they would like to talk to a guidance counselor. After you have a student's permission to talk to a counselor on his or her behalf, do so cautiously at first, until you are sure that the student will get the care that is needed. Many good school guidance departments insist on a psychological evaluation of the student, and counselors are in touch with other community agencies capable of giving the proper assistance. Some schools have an organized plan for crisis intervention that can help you as a teacher at the time of a crisis.

Response to Changing Family Needs

Formal schooling in America today includes a lot of training that in earlier times might not have been considered in the curriculum, and some of these new courses have been added as a result of changing family life. Schools commonly offer courses in sex education, drug and alcohol abuse, food and nutrition, and others in similar areas. The newest course may be parenting, whose purpose is to help young people be better parents. The schools in Tacoma, Washington, are in their fifth year of a parenting program that has resulted in opening better lines of communication between adults and teenagers about child rearing. The Tacoma program has a three-part structure: traditional academic instruction in child development, small group discussions with parents from the community, and firsthand experience in a nursery located at the high school (Brown, 1980). Many sex education courses include units on parenting; therefore, it is evident that schools, as they reflect society's needs in their curriculum, are not overlooking the parenting aspect of family life.

One-parent families are growing in America. In 1980, 18 percent of the nation's schoolchildren were living with one parent (Brown, 1980). In a study of one-parent families, Brown found that they accounted for 100 percent of the expulsions, 42 percent of the dropouts, 39 percent of the discipline problems, and only 9 percent of high academic achievement when compared to two-parent families and no-parent families (foster families and relatives). One-parent families and no-parent families represented only 25 percent of the total group, and so they were disproportionately represented in the negative statistics. Some concrete suggestions that were made at the conclusion of the study were that schools make provisions for single parents to have access to school personnel and activities after working hours, that school services be revised to better accommodate the unique needs of children from one-parent families, and that schools' adult education programs assume a major role in providing effective programs in the area of parenting (Brown, 1980). Whether they are composed of one or two parents living together or separately, many families need help, and the schools are a logical place for families to get the specific help they need.

As we move into the 1980s and beyond, educators should still be guided by one single purpose: *to do what is best for the students who come to them.* Parents are an integral part of the educational process and ought to be treated as such. If either the teachers or the parents fail in their coeducator's role, society will ultimately lose. Public criticism of schools is most often directed toward teachers and administrators, but parents have failed in their educational role at least equally. Educators often blame poor family situations for the students they receive and parents blame the schools for the poor education their children are getting, when both should be working together for the good of the children.

Response to Desegregation

When the desegregation orders were handed down by the various federal and district courts, school systems and communities knew that they must do something to prepare for the changes that were to come. Although white families had lived near black families and they had worked together for years, they had not been familiar with each other's cultural differences. Denial of equal educational opportunity to blacks in segregated schools had resulted in their having many learning deficiencies, but more important, their learning

Home—school advisers help with a wide variety of student problems. (*Photo used by permission of the Metropolitan School District of Lawrence Township.*)

expectations were very low. Now it was imperative for schools to gear their programs to meet these new teaching challenges. Schools had training sessions for their teachers and staff, community desegregation groups got together, and some important curriculum adjustments were made.

Human relations groups were set up to deal with teacher–pupil relationships within the schools. One ninth-grade student, who was a member of one of these committees, made the following statement (Bash, 1973):

> Why is it that people put blacks and whites in some kind of segregate categories?
>
> The students have fears and prejudices only because they were taught this. Even adults have this feeling and try to hide it instead of listening to the student's side of it. Why not let the teachers learn from their students sometimes? If teachers can learn from their students whom they are trying to teach, they will find they have a much better communication with people, Black and White.
>
> Let the child take the job for a while, listen to your students, each one, and your subject will be taught and learned. Talk to your class, you will find that more students in your class will let their feelings out about the subject or whatever is being talked about.
>
> Relate to people now!!! Don't wait. They will relate right along with you. (p. 16)

Not only did this young man have a good idea for bettering race relations, but he also hit on the good teaching technique of listening to your students. Many immediately useful suggestions, as well as long-lasting suggestions, on how to improve race relations have come from the human relations groups that were set up. Actually, by the time some of you reading this chapter have entered teaching, the work of the human relations committee may be on the back shelf, but one could benefit greatly by talking with former leaders and reading documents written by committee members.

Some research has been done on interracial acceptance in desegregated schools. The findings by Bennett (1979) in one large midwestern school district indicate that where there is a climate of acceptance, teachers do not distinguish between the learning potential of their black and white students. These teachers also tend to be strong and directing, fair, warm, spontaneous, and involved in the teaching profession. Bennett also found that although there was much student initiation in "acceptance" classrooms, the teacher still controlled the classroom interaction.

In the face of all the turmoil and change surrounding the process of desegregation, quality education is possible. Desegregation practices can have a positive effect on students, teachers, and administrators through changes in curricula, instructional practices, and attitudinal adjustments. Hawley (1983) suggested several strategies that are helpful in the desegregation process:

1. Desegregate as early as possible before racial prejudices are ingrained.
2. Employ instructional strategies that retain heterogeneous classes and work groups. These strategies deemphasize competition and encourage student interaction. Rigid forms of ability grouping should be avoided and possible misuse of special programs should be monitored closely.
3. Develop interracial extracurricular activities which provide contact in cooperative, nonthreatening situations.
4. Develop a rigorous but fair disciplinary program that can be enforced in consistent, firm, and equitable ways.
5. Involve parents directly in the education of their children. (pp. 335–336)

These are only a few ideas that have assisted in the desegregation process. If you find yourself in a school that is having some desegregation problems, the literature is full of helpful suggestions. Hawley (1983) wrote that desegregation is more than a challenge to the capacity of schools to provide high-quality education: it is a test of our national commitment to social mobility and to racial equality.

Busing and School Integration

Busing has been one solution used to solve the integration problem in our public schools. Busing has given many opportunities to both minority and white majority children to mix socially, athletically, and intellectually in the schools. The process of busing has occurred after extensive court litigation, some of which was bitter, and after the expenditure of millions of dollars for school buses and bus transportation. In 1978–1979, Los Angeles spent $375 per pupil on the mandatory busing program alone. In spite of all the busing efforts and all the other types of programs that have been devised to integrate our schools, the National Task Force on Desegregation says that racial bias is still pervasive and that government policies and practices that result in school segregation still exist (Summers, 1979).

Busing to achieve racial integration is an established, if still controversial, program in most metropolitan areas. (Photo used by permission of the Metropolitan School District of Lawrence Township.)

In 1972, several studies were published on the effects of busing. The Armor study (Ozmon and Craver, 1972) indicated that measured results had shown no improvement in academic skills, self-esteem, aspirations, or racial tolerance among the children tested (p. 32). The Armor study was done in selected districts from Boston to Riverside, California, and it was almost the only scientific study to indicate negative effects. On the positive side, this study in Rochester is one of many to report similar types of results:

> tests indicated that the academic performance of 135 ghetto youngsters attending school in the Rochester suburbs was dramatically higher than that of youngsters left behind in the city. There were also indications that white students developed better racial attitudes, and that white students in integrated suburban schools did better on tests and grades than whites in non-integrated suburban schools. (p. 33)

Magnet Schools and School Integration

One method of desegregation, which has worked to some degree in several school systems throughout the country, has been to establish magnet schools. The term *magnet* refers to the fact that certain schools, if made especially attractive to children and parents, attract students from all over the school district, thus assisting in the integration process. Magnet schools can be set up at all levels in the educational process and can include specializations that are limited only by one's imagination.

The magnet school plan in Houston has been one of the nation's most successful. In Houston's Independent School District, there are sixty-one magnet programs. One magnet school is for the performing and visual arts; and on this school's marquee, announcements of student performances in dance, drama, media arts, music, and the visual arts can be seen. Academic instruction is correlated with history, theory, and technique in each art area. The future artists of Houston and the United States are blooming here (McIntire, Hughes, and Say, 1982). Houston also has a program called Vanguard for the academically gifted, which begins in kindergarten and ends in high school. A definite measure of the success of Houston's magnet program is that the outstanding successes of these schools are attracting nonminority students back into the city. The greatest advantage of the magnet schools is that they are voluntary.

In Tucson, magnet schools have helped to successfully integrate the schools. Some magnet schools have tried innovations such as bilingualism. When successful, these innovations have spread to other magnet schools. Tucson has a large bilingual population; therefore, this type of magnet school has been very popular. (Grant, 1983).

In Boston, as many as one third of the school population attends magnet schools, which are racially balanced. Fantini (1982) wrote that although many magnet schools have committed themselves to basic academic skills, they also identify and cultivate talent and introduce the concept of education by choice, as does the alternative school program.

One of the keys to the success of the magnet schools is that they are more closely linked to the educational needs and interests of the students than are the traditional schools. These types of schools often have waiting lists, and children attending them have shown improved test scores. We are living in a complex society where many options must be tried to answer our population's diverse educational needs.

Response to Drug and Alcohol Abuse

Probably every countermeasure available to control the abuse of alcohol and drugs by teenagers has been tried by some school system in the country. School officials' responses vary from denying even that a problem exists to calling in dogs trained to find drugs or having some of their students strip-searched. No matter what we say and do as teachers, the problem will not go away. No one single attack seems to solve the whole problem because it is too complex, but the most successful programs seem to take a middle-of-the-road approach, using the best ideas from past experience.

The use and abuse of chemical substances is widely accepted in our society, and the schools must cope with this problem. Because teenagers crave acceptance among their peers, many drink alcohol or take drugs in order to be "sophisticated." Don't we as adults, with a leadership role in society, have a role to play to protect children from this dangerous force in our society? As teachers we are engaged in shaping minds, which, when under the influence of chemical substances, are unavailable to the whole purpose of education. Perhaps the most important question is how, as teachers, can we handle the alcohol and drug problem in ways that will produce the most positive results.

Students Against Drunk Driving (SADD) chapters have been established in schools across the country as teens try to combat alcohol abuse. (Photo by Axler.)

Xenia, Ohio, has a complete no-nonsense plan for dealing with alcohol and drug abuse. Xenia's plan works on approximately the following basis (Strong, 1983):

Students found to be under the influence of drugs or alcohol at school will not be tolerated. On the first offense, the student will be suspended from school for at least ten days *and* recommended for expulsion. The student may be permitted to return to school after ten days if—and only if—the student and parents agree to participate in a community treatment program. The local juvenile justice court will intercede against any student or family that does not comply. In addition, the student may not take part in any extracurricular activities for at least one season.

Punishment for the second—and each subsequent—offense must be even stronger. For example: "The student will be expelled from school for the rest of the semester, with loss of credit for the semester. Both student and parents must participate in a treatment program. Those who fail to comply will come under court order to do so."

In Xenia, we have toughly worded policies such as these, and we've made an agreement with the juvenile court. We inform the court when a student and family fail to comply with our requirement that they receive counseling and treatment. The court assigns a probation officer to the student and places the student under court order to follow through with rehabilitation. As a last resort, the court sends the student to a juvenile detention center. (p. 24)

Xenia's school officials know that they must also work with students in order to *keep* them from becoming chemically dependent on either alcohol or drugs; therefore, they conduct values clarification exercises, games, and simulations to help students find themselves. They believe that in order to be responsible to chemically dependent students, they must make these students accountable for their own behavior.

The schools in Corpus Christi, Texas, have a tough policy on drug use, but school officials warn that such a policy is difficult to administer. The present policy works as follows (Strong, 1983):

when a student is caught in possession of a suspicious substance, the substance is confiscated, and the principal automatically recommends a temporary suspension of from three to five days. Parents are notified immediately. During the brief suspension period, administrators conduct investigations, including asking for police analyses of the confiscated substances. Unless the police say the substance is *not* an illegal drug, recommendation for a semester's suspension follows, with further explanation to the parents. The student then may appeal to the superintendent—and finally to the board—for a decision. (p. 25)

Critics of the Corpus Christi policy warn that it does not have a rehabilitation clause in it, but others say that students can go for a fresh start the next semester. Others say that unmotivated youth may deliberately seek suspension so that they can skip school entirely. Critics say that in Corpus Christi, the policy has a disproportionate impact on low-income Mexican-American children. The greatest problem is proving that students are under the influence of either alcohol or drugs, as proof requires a trained observer and blood and urine tests. Any policy for dealing with a problem as complicated and entangled as alcohol and drug abuse is not going to be easy to administer. School officials need to decide how much they want to solve the problem and then act accordingly.

The nation's schools have allowed the alcohol and drug problem to enter through the front door and cause damage to thousands of young people. Unequivocally, abusers or distributors of mind-altering chemical substances have no place in a school. All school districts need a clear-cut plan for handling the alcohol and drug problem that includes rehabilitation options; ongoing general education on the dangers of drugs, alcohol, and other health problems; and firm discipline for offenders.

Response to Child Abuse

In Chapter 1, the problem of child abuse in America was defined. Schools and teachers are in an excellent position to help the victims of child abuse and, indirectly, the abusers.

Three steps are involved in protecting an abused child: (1) identification, (2) investigation, and (3) intervention. It is at the identification step that educators have the best opportunity to help. In some states, teachers and administrators are mandated to report all suspected cases of child abuse and neglect; therefore, legal action could possibly be taken against them for not reporting such violations. The important thing to remember is that by reporting suspected cases, one is not meddling in someone else's private problem but instead is helping to protect the life of a child: "Because we in America respect the privacy of the home, we have adopted a 'don't get involved' attitude that has sent many a child to an early grave" (Overton, 1979, p. 7). Suspected abuse cases are to be reported to the nearest office of the Department of Public Welfare, Child Protective Services Division, or the nearest police agency. Your job, as a teacher, is only to report and not to conduct a unilateral investigation.

As a teacher responsible for identifying a child abuse victim, look for any one or more of the following problems (Fraser, 1977):

One should suspect abuse if a child

is habitually away from school and constantly late;
arrives at school very early and leaves very late because he does not want to go home;

is compliant, shy, withdrawn, passive, and uncommunicative;

is nervous, hyperactive, aggressive, disruptive, or destructive;

has an unexplained injury—a patch of hair missing, a burn, a limp, or bruises;

has an inordinate number of "explained" injuries such as bruises on his arms and legs over a period of time;

exhibits an injury that is not adequately explained;

complains about numerous beatings;

complains about the mother's boyfriend "doing things" when the mother is not at home;

goes to the bathroom with difficulty;

is inadequately dressed for inclement weather with, for example, only a sweater in winter for outer wear;

wears a long-sleeved blouse or shirt during the summer months to cover bruises on the arms;

has clothing that is soiled, tattered, or too small;

is dirty and smells or has bad teeth, hair falling out, or lice;

is thin, emaciated, and constantly tired, showing evidence of malnutrition and dehydration;

is unusually fearful of other children and adults; or

has been given inappropriate food, drink, or drugs. (pp. 14–16)

Educators should also suspect child abuse if the parents (Fraser, 1977):

show little concern for their child's problems;

do not respond to the teacher's inquiries and are never present for the teacher's visits or for parents' nights;

take an unusual amount of time to seek health care for the child;

do not adequately explain an injury;

continue to complain about irrelevant problems unrelated to the injury;

suggest that the cause of an injury can be attributed to a third party;

are reluctant to share information about the child;

respond inappropriately to the seriousness of the problem;

cannot be found;

are using alcohol or drugs;

have no friends, neighbors, or relatives to turn to in crises;

have unrealistic expectations for the child;

are very strict disciplinarians;

were themselves abused, neglected, or deprived as children;

have taken the child to different doctors, clinics, or hospitals for past injuries;

show signs of loss of control or a fear of losing control; or

are unusually antagonistic and hostile when talking about the child's health problems. (pp. 14–16)

These problems and more will help you to identify victims and, hopefully, to start the recovery process so that these children can become productive citizens and much better students.

Response to Cultural and Ethnic Diversity

In this section, the school's response to cultural and ethnic diversity, is illustrated by multiethnic education, bilingualism, and value clarification.

Multiethnic Education

One of the main proposals for reforming education that emerged out of the social unrest of the 1960s and the early 1970s was multiethnic education, the type of curriculum that acquaints students with the many ethnic groups in our society so that they will become more familiar with and accepting of the diversity of the population in the United States. Advocates of multiethnic education feel that it should be an integral part of every social studies course from kindergarten through high school, so that our schools will reflect the reality of our society in the curriculum. Most American schools' curricula today represent the views of the dominant cultural group.

In conscience, at least, we believe in democracy and equality of opportunity for all Americans, but in practice, our schools, and our curricula in those schools, are not equal in their treatment of our diversity of cultures. Several things have happened in our nation's history to cause us to allow the curriculum to get into its present state. Puritan New England set the tone for education by being strongly in favor of education from the very beginning. Most of the trained teachers and early textbooks emerged from the New England area. Later, McGuffey's Readers influenced many more generations of schoolchildren, especially throughout the Midwest. Both the early school

Multiethnic education includes teaching children about the cultural heritage of different ethnic groups. *(Photo used by permission of the Metropolitan School District of Lawrence Township.)*

literature in New England and later the McGuffey's Readers espoused the dominant cultural group viewpoint of America, without the intentional exclusion of other groups.

When immigrants started arriving in large numbers, the dominant cultural influence on the school curriculum was not so innocent. The policy of assimilating new immigrants into American society became known as the "melting-pot" concept. New immigrants were forced to comply with certain national laws and to melt into American society. "Anglo-Saxon ideals were taught in the schools in order to bring these new people into the American race," according to Elwood P. Cubberley, a noted educational historian at the turn of the century (cited by Banks, 1977, p. 11). Despite the efforts of our government and our schools to make all ethnic groups into one new megaethnic group, mostly influenced by the dominant culture's philosophy, many ethnic groups settled into their own ethnic enclaves, where they could continue their unique cultural practices. Other cultural groups wished to become assimilated and become a part of their new country, therefore it was not always an unwilling participation by the newcomer.

Some Americans had become immigrants not because they chose to be, but because others had decided to bring them from Africa and force them into slave labor. Their descendants are our large ethnic group of black Americans. Lincoln's Emancipation Proclamation legally liberated them from slavery, but the *Plessey* v. *Ferguson* ruling by the U.S. Supreme Court in 1896 legitimized keeping them in an unequal position until the *Brown* decision in 1954. The *Brown* case set in motion numerous civil rights actions, both peaceful and violent, throughout the country, which eventually resulted in various forms of civil rights legislation, such as the 1964 Civil Rights Law and the 1965 Elementary and Secondary Education Act with all of its titles. During the upheaval, every established American institution was questioned, including our educational system.

Leaders in the multiethnic education movement realize that we are more a pluralistic nation than we are a monolithic nation, and that our cultural differences ought to be promoted and/or celebrated rather than diluted and lost. The first real evidence of a multiethnic impact on the curriculum came when there was an outcry for black history, which was first offered as a separate course to satisfy the demands of black students and civil rights organizations. Sometimes, history teachers inserted black history as an additional topic to be covered in their courses, but the course of study largely reflected the dominant culture.

As there were increasing signs of alienation among certain minority ethnic groups, particularly blacks, other steps were taken to change the curriculum and the school staff. For example, more and more minority teachers were hired; textbooks were written that reflected the contributions of most ethnic groups to our society; illustrations in textbooks were changed to show minorities fulfilling major roles; and in general, a much greater sensitivity was shown to ethnic and cultural diversity.

In addition to other obvious reasons for instituting multiethnic education, the busing of schoolchildren to achieve racial balance in our schools has resulted in an even greater need for multiethnic education. School districts are eager, for the most part, to meet the needs of all children in their schools, and most districts want their curriculums to be interesting and challenging to all their students. James A. Banks, an outstanding leader in multiethnic education, has suggested two exciting models for curriculum reform that offer the most inclusive and the most commonsense approach to multiethnic education. (See the accompanying illustration of Banks's model.)

According to Banks's diagram of curriculum reform, teachers in Model A talk only about mainstream perspectives of our history and culture. In Model B, the teachers use additives but retain mainstream emphasis. Banks suggested that teachers using Model A skip Model B and go to Model C, where the mainstream perspectives appear among several others and are in no way superior or inferior to the other perspectives. He called Model C the multiethnic model. Finally, in Model D, social or historical events are viewed in terms of other nations, and this type of curricular organization helps students to better understand the lands and cultures from which the various groups have come.

What the future holds for multiethnic education and other related federally sponsored programs is difficult to estimate, but a real need for such reforms has been well documented. There remain horror stories of how our native Americans are treated on and off their reservations, and the Chicanos and blacks still have to fight for rights that ought to be the same for all Americans. All minority ethnic groups must strive, to some degree, for acceptance, and there is no doubt that sound, well-thought-out, school-system-wide multiethnic curricular programs would be very helpful.

Innovative Strategies for Ethnic Studies

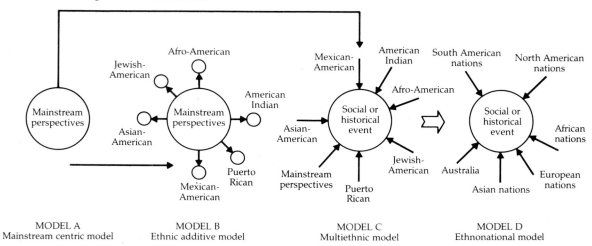

All Americans, indeed all planet Earth dwellers, fall somewhere on a continuum of acceptance of those who are different from themselves. The degree of acceptance ranges from none at all to total acceptance of other groups. The authors believe that the Banks typology, or study, of ethnic acceptance offers the reader a road map for understanding where individuals are "coming from" and where individuals might "go" in becoming more accepting of diversity. The figure on page 52 illustrates Banks's (1977) "Emerging Stages of Ethnicity":

Stages of Ethnicity

We often assume that ethnic groups are monolithic and have rather homogeneous needs and characteristics. Rarely is sufficient attention given to the enormous differences within ethnic groups. We also tend to see ethnic groups as static and unchanging. However, ethnic groups within modernized democratic societies are highly diverse, complex, and changing entities. I have developed a typology that attempts to describe some of the differences existing between individual members of ethnic groups. The typology assumes that individual members of an ethnic group are at different stages of ethnic development and that these stages can be identified and described.

The typology is a preliminary ideal type construct in the Weberian sense and constitutes a set of hypotheses based on the existing and emerging theory and research, and on my observations and study of ethnic behavior. The typology is presented here since it can be used as a departure point for classroom discussions of ethnicity. *However, its tentative and hypothetical nature should be emphasized in class discussions.*

Stage 1. Ethnic Psychological Captivity: During this stage, the individual has internalized negative ideologies and beliefs about his or her ethnic group that are institutionalized within the society. Consequently, the Stage-1 person exemplifies ethnic self-rejection and low self-esteem. The individual is ashamed of his or her ethnic group and identity during this stage and may respond in a number of ways, including avoiding situations that lead to contact with other ethnic groups or striving aggressively to become highly culturally assimilated.

Stage 2. Ethnic Encapsulation: Stage 2 is characterized by ethnic encapsulation and ethnic exclusiveness, including voluntary separatism. The individual participates primarily within his or her own ethnic community and believes that his or her ethnic group is superior to that of others. Many Stage-2 individuals, such as many Anglo-Saxon Protestants, have internalized the dominant societal myths about the superiority of their ethnic or racial group and the innate inferiority of other ethnic groups and races. Many individuals who are socialized within all-white suburban communities and who live highly ethnocentric and encapsulated lives may be described as Stage-2 individuals. Alice Miel describes these kinds of individuals in *The Shortchanged Children of Suburbia.*

Stage 3. Ethnic Identity Clarification: At this stage, the individual is able to clarify personal attitudes and ethnic identity, reduce intrapsychic conflict, and develop positive attitudes toward his or her ethnic group. The individual learns to accept self, thus developing the characteristics needed to accept and respond more positively to outside ethnic groups. Self-acceptance is a requisite to accepting and responding positively to others.

Stage 4. Biethnicity: Individuals within this stage have a healthy sense of ethnic identity and the psychological characteristics and skills needed to participate in their own ethnic culture, as well as in another ethnic culture. The individual also has a strong desire to function effectively in two ethnic cultures. We may describe such an individual as *biethnic.*

Stage 5. Multiethnicity: Stage 5 describes the idealized goal for citizenship identity within an ethnically pluralistic nation. The individual at this stage is able to function, at least at minimal levels, within several ethnic sociocultural environments and to understand, appreciate, and share the values, symbols, and institutions of several ethnic cultures. Such multiethnic perspectives and feelings, I hypothesize, help the individual to live a more enriched and fulfilling life and to formulate more creative and novel solutions to personal and public problems.

The Emerging Stages of Ethnicity: A Preliminary Typology

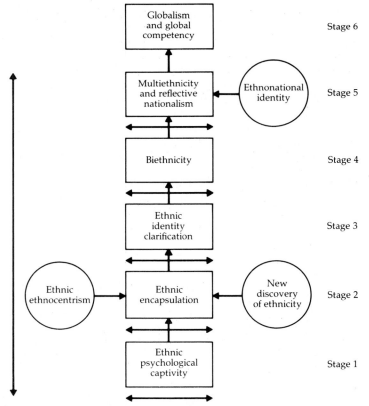

Source: Adapted by permission, from Banks, J. A. (1977). *Teaching strategies for ethnic studies* (3rd ed.). Newton, MA: Allyn and Bacon, p. 58.

Stage 6. Globalism and Global Competency: Individuals within Stage 6 have clarified, reflective, and positive ethnic, national, and global identifications and the knowledge, skills, attitudes, and abilities needed to function in ethnic cultures within their own nation as well as in cultures within other nations. These individuals have the ideal delicate balance of ethnic, national, and global identifications, commitments, literacy, and behaviors. They have internalized the universalistic ethical values and principles of humankind and have the skills, competencies, and commitments needed to act on these values. (pp. 55–56)

The important thing to remember when reading about these stages is that they are just stages and that no person need remain fixed in a stage. Movement either horizontally or vertically is taking place in all of our lives most of the time. The ultimate goal for most of us would be to reach Stage 6, but Stage 5 or Stage 4 is more realistic for most Americans. However, the more urgent goal in the 1980s, to avoid nuclear holocaust, might well be for all educators and for all of the world's people to strive for a Stage 6 identification.

It is important for all teachers and educators to recognize that they do live in a very pluralistic nation. The spirit of the 1960s and the early 1970s caused all of us in America to realize that discrimination toward minority ethnic groups can result in violence if we do not treat every group with fairness and dignity. For many reasons, children often come to school with attitudes that place them at either Stage 1 or Stage 2 in Banks's typology. Teachers can and do have a role to play in helping children, through multicultural and multiethnic education, to advance up the typology from Stages 1 and 2.

Bilingualism

Related to multiethnic education is bilingual education. Bilingual education was developed to help Latino students or those students of Spanish descent to better understand standard English curricula and to obtain for themselves an improved chance to compete for economic and social advantages in the mainstream of society. As we go about our busy lives, progressing through school and obtaining economic success, we often overlook the feelings of others, especially those less fortunate than we are. Latino children often come to school and face teachers and other children who not only do not know their language but also do not understand their culture. Latino children, without assistance, may not be able to master their language and a new one (English) at the same time; hence, they may become early dropouts because of their lack of understanding of the new language and culture.

Bilingualism and biculturalism are a way of reaching out to these disadvantaged students and giving them a better chance (Valverde, 1978):

Language is learned in the intimacy of one's family and around those we care about and cherish. It is in these comfortable surroundings that we express our most intimate feelings and emotions. Educators must accept and nurture, both verbally and nonverbally, the language children bring with them from the home. In doing this, not only do we indicate that the child's language is worthwhile, but also that the child is a worthy individual. As children sense this worth, educators can help them develop and reinforce a sense of efficacy. (p. 9)

In bilingual-bicultural programs, the child's native language is used as a mediator between the child's culture and that of the school and the society at large. As we understand the student better, we build important bonds of trust between the student and the teacher, which results in a greater readiness to learn the second language (Valverde, 1978).

An often-heard complaint is that bilingualism and biculturalism are bad for the child who is trying to learn a second language, but the contrary is actually true. We have learned that bilingualism and biculturalism are not detrimental to cognitive development, and that cognitive skills are transferable across cultures and languages (Ovando, 1983).

Another problem with bilingualism—and it is a political problem—concerns the enactment of Title VII of the Elementary and Secondary Education Act in 1968. The intent of Congress with this bilingual legislation was to get students to learn standard English as soon as possible and to drop their first or home language instruction. The result of dropping the first language was that the schools were no longer really encouraging a pluralistic development of our society. The 1968 legislation was not intended to maintain the rich linguistic resources that these children represented (Ovando, 1983). One of the great debate issues regarding bilingual-bicultural education, therefore, is maintaining the child's home language versus keeping bilingual instruction as short as possible.

The public is very concerned about new immigrant groups' having divided linguistic and cultural loyalties. Many people new to our society are finding that they can move into the mainstream without losing their first language and their cultural traditions. The political issue in regard to the cultural loyalty surrounding bilingualism and biculturalism is not resolved. The question asked is "Should linguistic minority groups have the right to participate fully in American life without being completely assimilated into the mainstream culture?" (Ovando, 1983, p. 567). The whole issue of cultural loyalty seems to be one of trust; thus, time will tell us whether this situation will present a serious problem.

Although funding for bilingual-bicultural education is still coming from the federal government, state legislatures are now prepared to assume funding for bilingual education. According to Ovando (1983), "It would be pedagogically unsound and sociopolitically imprudent to return to the sink-or-swim methods of the past" (p. 567). In fact, bilingual instruction could be the wave of the future because it can be personally satisfying to all students involved and can help students develop the interpersonal skills and attitudes that are essential to a healthy society. Bilingual-bicultural education could play a major role in helping us to prepare ourselves to participate in a global society.

Values Clarification

Values are changing in our society for many reasons: Some citizens in America are making a big effort to understand the diverse ethnic groups that live within our pluralistic nation. Also, the dominance of the church and the family are no longer as strong as they were before World War II, and thus, values that were once stressed at church and in the home are being lost. A one-school-district study in Minnesota, including interviews with 300 veteran teachers and administrators about changes in children over the past ten to twenty years, produced this comment (Hedin & Conrad, 1980):

> This passivity and dependence described by elementary teachers becomes in-grained by adolescence and, according to high school teachers, tends to harden into a generalized pattern of self-centeredness and lack of social con-cern. (p. 703)

The change of values indicated in the Minnesota study appears to corroborate the opinion held by some that ours is a materialistic society that is based on instant gratification and that places too much emphasis on what makes one "happy" in the short run. An example of the "me society" might be the increasing difficulty of finding people who want to dedicate their professional lives to teaching—a service occupation.

As teachers, we cannot suddenly overturn the "me society" model and insert a societal-concern model, but we can help students to look at the values they choose with much greater consideration. Harmin (1977) suggested a method of helping students to think more clearly about the value choices they make in life by including choosing, prizing, and acting in their deliberations:

Choosing

There are three elements in choosing: 1) making one's own judgments, 2) searching out alternatives in the choice situation, and 3) considering the conse-quences that will likely flow from each alternative. A word about each:

1. Free choice. Looking at this first part from its opposite side, I would say that a student would not be well prepared for value growth if he sought ways to avoid choices, perhaps by withdrawing from issues or timidly fol-lowing the lead of others. I believe it is better for students to learn to weigh evidence and to make choices independently.
2. Alternatives. Students should hunt for alternatives when faced with a choice situation. If a student approached issues as if they were simply either/or propositions or as if all the options were already known, he would not be well prepared to deal with values issues. The best way to find a good idea is to examine lots of ideas.
3. Consequences. Students should not conclude a survey of options with an impulsive or random choice. They should know how to think ahead, ma-nipulate abstractions, make predictions about what will happen if one op-tion or another were selected. It is on the basis of anticipated conse-

quences, not on the basis of chance or impulse, that I prefer students make their value choices.

Prizing

It is not enough that one's rationality be engaged in value situations. One's feelings, intuitions, and deepest senses must also be engaged if values are to be completely appreciated or fully internalized. Thus the deliberation process I recommend has an element called prizing, which asks two kinds of questions: 1) How do the options in value choice feel to you? Or which choices are you most likely to prize and cherish? 2) Which options would make you feel most proud to stand up and announce as being your choice? Or which options would you feel most comfortable in being publicly associated with? A word about prizing and affirming.

1. Prizing. Students would not be well served in their value growth if they did not know how to get in touch with their emotional or intuitive preferences or to include those preferences in their deliberations. This is not to suggest that one should always choose what one feels like choosing. But it is to suggest that one is better served by knowing how one feels and what one's conscience may be saying than by not knowing.

2. Affirming. There are important advantages to students being able to share with others their personal evaluations, especially the extent to which an option feels right to them. In one sense, an opportunity to share one's values with others tests the strength of those values. When we feel proud to tell those whom we respect about a choice we made, it is a signal to ourselves that we feel positive about that choice. When we feel ashamed to tell about it, if we would rather that even our best friends knew nothing about it, it suggests that we do not feel positive about the choice. Thus, one way to get positive feedback from our subconscious selves is to ask ourselves to what extent we would be proud of others knowing about that choice. In another sense, the more we learn about how to share our values proudly and straightforwardly, the more informed our society's collective choices can be. The more we are able to take advantage of each other's insights and wisdom, the less likelihood of a demagogue leading us astray. Students who learn when and how to stand up and be counted for the things they believe in learn something important about making democracy work. They learn to maximize collective support when support is available for their position and, when it is not, they learn how to take advantage of others' thoughts in making their own decisions.

Acting

Values issues are not abstract issues. They influence what we do with our limited time and energy. To divorce value deliberations from human behavior is to divorce values from the real world. So value deliberations should include the issue of "So what?" What does a deliberation mean in terms of behavior?

Looking at this from a negative perspective, I would say that students who have not learned how to take value deliberations beyond choosing and prizing, who do not ask themselves what, if anything, it all has to do with how they spend their days, have not learned complete valuing skills. I want students to be able to look at their behaviors, both their occasional acts and the general patterns of their actions, and to compare those behaviors with what their minds tell them are intelligent choices and what their hearts tell them are choices of which they can be proud. Our minds, our feelings, and our actions must be integrated if we are to live comfortable, value-directed lives.

Briefly, then, students are helped to deliberate on values issues when they are helped to develop skills for: 1) choosing freely, 2) searching for alternatives, 3) weighing predicted consequences. (pp. 25–27)

If children can be taught to practice using the Harmin model, they will not only be taught the values clarification process; more important still, they will be taught to act on their choices. The actions the students take will teach them about the consequences of their choices. The students using the Harmin model will develop skills in problem solving and they will be more actively involved in the learning process. The choice teens make to use or not to use drugs, to drink alcoholic beverages, to smoke cigarettes, or to get involved in premarital sex can be tested out by the Harmin process. Much more information is available on values teaching in *Values and Teaching* (1966) by Raths, Harmin, and Simon.

Literature is filled with examples of how citizens have had to make moral and ethical choices in life. Students need to be exposed to literature where delicate ethical decisions had to be made. The literature of the Holocaust has produced some very significant stories to help students clarify their own values. James Farnham (1983) wrote about the use of the Holocaust literature in helping students to clarify ethical and moral values. Farnham likes the story in *The Sunflower,* written by Simon Wiesenthal: A Jewish prisoner who is assigned to

work in a nearby hospital is taken by a nurse one day to the bedside of a young S.S. dying of wounds. The German had a pious Catholic upbringing and is now torn with genuine remorse for the atrocities he has participated in. The Jew listens quietly, giving him the solace of confessing his sins; but, when finally he must decide to forgive the German or not on behalf of all Jewish victims, he walks wordlessly from the room. Has he done the morally right thing or not? The Jew himself is not certain. This is the hard, ambiguous ethical core of *The Sunflower.* The value of the book is enlarged by a symposium which follows the tale itself in which thirty-two eminent people offer short opinions on the Jew's silence, providing students with an example of how good will and reasoned thought can be brought to bear on vital and ambiguous ethical issues. (p. 67)

The discussion that could follow such a reading would be valuable in bringing out the ethical implications of the Holocaust. Farnham (1983) wrote, ''Teaching students the historical and sociological facts of the Holocaust is of little value unless the ethical implications of the facts are raised" (p. 67). Teachers often teach meaningless facts without confronting the real moral and ethical issues in our society, and these opportunities are often there in our textbook literature.

Although the literature may be one source of values to talk about in class, our daily experiences are also filled with examples. One of the authors remembers stories about cheating on tests, violations of fish and game laws, highway litter problems, and many more that have served as illustrations for the purpose of clarifying values. One cheating story involved one of the authors when he was in the third grade on a day when he had failed to remember his spelling words for a test. He put together a small list of spelling words and slipped them in his desk under an empty inkwell, where they would be fully visible to him, but not to the teacher. After the test started, the teacher caught him immediately and sent him to the back of the room. Later, another cheater, who was known as the worst-behaved boy in the school, was caught by the teacher and sent to stand in the back of the room also. The original culprit stood there mortified by all of the embarrassment, but he was determined that it would never happen to him again. This is an example of learning by the world of "hard knocks."

Values emerge from our daily experiences everywhere, and as they emerge in your teaching experience, don't back away from discussing them in class. We cannot moralize as teachers, but we can involve students in ethical and moral value thinking. There is a lot of difference between telling children not to smoke because it is evil and explaining what cigarette tars will do to their lungs, and letting them decide for themselves.

Another example of an exercise in value clarification is that of the Sanchez family and the dilemma they faced concerning a possible strike (Banks, 1984):

The Sanchez Family and the Grape Strike

Mr. and Mrs. Sanchez and their seven children came from Mexico to live in California four years ago. Mr. Sanchez had been told by relatives who had been to the United States that he could make a lot of money very quickly if he came to California. When Mr. Sanchez arrived in California, he found that it was very hard to make a living working in the fields. Since the Sanchez family has been living in California, it has had to move many times in order to follow the crops and find work. The family has traveled as far as Texas and Michigan to work in the fields.

The work in the fields is very hard. Everyone in the family, except little Carlos, works in the fields so that the family can make enough money to get by with. Even Mrs. Sanchez, who used to stay at home and take care of the home when they lived in Mexico, now must work in the fields. The pay for the work is very low. Mr. and Mrs. Sanchez find that they get further and further into debt each year.

The Sanchez family is now living in the San Joaquin Valley in California. The family went to live there to work in the grape fields. For a while everything there was okay. Recently, a lot of things have been happening in the valley that Mr. and Mrs. Sanchez do not fully understand. Most of the field workers have said that they will not work next week because the Mexican American Union, led by Juan Gonzales, who is very popular with the workers, has called a strike. The union is demanding that the owners of the grape fields pay the workers more money and give them better worker benefits. The workers who belong to the union are threatening to attack any worker who tries to go to work while the strike is on.

Mr. Sanchez is not a member of the union. He wants very much to go to work next week. He has a lot of bills to pay and needs money for food and clothing. The family simply cannot get by with the small amount of money that the union has promised to give Mr. Sanchez if he joins it and refuses to work next week. Mr. Sanchez also realizes that if the grapes are not picked within the next two weeks, they will rot. He has heard that these strikes sometimes last for months. His boss told him that if he wants to go to work next Monday morning—the day the strike is to begin—he will protect him from the unionized workers. Mrs. Sanchez thinks that Mr. Sanchez should support the strike so that he can make higher wages in the future.

Questions

1. Do you think that Mr. Sanchez and his family will go to work in the fields next Monday? Why or why not?
2. If Mr. Sanchez does go to work, what do you think will happen to him and his family?
3. If Mr. Sanchez does not go to work in the grape fields next Monday, what do you think he might do to earn money?
4. What do you think Mr. Sanchez should do? Why?
5. What would you do if you were (a) Mr. Sanchez, (b) Mrs. Sanchez, or (c) the children? Why?
6. Tell whether you agree or disagree with this statement and why: The head of a family should never let his or her spouse and children do without food and clothing need. (p. 272)

Students can read about the Sanchez dilemma, answer the questions at the end, and really have a very sensitive value-based discussion. Many Americans have never had to think about the values discussed in these questions, but discussions like these help all of us to be more sensitive to each other, no matter what our cultural and ethnic origins might be.

Response to the Women's Movement

In your role as a teacher, you will influence children not only in a positive way; you will have many opportunities to influence them in a negative way as well. Negative results occur when teachers continue to reinforce old sex-role stereotypes. It is difficult for teachers to overcome the media image, which seems to reflect commonly held stereotypical views. The media often picture

Women in administrative roles in education serve as role models for students. *(Photo by Axler.)*

women in the roles of housewives or sex objects. Men are pictured more often in decision-making roles as bankers or business executives.

The sexist printed resources used by teachers are another difficulty that is hard to overcome. Gough (1976) made a study of basal readers published for the third grade in 1972 and 1973 and found that males outnumbered females both in content and in illustrations. The great heroes in history are generally depicted as males, and some textbooks even go so far as to intimate that girls lack competence in math: "Jane couldn't figure out how to do . . . , so John helped her" (p. 19).

As in all forms of unfair treatment, society loses. The people with top ability, whether they be girls or boys of whatever race, need to be encouraged to rise to their potential in any career opportunity. In 1972, the federal government took some action to end discrimination against females; Congress enacted Title IX, which says, "No person in the United States shall, on the basis of sex, be excluded from participation in, be denied the benefits of, or be subjected to discrimination under any education program or activity receiving financial assistance." As a result of this Title IX legislation, girls have received much better treatment in the athletic programs of our nation's public schools. In some states, where the boy's basketball tournament was the high-school event of the year, there is now a state girl's basketball tournament, and girls as well as boys now participate in an annual all-star game. Equality of treatment in athletics appears to be ahead of the academic programs in schools.

No solid evidence (Gough, 1976) indicates that men and women are born with psychological differences that cause them to behave in different ways. It follows, then, that cultural influences have the greatest impact on determining sex roles. Research (Gough, 1976) seems to indicate that sex-role expectations are repressive for members of both sexes, inhibiting both boys and girls from achieving their full psychological and intellectual capabilities. Careers for women in our society are primarily limited by the sex roles that are imposed on them by society: "Choices for women in our society are limited today only by interests, talents, motivations, and attitudes, and the school can play a part in influencing each of these" (Gough, 1976, p. 37). Schools and teachers can play an important part in helping to change traditional sex roles, thus freeing children of both sexes to become what they really want to be.

On so many issues, schools wait until there is a public awareness or a public outcry before anything is really accomplished because schools tend to reflect society's needs. Feminists and others like them think that schools should be more on the "cutting edge" than on the "trailing edge." The authors wonder if progress in human rights or equality in educational opportunity would advance more rapidly if teachers would take a more active role.

Some concrete suggestions by Foxley (1979) are offered to help teachers eliminate sexism in our schools. In the area of self-awareness, Foxley suggested the following activity:

> Much of the literature dealing with sex role stereotyping in the schools tends to focus on the problems rather than directions for constructive change. Yet, there is a great deal teachers can do to help free the student's environment of sexist elements. The purpose of this article is to highlight actions teachers can take in three areas: (1) self-awareness, (2) classroom practices and behaviors, and (3) out-of-classroom efforts.

Self-Awareness

In order to help others overcome the detrimental effects of sex role stereotyping and become fully aware, functioning, and human persons, we as teachers must first be able to recognize our own biases and work to change them—for our own benefit as well as that of our students. There are many ways to begin this self-assessment regarding sex bias. The following activity is one way.

Awareness and Assessment Activity. Listed below are sex role stereotypic characteristics which have generally been attributed to men and women, girls and boys. Read through the lists carefully.

Characteristics Generally Attributed to Men/Boys	*Characteristics Generally Attributed to Women/Girls*
1. aggressive	1. passive
2. independent	2. dependent
3. dominant	3. talkative
4. good at math and science	4. emotional

Teachers have an impact on the sex-role expectations of their students. *(Photo used by permission of the Indiana State Teachers Association.)*

Characteristics Generally Attributed to Men/Boys

5. mechanical ability
6. good at sports
7. competitive
8. skilled in business
9. worldly
10. adventurous
11. outspoken
12. interested in sex
13. decisive
14. demonstrates leadership
15. intellectual
16. self-confident
17. ambitious
18. autonomous
19. strong
20. unemotional

Characteristics Generally Attributed to Women/Girls

5. considerate
6. easily influenced
7. excitable in crises
8. tactful
9. gentle
10. helpful to others
11. home oriented
12. sensitive
13. religious
14. neat in habits
15. indecisive
16. supportive
17. submissive
18. devoted to others
19. conforming
20. concerned about appearance

—Do you agree with the categorizing of these characteristics for men and women in general?

—Do you see yourself as having more of the stereotypic traits of your sex than those of the opposite sex?

—Do you view your spouse and/or other members of your family (parents, siblings, children, other relatives) as having the characteristics generally attributed to their sex rather than those of the opposite sex?

—Do you view your friends and colleagues as having the sex role stereotypic characteristics?

—Do you view your students as having the sex role stereotypic characteristics? (p. 316)

After taking this simple test, readers should feel more in tune with themselves and how they perceive this problem. In Chapter 1, we talked about the intelligent young lady belittling her accomplishments and lowering her aspirations or goals. The reason girls often act this way is that they want to comform to the usual expectations that teachers, and particularly their peers, have for them. We may be losing a fine physician or an outstanding research scientist by not recognizing the problems that these young women have to overcome. By being aware that a young woman can have, and indeed often has, many of the characteristics generally attributed to young men, we as teachers can encourage nonsexist education in our schools.

Response to the Media

The negative impact of the media on the children we teach is profound. Teachers and schools can, however, turn some of these negative influences into stimulating intellectual topics for the benefit of their students. For example, the use of the foods poor in nutrition that are advertised on TV can be used as a topic of discussion in many classes. Some creative teachers have been known to form nutrition committees composed of administrators, teachers, parents, and children to look into the eating habits of students and the nutritional composition of the school lunches. The poor use of safety belts in TV movies can be a stimulus for a discussion on the advantages of buckling up for safety. Students might also get involved in a study of the use of safety belts and the use of nutritious foods through a problem-solving approach. Many negatives can form the curricular content for positive class activities.

Parents need to be shown how to help their child to learn by watching TV. Some thought-probing TV shows might be watched by both parents and children, with the parents reinforcing certain key concepts. To aid parents, teachers might send home special papers on important points for discussion brought up in a TV program. The socializing that parents and children do as they learn together by watching and discussing a TV show could be both educationally and personally beneficial.

The broadcast media have tremendous resources and produce some very valuable documentaries. Using this material as a resource can bring classroom discussions to bear on information and ideas unavailable in traditional school materials. Assignments for older students can include viewing a program for discussion in class the following day. A dramatization such as one done in 1986 on Peter the Great can be an immense help to social studies teachers.

Television can be a positive educational tool if only we can learn to use it properly.

Summary

Unit I on sociology and education was designed to alert you as a prospective teacher to some of the important social concerns in our society and the implications that these concerns have for schooling in America. The school does not exist in a vacuum; rather, it is an integral part of our complex society. Poverty, racial prejudice, and child abuse are all present in our communities, and the effect of all three are felt in the schools. Teachers must teach, but they must first get the attention of their students. Often, a student is inattentive because of problems that lie completely outside the school setting. Teachers who are aware of these problems and have strategies for dealing with them can better serve the students they teach.

Questions

1. In your opinion, what are some of the causes of teenage suicides? What can the schools do to alleviate these causes?
2. How have the school officials in the urban area nearest to you handled the desegregation mandate? In your mind, how is school desegregation progressing in this same urban community today?
3. What is the effect of drug and alcohol abuse on the schools? What are the schools doing to educate students to prevent these problems?
4. How do you feel about the melting-pot theory? Why do people question the value of total assimilation of minority cultures? What is an example of a minority culture that has not been assimilated?
5. Banks describes six stages of ethnicity. Using Bank's typology, describe your own ethnic stage of identity. In terms of the typology, what goals do you see for yourself and for society in the future?
6. What are some of the reported advantages and disadvantages of bilingual education? How does this relate to sensitive diverse cultures on one side and to becoming part of the mainstream culture on the other side?

Activities for Unit I

1. Choose any social issue that impacts on the schools, define the problem, gather data about the problem, and draw conclusions about how the problem could be solved.
2. Identify a school using Title I funds, visit the school, and report to the class on the status of the program.
3. Interview a social worker and/or a probation officer about his or her perceptions of how the criminal justice system works.
4. Read and report to your class on Phi Delta Kappa Fastback No. 46, titled *Violence in Schools: Causes and Remedies.*
5. Read and report to your class on Phi Delta Kappa Fastback No. 26, titled *The Teacher and the Drug Scene.*
6. Examine some selected school textbooks on your subject or at your grade level for sex bias in text and illustrations.
7. Invite a local authority on child abuse to talk to your class, and/or visit a local family-support center.
8. Look up the national statistics on teenage suicides and compare those figures with the rates in your own community.

THE
HISTORY
OF
EDUCATION

3

Origins of Educational Thought

OBJECTIVES

After reading Chapter 3, the student will be able to:
- Have a historical perspective of the roots of American education.
- Recognize why the emergence of the written language about six thousand years ago made a more formal type of schooling and education possible.
- Identify noteworthy accomplishments of the Greeks and the Romans.
- List specific periods and individual leaders who made significant contributions.
- State why certain historical advances in education were important to American accomplishments in education.

Introduction

The main goal of this chapter is to discuss the influence that developments in other countries have had on American education. Two events seem so obvious and so essential to us today that they hardly need to be mentioned; the development of written language and the invention of the printing press. These two happenings were five-thousand years apart, yet without them education would not have progressed as it has in America.

The Development of the Written Language

About five thousand to six thousand years ago, nomadic tribes began to grow their food rather than to hunt for it. The agricultural revolution led to the rise of cities as the new and expanded food sources led to an increase in population. Surplus food was traded with other newly emerging towns and cities, and writing was invented to keep commercial records. The new social order that grew out of the agricultural revolution had to develop new social institutions; among these institutions, one of the most important was education, not only to teach reading and writing but to instill the cultural heritage in the young members of the society. The Sumerians developed the first written language five thousand to six thousand years ago. Perhaps six thousand characters were used in the Sumerian language, a few of which are shown in the accompanying illustration.

The impact of the development of the written language on the growth of education is obvious. But we seldom recognize that it was some six thousand years ago that the trend began toward moving education from an almost total family responsibility to a responsibility of society. In the 1980s, more and more instruction outside the home is being demanded, and many advocate earlier nursery-school experiences.

Just as nomadic tribes came together in early times to achieve a better social order, and higher agricultural production, people today organize for many of the same reasons. As a result of diverse groups coming together, our language has continued to evolve, and more important, understanding languages other than our own has become a necessity to transact world com-

Early Sumerian Pictographs

| Plow | Boat | Chisel | Ax | Saw |

Source: Kramer, S. N. (1963). *The Sumerians.* Chicago: University of Chicago Press, p. 102.

merce, to establish cultural ties, and to achieve greater human understanding and world peace. Our world is exciting because we can communicate, but the world situation can be frustrating when we cannot find adequate avenues of communication. To the degree that we as educators can facilitate human understanding, we can aid in the peace-making process.

The introduction of written languages helped to make society more sophisticated, orderly, and predictable. The first teachers, who were probably also scribes, emerged about the same time that written languages were invented at the beginning of the Sumerian and Egyptian civilizations.

The Printing Press (Fifteenth Century)

Johannes Gutenberg, a German, is given most of the credit for inventing a press using movable metallic type in the mid-1400s. Gutenberg and others improved the printing press and refined the papermaking and inkmaking processes. The implications of the development of the printing press were enormous, and had it not been for this mechanical invention, the dissemination of the writings of scholars during the Renaissance, the Reformation, and since would not have been possible. The current computer suggests a close parallel to the original printing press in that both were and are revolutionary for their time periods.

Contributions of the Greeks

The ancient Greeks, during the Golden Age of Athens, gave us great advances in art, literature, and philosophy. Philosophers such as Socrates (470–399 B.C.), Plato (427–347 B.C.), and Aristotle (384–322 B.C.) were responsible for advanced thinking that has affected education up to the present time. Advanced thinking for these Greeks meant that they possessed wisdom far beyond what humans had experienced before their time.

Socrates

Socrates used a logical method of argumentation known as the *dialectical method*, more often called the *Socratic method* because of Socrates' finely tuned ability to use the process. Socrates wanted people to think logically; therefore, he used the dialectical method or logical discussion to cause them to think. His goal was to have a more ethical and moral society. An example of the Socratic method follows (Meyer, 1975):

"Do you believe," Socrates would ask an unsuspecting victim, "that Zeus leads a stainless life?"

Socrates advanced Greek wisdom by using his dialectical method to cause people to think logically. This skill is important for all teachers. *(Photo courtesy of the Library of Congress.)*

"Of course I do," comes the swift retort.

"And do you believe," Socrates leads on, "that Zeus had intercourse with certain mortal women?"

The man can but affirm, for long ago his elders had told him tales of the god's amorous adventures with mundane females, and the resultant increase in the Hellenic population.

"Is it your belief then," Socrates drives on, "that Zeus is an adulterer?"

The hard-pressed respondent begins to fidget, for he knows full well that Zeus is a married god, and so, whether he likes it or not, he emits a doleful affirmation.

The implications are obvious. If Zeus committed adultery, then his life is not without stain, and his divinity must be suspect. But remark how different the business would have been had Socrates accosted the stranger with the blunt query, "Do you believe that Zeus is a god?" The very question breeds alarm and, maybe, even a call for the police. (p. 8)

Socrates' method of questioning emphasized that mental discipline is necessary for acquiring knowledge, which has had an everlasting effect on education. The questioning approach used by Socrates was the forerunner of the inquiry approach used in education today, in social studies and in the sciences.

Plato

Plato was a student of Socrates. He came from the upper class, whereas Socrates came from the middle class. Plato's aristocratic ideal included dividing the state into three classes. He wrote that the masses were fit for doing the work of the state; the courageous and physically developed were to do the fighting and protecting; and the intellectually gifted were to be the kings or rulers.

Plato believed in the conditioning process for shaping the child's mind. Today, Plato and B. F. Skinner would have much in common as advocates of the manipulation of pleasure and pain to educate the child.

Plato believed that shaping young men (women were not educated at this time) was the best way to find the roles for them to fill in adult society. All instruction was based on what was best for the society. He attached great importance to the physical aspect of education, but games and sports were to be used for practical purposes and not for pleasure and entertainment as they are today. The practical philosophy of Plato is also found in the type of music he recommended for the young. Musically, pupils should be allowed to hear the two modes that expressed manliness and temperance, but never for pleasure or entertainment. The educational methods and curriculum ideas of Plato were well summarized by Butts (1955): "Plato doubtless did a great service in showing that a system of education is integral with the welfare of the state, but he also doubtless did a great disservice to democracy by idealizing an antidemocratic kind of state (p. 31).

Philosophically, Plato believed in the existence of a body of absolute, unchanging, spiritual ideas, which could be absorbed only by some men through contemplation. He believed that only as a man concentrated on the external truth could he cultivate his intellect. Such subjects as mathematics and philosophy were the best subjects to help students achieve intellectual discipline. The effect on Western education of Plato's idealist philosophy has been profound.

Aristotle

Many feel that Aristotle was the wisest of all Greeks. He had an inquiring mind that probed into every facet open to intellectual examination. He was a student of Plato, but he believed in empiricism as the road to knowledge, whereas Plato believed in the concrete embodiment of ideas. Both Plato and Aristotle stressed intellectual discipline as the mode of accumulating knowledge.

Perhaps more than anything, we owe a debt of gratitude to Aristotle for his introduction of scientific thinking. He was the first person to organize logic into a technical system of thought (Meyer, 1975). After Aristotle, most teachers taught logic as formal mental discipline. He gave us the tools to find rational explanations for complex matters.

Solon and Pericles

Solon (*ca.* 630–*ca.* 560 B.C.), another Greek, was considered the first great lawgiver in Athens. As a leader, Solon improved the lives of the lower classes by changing such practices as imprisonment and slavery for debt. The lower classes under Solon were admitted to citizenship and were given a place in the assembly, and the power of the aristocrats was weakened. As the common people in Athens gained economic opportunity, political democracy in Athens throve (Butts, 1955).

Pericles led the Athenian Greeks between 460 and 430 B.C. during the so-called Golden Age when democracy was at its height. Education also evolved and was most vital and rewarding during this period (Butts, 1955). In the beginning of our republic, when Thomas Jefferson stressed broad educational opportunities, he must have understood this lesson from the Greeks. But just as the Greeks became very democratic for their times, they also lost some of their momentum through excessive individualism.

Contributions of the Romans

The Roman Empire spread throughout the known world, where it eventually extended a common religion and a common language with the aid of a common political bond. During the Hellenistic period from the third century B.C. to the first century B.C., Greek culture and influence spread throughout the area conquered by Alexander the Great. Along with the Roman conquests, the Romans acquired a system of schools with a large Greek influence by the end of the third century B.C. The elementary school in Rome was known as the *ludus,* and in it, children aged seven to twelve were taught how to read, write, and count. The secondary schools were entirely Greek in character. They were called *grammar schools,* and the teacher was known as a *grammaticus.* Between the ages of twelve and sixteen, boys were taught Greek grammar and literature; thus, the first secondary schools in Rome were foreign language schools. During the first century B.C., Latin grammar schools developed as well. Emperor Vespasian (A.D. 9–79) made the first efforts toward establishing higher education in Rome by setting up library facilities with endowed chairs of rhetoric in Greek and Latin.

Quintilian

By far the most outstanding educator in Roman times was Quintilian (A.D. 35–95). He believed that the purpose of education was to uphold and protect society. He also believed that education could improve society. Quintilian was chosen as rhetor from Spain, a part of the Roman Empire, and he eventually rose to the rank of senator in Rome. His high rank was due to his intellect, to his teaching, and, no doubt, to the admiration of the emperor Vespasian. Some of Quintilian's ideas on education are worthy of our consideration today.

Quintilian's tenets included the importance of the teacher's being a good model for students and the value of the study of a foreign language to help one learn one's own language better. Quintilian was also an advocate of group schooling rather than private tutoring, for he felt that there was great value in socialization and comradeship.

These educational ideas of Quintilian come from his famous book *Institutes of Oratory,* which is primarily about what an orator needed in the way of education and training in order to be successful in Roman society. During the Renaissance, the *Institutes* were rediscovered, and it became the educational bible for generations of Humanist educators (Butts, 1955). Quintilian also advocated a list of great books to be read for a liberal education.

Meyer (1975) summarized best the contributions of this great educator when he outlined some of Quintilian's lasting contributions:

> the importance of the home in the child's early education; the necessity of understanding the peculiar nature of the individual child, and, by corollary, the recognition of his rights and dignity as a human being, even though he is not yet fully formed; the value of play and joy as spurs to learning; the desirability of learning not from books alone, but from experience as well; and so on. The memory of the planter of these and other seeds of progression may have faded, but his pedagogy in the main has been kept alive. (p. 52)

The importance of the Roman period in world educational history is that the Romans not only preserved some of the important ideas of the Greeks but spread these ideas throughout the known world. The contributions of Quintilian are noteworthy because they were no doubt read by Jean-Jacques Rousseau, Johann Heinrich Pestalozzi, and other subsequent educational reformers. The strong authority of Roman rule did not, however, contribute positively to the development of democratic forms of education.

The Middle Ages (A.D. 480–A.D. 1350)

The church, the monastery, the manor, and the guilds were all important institutions of the Middle Ages. The pope exercised control over the kings; thus, it was important for all people to please the church in Rome.

The Emperor Charlemagne (742–814) was a strong political leader of the era; he was able to establish a central government over most of western Europe. Charlemagne became Roman emperor in 800 A.D., when he was crowned by the pope. Under Charlemagne's rule, improvements were made in economics and agriculture, and reforms in religious and educational matters were achieved. Charlemagne invited one of the greatest scholars and teachers of his age, Alcuin of York, to be his educational adviser. The palace school that Alcuin established was attended by young members of the court and by Charlemagne himself, although he never personally learned to read and write. Along with Alcuin, other scholars were invited to teach the clergy and other officials of the government. A serious attempt was made to improve learning among the privileged classes.

The Middle Ages lasted another six centuries after Charlemagne's death. Feudal emperors ruled their individual domains through their vassals, and the lack of a united empire under a strong king contributed to the continuation of the feudal system.

The work of the monasteries during this period was to keep religious spirit alive and to preserve and copy ancient manuscripts. As a result, ancient documents were available to the many lay people who became interested in them in the Renaissance. The world owes a great deal to the patience, wisdom, and scholarship of these medieval monks.

Charlemagne improved education for the clergy and the ruling classes in his domain. *(Photo courtesy of the Library of Congress.)*

During the Middle Ages, there was so much stress within the church and society that life after death took on prime importance rather than life on earth. The development of the individual, through education, for life in the society in which he or she lived was mostly absent in the Middle Ages. It is an important lesson of the Middle Ages that we keep the act of learning and development of the individual alive, as well as maintain a keen sensitivity to anyone's possible disenfranchisement from an educational opportunity.

The Renaissance (Fourteenth to Seventeenth Centuries)

The Greeks, at their peak of power and influence, had altered the perspective of human thought, focusing on life in the present and viewing nature from a scientific rather than a mystical viewpoint. In the Middle Ages, however, the pendulum swung back to a focus on the hereafter and a more mystical outlook. But a new revolution of thought began during the fourteenth century. The rediscovery of classical civilization, the increase in trade and commerce, the revitalization of science and technology, and the rise of a new aristocracy whose wealth came from trade and banking rather than land and whose base of power lay in the cities signaled the beginning of the Renaissance. Life again became centered on earthly existence rather than the hereafter. The newly emerging Italian Renaissance witnessed the appearance of a new political, social, and economic order that would sweep across Europe, ending forever the old feudal system. Florence, Italy, under the stimulation of the very wealthy Medici family, was a major center of the newly emerging Renaissance culture.

When the Renaissance began, the church was dominant, but this was to change as the kings built strong national states. Further weakening in the church occurred after the Protestant Reformation began in 1517. The breakdown of the church contributed to the dissolution of the feudal system that held so many people in virtual slavery. Many serfs found new opportunities in the lively new cities that were springing up, where increased commercial trade was giving new growth and vitality to city life. Art and architecture, with brighter colors and inspiring designs, also helped to give a lift to city life.

The Greeks had focused on humans and what they could do with art, literature, science, education, and other facets of life just as the Humanist writers of the Renaissance focused on humans rather than on the church. Bonds that held people to the church were broken in favor of more secular approaches to life. The Humanists of this period were people who found new interest in human nature, thus freeing them from the restricting demands of the church, the guilds, the manors, and the monasteries. Scholars could now think more independently and with fewer restrictions.

Erasmus was an independent thinker, the foremost humanist of the Renaissance. *(Photo courtesy of the Library of Congress.)*

Desiderious Erasmus (1466–1536) of the Netherlands, one of the greatest scholars of the period, is considered the foremost Humanist of the Renaissance. Like most scholars of that era, he believed that human nature was perfectable if only it was allowed to develop through an understanding of ancient classics. Among his accomplishments was the first critical version of the New Testament, which marked the beginning of modern higher biblical scholarship. His *Praise of Folly*, written in little more than a week, gave him an international reputation. In this book, Erasmus wrote lines that were considered humorous and innocent at the time but that, in fact, were critical of the church and of what he perceived as corruption within the church. The book contributed to the spiritual rebellion that is now known as the Reformation. Erasmus also wrote the *Colloquies*, which were schoolbooks for children, containing many suggestions for the child to lead an upright Christian life. As in The *Praise of Folly*, the *Colloquies* also criticized the established church, but

Erasmus would not join the leaders of the Reformation in using his powerful pen to help their cause.

The Renaissance gave the world back the freedom of individual thought that had been lost before Europe had settled into the Middle Ages. Institutions such as the church, the arts, music, the sciences, and education would never be the same. The spirit of the Renaissance needs to be preserved by modern-day educators as they stimulate young learners to discover the wonders of the world.

The Reformation (Sixteenth Century)

The Reformation grew out of a seed planted in the Renaissance. For years before the Reformation, there had been many rumblings of discontent with the established church. One of the leaders of this discontent was a priest named Martin Luther (1483–1546), a very popular professor of religion at the University of Wittenberg. The pope, through intermediaries, authorized the selling of indulgences (spiritual pardons). One of the conditions for gaining an indulgence was to give a money donation for the building of Saint Peter's Church at Rome. Luther was very upset and, in 1517, he proceeded to nail ninety-five "theses," concerning problems with the church, to the church door at Wittenberg. This act officially signaled the beginning of the Protestant Reformation, which has never ended. Although Luther, at first, wanted to reform the church from within, many Reformation forces rejected the church altogether. Protestants, searching for their own interpretation of Christianity, formed numerous denominations: the Lutherans, the Presbyterians, the Anglicans, the Baptists, the Quakers, and many others.

Education benefited greatly from the Reformation. Luther insisted that solely through our faith in God could we be saved; therefore, it was imperative that we learn to read and interpret the Bible for ourselves. Luther suggested that every prince should provide primary schools for both boys and girls, and he translated the Bible into peasant German for them to understand. Later, in 1528, Luther wrote his famous Catechism, which became the child's basic book for religious instruction. Unfortunately, Luther was not able to get all of his followers educated quickly because most education still took place in the home, where many of the parents were illiterate.

Perhaps the true importance of the Reformation was that it sowed the seeds for the democratic type of education that emerged in the late eighteenth and the nineteenth centuries (Butts, 1955). The reformers, including both Luther and John Calvin (1509–1564) gave lip service to universal education for all, but they ended up supporting the more classical type of secondary education for the upper classes. Democratic education emerged several centuries later in America about 1840, where equal opportunity was afforded to all except a few minority groups.

Martin Luther marked the beginning of the Protestant Reformation when he nailed his ninety-five theses to the door of the church at Wittenberg. *(Photo courtesy of the Library of Congress.)*

No matter what trials and tribulations Luther and his fellow reformers had with education, the precedent had been set that being able to read the Bible or a catechism was the pathway to salvation. The Puritans and other religious groups arriving in America established schools for their children so that they could read the Bible.

As a reaction to the Protestant Reformation, the Catholics also began to use education as a means of countering the growth of Protestantism. Ignatius of Loyola (1491–1556) started the Society of Jesus, more commonly known as the Jesuits. The Jesuits' weapon against the spread of Protestantism was superior education. They established schools to train teachers all over the world, and as a result, they became a successful Counterreformation agency.

The Reformation has been and continues to be a stimulus to mass or public education. Currently, in America, education is regarded as a major pathway to social mobility and economic security, but the Puritans and other religious groups originally intended only that their children be able to read and write in order to read and interpret the Bible. In some religious groups, schooling is still first and foremost in promoting their faith. In recent years, private, church-based Protestant schools have been established across the country to give religious training similar to that given in the long-established

Catholic and Lutheran schools. The results of the Protestant Reformation are still very much a part of what is happening in education today.

The Development of Science and Reason

The study of science was condemned by Martin Luther as "that silly little fool, that Devil's bride, Dame Reason, God's worst enemy" (cited in Butts, 1955, p. 217). People were burned at the stake for advocating scientific explanations of natural and supernatural phenomena. Both Catholics and Protestants advocated a strict and narrow curriculum, mainly consisting of God's Holy Word. However, reformers such as Luther could not control all people's minds; thus, the individual thinking of Luther had opened the door to questioning traditional ways of thinking. The scientific spirit was one of the most long-lasting nonconventional phenomena to emerge from this period.

Sir Francis Bacon

Because of his writings and his influential political position as lord chancellor in England, Sir Francis Bacon (1561–1626) was able to popularize the scientific method. He determined that through the scientific investigation of known facts, one could make some generalizations that would fit many situations. In *Novum Organum* (1620/1901), Bacon set down his theories: the following example is an important part of the inductive process that he is famous for enunciating:

> CVI.   In forming our axioms from induction, we must examine and try whether the axiom we derive be only fitted and calculated for the particular instances from which it is deduced, or whether it be more extensive and general. If it be the latter, we must observe, as it were, in pointing out new particulars, so that we may neither stop at actual discoveries, nor with a careless grasp catch at shadows and abstract forms, instead of substances of a determinant nature: and as soon as we act thus, well authorized hope may with reason be said to beam upon us. (pp. 83–84)

In this instance, Bacon was warning his readers not to be taken in by the first set of observations, but to test the axiom to see if it fits just a particular instance or whether it can be generalized further:

> Today Bacon would be criticized for recording masses of useless data just because he observed them and for a neglect of the supreme importance of mathematics in modern science. Nevertheless, his insistence that knowledge arises out of experience rather than through traditional authority and his perception of the use of a controlled method of investigation were of supreme importance. (Butts, 1955, p. 219)

Bacon was not the first person to use these procedures as a method of investigation, but because of the important political position he occupied, he was able to popularize the method and make it respectable.

The meaning of Bacon's contribution to education and to science today is the growth of scientific inquiry as a discipline. As a result, the causes of some of our worst diseases, as well as answers to some of the most perplexing problems in our universe, have been discovered or are undergoing analysis. As a teacher and a promoter of a point of view, one never knows what long-range effect he or she may have on others—evidence the writings of Bacon.

The Origin of Secular Education

Students often ask when religious teachings and God as the center of the curriculum faded from our schools. The concept that children should be prepared for life in general and not just for entering the heavenly gates entered our thinking soon after the Reformation. John Amos Comenius (1592–1670) was a Moravian bishop who believed that children were not born human but became humanized through being educated in society. Eventually, Horace Mann (1796–1859) borrowed some of these secular ideas as he designed and modeled for us in America our common school system; however, both Comenius and Mann were very devout Christians.

Comenius was considered the most distinguished educational reformer of his time. His most famous textbook, the *Visible World,* was published in 1658. It was among the first illustrated schoolbooks ever written. Comenius felt that the best way to learn about the things of the world was to observe them firsthand, and that the next best way was through pictures. He felt it was the purpose of education to prepare children for happiness on earth as in heaven, thus breaking with the tradition of the Middle Ages of preparing one for life after death. Comenius also felt that learning was within the reach of every child, rich or poor, and girls as well as boys.

Secular education originated in this early period because of the logic of educating the child for all of life rather than just for the church. The candle of religious fervor within the schools did not burn low until more recent times. The curriculum and schools gradually became less religious; however, the *New England Primer,* used as a text in colonial Massachusetts is a reminder that the Puritans were one religious group that did not ride the Comenius bandwagon. It was difficult to shed the effects of the medieval period of pious religious teachings, but most of the public high schools in America today are virtually devoid of direct religious influences.

Comenius wrote a special handbook for mothers, *The School of Infancy,* to instruct them on how to teach their children at home. In the book, he urged mothers to teach their children values as soon as they were able to understand. Comenius also described a vernacular school for teaching the basics, which included a lot of moral and ethical education for the learners to digest.

IOHAN·AMOS COMENIVS, MORAVVS·A°·ÆTAT 50: 1642

John Amos Comenius believed in education for life and learning through experience. *(Photo courtesy of the Library of Congress.)*

He also suggested a Latin school and even a school of higher learning. Some of his schoolbooks continued to be used one hundred years after his death.

Comenius firmly believed in learning by practice. Like Jean-Jacques Rousseau, he believed in sense experiences to stimulate the students' intellect. The following is what Comenius had to say about what we now call in educational circles *hands-on-experiences*:

> Artisans do not detain their apprentices with theories, but set them to do practical work at an early stage; thus they learn to forge by forging, to carve by carving, to paint by painting, and to dance by dancing. In schools, therefore, let the students learn to write by writing, to talk by talking, to sing by singing, and to reason by reasoning. In this way schools will become workshops hum-

ming with work, and the students whose efforts prove successful will experience the truth of the proverb: "Our work makes us." (Cited in Piaget, 1957, p. 88)

The Effect of the Age of Reason and Enlightenment

By the eighteenth century, people in Europe were weary of the authoritarian regimes that had appeared during and after the Reformation. Arbitrary rule by kings in the various countries, as exemplified by the reign of Louis XIV of France, continued to keep the common people from participating in government. All monarchs (some were women) were elitists who maintained their power by supporting loyal armies and a privileged nobility. As a result of the disenchantment that the people, particularly the emerging middle-class, felt with the noble classes, the "Enlightenment" was born.

Reformers during the Enlightenment period protested the domination of the nobility, who thought their inherited rights put them above the law. Leaders of the Enlightenment emphasized the natural rights of all human beings, which were encouraged by the new scientific conceptions of the world. Hereditary rights eventually gave way to more democratic forms of government.

One reformer, John Locke (1632–1704), was among the intellectual giants of the period. Locke was born into the aristocratic class in England, but as a philosopher, he produced some very democratic ideas for government. He supported the social contract theory of government whereby citizens delegate authority to the government, in turn for which the government agrees to protect the natural rights of all citizens. Locke's social contract theory greatly affected the framers of the American Constitution. As our government is basically democratic, his influence has indirectly affected our need in America to sustain a good educational system to produce citizens who are intelligent voters.

In his educational theory, Locke emphasized education through the senses rather than from memory. He attacked narrow classical training and favored curricular items like arithmetic, writing, science, carpentry, gardening, and sports. He gave wide popularity to the famous conception of education as being the achievement of "a sound mind in a sound body." He was not the first nor the last of the great thinkers to emphasize the senses as the road to knowledge.

Jean-Jacques Rousseau (1712–1778) was another writer and philosopher during this era who was a child of the Enlightenment period. It was characteristic of him—and of the Enlightenment—that he said the best way to do things in the future was to do them exactly opposite of the way that they had been done in the past, showing a real contempt for authority. The practice or the emphasis in schools during his day was to think of the child as evil and sinful; therefore, the job for the teacher was to drive all of this evil thinking from the child. Rousseau said that the child is born with inherent impulses that are right, a philosophy the exact opposite of the one of his day.

Teachers and others inspired by Rousseau began looking at children in an entirely different and more positive way. From this basic idea emerged the principle that human nature is perfectable and can be constantly improved. Key words that crept into Rousseau's writings were *naturalism, freedom, growth, interests,* and *activity,* which were all later a part of John Dewey's progressive educational philosophy at the turn of this century. Rousseau argued that education should be designed to follow the natural stages of development of the child. In the infancy stage, Rousseau suggested free play and activity, and he had various other advanced ideas for children as they matured into the later stages: "In general, Rousseau did a great service in directing attention to the desirability of studying the child so that education can be adapted to the child's characteristic needs" (Butts, 1955, p. 291).

Rousseau wrote about what he felt was the ideal teaching–learning situation in a book called *Émile* (1762). This very famous book describes in detail how the boy Émile is to be brought up in life and nurtured into manhood. According to Boyd (1963), the book indicates many parallels to Rousseau's own life as a child. Even though Rousseau was not an educator and his philosophy, as noted in *Émile,* was never put into practice, his words influenced the works of many other educational reformers.

One of the great educators in history was Johann Heinrich Pestalozzi (1746–1827), who was very much an admirer of Rousseau's ideas on the natural development of the child. Unlike Rousseau, Pestalozzi was a practicing educator who actually tried out his ideas. Some experiments with education that he tried failed, for any of a number of reasons, but eventually, he was successful and gained many followers all over the world, including in America.

Pestalozzi believed that religion and moral instruction were very important but that they should be developed from within the individual and not stamped on him or her from without. He emphasized individual development, saying that every faculty of the body and mind should be harmoniously and uniformly developed. Society, he felt, could be improved if individuals were helped to develop their own powers, abilities, and feelings of self-respect and security. He was a champion of the poor and downtrodden and an advocate of discipline through cooperation and sympathy, not physical punishment. He was opposed to mere repetition as a means of learning, the method used in his day for learning the rules of grammar. He believed that experience had to precede or accompany learning, emphasized practical activities, and developed "object-teaching lessons" related to the step-by-step study of objects in the child's environment. The principles and ideas of Pestalozzi were used by other reformers to shape the schools in Germany and in America.

In a portion of a letter to a James Greaves, Pestalozzi wrote the following:

Johann Heinrich Pestalozzi was a Swiss educator who believed in education for all children to develop their individual talents through experience. *(Photo courtesy of the Library of Congress.)*

We must bear in mind that the ultimate end of education is not perfection in the accomplishments of the school, but fitness for life; not the acquirement of habits of blind obedience and of prescribed diligence, but a preparation for independent action. We must bear in mind that whatever class of society a pupil may belong to, whatever calling he may be intended for, there are certain faculties in human nature common to all, which constitute the stock of the fundamental energies of man. We have no right to withhold from any one the opportunities of developing all his faculties. It may be judicious to treat some of them with marked attention, and to give up the idea of bringing others to high perfection. The diversity of talent and inclination, of plans and pursuits, is a sufficient proof for the necessity of such a distinction. But I repeat that we have no right to shut out the child from the development of those faculties also which we may not for the present conceive to be essential for his future calling or station in life. (Cited in Anderson, 1931, p. 166)

This letter points out of the need for general education, which Horace Mann and others called for in this country in the 1840s. Mann was strongly influenced by the German educational system, which was influenced greatly by Pestalozzi.

The origin of the kindergarten goes back to Pestalozzi and one of his star students Friedrich Wilhelm Froebel (1782–1852). Froebel very much admired Pestalozzi, for whom he taught in Switzerland, but Froebel returned to his native Germany to carve out his unique contribution to educational history. Froebel believed that educational reform must start in the nursery school, and he dedicated himself to this task.

The early kindergarten was less regimented than schooling for older children. (*Photo courtesy of the Library of Congress.*)

Froebel made his kindergarten into a land of song, story, and play. The kindergarten was to be designed as the child's own world and not an adult world into which the teacher forced the child. Stress would be placed on socialization or helping the child learn to function freely and agreeably with his mates (females were not permitted to attend kindergarten). Among Froebel's curricular offerings were what he called "gifts," which were cubes, spheres, cylinders, and circles. All the "gifts" had symbolic meanings. Froebel's "occupations" were things that could be transformed when they were put to use, for example, sand, clay, cardboard, and paper. The story was also made a part of the kindergarten, and it stimulated interest in all areas.

Froebel's invention came to America as early as 1855 in Watertown, Wisconsin. Here Mrs. Carl Schurz, a former pupil of Froebel, opened the first kindergarten in America. Elizabeth Peabody of Boston opened the first English-speaking kindergarten in 1860, and the first public tax-supported kindergarten opened in St. Louis in 1873. Most public school systems in America today provide kindergartens, but it took more than one hundred years for this innovation to become standard educational practice. In the current curriculum of the kindergarten, one can still see the influence of Rousseau's naturalism and Pestalozzi's practicality.

Even though practice lags behind theory, sometimes hundreds of years, the Enlightenment brought us hope for democracy and the theory of the natural development of the child. Common people began to be recognized as persons who were important and worthy of being educated. The United States has demonstrated the ideals of the Enlightenment probably better than any other nation, but the United States as a country still has much additional progress to make before it can really be said that there is truly equal educational opportunity in American schools.

Summary

The ideas and events described in this chapter may seem long ago to most of us, but even six thousand years is only a fraction of a tick of the clock in the history of the human race. All of the people and events portrayed in this chapter were very influential in the development of education in America. The early symbols that made up the first written language were a start toward the development of modern language. The Greeks used languages to communicate and make great advancements in society, and the Romans spread their culture throughout the known world. The Renaissance was a reawakening of individual freedom and spirit. The printing press was and continues to be a catalyst in cultural development. The Reformation caused people to think about their individual salvation and thus about the need for common schooling. Science and the beginning of secular education promoted the concept that human beings could benefit from learning about life here on earth as well as life in the hereafter. And the Enlightenment brought us our government, our democratic way of life, a new way of looking at humankind, and the kindergarten.

Questions

1. When education moved from being entirely a family responsibility to more of a formal or outside-the-family responsibility of members of the tribe or community, what were some of the factors contributing to this change?

2. Why have the Greeks been admired for their educational contributions? What were some of the prime factors leading up to these contributions?

3. What does it mean to have a political leader, such as the Roman Emperor Vespasian, take a real interest in education? Are there some parallels to this leadership role at the local, state, and national levels of American government at the present time?

4. Quintilian had some ideas about education that are as relevant today as they were in Roman times. What were some of his ideas?

5. What were some of the problems of the Middle Ages that tended to slow down inquiry and the advancement of knowledge? Could these problems occur again? Why or why not?

6. Why has Erasmus been such an important figure in history? What did he do during the Renaissance that made his name synonymous with the period?

7. What changes that were immediate and long-lasting came about as a result of the Reformation?

4

Colonial and Federal Developments in Education

OBJECTIVES

After reading Chapter 4 the student will be able to:
- Describe the three basic areas of colonial development in America.
- Understand how the three areas of colonial development have influenced American education in different directions.
- Identify some of the early practices in education.
- Recognize the depth of federal involvement in education from 1785 to the present.
- Appreciate the role that the federal government has played in stimulating education.

Introduction

The focus of this chapter is the growth of schooling in the American colonies and the expansion of the federal government's role in education since the adoption of the U.S. Constitution in 1789.

The colonial period was marked by significant differences in the development of educational resources in the northern, middle, and southern geographic regions. Each area made lasting contributions to the nation's educational growth.

As America made the transition from being an aggregate of colonies to being a republic, the federal government took a very inactive role in education because of the Tenth Amendment to the Constitution. But over the years, the federal government has had tremendous influence on the growth and climate of education. U.S. Supreme Court decisions as in the *Dartmouth College* case and *Brown* v. *The Board of Education of Topeka* have affected all school systems. Acts of Congress such as the Morrill Act of 1862, the Civil Rights Act of 1964, and the Elementary and Secondary Education Act of 1965 have furthered education for many citizens. The executive branch has also been active, most recently with the study *A Nation at Risk* (U.S. Department of Education, 1983). The federal government has probably done more to influence the direction of education with less money spent than either the states or the local communities.

Colonial Developments in Education

Introduction

During the colonial period in America, from 1607 to 1784, educational practices reflected Old World traditions. Commager (1976), however, outlined three areas in which the colonies were different from the Old World. First was the enlargement of the scope of public education. Most of the expansion was in the New England area, but it occurred in other areas as well. The second difference was the substitution of morality for religion in the schools. Generalized religion was present in the schools rather than one particular religion. Third, schools provided more for students than just formal education (Commager, 1976). This section highlights developments in each of the three distinct geographic areas in colonial America and some early educational practices are noted. (See the Appendix for "Dates of Key Educational Events in America.")

The Northern Colonial Development

The first settlers in the northern colonies were the Pilgrims, who were of English descent, but who, because of religious persecution, had left England to go to Holland. The Pilgrims were of the Puritan faith, and most found life in Holland agreeable at first. However, some eventually returned to their homeland and, together with others from England, formed a joint stock company. The formation of the joint stock company made it easier for groups to get together and pool their resources: English farms were being turned into sheep enclosures, and farmhands were being put out of work; and vital natural resources, such as timber, were being depleted, so that it was increasingly urgent to find new resources. Many laborers were being put out of work, and because there was no help available from the government as we have today, the economic motivation to emigrate was as intense as the reli-

The 1908 schoolroom was ruled by the schoolmaster and was populated with scholars of all ages, studying and reciting their lessons. (Photo courtesy of the Library of Congress.)

gious motivation. Thus, it was a joint stock company of English and Dutch Pilgrims that left England for America on the *Mayflower* in 1620.

Once in America, the Puritans at first left education up to the church and the households, but in 1635, they established the first grammar school. And only a year later, in 1636, Harvard College was established in order to train the clergy. The colony needed the clergy, but only half of the first few years' graduates went into the ministry; thus began Harvard's role of training other professional groups.

Because by 1642 concern had been raised in the communities that the youth were not learning to read, the Commonwealth of Massachusetts decided to enact a law regarding education. The law of 1642 was the first law in America to establish the principle of compulsory education, but it did not specify any schools, nor did it require attendance. The "Old Deluder Satan Act" of 1647 was a tougher law: it called for every town having 50 households or more to offer reading and writing so that the children could avoid hellfire and damnation by being able to read the Scriptures. Also, the law of 1647 instructed towns with 100 households or more to provide Latin grammar schools to enable the young to prepare themselves for college. Thus, we see that the colony had enlarged the scope of education to include all children, whereas people in the Old World, especially England, had been concerned only about the education of certain elite groups.

The fact that education was specified by law did not mean that there was instant compliance. Nevertheless, there was a real interest in the communities in providing education at the basic levels. Apparently, the Massachusetts colonists complied better with the mandate for grammar schools than they did for basic schooling, for all twelve towns of over 100 inhabitants established grammar schools. In these early days, as in more recent times, farmers needed their boys at home to help with the work; therefore, they didn't encourage schooling as much for their sons as the city-dwellers did.

There was more unity in New England than in other colonial areas. The unity among people in the North was probably due to their common religious ties, their town meetings, and the fact that they lived in close proximity to one another. Although they didn't always agree on issues, there was better communication within their settlements, and the result was that they were quicker to support education than either the middle or the southern colonies.

The Middle Colonial Development

The colony of New Amsterdam was established in 1621 by the Dutch. From the very start, this colonial establishment was very parochial. The Dutch did their own teaching, as did the Anglicans, the Catholics, the Quakers, and others. Because of this lack of unity, a university (Princeton) was not established until 1746, or 110 years later than New England's Harvard.

Pennsylvania, another colony in the middle area, was established in 1681 by William Penn (1644–1718). Penn's influence and the Quaker belief in toleration of other religious groups led many other groups, such as Anglicans, Lutherans, Presbyterians, Dunkers, Mennonites, and Moravians, to move into the colony (twelve thousand by 1689). All of these groups made immense contributions to the society, but the different religious sects generally stayed to themselves, worshiping and educating their children in their own churches and schools. Thus, they also were very parochial in their educational activities.

William Penn expressed his idea of what education ought to be:

> We press their memory too soon, and puzzle, strain and load them with words and rules; to know grammar and rhetoric, and a strange tongue or two, that it is ten to one may never be useful to them; leaving their natural genius to mechanical and physical, or natural knowledge uncultivated and neglected; which would be of exceeding use and pleasure to them through the whole course of life. (Cited in Cremin, 1970, p. 305)

William Penn and the Quakers of Pennsylvania believed in equality for all, including blacks and American Indians. (*Photo courtesy of the Library of Congress.*)

Penn had a real concern that all children should be educated but he also felt that a college curriculum was unnecessary because of the impracticality of the courses.

The Quakers also brought with them the concept of human equality. The Quakers believed in working with and educating blacks and Indians. Penn himself tended to be rather paternalistic toward blacks and Indians, but later Quaker leaders came out very strongly against the evil of slavery. Quakers in the mid-1800s helped slaves escape through the underground railway system, and they were active in the abolition movement before the Civil War.

Benjamin Franklin (1706–1790), though he was born in Boston, the son of a candlemaker, spent most of his adult life in Philadelphia, Pennsylvania. A common theme that Franklin espoused most of his life was the need for self-education. Franklin himself was the perfect model of self-education, having had no more than two years of formal education. The rest of his education he had acquired on his own. He wrote and distributed *Poor Richard's Almanac,* which was filled with proverbs to encourage industry and frugality, as a means of obtaining wealth. Typical of these proverbs is (Cremin, 1970): "It being more difficult for a man in want to act always honestly, as it is hard for an empty sack to stand upright" (p. 374). The Almanac was widely disseminated and read by the average American, who understood the plain and simple commonsense proverbs.

Franklin's desire for practical education led to the establishment of the Junto Club in Philadelphia. The Junto was a club for mutual self-improvement and was put together by Franklin and his friends for that purpose. Franklin was influenced by John Locke, who had established a similar club for self-improvement in England. The club served Franklin for forty years as an intellectual sounding board for his creative ideas.

Franklin was also very interested in practical education, as was Penn. He reflected in his famous autobiography the pride he had had in establishing the Philadelphia Academy in 1751, which later became the University of Pennsylvania. In the academy, Franklin wanted his students to acquire a good education in the English language; thus, Latin and Greek were not high on his list. The curriculum included natural history and gardening, the history of commerce, principles of mechanics, physical exercise, experiments with scientific apparatus, and even field trips to farms for natural observations. The academy became the second type of secondary school established in America, the first being the Latin grammar school, and the third being the high school. (The first high school was established in Boston in 1821.)

The Southern Colonial Development

In the southern colonial area, Jamestown, Virginia, was established in 1607. This colony's basic motivation for settlement was economic. The settlers' interest in the land and in what it could do for them led eventually to the use of slaves as a source of cheap labor.

Private family tutoring was the main method of education for the sons of southern plantation owners in the colonial South. *(Photo courtesy of the Library of Congress.)*

The plantation system was not conducive to universal education because of the sparseness of population over a large geographical area. The planters installed private tutors in their homes to teach their sons and later sent them to Harvard, Princeton, Yale, William and Mary, or England for a university education. Poorer whites received very little education, but occasionally planters would get together and build a one-room school on an abandoned tobacco field—sometimes called an *old field school*. Generally, instruction was meager, and the teachers were ill prepared.

The institution of slavery itself set up to provide cheap labor, had a profound psychological effect on all who lived in the South, both white and black. To generalize, the whites developed a superior attitude, and as a result, the slaves suffered terrible indignities. Life in the South, and public education in particular, would lag behind the other areas of the country far beyond the colonial years.

One example of the degree to which this superiority–inferiority attitude existed is a whipping given a slave owned by Colonel Lloyd, the same man who owned Frederick Douglass (1877?–1895). The beating in question was witnessed by Frederick Douglass himself (cited in Preston, 1980):

> One of the most heart-saddening and humiliating scenes I ever witnessed, was the whipping of Old Barney, by Col. Lloyd himself. Here were two men, both advanced in years; there were the silvery locks of Col. L., and there was the bald and toil-worn brow of Old Barney; master and slave: superior and inferior here, but equals at the bar of God; and in the common course of events, they must both soon meet in another world. . . . "Uncover your head!" said the imperious master; he was obeyed. "Take off your jacket, you old rascal!" and off came Barney's jacket. "Down on your knees!" Down knelt the old man, his shoulders bare, his bald head glistening in the sun, and his aged knees on the cold, damp ground. In this humble and debasing attitude, the master—that master to whom he had given the best years and the best strength of his life— came forward, and laid on thirty lashes, with his horse whip. The old man bore it patiently, to the last, answering each blow with a slight shrug of the shoulders, and a groan. I cannot think that Col. Lloyd succeeded in marring the flesh of Old Barney very seriously, for the whip was a light, riding whip; but the spectacle of an aged man—a husband and a father—humbly kneeling before a worm of the dust, surprised and shocked me at the time; and since I have grown old enough to think on the wickedness of slavery, few facts have been of more value to me than this; to which I was a witness. It reveals slavery in its true color, and in its maturity of repulsive hatefulness. (pp. 69–70)

Slavery was a negative force in the South in the development of education, but there were positive factors in the South as well, such as Thomas Jefferson (1743–1826) and his creative mind. Jefferson's contributions to the young republic were many, but he should be remembered especially as a strong advocate of public education. Jefferson wrote a bill in 1779 for the Virginia Legislature, called the Bill for the More General Diffusion of Knowledge. Under the guidelines of the bill, Virginia was to be divided into parts, called *hundreds,* and each hundred was to provide elementary schools where reading, writing, arithmetic, and history were to be taught gratis to all free inhabitants. (The economic system in the South at this time hinged on the institution of slavery, and slaves were to be kept ignorant. Thus, slaves were left out of Jefferson's educational plan.) The bill went on to propose that Virginia build twenty grammar schools spread throughout the commonwealth to teach more promising students such subjects as Latin, Greek, and English grammar, plus more advanced arithmetic. The brightest scholars of the lower school whose parents could not pay tuition were to be granted scholarships to the grammar school. Finally, Jefferson's bill provided to ten scholarship students of the grammar schools free tuition, board, and clothing for three years of study at William and Mary College (Cremin, 1970).

The immediate results of the Bill for the More General Diffusion of

Knowledge for Virginia were disappointing, for the legislature failed to pass it until seventeen years after it was first proposed. Then, they left it up to the courts in each county to decide whether they needed to implement the law, and none of the counties wanted it. The inspiring words and the educational ideals written into the bill were not lost, however, as they eventually helped to bring free education to New England, the Midwest, the Far West, and eventually to Jefferson's own South (Brodinsky, 1976). The bill that Jefferson authored reflected the thinking of Locke and Rousseau, whose writings Jefferson was very fond of reading.

Jefferson's educational interest expanded to the University of Virginia, where he designed the buildings, organized the curriculum, and assembled a faculty. The university opened in 1825, a year before his death; the University of Virginia was truly "Mr. Jefferson's University" (Meyer, 1967, p. 128).

In an effort to expand education, the Society for the Propagation of the Gospel in Foreign Parts (SPGFP) was established in 1701 to educate slaves and Indians. This Anglican educational group felt that if they could teach these groups to read and write, slaves and Indians would have a chance at salvation. Naturally, the society had trouble in the South because of established groups that were against these motives of the society, for slaves, by law, were not to be taught, and Indians resisted SPGFP teachings. Eventually, the SPGFP was to have better luck in the middle and northern colonies.

Although public schooling was long in arriving in the South, southerners founded a secular college in 1693 in the town of Williamsburg, known as William and Mary College. Among other things, William and Mary was the first college to establish modern languages and modern history as part of the curriculum. The first chair of law, occupied by the famous George Wythe, who instructed Thomas Jefferson, was established at William and Mary. Here also was founded in 1776 the famous honor society known a Phi Beta Kappa.

The achievements in education in the southern colonies were mixed. The establishment of William and Mary College and the University of Virginia were landmarks in higher educational achievement. And the educational ideals of Thomas Jefferson were inspirational. Yet, forever overshadowed by the economic needs of the plantation system, the southern colonies lagged far behind the more northern areas in the development of public education.

Some Early Practices During the Colonial Period

Several practices during the colonial period were interesting from a historical point of view. Most of the practices had European origins, and some lingered on many years after the colonial period (Johnson, 1963):

The Hornbook

The hornbook was not a book in the usual sense of the word, but it was usually a piece of printed paper about three by four inches fastened on a thin piece of board. The name "hornbook" came from the fact that it was a custom in those days to cover the written material on the hornbook with the translucent covering from a cow's horn. Covering of the letters was important to save them from being smudged by little fingers. At one end of the board was a handle with a hole in it so a string could be attached; therefore, the youngster would be able to hang it around his neck. Generally, the alphabet was printed on the hornbook in both capitals and in small letters; and then in orderly array

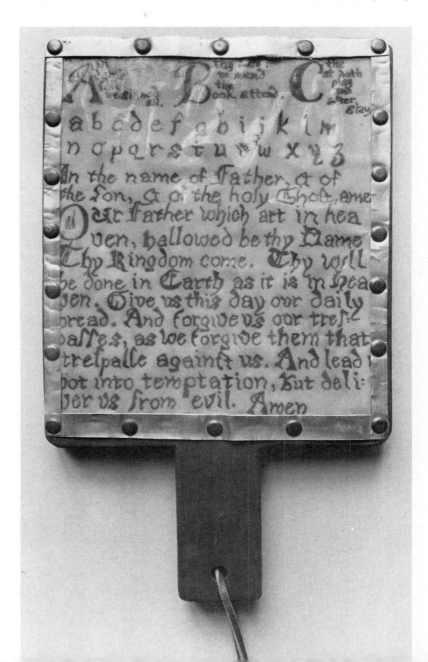

Paper was expensive and books scarce in colonial America, so young scholars studied their basic lessons from the hornbook. *(Photo by Axler.)*

the vowels, then double lines of ab, eb, ibs, and the benediction, "In the name of the Father, and the Son, and of the Holy Ghost. Amen." The remaining space was devoted to the Lord's Prayer, unless, as was sometimes the case, this was supplemented at the bottom by Roman numerals. (p. 28)

First Schoolhouses

The first school buildings were described by Johnson as having been built of logs exclusively. This type of log building was common even fifty years after the Revolution. Often the floors were bare and very dusty—especially when some young scholars would deliberately kick up some dust to amuse themselves and their schoolmates. Sticks were inserted around the walls on the inside of the cabin, and boards were nailed to them for desks. There was a fireplace at one end, and some windows were cut where greased paper was inserted to break the wind and cold and to let in some light. These early colonial schools had no blackboards and no maps. Some schools had globes, but there were no slates and pencils until much later. (p. 38)

Writing Practices

Most young scholars of this era learned the skill of penmanship very well. They generally wrote in "copybooks" which were hand-made and ruled by the students. Writing was done with quill pens and ink, and early schoolmasters needed to be experts on how to sharpen quill pens. Some schools made their own ink, while others used ink powder which was put to use by dissolving it in water. The most important thing for a schoolmaster to teach was penmanship; spelling mattered little. (p. 40)

The New England Primer

Like the hornbook, the *Primer* was brought over from England. It was first published in Boston about 1690 and was used as late as 1806. The *Primer* was a very small book, three by four inches in length and breadth and ninety pages thick.

Every *Primer* had a page devoted to the alphabet, followed by two pages of curious word fragments called "Easy Syllables for Children," like *ba, be, bi, bo,* and *bu.* There were then three pages of words from one syllable up to six syllables. The rest of the book was filled with religious and moral verses and prose, including the picture alphabet with a two- or three-line jingle after each letter. For the letter *A* there was

In Adam's fall
We sinned all.

For the letter *C* there was

Christ crucified
For sinners died.

For the letter *Y* there was

> While youth do cheer
> Death may be near.

The Puritans who used this book felt that their children were born in original sin and that much help was needed if it was to be driven from them.

Another part of the *Primer,* labeled "Lessons for Youth," laid down some extremely strict rules for children to follow. The following three verses illustrate how harsh the book was on the young scholars:

> Foolishness is bound up in the Heart of a Child, but the Rod of correction shall drive it from him.

> Liars shall have their Part in the Lake which burns with Fire and Brimstone.

> Upon the Wicked God shall rain a Horrible Tempest.

Modern-day teacher-educators would not agree with this Puritan idea of educating a child out of fear because most educators today believe, as Rousseau believed, that children are born innately good.

The Dame School

Another Old World practice that was carried to this continent was the dame school. The school dame was a woman who lived in the neighborhood and decided to teach reading. She received a modest fee for her efforts while she performed her normal housekeeping chores as well; as a result, she may well have been America's first home-economics teacher. Dame schools were an English institution and were described by the English poet George Crabbe in these words (Johnson, 1963):

> a deaf, poor, patient widow sits
> And awes some thirty infants as she knits;
> Infants of humble, busy wives who pay
> some trifling price for freedom through the day.
> At this good matron's hut the children meet,
> Who thus becomes the mother of the street.
> Her room is small, they cannot widely stray,
> With band of yarn she keeps offenders in,
> And to her gown the sturdiest rogue can pin. (p. 25)

Summary of Colonial Education

The colonial period was a difficult era in all three colonial locations, but important seeds were planted that influenced later educational developments. Among the most important colonial advances were the establishment of compulsory education in New England in 1642; the successful establishment of a practical rather than a classical secondary-school curriculum at Franklin's academy in 1751; and the enunciation by Jefferson of the educational theory of a more democratic educational system in 1779. It was also during this period that some of our nation's greatest universities were established, such as Harvard in 1636, William and Mary in 1693, and Princeton in 1746.

Federal Developments in Education

Even before the ratification of the U.S. Constitution, the federal government became involved in education with the Ordinances of 1785 and 1787. Although the Tenth Amendment to the Constitution placed the primary responsibility for education with the states, the federal government over the years has stimulated education by giving money back to the states for priority items considered crucial to the nation's best interest. The federal government has

The Ordinances of 1785 and 1787—Where Federal Aid to Education Began

Rectilinear System of Survey

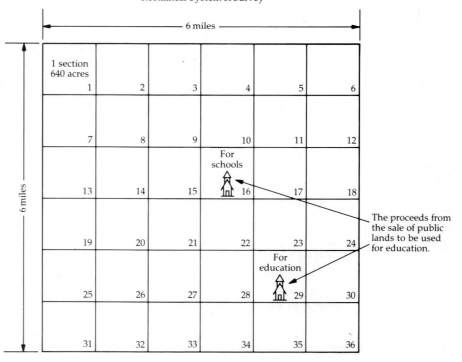

One Township

also influenced educational progress through the U.S. Supreme Court and its interpretation of the Constitution. Beginning with the Ordinance of 1785 and 1787 and continuing through the study of *A Nation At Risk* in 1983, highlights of federal action will be presented.

Ordinances of 1785 and 1787

As the western areas of the country were being developed, the Congress passed the Land Ordinances of 1785 and 1787. Under these ordinances, every township was to contain thirty-six sections, each with 640 acres; the sixteenth section of those townships was to be sold, and the money was to be used to support education. This aid to public schools was a very important precedent to establish and one very much supported by Thomas Jefferson.

In 1787, another land ordinance was passed, the Northwest Ordinance, which set aside not only the sixteenth section for schools but also two whole townships for a university. These two townships were to be taken from the entire 1,500,000 acres under the Northwest Ordinance. In addition to the provision for land to be sold and used for public education, Article III states:

> Religion, morality, and knowledge being necessary to good government and the happiness of mankind, schools and the means of education shall forever be encouraged. (Butts, 1978, p. 17)

Even though these ordinance rules were often not abided by because of greedy land speculators, they truly stimulated public education. These ordinances are examples of federal action for the general welfare of all citizens.

The Adoption of the U.S. Constitution in 1789

The matter of education was scarcely mentioned at the Constitutional Convention, thus the U.S. Constitution itself does not cover education anywhere within its contents. The precedent had not been set by any country that public education was a responsibility of the state. The feeling of most of the framers of the Constitution was that education was mainly a private matter, and generally under religious control. The Tenth Amendment says that powers not delegated to the federal government by the Constitution, nor prohibited by it to the states, are reserved to the states, or to the people (Hicks, 1957). Therefore, education became the responsibility of the states.

It was unfortunate that at this time in our history, the states were not ready to establish an educational system. Most states had their own political and economic problems to keep them occupied during the early years of the republic, and the development of education in most states did not get started until the second quarter of the nineteenth century.

Morrill Land-Grant for Colleges (1862)

The Morrill Act of 1862 was one of the most notable congressional decisions in support of public higher education and for the general welfare. Since at least 1838, there had been interest in agricultural instruction, and some states established agricultural schools. Senator Justin S. Morrill of Vermont took up the cause to establish colleges where both agriculture and industrial education were to be taught. Senator Morrill reasoned that public lands could be sold, and that the proceeds from this giant land sale could be used to build colleges in each of the states. President Lincoln signed the Morrill Land-Grant Act into law in 1862, eventually endowing at least one land-grant college in

Justin Morrill advanced American higher education when he spearheaded the bill to establish land-grant colleges in each of the states. *(Photo courtesy of the Library of Congress.)*

each of the fifty states, the District of Columbia, Puerto Rico, Guam, and the Virgin Islands. The mandate to establish the colleges included the provision of agricultural and mechanical arts (engineering), as well as military science and tactics. Each state would receive the proceeds from the sale of 30,000 acres of public land for each senator and representative it had in Congress. So far, proceeds from the sale of about 11.4 million acres of our public lands have been used to finance these public colleges.

One might ask, "Has this noble experiment helped the United States acheive what it intended?" Today, over half the nation's scientists have been prepared in land-grant schools, many Nobel Prize winners have earned degrees at land-grant institutions, and such discoveries as hybrid corn, streptomycin, television, and talking pictures have emerged from these colleges (Meyer, 1967, p. 212). The first person to walk on the moon and many of our nation's astronauts have graduated from these public institutions of learning. According to Eby (1952), "The establishment and continued support of the land-grant colleges proved to be the most far-reaching educational measure ever taken by the Federal Government" (p. 648). The Morrill Act not only established public institutions of higher education but also caused a healthy competition between the public and private sector in higher education. Because of the lower tuition costs of these institutions, millions of Americans have been extended an opportunity for a higher education.

Plessy v. Ferguson (1896)

The Morrill Act served to increase educational opportunity, but in 1896 the Supreme Court made a decision that would severely restrict the educational and personal opportunities of millions of Americans for years to come. In the *Plessy* v. *Ferguson* case, the Court upheld the right of the railroads to segregate passengers according to their race. By so doing, the Court also endorsed segregation by race in the schools and affirmed the "separate-but-equal" doctrine. As a result of the *Plessy* v. *Ferguson* case, schools in the northern as well as the southern states remained legally segregated until the *Brown* v. *The Board of Education of Topeka* case of 1954.

The "separate-but-equal" doctrine proved in practice to be "separate but unequal." With inferior schools came inferior jobs and fewer opportunities for economic success for blacks. The personal indignities experienced by minorities as a result of legalized segregation were reprehensible. The civil rights guaranteed by the U.S. Constitution to all citizens were dealt a severe blow by the *Plessy* v. *Ferguson* decision.

Smith-Lever Act (1914)

By the early 1900s, the federal government had become concerned about the quality of country life in the United States, and President Theodore Roosevelt appointed a Country Life Commission to study the problem. As a result of the commission's report, the Smith-Lever Act was passed in 1914. The Smith-

Lever Cooperative Agricultural Extension Act provided for national aid to people desiring information on agriculture and home economics. People not attending college were to get instructions and practical demonstrations in agriculture and in home economics. This extension work is now done through the agricultural colleges in each state under the direction of the U.S. Department of Agriculture. The educational work, under the Smith-Lever Act, has been accomplished by the publication of informational pamphlets and papers. This act has resulted in the improvement of country life through the educational process. The dissemination of vital information to farmers and their families has made their lives easier and more productive.

Smith-Hughes Act (1917)

In 1917, Congress passed the Smith-Hughes Act to provide vocational education in schools below the college level. The act called for cooperation between the federal and state governments; thus, the states had to match federal dollars in order to comply. Vocational education includes courses in agriculture, home economics, trades, industries, and commerce. The Smith-Hughes Act was the first of many related acts that were to follow. Many rural communities owe a great deal to the work and dedication of the vocational agriculture teachers whose salaries were partly provided for by the act.

The Smith-Hughes Act and the Smith-Lever Act have greatly benefited rural and urban Americans. Today, less than 10 percent of our population is engaged in the production and distribution of food. American farmers are so efficient as a result of our great agricultural colleges, extension agents, and vocational agricultural education, that most Americans are free to pursue other goals. Industries and businesses as well are dependent on the trade and commercial skills developed by students in vocational programs in the schools.

The GI Bill of Rights (1944, 1952, and 1966)

The generosity of the federal government continued when, after World War II, Congress rewarded returning soldiers with free education. What occurred was the passage of the famous GI Bill of Rights of 1944. In 1946, enrollments in colleges were 45 percent higher than they had been in 1944, and in 1947, over a million former service men and women were in colleges across the nation (Good & Terrer, 1973). Not only did the former GIs get their tuition paid for at college, they also got subsistence pay and money for books and supplies.

More former GIs received benefits below the college level than at the college level. Training was given at various vocational training schools, at employment locations using on-the-job training, and on farms. Both of these programs, at the college level and below the college level, were administered by the Veterans Administration.

Since the initial Act in 1944, the GI Bill of Rights has been extended to include veterans of Korea (in 1952) and Vietnam (in 1966). The number of total participants is about sixteen million persons, with a total cost in excess of $34 billion. Many feel that the GI Bill is one of the best investments the country has ever made (Brodinsky, 1976):

> In the early days of the G.I. Bill veterans returned to the college classroom eager for learning; often impatient with dull professional techniques and institutional rules, the returning veterans helped change and invigorate higher education. (p. 73)

The whole process of the GI Bill has democratized education, enabling those from poorer economic backgrounds to climb the socioeconomic ladder.

Brown v. Board of Education of Topeka (1954)

The question of the legality of segregation on the basis of race, particularly segregation in education, once again came before the Supreme Court in 1954, sixty years after the *Plessy* v. *Ferguson* affirmation of "separate but equal." Because of the importance of this case, it is necessary to understand some of its background.

By chance, a young housewife from Merriam, Kansas, drove her maid home through a neighborhood where a dilapidated school building was located. Esther Brown, a white housewife, became outraged when the school board in that city refused to make any improvements at the dilapidated black school until a new, modern white school could pay its building debt, forty years hence. She made speeches in Merriam and throughout the state, decrying the school's lack of a gymnasium, a cafeteria, and an auditorium. She also mentioned the smelly earthen privy, which served both sexes; the lack of plumbing or adequate heating and lighting; and the generally run-down condition of the school. Eventually, she recruited campaign workers and collected money for legal fees (Teeter, 1983).

The legal case in Kansas was put together by an association formed by Esther Brown. Oliver Brown (no relation to Esther), a Topeka, Kansas, welder and part-time minister, sued the Board of Education, asking that his daughter be admitted to the town's all-white elementary school. First, the case was tried in the U.S. District Court, and then, along with four other similar cases, it was tried by the U.S. Supreme Court using Oliver Brown's name. Thurgood Marshall and a team of civil rights lawyers argued the case for Brown, and John W. Davis, one of the most able lawyers at this time, argued for continued school segregation. Chief Justice Earl Warren stated the majority opinion that segregated schools were inherently unequal, and that dual educational systems were to be abandoned. This case ended the rule of the "separate-but-equal" doctrine. It took a while for people to act on the new

Thurgood Marshall and Chief Justice Earl Warren made civil rights history in the case of *Brown* v. *Board of Education of Topeka* in 1954. *(Photos courtesy of the Library of Congress.)*

ruling, and there was a need for more action on the part of the Supreme Court and the Congress, but eventually schools were integrated.

Civil Rights Act (1964)

Related to the *Brown* decision, Congress passed the Civil Rights Act of 1964, placing all three branches of the federal government behind black equality in education. The Supreme Court had acted in 1954, and both President Kennedy and President Johnson were squarely behind the movement. Title IV of the Act enabled the U.S. Justice Department to initiate lawsuits on behalf of individuals in order to force compliance with the desegregation law. Title VI allowed the federal government to withhold funds from states and school districts that were not integrating their schools. As more and more funds from the federal level became available, withholding funds became a genuine threat. The Civil Rights Act of 1964 has proved to be a needed measure to ensure compliance with the intent of the *Brown* case in 1954.

Presidents John F. Kennedy and Lyndon B. Johnson were strong supporters of civil rights and federal aid to education. *(Photos courtesy of the Library of Congress.)*

The Elementary and Secondary Education Act (ESEA) of 1965

In order to help poor and minority children, Congress in 1965 took a giant step toward giving financial aid to the nation's public schools. When he signed this bill into law, President Johnson felt that it would have a tremendous impact on the future of the United States (Brodinsky, 1976). The act has extended the role of the federal government in elementary and secondary education as never before. No doubt, the passage of the bill hinged on the nation's interest in providing aid and assistance to poor people and minority groups. Political rhetoric at the time of the passage of the bill and the influence of civil rights groups were two factors not to be ignored.

The act is divided into nine titles, each one specific to certain areas of need and interest. For example, Title I, the main part of the ESEA, is for the purpose of educating poor children in metropolitan areas, in Appalachia, and in states where literacy rates have been low. The policy for Title I of ESEA is as follows:

Part I   Elementary and Secondary Programs
Elementary and Secondary Education Act of 1965

*Title I   Financial Assistance to Meet Special
Educational Needs of Children*

Declaration of Policy

Sec. 101. In recognition of the special educational needs of children of low-income families and the impact that concentrations of low-income families have on the ability of local educational agencies to support adequate educational programs, the Congress hereby declares it to be the policy of the United States to provide financial assistance (as set forth in the following parts of this title) to local educational agencies serving areas with concentrations of children from low-income families to expand and improve their educational programs by various means (including preschool programs) which contribute particularly to meeting the special educational needs of educationally deprived children. Further, in recognition of the special educational needs of children of certain migrant parents, of Indian children and of handicapped, neglected, and delinquent children, the Congress hereby declares it to be the policy of the United States to provide financial assistance (as set forth in the following parts of this title) to help meet the special educational needs of such children. (p. 1)

A Nation At Risk (1983)

Most of the events discussed so far concerning the federal government have been the result of actions taken by the congressional and judicial branches. The President and the executive branch of the government demonstrate leadership in various ways. The Reagan administration, through his then Secretary of Education, T. H. Bell, created the National Commission on Excellence in Education in 1981. The commission was directed to examine the quality of education in the United States. The federal government took this action in part because of the decline in college-entrance-exam scores and complaints by business and military leaders that they were having to spend millions of dollars on remedial education, such as reading, writing, spelling, and computation.

The commission was composed of eighteen people representing all levels of education and some outside the field of education. They listened and talked to administrators, teachers, students, parents, business leaders, and public officials, as well as read papers written by experts on a variety of educational issues. At last, they arrived at certain findings, and from these, they wrote their recommendations. Most college libraries have a copy of the commission's complete report. It contains many useful recommendations for education.

The following findings and recommendations are from the commission's report, called *A Nation at Risk* (U.S. Department of Education, 1983):

A Finding in Regard to Content

Secondary school curricula have been homogenized, diluted, and diffused to the point that they no longer have a central purpose. In effect, we have a cafeteria-style curriculum in which appetizers and desserts can easily be mistaken for the main courses. Students have migrated from vocational and college preparatory programs to "general track" courses in large numbers. The proportion of students taking a general program of study has increased from 12 percent in 1964 to 42 percent in 1979. (p. 18)

A Recommendation in Regard to Content

We recommend that State and local high school graduation requirements be strengthened and that, at a minimum, all students seeking a diploma be required to lay the foundations in the Five New Basics by taking the following curriculum during their 4 years of high school: (a) 4 years of English; (b) 3 years of mathematics; (c) 3 years of science; (d) 3 years of social studies; and (e) one-half year of computer science. For the college-bound, 2 years of foreign language in high school are highly recommended in addition to those taken earlier. (p. 24)

A Finding in Regard to Time

Evidence presented to the Commission demonstrates three disturbing facts about the use that American schools and students make of time: (1) compared to other nations, American students spend much less time on school work; (2) time spent in the classroom and on homework is often used ineffectively; and (3) schools are not doing enough to help students develop either the study skills required to use time well or the willingness to spend more time on school work. (p. 21)

Three Recommendations in Regard to Time

1. Students in high school should be assigned far more homework than is now the case.
2. Instruction in effective study and work skills, which are essential if school and independent time is to be used efficiently, should be introduced in the early grades and continued throughout the student's schooling.
3. School districts and State legislatures should strongly consider 7-hour school days, as well as a 200 to 220 day school year. (p. 29)

Summary

The preceding pages have illustrated how all three branches of the federal establishment have been involved in education. At the very beginning of our republic, in the Ordinances of 1785 and 1787, the federal government supported education even though in the Constitution's Tenth Amendment, the responsibility for education was left to the states. The Morrill Land-Grant Act of 1862 was a tremendous boon to state universities and to science. The Smith-Lever Act of 1914 and the Smith-Hughes Act of 1917 helped to improve rural life in the United States and to enhance the state agricultural colleges that trained vocational agriculture teachers and regulated the dissemination of information to rural people.

The G.I. Bill of Rights is an example of the federal government's involvement in helping those who have served our nation.

In the *Brown* case, the Supreme Court declared that all races must be treated equally, and the Civil Rights Act of 1964 placed the necessary power in the hands of the federal government to make changes in the schools. President Johnson's ESEA of 1965 set a precedent of sending huge amounts of federal aid to the schools in order to equalize educational opportunity. *A Nation at Risk* (U.S. Department of Education, 1983) was designed to influence the directions that education was to take in the United States.

In the 1980s the Reagan administration has been interested in turning back some of the responsibility for education to the states. The U.S. Department of Education had accumulated a great deal of responsibility for education during the 1960s and 1970s, mainly because of the need to help minority citizens by overseeing and implementing various federal educational grants and entitlements. Now the federal government, assuming that most of our minority citizens have their civil rights protected, want this responsibility to revert back to the states. The question still remains whether the states will truly be responsible for educating all of their citizens. Aside from the desire to make the states responsible, there is the current mandate to reduce federal expenditures. In the case of the ESEA of 1965, the federal government did in some cases get very close to giving general aid to the schools, but this aid has remained basically categorical, being earmarked only for particular programs. The federal government, then, has performed a vital role as a stimulator of educational innovations of all types and has often acted as a safety net for the poor and the disadvantaged. It will be interesting to see if state governments have matured in the 1980s to the point where they will be capable of handling most of the administrative and financial burden of education.

Questions

1. Psychologically speaking, what was wrong with the teaching approach used in the *New England Primer?*
2. Describe five current educational practices that can be traced back to the Puritans and other groups of early settlers.
3. Why was the northern colonial region more inclined toward learning and education for all of its citizens than the other two colonial areas?

4. Specifically, what were the contributions of William Penn and Benjamin Franklin to educational development in Pennsylvania?

5. What effects did the plantation system and the institution of slavery have on educational progress in the southern colonies?

6. Some of the ideals of Jefferson and Franklin were ahead of the realities of their times. What were some of the factors that caused this gap? Today, does progress within our educational institutions lag as a result of a similar gap between real and ideal?

7. Historically, what has been the nature of the relationship between the federal government and education in America? Do you feel that this role is changing?

8. Describe the legal milestones in the civil rights movement in America as they relate to education. How did each help or hinder the progress toward equal educational opportunity for all citizens?

9. What has been the significance of the Elementary and Secondary Education Act (ESEA) of 1965 on educational opportunities in the United States?

5

Private and Public Schooling in America

OBJECTIVES

After reading Chapter 5, the student will be able to:
- Appreciate the contributions of both private and public education to the overall progress of American education.
- Understand how public and private education became legally separate entities.
- Realize the importance of the common school movement in the mid-1800s.
- Recognize how difficult it was to win and continue tax support for public schools.
- List and describe important events in educational history, both private and public, that have brought greatness to the whole American experience.

Introduction

Private and public education have developed side by side since very early times in America. The resulting competition between these two groups has generally been good for the country. In this chapter, we outline some of the historical educational events that have taken place in both the private and the public sectors. Many early endeavors in education were private only because the financial arrangements were made without local, state, or federal government assistance; however, admission to these educational establishments was frequently open to all and often free for poor children. Public schools have brought education to the masses of our citizens, a task few other countries have been able to accomplish.

Private Schooling in America

The private sector has given the American educational scene several exemplary models from kindergarten to higher education. Notable educational events occurred in the early days of our republic at the private level, and they continue today. Some of the educational models that have emerged from the private sector are now examined.

Sunday Schools

The Sunday school movement was begun in England in 1780 by Robert Raikes. These schools were established during the Industrial Revolution, when children were employed in the factories from sunrise to sunset six days a week. The idea was to offer basic educational opportunities to children on their day off, Sunday. The idea spread to America, where Sunday school societies were formed. At first, the goal was to teach the children the basic three Rs in a secular manner, but then the churches took over and made the principal aim of this movement to give the children religious instruction.

Apparently, people felt sorry for these poor children who were deprived of their ABCs, and in fact, many children benefited from this philanthropic endeavor. The philanthropists benefited also, by not being taxed for education; thus, the fact that something was being done for the poor children delayed the passage of the public tax for education. The delay of the tax at this point in history led Meyer (1967) to say, "Philanthropy was a favorite stratagem of a puissant, self-interested minority in their effort to stay the establishment of the tax-supported school" (p. 143). Nevertheless the Sunday school movement did impress on the people the need for public education. The attitude of some taxpayers today toward paying for public education indicates that problems concerning this issue have changed very little over the years.

Monitorial Schools

Another English innovation was the monitorial school. Started in England by Andrew Bell in 1797, it was brought to America by Joseph Lancaster in 1818. The monitorial school system was organized around selected students known as *monitors,* who were chosen for their academic abilities. One paid school teacher was hired to teach a monitorial school having as many as three to five hundred students. The best scholars were then selected by the teacher, and these scholars, or monitors, became responsible for about ten other students. Directions and/or instructions were given to the monitors by the teacher, and they, in turn, delivered the lesson to their ten students. The school was run in a very military manner; often orders were barked out in a dictatorial fashion. Corporal punishment was abandoned in favor of the use of the dunce's cap, leg shackles, a wood log hung around the neck, or suspension from the ceiling in a basket. The schools were set up to be efficient and cheap, but they were also impersonal: numbers were used in place of names. Some books were reprinted on wall charts for use in group instruction in order to save money on materials. The curriculum generally consisted of the catechism, reading, writing, spelling, and arithmetic.

The contributions of the monitorial system were several. Mostly, it was cheap (as low as $1.06 per term), and thus, education became financially available for the first time to nearly everyone. Lancaster's efficient ways were innovative, but also restrictive. As a substitute for pens and paper, he used sand trays for writing lessons. These trays are being used today by teachers who work with dyslexic children. Selden (1975) wrote that "Lancaster above all, offered schooling to the poor at a time when they were otherwise denied it, and in doing so planted the seed of the concept of education as a fundamental right" (p. 27). Many teachers today use a type of monitor system when they ask some of their better students to help explain a previously taught concept to individuals or small groups within the class.

Infant Schools

From England, another response to the Industrial Revolution was the invention of infant schools to take care of the children of poor families who worked in the factories. Robert Owen, a Scottish manufacturer and socialist, was behind this movement. Besides being an advocate of reducing the hours of child labor, Owen was able to establish infant schools, including one for his own factory workers. These schools taught some religion and parts of the three Rs, but the schools concentrated on play, singing, dancing, and nursery care of the children. The infant school served three-, four-, and five-year-olds.

By the 1820s, infant school societies had been formed in the major cities in the United States.

Robert Owen went on to establish a socialist society in New Harmony, Indiana, and to assemble a learned group of scientists and intellectuals at that location. The infant school idea and related happenings promoted the belief that society's schools had a responsibility to very young children as well as to older children. However, commitment to the education of the younger infant-school-age group, is still not part of our tax-supported system in most areas. Butts (1955) stated that "from England came the Sunday schools, the monitorial schools, and the infant schools, all of which helped to provide a transition from private to public school sytems" (p. 491). These three exemplary private-school experiments show how private endeavors in education often do aid the development of public education.

The *Dartmouth College* Case (1819)

Legally, there was confusion in higher education about who controlled the colleges until the *Dartmouth College* case was decided by the U.S. Supreme Court in 1818. The question was whether Dartmouth College should remain private or be controlled by the state of New Hampshire. In 1816, the state legislature passed a law converting Dartmouth into a state university. This drastic change of events in the history of the college occurred when the liberal state legislature became upset at the firing of their liberal friend, John Wheelback, who had been president of Dartmouth for sixteen years. The legislature even installed a new liberal board of trustees. The old, more conservative board went to work to gain back its power to operate the college.

The old board first took its case to the New Hampshire Supreme Court, but the plea was denied. The old board then appealed its case to the U.S. Supreme Court after having hired an able lawyer by the name of Daniel Webster. In 1819, Chief Justice John Marshall wrote the decision that reversed the lower court's ruling. Justice Marshall said, in effect, that the original charter for the college came from the king of England and had the force of a contract that the state could not impair. According to Butts (1955),

> the decision had far-reaching economic and political ramifications, but it meant specifically for colleges that the philanthropic endowments of private colleges would be safe from encroachment by the states. This encouraged private donors to give money to the private colleges and stimulated the states to establish their own universities under state control. (p. 466)

As a result of the *Dartmouth College* case, the United States has a strong dual system of colleges, both private and public. Twenty state universities were established before the Civil War, but private universities had been the major influence until that time.

Dartmouth College was founded in 1769 under a charter from the English king. The *Dartmouth College* case in 1818 upheld the right of the college to remain a private institution, free from state control. *(Photo courtesy of the Library of Congress.)*

The Academy Movement (1800—1850)

Another precedent-setting educational institution was the academy. The academy movement in the United States began with Benjamin Franklin's Philadelphia Academy in 1751 and spread rapidly during the first half of the next century. One thing that greatly facilitated the academy movement was the *Dartmouth College* case in 1819 (Kraushaar, 1976). Academies were secondary schools that offered a variety of programs, including college preparatory education as well as programs that terminated at the end of a student's time at the academy. In general, the academies provided a broad, practical curriculum in tune with the great social, political, and cultural changes that were part of the growing young nation. The academy was the dominant secondary school until after the Civil War. Most of the academies were privately endowed, and with the rise of the public tax-supported high schools, only the best endowed of the academies survived (Cubberley, 1934). The Phillips Academy at Andover, Massachusetts, is probably the most famous survivor.

The academies boosted the importance of secondary education, and they offered a variety of educational opportunities. There was definitely an emphasis on English literature and grammar, as well as on the traditional Latin and Greek, plus newer subjects on the American scene like algebra, astronomy, botany, chemistry, U.S. history, surveying, and debating. The academies bridged the gap between the more elite type of Latin grammar schools that had come before them and the more democratic high schools that were to follow.

Education for Women

Pioneer efforts in the area of higher education for women were made about 150 years ago. The attitude of most people at this time was that the place for a woman was in the home, caring for children and taking care of other family needs. Because women's minds had not been tested, there was a feeling that women were intellectually inferior to men. Three women made notable contributions to the education of women in the early 1900s.

Emma Willard (1787–1870) Emma Willard received as much education as she was allowed, and she began her teaching career at the age of seventeen in Middlebury, Vermont. In her husband's medical library, she was able to continue her education on her own, and when her husband ran into financial difficulty, she responded by opening up a school for girls in her home. The curriculum began with socially acceptable types of subjects, such as music, drawing, and penmanship, and gradually expanded to include foreign languages, mathematics, philosophy, history, and literature. She called her school the Middlebury Female Academy, and it was a big success. Emma pressed for state financial support of female academies in both Connecticut and New York, but she was denied support in both places.

Eventually, the people of Troy, New York, invited her to start a school. She opened what became known as the Troy Female Seminary in 1821, when she was only thirty-four years old, and for the next fifty years at Troy, she dedicated herself to improving the education of women. The result of the success of the Troy Female Seminary and Willard's efforts can be seen in the formation of Vassar, Elmira, Mary Sharp, and other women's colleges. By 1837, Willard was able to get some small state support for Troy, and with the opening of Iowa State and Utah Universities to women, her influence had become far reaching. Moorefield (1974) summed up Willard's influence by saying,

> No college anywhere—not just in the United States but throughout the world—accepted women students in 1787. By the time she died in 1870, women were not only attending American high schools but many of the brightest and most determined among them were earning college degrees and launching professional careers. (pp. 30–31)

Catherine Beecher (1800–1878)   Catherine Beecher was part of a famous family. Her sister, Harriet Beecher Stowe, was a gifted writer, and her brother was Henry Ward Beecher, a well known pulpit orator. In 1828, she opened the Hartford Seminary, a school for girls in Hartford, Connecticut. Catherine Beecher also started a school in Cincinnati, Ohio, called the Western Female Institute for Women.

During the early 1800s, women were flocking into teaching as the only career field open to them. Beginning about 1830, Beecher dedicated herself to the recruitment and training of teachers willing to go to the western states to train the uneducated masses. She went on trips to New England to find young women who were willing to make the long trip to the West, and she worked with committees that were willing to work to support her cause. Her work helped to alert the public to the need for common schools and trained teachers. This pioneer woman educator organized the Woman's Education Association in 1852. Among other things, the association promoted providing liberal education for women and making women into successful wives, mothers, and housekeepers.

Mary Lyon (1797–1844)   Mary Lyon dedicated her entire adult life to education, and the last twelve years to the founding and the administration of Mount Holyoke College for women in South Hadley, Massachusetts. The college opened its doors in 1837 to serve women of limited means. A small tuition was to be supplemented by two hours of domestic work daily. Lyon thought of education as a means of performing social and religious services. Her students were encouraged to become missionaries, particularly in foreign missions.

All three of these women did some of the initial work necessary to prove that higher education for women was worthwhile. In those days, it was necessary to mix higher education with housekeeping and other socially acceptable career areas in order to launch the concept of women in college. The past 150 years have seen a growing acceptance of women in colleges and universities, but the last twenty years have seen a tremendous growth of the acceptance of women into the major professions.

The Development of the Kindergarten

Kindergartens are not universally supported by the public tax dollar even to this day, but the private endeavours in this important area have been tremendous. It could be, as in the case of the Sunday school, that the very success of private efforts have delayed public support. Froebel's kindergarten came to the United States as a private institution in 1855. (Froebel's kindergarten and the American adaptions of it were discussed in detail in Chapter 3.) The kindergarten curriculum has always focused on the child, so the kindergarten movement, when it came to the United States, laid the foundation for the "child-centered" elementary school (Butts, 1955, p. 404).

Mary Lyon, who founded Mount Holyoke College for women, was one of America's great female educators. *(Photo courtesy of the Library of Congress.)*

Hampton Institute (1868)

After the Civil War, one of the northern generals, Samuel Chapman Armstrong, founded the Hampton Institute in 1868. General Armstrong believed that the best education for blacks was a practical type of education that would get them jobs in the post–Civil War days. According to Butts (1978), "General Armstrong argued from a humanitarian but paternalistic attitude of white superiority that the racial differences as well as the economic disabilities of Negroes required a special kind of education" (p. 212). Specifically, the types of skills taught at Hampton were woodworking, metalmaking, cooking, and serving. Students at Hampton were also taught such academic subjects as English, arithmetic, geography, and history at the secondary level. The significance of Hampton was that it was here that Booker T. Washington attended school and learned from his mentor, General Armstrong, how to set up his own Tuskegee Institute in 1880.

Booker T. Washington was the outstanding educator and spokesperson for black rights and education in the late 1800s. *(Photo courtesy of the Library of Congress.)*

Booker T. Washington developed his Tuskegee model after the Hampton Institute with a very strong emphasis on industrial education. He believed that blacks would be served best by a practical or vocational education rather than a liberal arts education. Other white and black leaders of the period believed that a good liberal arts education would best serve to bring blacks out of slavery into modern society. The most prominent black leader opposed to Washington's views was W. E. B. DuBois.

Hampton Institute was a start for black education, but the direction it took, according to many modern scholars, appears to have been wrong in that blacks were given one type of educational opportunity (industrial, leading to blue-collar jobs), whereas whites were given another (liberal arts training, leading to the professions). Some would say that the direction that Armstrong and Washington took was the only one available at the time and, pragmatically, the only sensible way to move considering the social status of blacks in the South during this period. By 1900 fourteen hundred Tuskegee graduates had found jobs in thirty different industries, and the Hampton Institute model of industrial education spread to many more schools in the South besides Tuskegee.

The education of blacks to improve their economic standing was the main thrust at Tuskegee Institute, founded by Booker T. Washington. (*Photo courtesy of the Library of Congress.*)

The Dewey Laboratory School and the Progressive Education Movement

Another significant happening in private education was the establishment in 1876 of the laboratory school at the University of Chicago by John Dewey (1859–1952). The entire University of Chicago had been financed privately by John D. Rockefeller, and it was here that some of the most significant experiments in education were to be carried out under the guidance and direction of John Dewey. Although Dewey gave credit to Francis Parker (1837–1902) for being the father of progressive education, effective publicity for the movement orginated from the laboratory school in Chicago. Some of the experiments in different parts of the country were labeled as progressive, but later were to be condemned by Dewey as being unsound educationally. The details of the Dewey philosophy will be explained in Chapters 6 and 7.

The progressive movement in educational history is noteworthy because most educators up to this time had thought of only one way to teach: the traditional method. Francis Parker had tried out some progressive ideas in the public schools in Massachusetts, but Dewey's ideas were revolutionary. The concept of the child and how she or he learned would now become more important than forcing subject matter to be memorized. This reform did not take place at once, but as the years have unfolded, we have seen an increasing acceptance of these ideas.

Experimental Private Schools of the 1960s and 1970s

During the 1960s and the 1970s, many experimental private schools were founded. No doubt, many of these schools were stimulated by the progressive school movement of an earlier era. The Harlem Preparatory School was one of several private street academies whose purpose was to rescue bright young black people from failure. Schools like Harlem Prep specialized in instilling self-confidence in the students and in getting them to understand that through a college education, they could lift themselves up the socioeconomic ladder.

Other private schools were established on the Montessori or Summerhill model. The Montessori schools stress respect for the child and place emphasis on his or her interests. The Summerhill model places emphasis on freedom of the child to decide on his or her own learning. These two models were often more enthusiastically supported than thought out, but many of these schools show signs of stability today (Kraushaar, 1976). Private alternatives to public schools keep the spirit of competition alive, and private school ideas are being adopted by the public schools; for example, several public systems now have Montessori types of schools.

The diversity within private schools today is nearly as great as it is in the public schools. The church schools include not only Catholic and the Lutheran schools, but schools of almost every other Protestant denomination as well. Hebrew schools were small in number before 1940; 90 percent of the present five hundred or so were formed after this date (Kraushaar, 1976). There are Black Muslim schools in some of our largest cities. Some other private or nonsectarian schools prefer to carry the label of *independent* rather than *private* because of the elitist connotation that comes with the label *private*.

Public Schooling in America

There were compulsory school laws in New England as early as 1642, but these schools were not public as we understand that term today. The mandate that Massachusetts placed on its citizens to send their children to school was a helpful precedent for the future of public schools, but schools were not free. The concept of free public schools eventually won out, but it was a long, hard struggle, one of this nation's finest and most noteworthy achievements. Some of the important milestones in the development of the free public school are discussed here.

The struggle continues today as we try to maintain the public schools amid cries that they are failing to educate our children and are in a state of disarray. Some questions must be asked: Are they worth all our efforts, or should we now change our stance to a greater emphasis on the private types of schools through vouchers or tuition tax credits? What about poor people's education and equal educational opportunity? Where do we go from here? We hope to provide some of the answers in the following pages.

Jefferson's Model (1779)

We have written in Chapter 4 how Thomas Jefferson provided a plan for public education. His plan for Virginia served to stimulate others interested in education, such as De Witt Clinton of New York, even though Virginia did not adopt Jefferson's ideas.

De Witt Clinton

The New York Free School Society was organized in 1805 under the leadership of De Witt Clinton (1769–1828), then mayor of New York City and later governor of the state. The society was organized for the purpose of educating the poor children in the City of New York. The society was able to secure funds from the city council and the state legislature, to build schools, to train teachers, and, most of all, to get the people interested in free public education. (Other free societies were formed during this same period. One in Washington, D.C., had Thomas Jefferson as a board member and a financial contributor.) De Witt Clinton was a great believer in the monitorial system of education (see the discussion earlier in this chapter), which prospered in New

York with his enthusiastic approval. Eventually in 1853, the society turned over its system of schools to the city to be used as its regular public schools.

In his two terms as governor of New York, Clinton was a dedicated crusader for educational improvements throughout the state. Through his efforts, popular interest in education was intensified (Eby, 1952). Many governors today face a similar struggle in trying to reform public education in their states.

Jackson's Presidency (1829–1837)

In 1829 Andrew Jackson (1767–1845) became president of the United States, the first president to be elected by the people in general, excluding, of course, slaves and women. The advocates of popular elections had fought battle after

The son of poor farmers, Andrew Jackson and his rise to the presidency symbolized the opportunities of America. (*Photo courtesy of the Library of Congress.*)

battle to achieve their goal, known as *white manhood suffrage*. The country was now fulfilling the spirit and the intent of the doctrines of the American and the French Revolutions (Hicks, 1957). The march toward democracy was well on its way with white manhood suffrage; still there would be a long wait for universal suffrage.

Before Jackson, all presidents had been elected from the elite classes of the eastern states. With Jackson, the frontier states saw one of their own elected to the presidency: "The Jackson inauguration symbolized for many the triumph of the common man" (Hicks, 1957, p. 367). Now men who made their living by plowing the land, mending shoes, or working in a factory could vote along with the wealthier classes. Once access to the ballot box was assured, interest in pubic education began to spread. The matter of white manhood sufferage was a significant step for America.

The Cousin Report (1831)

In the late 1820s, Prussia was among the strongest countries in Europe. Encompassing much of present-day Germany and of present-day Poland and parts of Russia, Prussia had a strong educational system that was to influence educational reform in many countries. Victor Cousin, a Frenchman, was instrumental in writing a report on the value of Prussian education. The Cousin Report resulted in a French school reform law, but more important for the United States, it was translated and printed here and read by many educated people:

> What the Frenchmen liked about the Prussian System of Education was its national authority over education; its centralized secular control; its trained and expert teachers; its up-to-date methods; its planning, financing, and supervising; and finally its bold and outspoken employment of the school as an instrument for national ends. (Meyer, 1967, p. 178)

Through his writings, Cousin stimulated school reform on two continents.

The Stowe Report (1837)

Near the conclusion of the Jackson presidency, in 1836, Calvin Stowe, an Ohio theologian, was sent to Prussia to bring back an American report on the schools. He liked what he saw in Prussia, particularly the thoroughness of instruction, teacher education, and the Pestalozzian methods that were being used. The Ohio Legislature must have been somewhat excited because they ordered ten thousand copies of the report printed, but Ohio took very little action. The Stowe Report did find its way into notable journals of education, and it was reprinted and circulated to other states, including Massachusetts.

Horace Mann

Like several others who had gone before him, Horace Mann (1796–1859) visited and reported on the Prussian schools in 1843. Unlike most previous visitors, he included in his report both praise and criticism of the Prussians. While he was in Europe, he also took time to visit England, Belgium, Holland, and France. He rated Prussia first and England last because England lacked a national system of education in which all of the people could participate. When he returned, Mann said, "There are many things abroad which we at home should do well to imitate" (Cubberley, 1934, p. 362).

Horace Mann was a dedicated public servant. Before becoming a leading educator in Massachusetts, he was president of the State Senate and was headed for the governorship. As a legislator, he led humanitarian crusades for such noble causes as psychiatric treatment of the insane, abolition of

Horace Mann's contributions to public education in Massachusetts gained him the title "father of the common schools." (Photo courtesy of the Library of Congress.)

imprisonment for debtors, better prison conditions, and temperance laws. When Mann had an opportunity to organize the newly formed state school board in Massachusetts, he resigned from the legislature to become the first secretary of the Massachusetts school board. The remainder of his life was dedicated to improving public education. He spent his last years as president of Antioch College in Ohio.

Because he was the first secretary of the Massachusetts Board of Education, Mann had great freedom in defining his position. He created a tremendous model for all school systems in the United States to follow. One of his first tasks was to inspect the schools and to assess their state. He criticized education in Massachusetts as having shanty school buildings without the slightest sanitary facilities, stupid and incompetent teachers, dilapidated equipment, and supervision that was in full collapse (Meyer, 1967). Some of today's reformers have been heard to say some equally inelegant things about current school practices.

On Mann's return from Europe, he instituted many needed reforms. New schools were built at a cost of $2 million—a large sum in those days for a state to spend. Teachers' salaries were raised 62 percent for men and 54 percent for women, and three new teacher training institutions or normal schools were built, the first of their kind in America. Mann proceeded to improve the quality of teaching in the state by making personal addresses, authoring twelve annual reports to the legislature, writing in the *Common School Journal,* and continually visiting the schools while in office (Monroe, 1940).

Schools grew in the early 1800s from isolated cabins with a few pupils to larger buildings serving many more children. *(Photo courtesy of the Library of Congress.)*

Leaders like Horace Mann come along very infrequently. Reforming the schools as he did in Massachusetts was one of the most democratizing moves ever made in American history. Building up good common or public schools was a bold and courageous move because, at the time, many people felt that we should have different classes of citizens. Mann, however, was not an elitist and had not forgotten his own ordinary roots. This was the beginning of our public school system, where every child would be offered an opportunity for a formal education. Keppel and Messerli (1975), during our bicentennial celebration, wrote in reference to Mann, "Our national pantheon is peopled by few visionaries and many men and women of action; but it is the rare occupant who has been both a dreamer and a doer" (pp. 18–21). Some have even honored Mann by referring to him as the "father of our common schools."

Other Public-School Reformers

Another very important school reformer of the period was Henry Barnard (1811–1900). Barnard, who did in Connecticut what Mann had done in Massachusetts, eventually became the first U.S. Commissioner of Education in

Henry Barnard was an educational reformer in Connecticut, who published and edited *The American Journal of Education. (Photo courtesy of the Library of Congress.)*

1867. Barnard founded the American Association for the Advancement of Education, whose publication was known as *The American Journal of Education*. As editor of the journal, Barnard publicized the merits of public education and gave details on ways to accomplish the task. The journal supported every educational reform of consequence that occurred before the 1880s (Meyer, 1967). In addition to Connecticut and Massachusetts, other states picked up on the trend that was sweeping the country, and reformers emerged in many areas, notably, Robert J. Breckenridge of Kentucky, Calvin Stowe of Ohio, Caleb Mills of Indiana, and Jonathan Swett of California.

Catalysts in the Public School Movement

A discussion of the public school crusade, spearheaded by Mann and others, would not be complete without mention of other important forces or events that acted as catalysts in the process. Previously mentioned items such as Jacksonian democracy, the monitorial system, and the use of educational or pedagogical journals were all instrumental in aiding public schools. Newspapers, then costing a mere cent, were cheap enough so that nearly everyone could afford them, and the urge to read them sparked an interest in schooling. Josiah Holbrook's American Lyceum was begun in 1826 for the purpose of stimulating citizens with lectures on varied topics, and the lecturers always sang the praises of the common schools. From the start, the labor movement favored free public education, and members demanded that the states accept full responsibility for providing schools at public expense. During this period, internal improvements, consisting of the building of canals, railroads, and turnpikes, helped to spread the news from one part of the nation to another. Speakers of note, such as Ralph Waldo Emerson, talked of unrestrained individualism that would allow one to rise to endless heights, inferring that the best way to rise was through schooling.

The first *McGuffey Readers* were published in 1836, and they continued to be used until 1920. The *Readers* were truly American, not like many previous books that related more to European origins and to New England. The standards of social life set up in the *Readers* pleased a majority of the Americans, particularly those who were living on the frontier. Many of the stories were pleasant, and few were designed to frighten children about going to hell as earlier texts had done. The stories used by McGuffey included many of top literary merit. These improved textbooks and others helped to popularize the public schools.

Immigration, mostly from European countries, was a large factor in the increasing use of the public schools. Those who now referred to themselves as "native Americans" feared that conflicts and disputes might result from having so many immigrants in the work force building canals and railroads. Some feared the political influence of the foreigners, but eventually, the wise and broad-minded realized that assimilating these immigrants through education into the democracy, rather than excluding them, would be the best

Ralph Waldo Emerson expounded in his philosophy of humanism the value of learning both from schooling and from life, as well as the importance of independent thinking. *(Photo courtesy of the Library of Congress.)*

policy (Monroe, 1940). One significant result was that the native population saw education as an effective means of making democracy work; therefore, the great immigrations into this country aided the development of education.

Pauper Schools and Public Taxation

The ideal of having public schools was one thing, but paying for them through taxes was another issue entirely. Unfortunately, the precedent set abroad was not helpful. In England, school reformers thought of public schools only as charity schools. This concept predominated in the thinking of most people in the colonies during the eighteenth century, and it was a difficult idea to erase. Overcoming this barrier was necessary in order to establish the free and open democratic school system that was to follow. Benevolent societies and individuals did perform a service by aiding the pauper schools, but their act carried with it the stigma of elitism.

Gradually, the view that the teacher might be paid by the people in general or through public taxation was accepted (Monroe, 1940). The 1809 law in Pennsylvania that provided free education to the poor made few friends, as the poor had to declare themselves as lowly paupers to qualify, and property owners objected to paying the tax (Meyer, 1967). Pennsylvania later became a model for doing away with the pauper school custom when it enacted the Free School Act in 1834. The trend that emerged was to use local and county taxes for schools, with some additional help from the state.

In most states, the rate bill or tuition tax was charged to every child whose parent was able to pay. The rate bill system of collecting money for schools grew out of the Old Deluder Satan Act of 1647 in Massachusetts. This system of collecting tuition kept many children from obtaining an education, either because they could not afford the rate or because they were too proud to ask for charity. Many states would allow a certain number of free attendance days; after this period, the parents had to pay the rate. This later practice encouraged some parents to hold their children out of school. The rate bill forced some poor parents to send only one child at a time (Monroe, 1940). Massachusetts ended their system of rate collection in 1827 and Delaware did so in 1829, but other states did not end the practice until much later—some even after the Civil War.

Even though the rate bill or tuition practice has ended, some public schools are not completely free today. One large public school system in a major midwestern city charges fees for books. Other systems are known to charge fees for certain extras, thus often placing those who are unable to pay for those extras in an embarrassing position. The maintenance of "free" public schools is still a live issue.

Compulsory School Attendance Laws and Child Labor Laws

One of the most important changes to affect the growth of the public school system was the passage of compulsory-school-attendance laws. The first of these laws was drafted in Massachusetts in 1852, but it was 1918 before compulsory attendance legislation had been passed in all states. The first decree in Massachusetts was for a period of only twelve weeks. The enforcement of most of these laws was weak because the states did not have the administrative machinery to enforce them (Katz, 1976).

Compulsory schooling regulations changed greatly between 1900 and 1930. The previously simple statutes requiring school attendance for a fixed number of days each year became a complex network of legal rules. Added to the school attendance rules were rules for hiring truant officers and defining their duties, and for establishing truant schools, delegating jurisdictional power, and dealing with child labor laws. The child labor laws, the first of which was passed in Rhode Island in 1840, often required school attendance as a prerequisite for the employment of children or disallowed employment altogether for some youth during their schooling. After the passage of the child labor laws, 90.6 percent of the children legally designated as too young to work were attending school (Katz, 1976). Average daily attendance helped to improve compliance with compulsory attendance laws. Some children were sent to reform schools after being convicted of truancy.

The child labor laws and the compulsory attendance laws were crucial in furthering the development of the public schools. Today, the benefits to the growth of their children both socially and mentally motivates most parents to support their children's education, but the compulsory attendance edict is still needed for the benefit of all society, and many states are currently considering extending the age of compulsory education to eighteen.

The *Kalamazoo* Case (1874)

It took the action of the supreme court in the state of Michigan in 1874 in *Charles E. Stuart and others* v. *School District No. 1 of the Village of Kalamazoo and others* to finally decide that the public high school was a legitimate part of the public school system. Some prominent citizens of the city of Kalamazoo, Michigan, objected to paying taxes to support the local public high school. Charles E. Stuart, a former U.S. Senator, was one of the citizens who objected to the tax-supported secondary school. He felt that an elementary-school education was enough for the taxpayers to provide, for he, after all, had made it all the way to the Senate with only an elementary-school diploma.

Judge Thomas M. Cooley, an associate justice of the Michigan Supreme Court, argued that a liberal education, including instruction in the classics, was an important practical advantage to be supplied to all and not just to those whose accumulated wealth enabled them to pay for it (Selden, 1975). In addition, Judge Cooley cited, among other legislation, the Northwest Ordinance of 1787, which states that "schools and the means of education shall forever be encouraged." The effect of the *Kalamazoo* case was far-reaching. After 1874, in states across the nation, courts turned to the *Kalamazoo* decision as a precedent when faced with challenges to the public high schools. In the fifteen years following Judge Cooley's decision, the number of high schools in Michigan rose from 107 to 278, and there was a similar expansion in other states (Selden, 1975).

Considering the general acceptance of the public high school as a part of our American educational system, it is hard for us to realize how hard a fight was necessary to win approval for its existence: "Even at the beginning of the twentieth century public high schools enrolled only 11% of all youth eligible to attend" (Brodinsky, 1976, p. 23). As we well know the debate continues about what the high-school curriculum should be, but the right for it to exist was settled in the Kalamazoo decision.

The Committee of Ten (1892)

The proper curriculum for the high school was clarified and defined by the Committee of Ten in 1892. This committee was formed by the National Education Association for the purpose of improving the relationship of the secondary schools to the colleges. The committee was chaired by the legendary president of Harvard University, Charles Eliot. The rest of the membership was composed of male college presidents, professors, and teachers, mainly experts on the college preparatory curriculum. The members felt unanimously that high schools should offer academic subjects and that high-school students should be subjected to academic rigor.

The committee of ten selected nine subcommittees, each composed of ten members, and assigned a field of study then taught in the high schools. These subcommittees took on the task of deciding where in the high-school program to place each subject, how long each subject should be studied, and by what methods each of the nine subjects should be taught. According to Eby (1952),

> This was the first time in American education a group of 100 educators had undertaken to formulate a unified system of instruction for children and youth from six to 18 years of age. The report was one of the most important educational documents ever issued in the United States. (p. 592)

As a result of the work of the Committee of Ten, the curriculum of public secondary schools became more standardized than it had been in the older academies. Despite the committee's goal of treating everyone the same, whether they were college-bound or not, the suggested curriculum was dominated by college-preparatory courses. The committee did not study pupil abilities, social needs, interests, or capacities for learning (Cubberley, 1934). The domination of colleges over the secondary-school program is still very much in evidence, and battles remain to be fought to improve programs and attitudes toward programs for the non-college-bound student.

Public Education and the Role of Religion

By the turn of the century, public education for all was well on its way to becoming an established reality in America. You will find modern developments in public education explored throughout this text, from the social issues discussed in Chapters 1 and 2 to the foundations and issues of school law, governance and control, finance, and curriculum to be presented later.

One additional topic should be explored as a twentieth-century concern, seen in the light of history. The issue of religion in the public schools has been and continues to be a matter for heated debate in America. In order to further your understanding of this controversy, the following paragraphs present some historical and legal facts.

In western and central Europe during the Middle Ages, only one established Christian denomination, the Roman Catholic Church, set the moral values and standards of behavior. The new social, political, and economic relationships that marked the Renaissance helped to lead to the Reformation and a split in the church and many new Christian denominations emerged. The dilemma that we face today in our public schools was partly and indirectly caused by the division of the Christian church during the Reformation and the idea of the separation of church and state, which originated during the Enlightenment.

Diversity of religious thought did not alone cause the move away from religion's being the basis for education. Educators like Comenius believed in educating the child for all of life and not just for entry into heaven. Thinkers like Comenius and Luther—and later, in the Enlightenment period, Rousseau—set in motion a chain of events that has led us into teaching only secular curricula in our public schools today.

The movement toward secular education in America is where it is today for a number of reasons. The First Amendment of the U.S. Constitution was adopted in order to give everyone an opportunity to practice the religion of her or his choice, free from the restraints of the government. This noble idea, set down by the Founding Fathers, was meant to protect citizens from feared encroachments by federal, state, or local governments on personal religious beliefs. In addition, Horace Mann and other school reformers in the 1840s obtained their model for public-school reform from Prussia. The Prussian system of schools was completely under secular control.

During colonial times—and in some areas for a great many years after—the public schools were located in homogeneous communities with only one or two religious denominations. The practice of religion in the schools was logical and generally without controversy. But most communities grew and diversified in the makeup of their citizenry. In our present-day pluralistic society, the practice of any one particular religion in a school causes great controversy, and it was declared illegal by the U.S. Supreme Court in *Abington* v. *Schempp* and *Murray* v. *Curlett* in 1963.

Today, in our country, many groups and individuals are saying that the values of our young people are not what they should be, and that eliminating religious training from the schools has also removed moral and values training from our children's education. Solutions for this problem vary from those that suggest a values clarification approach to those that propose that churches work with the schools to improve the children's value base. Some organizations, such as the National Council on Religion and Public Education (NCRPE), point out that the Supreme Court ruled in 1963 only against reading from the Bible and the use of the Lord's Prayer in the public schools. The court specifically said that study of the Bible or religion as a part of the secular school curriculum was consistent with the intent of the First Amendment. Thus, the NCRPE suggests that schools use the Bible as literature and for stories on values, that comparative world religions become a part of social studies, and the study of the arts include religious subjects.

The issues of religion in the public schools and the move toward secularism are still to be resolved, for not only are the many Christian denominations involved but also the Jewish community, many non-Christian sects, and even atheist groups. As the controversy continues, it is important for teachers to know where they stand personally on this issue and what the current laws and rules of their school district are in relation to the religion issue.

Summary

This chapter first gives some examples of the contributions of private education in the United States. Many of these examples paved the way for changes that were later picked up by the public schools. Privately, many schools operating today offer alternatives to the public schools that may one day be adopted by the public schools. As long as there is a proper balance between the two systems, each of them actually helps the other. Kraushaar (1976) stated it best when he wrote:

> The new goal is to recognize the spheres and validity of public and private schools and that the dual system adds alternatives, richness, and diversity to the opportunities open to the young, while it strives to bring the two spheres into harmonious working relationship. (p. 52)

Public educational development winds its way historically from New England's quasi-public schools to the more free and open public schools we have today. These early schools were quasi-public schools because they charged a rate or a tuition even though they were open to most of the people. The great public-school movement headed by Horace Mann consolidated public opinion in favor of free public education, and after the *Kalamazoo* case, we were assured of free public high schools as well as elementary schools. Many important people helped to shape the events that have built the public school system into the vast network it is today.

Questions

1. Were there any early practices in education that you would like to see teachers make use of today?
2. How have educational practices begun in the private sector affected the public schools?

3. Compare the influence of the *Dartmouth College* case with the *Kalamazoo* case on the use of public money for education.
4. Compare the emphasis of the academy movement with the previous grammar-school movement and the subsequent high-school movement.
5. Describe the impact on minority education, particularly higher education, of the work of Emma Willard, Catherine Beecher, Mary Lyon, and Booker T. Washington.
6. How have the progressive education movement and the experimental private schools of the 1960s and 1970s affected the public schools?
7. How did European school systems, particularly the Prussian system, influence American education in the early 1800s?
8. What was the significance of each of the following for the growth of public education in America?
   a. Pauper schools.
   b. Child labor laws and compulsory attendance laws.
   c. Public taxation for education.
9. Describe the controversy over religion in the public schools.

Activities for Unit II

1. Write a paper on the contributions of Friedrich Wilhelm Froebel. Compare what is done, in a curricular way, in present-day kindergartens to Froebel's kindergarten in Germany.
2. Construct a model of an early educational device such as a hornbook, a copybook, or a quill pen.
3. Try to simulate in class what the Socratic method of teaching might have been like. What are some implications concerning the Socratic method that would work today in teaching?
4. As a class, rediscover the exuberance of the Renaissance by designing new learning activities for children that will truly "light their fire." These activities could be put to use in some school during your pre-student-teaching experience.
5. Choose an educator such as Sir Francis Bacon, John Amos Comenius, John Locke, Jean-Jacque Rousseau, Johann Heinrich Pestalozzi, or Friedrich Wilhelm Froebel and report to the class on how he made a significant impact on learning and education.
6. Role play what it may have been like in an early one-room school. One student will be the master and the rest of the class will be divided into eight grades. The members of each grade will devise a "curriculum" for themselves.
7. Invite a retired teacher to talk about the methods he or she used in teaching. Have the teacher bring to the class any historical textbooks she or he might have.

8. Locate an old McGuffey Reader and compare the values taught by it with the values taught in a modern textbook for the same grade level.
9. Create a drama illustrating the common school movement in education. Include media events, foreign influence, and men such as Horace Mann and Henry Barnard. Create minor supporting roles for interest.
10. Interview a local school official concerning the use of Elementary and Secondary Education Act (ESEA) funds. Attempt to find out the amount of funds received locally and the purposes for which the funds are used.

THE PHILOSOPHY OF EDUCATION

6

Traditional Philosophies

OBJECTIVES

After reading Chapter 6, the student will be able to:
- Speculate about the reasons for studying philosophy.
- Define and give examples of the philosophical questions posed in the four major branches of philosophy.
- Compare and contrast the educational beliefs and principles of the five pure philosophies.
- Identify the contributions of major philosophers in each of the pure philosophies.
- Decide which philosophy or philosophies incorporate the student's philosophical position.

Introduction

As a student of the education process, you have learned that a teacher is required to make decisions about what should be taught, what methods should be used in the instruction, what learning activities should be included in each lesson, whether learning should be by group activity or individual project, and what techniques should be applied to evaluate this learning. Thus, education involves the investigation of a multitude of problems and questions, and the possible answers to all of these questions are based on the teacher's beliefs about people, about the world, about how students learn, about how students think, and about values. Every decision the teacher makes, from how the classroom should be arranged to how the learning should be evaluated, involves the teacher's philosophy of life and his or her philosophy of education. Discipline and classroom control practices are especially dependent on the teacher's belief system and philosophy of education. Teaching without developing one's own philosophy of education would be analogous to building a house on sand instead of on a firm foundation, or to taking a trip without a road map.

Definition of the Term *Philosophy*

What is a "philosophy"? The word comes from two Greek words meaning "love of wisdom." In practical terms, philosophy is the belief system that a person develops concerning existence, reality in the world, truth and knowledge, logic or thought processes, and aesthetic and ethical values. A philosophy answers such questions as "What is real?" "How do we gain a knowledge of what is true?" "What is our view of the world?" "Are humans basically good or evil?" "How do we learn?" "What are the principles of correct thinking?" "What ethical values should guide us in our actions?" And "Of what does beauty consist?" Philosophy, then, is a person's fundamental belief system, on which he or she bases the answers to life's (and education's) most perplexing questions.

Why Study Philosophy?

As mentioned in the introduction to this chapter, many of the pressing problems in education today are related to and can be answered by one's personal philosophy of education. Many of these questions are related to the three crucial areas of discipline, methods, and evaluation. What classroom control techniques should be used with students at a specific age and maturity level? Are humiliation and sarcasm ever appropriate as discipline methods? Should subject matter be used as punishment ("Johnny, do twenty more addition problems because you talked without raising your hand")? How effective are logical consequences and assertive discipline techniques in controlling the aggressive behavior of students? Are detention and isolation techniques harmonious with the teacher's general philosophy of education? Should corporal punishment be used as a last resort? The answers to many of these questions concerning classroom control depend on one's view of the student as basically good or evil and on one's ideas about how correct behavior is best learned and internalized.

What questions arise in the area of teaching and learning methods? Should instruction concentrate on group work or individualized learning experiences? Do you favor individualized learning contracts? Is peer tutoring an effective method for a particular age or learning level? Are calculators and computers an aid to learning math, or do they make students too dependent on machines to do their calculations for them? How do you feel about programmed instruction and teaching with television? Are current television programs an aid or a hindrance to classroom learning? How should commercial television programs be used to supplement classroom learning? What percentage of instruction should be by practical hands-on experiences in comparison with the percentage of theoretical concepts taught in the classroom (philosophers have very definite opinions on this question)? Is your aim as a teacher to cover all the known subject matter in a survey fashion, or should students study fewer topics in greater depth by "postholing"? Should subjects such as history be chronological or topical in arrangement? Should the study of biology be organized by the classification system (phyla) or by the practical use of each plant or animal (niche approach)? What is "basic" for pupils to learn at a specific level in elementary school? Are physical education, music, and art basic to the learning process in elementary schools?

How should students be evaluated? Should academic test scores be the only method of evaluation? How much should academic ability, attitude, and effort be considered? Should evaluation be subjective, objective, or a combination of both? Would you recommend "extra-credit" projects for slower students, for better students, or for all students? Would you use essay or objective exams in your subject area or grade level? What is the importance of success or failure to the self-concept of the student? Should students be passed from grade to grade with their peers whether or not subject-matter mastery is attained? Is competency-based education an answer to this problem?

Numerous other examples could be given, but let these illustrations prove the point that all questions in education are basically philosophical questions.

Even the physical arrangement of classrooms should be based on a philosophy of education. Is the teacher's desk in the front, at the side, or at the rear of the classroom? Should students' seats be in rows, in a circle, or in a U-shaped arrangement? Should three or more classes be grouped together in open-concept "pods" or separated into single classrooms?

Philosophy is truly the most practical of subjects because every question is in essence a philosophical question. This chapter on philosophy will help you to form a philosophy and to rely on it to answer these and other questions in everyday educational practice.

F. Bruce Rosen (1968) stated that there are very few new problems in education. Therefore, we educators need to study philosophy to clarify these age-old problems, such as the problem of how to educate students for citizenship (studied by Plato and by education students today). Rosen wrote:

> One of the most immediate values in the study of a variety of philosophies of education is that it allows one to see a number of different and alternative solutions to a single problem. Each of the solutions is part of a broader framework of educational thought which in turn is part of a philosophical system. Thus, each solution is a part of a consistent view point. . . . Each point of view provides us with a different measuring stick for current educational practices. (p. 8)

Rosen sees philosophy as a person's attempt to give meaning to life and to search for answers to the basic problems in existence and education (p. 3). Thus, the authors of this text believe that students of education should engage in acting as well as thinking. Students are seeking in this chapter the personal beliefs and values that will serve as a foundation in their search for answers to present and future educational problems. A student's philosophy will enable him or her to make and to justify consistent choices in a future educational career.

The Language of Philosophy

Before the major pure and educational philosophies can be studied, the education student must become familiar with the special terminology of philosophy. At first this process may seem like studying a foreign language, but as you use these terms, they will become clear. Do not be fearful of them, and use the simple equivalent question given for each term to help you.

Metaphysics

The first of the four major divisions of philosophy is metaphysics. Metaphysics concerns the universe and humankind. The main question posed in metaphysics is "What is real?" or "What is reality?" Concerning the world, metaphysics includes the question of what causes events in the universe to happen, including the theories of creation and evolution. Metaphysics also involves questions concerning the nature of humans. Is the basic human nature physical or spiritual? What is the relation, if any, of mind and body? An additional question is whether we are free or determined. In other words, does a person make free choices, or do events and conditions, such as mental ability, poverty, and financial resources, force one into basic decisions? Other aspects of metaphysics encompass questions about a person's existence, about the nature and existence of God, about whether there is purpose in events of the universe, and about whether ultimate reality is singular or plural: Is reality one substance (mind or body), two substances (mind and body), or more than two substances?

The questions in metaphysics are extremely relevant to teachers and students of education, especially questions about humanity and the universe. Theories about how the universe came to be and about what causes events in the universe are crucial to the sciences, especially biology. The questions about humankind in metaphysics are important at all grade levels and in all subjects. How much can students influence and control their own lives (freedom versus determinism)? Are humans "little animals" to be treated only as physical beings, are they only a composite of the ideas they hold, or are they a combination of both? The answers to these questions will influence the teacher's behavior in disciplining students, in emphasizing physical conditioning of the body versus developing the mind, and in deciding how much emphasis to place on student's learning decision-making skills.

Epistemology

The second major division in philosophy is epistemology. Epistemology deals with "What is true?" and "How do we know?" Epistemology includes the possibility of knowledge, the kind or types of knowledge, and the ways of knowing. In connection with the possibility of knowledge, an agnostic would believe that it is impossible to have knowledge of ultimate reality, whereas a skeptic would question whether such knowledge is possible. The two major types of knowledge are knowledge that is based on observation and experience and knowledge that is self-evident and does not require proof. However, the major contents of epistemology for the teacher are the five ways of knowing. The first way of knowing is by revelation from God, or such as the Ten Commandments. The second is by authority: one relies on an expert for knowledge. The third way of knowing involves reasoning ability within the mind of the individual, and the fourth is knowledge gained through sense perception by the individual (the scientific method). The fifth way of knowing is by intuition: after study of the topic, one skips the ordinary steps in the discovery process when insight comes (as in a brainstorm of ideas in the middle of the night, for example).

How we know, or epistemology, is of paramount importance to teachers because their beliefs about learning influence their classroom methods.

Should teachers train students in the scientific method, deductive reasoning, or both? Should students study logic and fallacies of the reasoning process? Under what conditions can one believe an authority figure (an athlete or a movie star) on television? Is the "grand leap" of intuition a legitimate source of knowledge? Is intuition involved in major scientific discoveries (such as the discovery of pasteurization)? Teachers' knowledge of how students learn influences how they will teach.

Logic

Logic, or how one thinks, is the third major division of philosophy. It is closely related to epistemology and includes two major subdivisions: deductive logic and inductive logic. When one starts with a general principle and "deduces" specific facts or behaviors, one is using deductive logic. When one begins with a multitude of specifics and eventually formulates a general rule from them, one is using inductive logic. Although the scientific method encompasses both deduction and induction, it places great emphasis on the inductive method. As will be explained later, idealists tend to emphasize deduction, whereas realists and pragmatists rely on induction and the scientific method, using the systematic observation of experience. John Dewey's *How We Think* (1933) deals with this question of the scientific method. Immanuel Kant, an idealist, is associated with deduction, whereas Francis Bacon, a critical naturalist, and other scientists emphasize induction.

Axiology

The fourth major division of philosophy is also of crucial importance to teachers and schools. Axiology includes the questions "What is morally right?" and "What is beautiful?" It covers ethics and moral values, topics that many people think schools should emphasize. Good citizenship, honesty, and correct human relations are all learned in schools. They are not always taught directly but are learned as a by-product of other learning. Often, students learn ethics from what the teacher "is" as well as from what the teacher "says." Cheating on exams and instances of academic dishonesty have also become major problems in some schools. Watergate and other instances of government corruption have placed much pressure on the schools to increase instruction in ethics and moral values. One major question to be examined is whether the end (goal) justifies any means (methods) of achieving it. In the Watergate scandal, getting a particular president of the United States reelected seemed to be more important than the methods used to accomplish this goal, and basic violations of ethical principles and basic civil rights resulted.

In summary, problems in philosophy can be divided into questions of being (existence), knowledge, logic, and values. Questions such as "Who am I?," "Why am I here?," "What is real?," "What is good?," "What is beautiful?," and "How can students learn?" are crucial to education and to teachers. The reader is now introduced first to the various positions of the pure philosophies and then to the related educational philosophies to see how each philosophy answers these relevant questions.

Pure Philosophies

The four major "pure" philosophies are naturalism, idealism, realism, and pragmatism. In addition, existentialism is included here in the pure philosophies, and its major tenets are discussed in this section. These pure philosophies are related to the educational philosophies of perennialism, essentialism, progressivism, and reconstructionism, which are discussed in the next section of this chapter.

As will be seen, naturalism and realism share a belief in the external physical world as being the real world, but they differ in that naturalism has little theory of knowing whereas realism has an epistemology based on the scientific method. Realism emphasizes the correspondence theory of truth (that something is true if it corresponds to the external world as it appears to our senses). For idealists, on the other hand, reality is an idea in our heads, not in the external physical world. Idealists emphasize the consistency (or coherence) theory of truth, which states that an idea is true if it forms part of a "system" of ideas. Idealists place much emphasis on deductive reasoning and much less on the senses and the scientific method. Pragmatism (also called *experimentalism* or *instrumentalism*) places its emphasis on change as the only reality to be counted on. For pragmatists, everything is relative and situational, including ethics. Existentialism is oriented toward the individual and is concerned with two basic issues, individual freedom and death. Freedom of choice is crucial for the existentialists. Each of these pure philosophies is now examined in more detail.

Naturalism

Naturalism is the oldest of the major pure philosophies, dating back to ancient times. Naturalism is also the simplest of the major pure philosophies, with its belief that the physical world as it appears to one's senses is true reality. Naturalism shares this belief in the external physical universe with realism, but naturalism differs from realism in that naturalism does not emphasize questions concerning knowledge or epistemology. Instead, naturalism places its emphasis on metaphysics (what is real). Naturalism is best conceived of as opposing "supernaturalism" because true naturalists believe that there is nothing beyond the physical world that a person sees. For the pure naturalist, there is no god outside or above nature. The closest approach they have to a god is pantheism, where the totality of nature approximates "god." As Butler (1968) put it, "Naturalism is a distinct philosophy by virtue of its insistence that reality and nature are identical, and that beyond nature there is no reality" (p. 73). Naturalists believe that the human being is a child of nature, not of society. They emphasize living in harmony with nature and using the scientific (inductive) method of logic. Society, they believe, results from individuals' binding themselves together in a social contract to avoid anarchy. Naturalists believe that science yields items of knowledge that make up a dependable source of scientific information.

Thomas Hobbes and Herbert Spencer both contributed much to the development of naturalism. Hobbes (1588–1679) believed that humans are in continual competition with others (a war of everyone against everyone). When one says, "It's a cruel and competitive world out there," she or he is espousing Hobbes' philosophy. According to Hobbes, schools should emphasize competition, not cooperation. He would emphasize high academic standards, science fairs, spelling bees, and other forms of competition, especially letter grades. Hobbes believed that "justice is exacted of men by a terror of punishment which is greater than the benefit they [students] would gain from a breach of the law" (Butler, 1968, p. 60). Thus, Hobbes's major classroom discipline technique would be the fear of punishment.

Spencer (1820–1903) was a scientist who participated in the development of the theory of evolution. He believed that the child is a little animal who must be educated according to the natural rhythms of growth and development. Scientific knowledge, he believed, was of the most worth, and the long infancy of humans makes education a necessity. Spencer wrote specifically about education in *Education: Intellectual, Moral, and Physical* (1861). He called his theory the synthetic philosophy, involving the principles of evolution and dissolution, and he was very objective in collecting and organizing facts by the scientific method. He was an energist and an agnostic, believing that ultimate reality is a force and that it is unknowable. Spencer's eight principles of the education process included the following (Butler, 1968):

1. Education must conform to the natural processes of growth and mental development.
2. Education should be pleasurable . . . [with an emphasis on readiness and interests].
3. Education should engage the spontaneous self-activity of the child. . . . The child educates himself in a great measure [the use of native self-activity].
4. Acquisition of knowledge is an important part of education.
5. . . . education is for the body as well as the mind. . . . Mind and body must both be cared for and the whole being of the pupil unfolded as a unit.
6. . . . education practices the art of delay . . . [in harmony with the rhythms of nature and maturation].
7. Methods of instruction should be inductive.
8. Punishment should be constituted by natural consequences of wrong

deeds; should be certain, but tempered with sympathy. Punishment should fit the crime, be consistently administered, and avoid anger. (pp. 92–94)

Jean-Jacques Rousseau (1712–1778) was probably the greatest modern naturalist, from the educator's standpoint. Rousseau believed that the individual is innately good but is corrupted by society. He condemned society and preferred the simple life lived close to nature. He wrote *Émile* (1762), a book describing the education of the son of a wealthy person through private tutoring, and *The Social Contract* (1762), his work on politics. Rousseau opposed the contemporary emphasis on habit formation and behavioral conditioning. He believed that the impetus for growth and maturation of mind and body comes from within and that students should be cultivated much as the gardener tends a plant, providing the proper environment and nourishment, while preventing harmful outside influences from the world. Rousseau be-

Jean-Jacques Rousseau's philosophy of naturalism influenced the educational and political thought of his times. *(Photo courtesy of the Library of Congress.)*

lieved in a practical education through action rather than talking. He believed that students should not be exposed to society until they had learned how to handle this experience. Thus, he wanted to teach the student moral principles before introducing her or him to society. Rousseau believed that a person should place emphasis on studying his or her relationship to the environment. In Rousseau's words,

> The real object of our student is man and his environment. To my mind those of us who can best endure the good and evil of life are best educated; hence it follows that true education consists less in precept than in practice. We begin to learn when we begin to live; our education begins with ourselves, our first teacher is our nurse. (Cited in Gruber, 1973, pp. 108–109)

Rousseau's belief in the goodness of man and in the evil of society is evident in this statement (Gruber, 1973):

> God makes all things good; man meddles with them and they become evil. He forces one soil to yield the products of another, one tree to bear another's fruit. He confuses and confounds time, place, and natural conditions. He mutilates his dog, his horse, and his slave. He destroys and defaces all things; he loves all that is deformed and monstrous; he will have nothing as nature made it, not even man himself, who must learn his paces like a saddle horse, and be shaped to his master's taste like the trees in his garden. (pp. 107–108)

Rousseau further stated, "Plants are fashioned by cultivation, man by education" (Gruber, 1973, p. 108). He obviously put great emphasis on education, but it must be noted that his opinions on women's role in society are dated because he devoted only one chapter at the end of *Émile* to women's role, which he stated was to be a helpmate for the Émiles rather than to be educated for careers of their own. In spite if such weaknesses, Rousseau was very influential in the philosophy of naturalism and was the philosophical father of Johann Friedrich Herbart, Johann Heinrich Pestalozzi, and Friedrich Froebel, as shall be seen later in this chapter.

The "back-to-nature" trend in the last few years in the United States is an example of naturalism. Backpacking, camping, and survival training are examples of this trend, as is the "natural look" in cosmetics and dress. We all seem to yearn for a return to the simple life in the rhythms of nature. Anything that is artificial and unnatural seems to repel us. "Earth tones" have been popular in interior decoration, and even suburbs have resulted from a trend to "get back to nature" and away from pollution. In fact, the entire environmentalist movement parallels the ideas of naturalism. Examples of this movement range from the protection of wilderness lands to a trend toward heating homes with wood and solar energy rather than with fossil fuels. As can be readily seen, naturalism has been the "in" philosophy in recent years.

Philosophies and Roles in Education

Naturalism	
Student	Teacher
Little animal to be kept attuned to nature.	A. Protector from evils of world. B. Transmitter of knowledge so child can cope. C. Competitive mentor and strict disciplinarian. (Views differ.)

Idealism	
Student	Teacher
A mind to be nurtured and protected.	Model for students. Emphasizes lecture and discussion of ideas. Transmitter of cultural heritage.
Parent	
Protector from evils of the environment.	

Realism	
Student	Teacher
"tabula rasa." Blank page. Passive organism.	Forms correct habits in students ("conditioner"). Connects new information to old.

Pragmatism	
Student	Teacher
An active problem-solver moving toward the goal of an independent learner.	Guide and resource person.

Existentialism	
Student	Teacher
Active questioner searching for self, responsible for own learning.	Helps students to make their own choices and to become their own person.

Naturalism has both strengths and weaknesses as a philosophy. According to Butler (1968), the simplicity of naturalism is both a strength and a weakness. In calling people back to nature, it is a simplifying influence on the hectic pace of modern life. However, naturalism is too simple in that it does not have an adequate theory of knowledge (epistemology); thus, it is not a comprehensive philosophy. It ignores the fact that nature is not all rhythm and harmony because it includes tornadoes, earthquakes, and floods. For naturalists, there is no supernatural, and the pupil remains a "little animal" with slight emphasis on mental development. Thus, physical conditioning of the human body becomes very important for the naturalists.

Idealism

Idealism is the second pure philosophy. Idealism is important both because of its own beliefs and because pragmatism and realism were developed as counterthrusts to idealism. Idealists believe in the reality of the spirit, the mind, the soul, and ideas. As Rosen (1968) pointed out, "Idealism is a philosophical position which adheres to the view that nothing exists except as it is an idea in the mind of man, the mind of God, or in a super- or supra-natural realm" (p. 12). Thus, idealism could be more accurately called *idea-ism* without the *l*. Although idealists do believe in ideals, as shown by their belief in God and the supernatural, their main emphasis is on ideas and the human mind. As contrasted with naturalism, which includes a belief in the physical world and a lack of belief in supernaturalism, idealism has completely opposite beliefs. For idealists, the idea of a physical thing, such as a building, in the human mind is what is real, not the physical structure itself. Also, most idealists have a firm belief in God, whereas most naturalists do not believe in any supernatural power that is of a higher order than nature itself. George Berkeley (1685–1753), the consummate idealist, had trouble with the question of whether the sound of a tree actually existed when it fell in a forest if there was no human mind there to perceive it. For Berkeley, "to be was to be perceived," and he solved the problem by maintaining that God (the mind of God) was always there to perceive the sound of the tree falling.

Idealists believe in the power of reasoning (in the mind), particularly deductive reasoning, and they deemphasize the scientific method and sense perception, which they hold suspect. They believe that we look inside our own minds for the truth. They search for universal or absolute truths that will remain constant through the centuries. Rosen (1968) summarized this idealist view when he wrote that the senses deceive us and make us believe that the purely transitory world is the real world, and that therefore, we must suppress the senses as much as possible. Idealists often define education as helping humans to conform to the will of God. Idealist educational beliefs include an emphasis on the study of great leaders as examples for us to imitate. For idealists, the teacher is the ideal model or example for the student. Teachers pass on the cultural heritage and the unchanging content of education, such as studying the great figures of the past, the humanities, and a rigorous academic curriculum. Idealists emphasize the methods of lecture, discussion, and imitation; and finally, they believe in the importance of the doctrine of ideas.

Plato, Immanuel Kant, and Georg Wilhelm Friedrich Hegel were three very important idealists. Plato was intent on separating the permanent from the temporary, shadows from real objects, and the perceptions of our senses from realities. What one's senses perceive are illusions compared to the real world of ideas in the mind. This idea is perhaps best seen in Plato's allegory of the cave (cited in Rosen, 1968):

> There is a cave in which men are chained facing a wall. On a ledge behind those who are chained, another group of men walk carrying things. Behind the men on the ledge is a fire which casts their shadows on the wall for the chained men to see. . . . Plato's analogy indicates that the world we know, the world of our senses, is like the shadows. It is unreal but we believe it to be the true reality because of habit and because it is the only reality with which we are familiar. The Real World, the World of Ideas, is of a different order, just as the men on the ledge are of a different order than their shadows. (p. 13)

Kant and Hegel carried Plato's ideas further. Kant (1724–1804) emphasized the universal moral law, which he believed human beings naturally tend to fulfill. Kant's universal moral law, or categorical imperative, states that we should behave according to principles that we would want to be universal laws for everyone; for example, "Don't cheat on your income tax unless you expect everyone to do so." Also, persons must act correctly because it is right morally, not because other people will praise or condemn them for these actions. Hegel (1770–1831) believed that an individual fact or idea has no value until it fits into a system with other facts and ideas. This idea is sometimes called the *coherence theory of truth* because the facts or ideas have to stick to each other to become meaningful. Hegel also believed that most thought patterns begin with an idea (a thesis), then progress by contrasting this idea with its opposite (antithesis), and finally find the real truth in a combination of the thesis and the antithesis (the synthesis). Hegel would look at the idea that only the subject matter is important in schools (thesis), examine the opposite idea that only the child is important (antithesis), and conclude these ideas are equally important in learning (synthesis). As far as Hegel's ideas on education are concerned (Gruber, 1973):

> Hegel's educational theories grew directly out of his absolute idealism. He considered education to be a life process, a mental discipline that makes man religious, moral, cultured, and rational. Education should be compulsory through the state and for the state because only through education is the Will of God transmitted. (p. 133)

One of the idealists who had the greatest impact on education was Friedrich Froebel. He studied under Pestalozzi, established a school for boys, and opened the first kindergarten ("child's garden") in Germany in 1837. He then spent the rest of his life on the preparation of teachers in the area of early childhood education. Froebel's unhappy childhood probably influenced his ideas on education. His father, a minister, paid little attention to his son, and his stepmother favored her own children. Gruber (1973) stated, "This early

Friedrich Froebel, who established the first kindergarten, felt that early childhood was an important time, when children should be nurtured and given many and varied play experiences. *(Photo courtesy of the Library of Congress.)*

unfortunate childhood probably shaped the whole course of his life and was influential in centering his interest on early childhood education, making him sympathetic to and understanding of the problems of the very young'' (p. 145). Froebel, like Rousseau, believed that the child develops from the inside out and that the child should be nurtured like a plant in a garden. Gruber (1973) wrote:

> He [Froebel] likened education to a garden and believed that the school should cultivate and develop the potential in each child as a horticulturist tends each tender plant. To this end he used color, motion spheres, cubes, and other geometric forms and figures for their symbolic meaning. For example, a sphere taught the child the unity of mankind to God. (pp. 146–147)

Froebel recommended that an actual garden of living plants be part of every kindergarten, and he emphasized vocations as an important part of a child's learning. He recognized the importance of the parents' role in educating the child, writing a songbook for mother and child. However, the role of the parent was to protect the child from the evils of the environment, not to prescribe exactly what the child should learn and do. Froebel emphasized the social aspects of learning by group activity because he thought that every human act has social implications (Gruber, 1973):

> Possibly Froebel's greatest contribution to educational method was the doctrine that play was itself educational. He believed that play and free self-activity were nature's way of developing the child and that the child's activities should be prompted by the development of his own nature. (p. 147)

Froebel's kindergarten in German led to the first American German-speaking kindergarten, established by Mrs. Karl Schurz in Watertown, Wisconsin, in 1855, and to the first English-speaking kindergarten in Boston in 1860. Gruber (1973) concluded,

Modern kindergartens provide many of the types of experiences recommended by Froebel in the 1800s. *(Photo used by permission of the Indiana State Teachers Association.)*

> Although he [Froebel] differed in many respects from Rousseau and his teacher Pestalozzi, he shared with them a concern for the continuous development of the individual from infancy. He aimed to rear free-thinking, independent men through developing the inner nature of the child, and believed that all learning should be oriented in the direction of the child's interests and capacities. (p. 146)

Many criticisms of idealism can be identified. It seems to ignore the physical aspects of human nature. It fails to place importance on information available through the senses. Idealists place an overemphasis on perfection and unattainable goals, and they tend to emphasize the humanities to the detriment of the sciences. Some philosophers would also criticize its goal of preserving the past and of transmitting our cultural heritage to future generations. In spite of these possible deficiences, idealism has had a great influence on American education. Hiring officials tend to seek teachers whose personal qualities can be used as examples for students, and Hegel's system of thesis, antithesis, and synthesis is widely evident in American education. Kant's universal moral laws have also influenced values education in schools in the United States. In fact, an entire nineteenth-century movement of idealists in the United States, called *transcendentalism,* has influenced our values and literature. Transcendentalism received its name from the transcendentalists' belief that reality is to be found "beyond" the physical environment and the physical nature of a person.

Idealism was also important, as has been mentioned before, because it led its opponents to develop the philosophies of realism and pragmatism.

Realism

Realism is the third of the pure philosophies. One way to understand realism is to compare it with idealism and naturalism. Rosen (1968) wrote about realism:

> Where an idealist would say that a tree in the middle of the desert exists only if it is in some mind, or if there is knowledge of it, the realist would hold that whether or not anyone or anything is thinking about the tree, it nonetheless exists. The realist has revolted against the doctrine that things that are in the experiential universe are dependent upon a knower for their existence. (p. 28)

Concerning the relationship of realism to naturalism, realism is in many ways similar to naturalism, but naturalism has a better-developed theory of knowledge (how we learn). Both realists and naturalists believe that the real world is the physical world as it appears to our senses, not the world of ideas in our minds. Both emphasize the senses and the scientific method.

What are the philosophical beliefs of the realists? To the realists, as has been said, the physical world, as it appears to our senses, is the real world.

The realists also believe that the universe is governed by an orderly system of natural laws. Thus, they emphasize the natural sciences and a dependable fund of scientific knowledge. They place much faith in inductive logic and the scientific method, differing from the idealists, who place emphasis on deductive logic and reasoning instead of the scientific method of inquiry. A further way in which realists differ from idealists is in their belief in a mechanistic universe, a universe governed by natural laws and cause–effect relationships, and not necessarily by a supreme being. Realists do, however, agree with idealists in their belief in absolutes. Realists reinforce the idealists' belief that

Aristotle was a realist, believing that unchanging physical realities should be studied through inductive logic and scientific investigation. *(Photo courtesy of the Library of Congress.)*

the purpose of education is to conserve and transmit the cultural heritage to future generations. Humans are, however, more passive spectators than active participants in the events of the universe. In the realist view humans are analogous more to a radio wave receiver than to a transmitter. Whereas the idealist Plato was interested in ideas and universal truths, Aristotle, the realist, was concerned about specific facts discovered by the scientific method. Aristotle believed in unchanging, objective, external realities. As Butler (1968) put it, "This confidence in abiding, objective, and external realities which, like the pyramids, stand unaffected by the passing processions, whether of time or inquisitive minds, is the prime confidence of realism" (p. 76). The educational beliefs of the realists are that neither teachers nor students are free; they are subject to natural laws and are spectators in the universe. The subject matter of schools, according to the realists, is the physical universe, and the scientific method and inductive logic should be used to discover and master facts. In fact, "the whole concept of teaching machines is compatible with the [realists'] picture of reality as a mechanistic universe in which man is simply one of the cogs in the machine" (Rosen, 1968, p. 41).

Realists can be divided into two groups: new realists and critical realists. The new realists believe that the objects of the real world are just as we perceive them. They believe in the correspondence theory of truth, which says that a thing is true if it "corresponds" to the real world. By contrast, critical realists have a representational view that, as in Plato's allegory of the cave, one never sees the real objects but only their shadows or "representations" of reality. As Rosen (1968) stated,

> Critical Realists felt that man could not know the world directly but only through certain vehicles or essences. Thus, objects are not presented directly to consciousness but are represented. We do not have direct knowledge of any object except as it is carried to us by our senses. It was felt by the Critical Realists that this position was the only way to explain errors of perception. (pp. 33–34)

Thus, new realists believe that one sees the world directly, whereas the critical realists believe that it is seen indirectly.

John Locke, John Amos Comenius, and William James are examples of the realist tradition. Locke (1632–1704) believed in the "blank-tablet" view of the mind, a belief that there are no innate ideas in the mind. Locke stated that the mind of a person is blank at birth and that the person's sensory experiences write impressions on this blank tablet. Comenius's view of the human mind was that it resembles a spherical mirror (of the ball type used in dance halls of the 1920s to reflect the lights). This view of the mind means that it receives images or signals in a passive way rather than originating or transmitting them. Because the mirror is composed of small pieces of glass, it also distorts the images and results in errors of perception. William James (1842–1910) is classified as both a realist and a pragmatist, as we shall see later in this

John Locke, a realist of the seventeenth century, believed that ideas come to the mind only through experience with the world. *(Photo courtesy of the Library of Congress.)*

chapter. His realist ideas included his emphasis on habits, which he defined as tendencies to act in certain ways, and his emphasis on building useful systems of association in the pupil's mind. On the topic of habits, Gruber (1973) presented James's view in the following words:

> James' *Talks to Teachers* [1898] is a popular simplification of his monumental *Principles of Psychology* prepared especially for classroom teachers with little or no technical knowledge. . . . James writes that pupils can easily understand at an early age that our lives are but a mass of habits. He agrees with Aristotle that habit is man's second nature and with Kant that education is for behavior and habit. . . . Like many modern psychologists, he advises the person to accumulate all the possible connections (or assumptions) that will reinforce the right motives and warns that deferring the establishment of a new habit lessens the chance that it will ever be formed. (p. 176)

In education, the realists are represented by the works of Johann Heinrich Pestalozzi and John Friedrich Herbart. First, let us look at the realistic ideas of Pestalozzi. Pestalozzi was influenced by Rousseau in his belief that the teacher is like the gardener who tends the plants and that growth comes

William James, who is classified as both a realist and a pragmatist, believed that education is the formation of habits. *(Photo courtesy of the Library of Congress.)*

from within. The teacher cannot make a student learn but can only protect the student from harmful outside forces and provide the proper environment for learning:

> Basing all learning on sense perception and activity, Pestalozzi developed a curriculum made up of object lessons, development of language skills, arithmetic, geography, music [especially singing], drawing and modeling, geometry, gymnastics, and manual training. He rejected, as did Rousseau, the study of history, myth, and literature because they had no direct connection with sense perception. (Gruber, 1973, p. 125)

In *How Gertrude Teaches Her Children* (1801), Pestalozzi emphasized a natural education and opposed education based on memorization and the mental discipline theory of learning. Pestalozzi believed that ''the child's innate capacities should be awakened by a series of experiences arranged according to his maturation and that method should follow the order of nature" (Gruber, 1973, p. 125).

Herbart (1776–1841) was born in Germany but took a job in Switzerland as a tutor. Here he was influenced by Pestalozzi, the Swiss educator. Both Herbart and Pestalozzi emphasized the importance of sense impressions, but they had many differences, as shown in the following comparison (Gruber, 1973)

> Pestalozzi was active, impulsive, and developed his pychology in actual practice; Herbart, on the other hand, was thoughtful, scholarly, systematic, and developed his theory of psychology in connection with his teaching of philosophy. While Pestalozzi was interested in the education of childhood and youth through sense perception, Herbart was interested in the intellectual development of the secondary school pupil and the university student. (p. 139)

One of Herbart's major beliefs was that the learner can be conditioned to correct behavior, and Herbart agreed with John Locke that experiences write impressions on the blank tablet of the mind. Like William James, Herbart was interested in psychology, especially the conscious and unconscious states of the mind. Herbart believed that interest can call an idea or experience from the unconscious to the conscious state.

Herbart's main contributions to education are his five formal steps of methodology. The first is to prepare the student to receive new information, and the second is to present the new knowledge. The third step is association in which new material is compared to knowledge already in the brain, or "apperceptive mass," as Herbart called it. The fourth step is generalization, an attempt to discover a general rule, and the fifth is application of the concept learned to new situations. Rosen (1968) summarized Herbart's ideas in the following words:

> Herbart argued that all subjects are related and that knowledge of one helps strengthen knowledge of the others. As the mind acquires new contents they are assimilated with the existing contents [in the apperceptive mass]. . . . The relationship between new ideas and old ideas occurred in what Herbart called the apperceptive mass. Within the mind, new apperceptions or presentations united with older apperceptions and struggled to rise from the unconscious level of the mind to the conscious. Obviously, any teaching must be aimed at making the greatest number of connections between new ideas and those which were already held in the apperceptive mass. (p. 32)

This discussion of the major ideas of realism has uncovered both strengths and weaknesses in this philosophy. Its strengths include its support of habits and behavioral conditioning, its emphasis on cause-and-effect relationships, and its emphasis on psychology. Criticisms include its treatment of the mind as a passive receptor of knowledge and experiences, its emphasis on

A Comparison of the Steps in the Learning Process Between
Dewey and Herbart

Steps to Knowledge		
Dewey's Pragmatism (student-based)		Herbart's Realism (teacher-based)
Test all hypotheses and choose a "best" solution for this situation.	5	Application of the general rule to a new situation.
Consideration of possible positive and negative consequences of all hypotheses.	4	Generalization—formation of a general rule.
Formulation of hypotheses.	3	Association of new knowledge with previous knowledge.
Definition of the problem in terms of all participants can accept.	2	Presentation of new knowledge.
Recognition of the problem by students: "felt need."	1	Preparation of students to receive new knowledge.

cultural heritage rather than change, and its overdependence on cause-and-effect relationships, which seems to diminish a person's ability to control his or her own life. Whatever the strengths and weaknesses of realism, realist educators such as Herbart and Pestalozzi made an enormous contribution to educational thought and methodology.

Pragmatism

The fourth major pure philosophy, pragmatism, is the only one that originated in the United States. Pragmatism, sometimes called *experimentalism* or *instrumentalism*, was developed in opposition to the principles of idealism. Ideas alone are not sufficient for reality, said the original pragmatists; action on these ideas is necessary to determine their value. For the pragmatists, the only test of truth is what works best and what ideas can be used to solve problems satisfactorily. The pragmatists were oriented more toward the present than toward the past, which is prominent in idealism and realism. They grounded their thinking in present actualities and used the scientific method to solve present problems: If the idea "works" and the problem is solved,

The Relationships Among the Traditional
Philosophies and Science

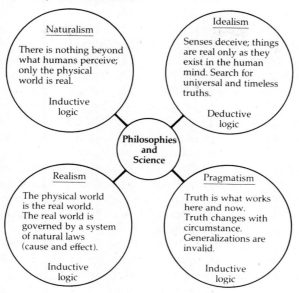

then truth has been discovered. Truth, then, is relative to present conditions and circumstances, not an absolute as the idealists and realists believed. For pragmatists, "experience" was the medium in which thought (ideas) and action mix. They formulated the principles of interaction and continuity of experience. Americans are a very pragmatic people who like the ideas of learning by doing, engaging in practical tasks, and determining truth in each problem situation as it comes along. The pragmatists believed that change is the only thing that can be counted on to be permanent and that truth, reality, and values are all relevant to circumstances. Furthermore, the pragmatists did not believe in absolutes and tended to doubt that rules can be generalized over many specific situations. For the pragmatists, society and the social aspects of culture were also very important.

What are the educational principles of current pragmatists? Pragmatists see education as the reconstruction and reorganization of human experience. Educators should provide conditions that allow students to grow. They see the student as an organism capable of solving problems. The teacher, for the pragmatist, is also a continuous learner who aids and guides others in the learning process without pretending to be the only source of knowledge. Teachers do not abdicate their responsibilities; they arrange conditions for learning related to students' needs and interests.

The curriculum of the pragmatists would consist of any experience contributing to growth and would be based on the needs and interests of the learner. Thus, the subject matter is centered on the problems and needs of the learner, not on universal moral laws as the idealists advocate or on the cause–effect relationships championed by the realists. The project method, individual problem-solving research, and class discussions comprise the methods of the pragmatists, who encourage students to become self-directed learners. As Rosen (1968) wrote, "Pragmatic method is rooted in the psychological needs of the students, rather than in the logical order of subject matter. Thus, method is nothing more than the helping of the students to use intelligence and the scientific method in the solution of problems that are meaningful to the child" (p. 82). As one pragmatist has asserted, "Interest is not enough. It is a necessary, but not a sufficient, condition for selecting an area of concern. It should also offer a challenge and significant educational value" (Rosen, 1968, p. 82). Thus, instead of studying biology in terms of phyla, for example, the pragmatist would help students to organize the subject in terms of significant problems of interest to the students, such as ecology, acid rain, and damage to the environment. The social consequences of our actions are of pressing importance to the pragmatists, who see every action and decision as having an effect on society at large.

The pragmatic method involves the five steps of the scientific method. John Dewey himself outlined them in the booklet *How We Think*. The first step is a recognition of the problem. It begins with an uneasy feeling that something is wrong, which Dewey called the "felt need." The second step is to define the problem in terms that all participants can accept. The authors of this text see this definition stage as one of the most crucial in problem solving because a problem cannot be solved if group members are, in effect, working on different definitions of the problem. The third step is to formulate hypotheses or tentative solutions to the problem. Considering both the positive and the negative consequences of each possible solution is the fourth step in the process. The final step is to test each of these possible solutions and to choose one "best solution" based on the consequences of trying them all in actual practice. It should be added at this point that pragmatists are very suspicious of broad generalizations. They believe that truth is valid only for a single set of circumstances, which are never identical from one situation to another. Pragmatists could truly say, "Never trust a generalization, including this one!"

Numerous American leaders of pragmatism can be identified, such as William Heard Kilpatrick, Boyd Bode, and George Counts, but William James (already discussed under "Realism"), Charles Sanders Pierce, and John Dewey are the most influential names in this movement. Pierce, for instance, formulated the pragmatist idea that the consequences of an idea determine its meaning. However, John Dewey is discussed here as the foremost leader of the pragmatists.

Who was John Dewey, and what were his major philosophical ideas? John Dewey was born in 1859 in Burlington, Vermont, and lived until 1952. He came from a line of pragmatic Vermont farmers and attended local public schools. After he graduated from the University of Vermont, Dewey taught in

John Dewey, America's foremost pragmatist, said that learning occurs through experience and that knowledge is related in the world and thus should not be segregated in schools into isolated subjects. (*Photo courtesy of the Library of Congress.*)

a Vermont high school for only three years and then went back to school to earn graduate degrees. First, he studied under George Sylvester Morris and G. Stanley Hall at Johns Hopkins University. Dewey studied idealism under Morris and learned educational psychology from Hall. Gruber (1973) summarized Dewey's professional career as follows: "He taught philosophy at the University of Michigan and Minnesota, was professor of philosophy and pedagogy at the University of Chicago from 1894–1904, and was professor of philosophy at Columbia University from 1905 until his retirement in 1931"

(p. 183). After his retirement, he remained active by traveling and lecturing until his death in 1952.

Dewey rebelled against the educational ideas of his time and made a radical departure in his educational thought. He opposed the ideas that education is a preparation for life and that facts must be stored up before thinking can occur. Dewey believed that education is life and that facts are discovered as one works on solutions to significant problems. Dewey analyzed the human thinking process and investigated the interrelationships of a great number of dualisms, such as interest and effort, mind and body, and change and permanence. In his belief, every idea was conditional, a hypothesis to be tested in practice. Instead of being absolute and universal, as the idealists believed knowledge to be, Dewey emphasized that knowledge is relative and situational, requiring a constant reevaluation and reconstruction of experience. Dewey called his philosophy "instrumentalism" because he saw ideas as instruments of living rather than as ends in themselves. Gruber (1973) wrote, "For Dewey, then, reality is change, the universe is process, and man is coexistent with nature" (p. 184).

What are Dewey's major educational contributions and his legacy to American education? Dewey held a strong belief in democracy, and he believed that schools should teach democracy by using democratic principles themselves. He was also a proponent of the problem or project method of teaching and learning (Gruber, 1973):

> while the student with a proper "project" is intellectually active, he is also overtly active; he applies, he constructs, he expresses himself in new ways. He puts his knowledge to the test of operation. Naturally, he does something with what he learns. Because of this feature the separation between the practical and the liberal does not even arise. (p. 191)

As one can readily see, Dewey influenced American education in very practical directions. The following quote from Dewey (cited in Gruber, 1964) illustrates his criticisms of schooling that is unrelated to life experiences:

> The failure [of schooling] is again due, I believe, to the segregation of subjects. A pupil can say he has "had" a subject, because the subject has been treated as if it were complete in itself, beginning and terminating within limits fixed in advance. A reorganization of the subject matter which takes into account outleadings into the wide world of nature and man, of knowledge and of social interests and uses, cannot fail save in the most callous and intellectually obdurate to awaken some permanent interest and curiosity. Theoretical subjects will become more practical, because they are more related to the scope of life; practical subjects will become more charged with theory and intelligent insight. Both will be vitally and not just formally unified (p. 425)

From this quotation it can readily be seen that Dewey was interested in the theoretical versus the practical and in interest and effort. Dewey further maintained that one problem with schools and their curricula was that cohesive and unified learning was artificially splintered into separate courses. We can understand the problem that Dewey was confronting when we hear a student say, "Why should I have to use correct spelling and grammar? My report was for science, not English."

Dewey's impact on the progressive education movement in America is much debated. Dewey and the pragmatists originally gave the impetus to the progressive movement. However, in Dewey's view, his followers often misinterpreted his ideas and carried them too far. As a result, in 1938, Dewey issued a statement ending his association with the progressive education movement. In fact, he became a critic of progressive education in the United States. Gruber (1973) summarized Dewey's influence in the following words:

> John Dewey's influence in American education has been considerable, not only in the mainstream of public education, but among the traditionalists and essentialists who opposed him. The impact of his writings can be traced to the fields of law and art as well as the social sciences. . . . He was not as analytic as Pierce nor as fluent a writer as James, but his often difficult style has gotten through to the minds of his countrymen and has influenced every department of American thought. (p. 189)

Dewey is often censured as responsible for the so-called progressive education of our modern schools, but Brickman (1966) made the following assessment of the responsibility for the problems that developed:

> Adverse criticism of Dewey, in relation to our modern education, is due to the failure by school officials to interpret and apply adequately his principles to practical problems in the conduct of our schools. Deficiency is not in Dewey as a philosopher but in school officials as administrators of his philosophy. (p. 22)

Whether one worships Dewey or hates him, it can readily be seen that his ideas have had a great effect on American education.

Existentialism

The last pure philosophy, which is examined here only briefly, is existentialism. For existentialists, existence (being) precedes essence (meaning). Individuals always have a choice in any situation and should make the most of the situation in which they find themselves. For instance, if you were being held as a prisoner of war by an enemy army, you could still control your thoughts and even your reaction to enemy torture. Another example in a school situation would be your attitude toward taking a subject you dislike. You can either oppose all learning in this subject, or you can attempt to be positive in taking what is valuable to you from the lessons in this subject. If, in another instance, two children are born in the ignorance and poverty of a large-city slum, one could seek education and fight his or her way to a better life, while the other could continue as part of the welfare system. For existentialists, the future depends a great deal on one's choices and one's attitude toward the future. Existentialism emphasizes human individuality as much as pragmatism and reconstructionism place their trust in the importance of social problems. Existentialists see people as alien beings in a world foreign to their spirits, and anxiety, loneliness, and uneasiness are central to their thinking about humankind and reality.

Educational beliefs are not the main product of existentialist thought, but the existentialist student would have a questioning attitude and would be immersed in a continuing search for self and reasons for her or his own existence. The existentialist teacher would help students become what they themselves want to become, not what outside forces such as society, teachers, or parents want them to become. The authors of this text have seen many pressures from parents who are trying to fulfill their own dreams and aspirations through their children. Existentialist educators would deplore this interference in the child's own existence and would believe that the students should make these choices for themselves. In much the same manner, existentialists question the validity of educational objectives imposed on students from outside forces such as teachers or the school system. Existentialists place a great deal of emphasis on the individual and are very suspicious of any social and group activities. Thus, existentialists would welcome alternative education opportunities but would deplore behavioral objectives as another form of conditioning that usurps individual freedom of choice.

Existentialists believe that tragedy should be faced openly and directly, and thus, they would applaud death education units as meeting directly a part of life with which all of us must deal at some time. Death for existentialists is something personal that happens to the individual. For them, life and death are two sides of the same coin. They emphasize authentic experiences in education as moments of truth dealing with the very meaning of human existence. For existentialists, the individual seems to be thrown into a world beyond his or her control, and existentialism seems to flourish in a situation where ideologies have fallen apart, such as in Germany before World War II or in the age of the atomic bomb.

Existentialism can be divided into two strains, and its followers are a diverse group. The Christian or theistic existentialists are best exemplified by Søren Kierkegaard, and the atheistic existentialists are represented by Jean-Paul Sartre (1905–1980) and Albert Camus (1913–1960). Gruber (1973) summarized the origins of existentialism in the following words:

> Although existential philosophy has been traced back to Plato and St. Thomas Aquinas, it is generally agreed that the modern movement arose from the revolt of the Danish theologian Søren Kierkegaard (1813–1855) against the absolute idealism of Hegel and the authoritarianism of church and state. . . .

This philosophy states that existence [being] precedes essence [meaning] and attempts to create authentic individuals who are free from the tyranny of the group. Present-day interest in existentialism grew out of the destruction and despair of the concentration camps in Germany and the occupation of France in World War II. (p. 220).

Buber (1878–1965), one of the theistic existentialists, emphasized the importance of the relationship of the teacher and the pupil. Friedman said of Buber's philosophy: "This meeting of pupil and teacher as two unique individuals is what is educative. The relation of teacher to pupil is the meeting of one who has found direction with one who is finding it" (p. 181–182). The English educator A. S. Neill (1883–1973) established a school, Summerhill, which further embodies existentialist principles. At Summerhill, students have much freedom. There are no rules, no requirements, no homework, no grades, no tests, and no dress codes. Neill was trying to rehabilitate students who hated authority by making the student responsible for his or her own learning. Neill found that many students abused the freedom at first but that, after a recovery period, they began to plan their own learning.

In an evaluation of existentialism as a philosophy of education, its individualism is both a strength and a weakness. Can institutions supported by the society at large be this amenable to the wishes of each individual? Can schools avoid overall objectives and group activities? Yet, the freedom of the student to become what he or she desires to become has widespread support in the general statements of goals for schools in the United States.

Summary

In this chapter the term "philosophy" as well as the major divisions of philosophy, such as metaphysics, epistemology, axiology, and logic, were defined. The questions examined by philosophers were noted, and the reasons for studying philosophy were suggested. The major tenets of the four major pure philosophies of naturalism, idealism, realism, and pragmatism were delineated. Naturalism and realism share a belief in the external world as being the real world but differ in that naturalism has little theory of knowing while realism has an epistemology based on the scientific method. Idealism is based on reality as in a person's head, not in the eternal physical world. Pragmatism places its emphasis on change as the only reality. The major ideas championed by John Dewey as well as his contributions to education were examined. Finally, existentialism's beliefs in the importance of personal choices, anxiety, and loneliness were shown in relation to the educational contributions of this philosophy of individualism.

Questions

1. Define and differentiate among metaphysics, epistemology, axiology, and logic as divisions of philosophy.
2. After having read the section entitled "Why Study Philosophy?" in this chapter, describe in your own words the rationale behind the study of philosophy.
3. Compare and contrast idealism with both realism and pragmatism. What is the relationship of these three philosophies?
4. What naturalistic influences do you see in today's society? (For example, the environmentalist movement and the "back-to-nature" movement.)
5. Explain in your own words what Plato meant in his allegory of the cave. What was the significance of the allegory in Plato's philosophy?
6. Explain a major philosophical idea associated with the three major realist philosophers: Locke, Comenius, and James.
7. Explain a major philosophical idea associated with the three major naturalist philosophers: Hobbes, Rousseau, and Spencer. Then evaluate these three philosophical ideas.
8. What were the major contributions of John Dewey to the pragmatist philosophical tradition? Do you agree with these educational ideas?
9. Describe the existentialist attitudes toward individualism and group activity.
10. Name and describe the two types of existentialism and some major existentialist philosophers associated with each type.

7

Educational Philosophies

OBJECTIVES

After reading Chapter 7, the student will be able to:

Conceptualize the relationship between the pure philosophies and the educational philosophies.

Compare and contrast the differences between the conservative and liberal philosophies.

Identify the contributions of major educational philosophers in each of the educational philosophies.

Trace present-day movements in education to one or more of the educational philosophies.

Decide which educational philosophy incorporates her or his philosophy of learning.

Introduction

How are the educational philosophies of perennialism, essentialism, progressivism, and reconstructionism related to the pure philosophies already discussed? Rosen (1968) explained the relationship as follows:

> Educational philosophizing concerns itself with many of the same questions as "pure" philosophy. Even where the questions are not the same they are often no more than variants. For example, while the "pure" philosopher may ask, "How does a person come to know something?" the educational philosopher may go one step further and ask, "What are the specific classroom conditions under which a person is most likely to learn?" (p. 6)

Dupuis (1966) categorized educational philosophies as either "liberal" or "conservative" based on the answers to four philosophical and five educational questions. He sees the conservative ideas as controlling educational practices until Jean-Jacques Rousseau and his followers revolted against these conservative views. Even these more liberal views of Rousseau were not as effective in changing educational practices because of a lack of unity between these liberal philosophical principles and the educational practices of his time. This unity of education and philosophy was accomplished by John Dewey. However, there was a conservative "counterrevolution" to Dewey's liberal ideas, and Dupuis sees the problem today as one of finding a solution to this "either-or" dilemma between liberal and conservative ideas in education. Dupuis (1966) also stated that the split personality in the philosophy of American education is partly responsible for the problems in education in the United States. Of the four educational philosophies that are examined in this chapter, perennialism and essentialism are classified as conservative, and progressivism and reconstructionism are denoted as liberal educational philosophies. Now we examine each of these educational philosophies in greater detail to see why they are classified in these ways.

Perennialism

Perennialism, like essentialism, places its emphasis on the past. For the perennialists, truth is logical, permanent, and unchanging (Rosen, 1968):

> Perennialism is a modified form of realism which is an outgrowth of the thought of St. Thomas Aquinas. Many of its tenets are, however, still deeply rooted in the Aristotelian tradition of realism. But this Aristotelian world-view has had added to it the concept of God as usually defined by the Roman Catholic Church. (p. 47)

174

Perennialism places emphasis on everlasting values and is composed of two branches. The ecclesiastical (religious) perennialists are exemplified by Saint Thomas Aquinas (1225–1274), and the lay perennialists include Mortimer Adler (1902) and Robert Maynard Hutchins (1899–1977). The lay branch of perennialism places its emphasis on reason as the major way of knowing truth, whereas the religious branch relies on revelation. The lay group's main goal is to develop the intellect, and the religious branch has the goal of moral and religious development. The perennialists emphasize detailed study of the classics, and their curriculum would be based on the great books. As Rosen (1968) stated, perennialists believe in faculty psychology in which "the faculty of reason is trained through the formal discipline of those subjects with the most logical organization" (p. 58). For them, the study of subjects such as Latin would exercise and train the mind in preparation for future scholastic activity. Their criteria for studying a subject would be this "mental discipline" rather than whether the subject is immediately useful or interesting to the student. The perennialist teacher would have highly developed skills of reasoning and would rely on the lecture method of passing along the truth from the past.

Perennialism was a counterrevolution to progressivism, but many of its themes originated earlier. For perennialists, permanence, not change, is real. The perennialists urge the study of the great masters, such as Plato and Aristotle, and of our timeless cultural heritage. Students, they say, should not follow current fads but should adjust themselves to eternal truth. The perennialists believe that people seek to answer the same questions about the meaning of life today as in the ancient writings of Plato and Aristotle: What does it mean to be a good and virtuous person (a question as appropriate in the time of the Watergate scandal as in the time of Plato)? Does power corrupt, and who should rule a country? Perennialists believe that the problems of humankind, such as greed, ethical decisions, and the proper uses of power, are the same today as they were in ancient Greece or Rome.

Educational Ideas of Perennialists

What are the educational ideas of the perennialists? They believe, as has been stated previously, that human nature has not changed since the beginning of time. Because a person faces the same problems and dilemmas now as then, a classical education for every student is the proper training for addressing these issues. Perennialists emphasize the use of reason, saying that students must learn to control their basic urges through reason. The job of education for the perennialists is not to adjust people to society or current trends in the world, but to adjust them to eternal truth. In opposition to the progressives, perennialists claim that schooling is merely a preparation for life and can never become a real-life situation. They would teach the three Rs, the liberal arts, and the cultural heritage of literature and history of the United States and the world, not what students desire to learn at a particular moment or

Robert Maynard Hutchins, as president and chancellor of the University of Chicago, expounded the perennialist ideas of knowledge as eternal and as the chief goal of education. *(Photo courtesy of the Library of Congress and the University of Chicago.)*

subjects that become temporary fads. The curriculum of the perennialists would include the great books that are classics for all time and contain attempts to answer the age-old questions of concern to human beings. Hutchins (1936) summarized this view of education when he wrote, ''Education implies teaching. Teaching implies knowledge. Knowledge is truth. The truth is everywhere the same. Hence education should be everywhere the same'' (p. 66). Kneller (1971) further summed up perennialist views in the following words:

> In short, say the perennialists, the minds of most young Americans have never really been exercised in intellectual matters, largely because teachers themselves are indifferent and give up too quickly. It is much easier to teach students at their own pace and in accordance with what they want to learn.

Yet, in allowing the child's superficial inclinations to determine what he learns, we may actually hinder him from developing his real talents. Self-realization demands self-discipline, and self-discipline is attained only through external discipline. (pp. 45–46)

What are the major criticisms of the perennialist viewpoints as they concern education? First, the perennialists are assailed for their focus on the past. Critics accuse them of not empathizing with the current interests of learners, with the present problems of society, and with preparing students for the future. Rosen (1968) wrote, "The perennialists, despite their many claims to the contrary, are advocates of a regressive social philosophy. They would have us solve our twentieth century problems by turning back the clock to a system of beliefs prevalent in the thirteenth century" (pp. 55–56). Another of the criticisms of perennialism is that it is unfair to force all students into a system of education fit only for a few elite students. Even Plato in *The Republic* advocated this type of classical education only for the elite ruling class. Kneller (1971) summarized this criticism of perennialism as follows:

Perennialists may be accused of fostering an "aristocracy of intellect" and unreasonably restricting their teaching to the classical tradition of the Great Books. They fail to appreciate that, although many children lack the particular intellectual gifts perennialism emphasizes, they nevertheless become good citizens and productive workers. To subject them to the same sort of rigorous academic training as that given to students of university caliber is to ignore this difference and perhaps to injure their personal growth. (p. 46)

Essentialism

The essentialists have some beliefs in common with the perennialists, but the essentialists also have some emphases all their own. Both look to the past for guidance. However, the essentialists place their faith in the three Rs instead of the great books emphasized by the perennialists. The essentialists place more emphasis on the present than the perennialists. Essentialists thus aim at using basic skills to help students adjust to the real world of present society as it is. In Kneller's (1971) words,

How does essentialism differ from perennialism? First, it advocates a less totally "intellectual" education, for it is concerned not so much with certain supposedly eternal truths as with adjustment of the individual to the physical and social environment. Second, it is more willing to absorb the positive contributions that progressivism has made to educational methods. Finally, where perennialism reveres the great creative achievements of the past as timeless expressions of man's universal insights, essentialism uses them as sources of knowledge for dealing with problems of the present. (pp. 60–61)

Essentialists place much more emphasis on the present than the perennialists, who have the greatest faith in the past. Perennialism and essentialism do both share an emphasis on basic skills. However, whereas the main emphasis of perennialism is the great books approach, the chief ideas of essentialism revolve around basic skills. Essentialism shares with idealism and realism the view that truth is immutable, permanent, and unchanging, but it differs from idealism in its view of what is real.

Essentialists maintain that there are certain essentials that all people should know if they are to be educated, and these are usually defined as the basic skills of reading, writing, and arithmetic. Thus, as will be discussed later, the essentialists were the forerunners of the current "back-to-basics"

Essentialists see the learning of the basic skills as the goal of education. (*Photo used by permission of the Indianapolis Public Schools.*)

movement in American education. The essentialists focus on the effort and hard work involved in learning, in opposition to the "learning-can-be fun" attitude of the progressives. They see the teacher as a mediator between the student and the basic skills, and they promote intellectual standards. They see subject matter as the heart of education and accept the traditional methods of "mental discipline." They accentuate self-discipline as the best discipline and promote social values rather than individual experience in education. Essentialism, unlike perennialism, is opposed not to progressivism as a whole but only to certain aspects of it. Essentialists see learning by doing as *a* method but not as *the* method of learning. According to the essentialists, learning by doing should support the total learning of the student, but they caution against overgeneralizing from a few specific experiences.

The most prominent essentialist philosophers were William Brickman (1913), editor of *School and Society* magazine, and Arthur Bestor (1908) and Mortimer Smith (1906–1981), both active in the Council for Basic Education. Essentialists such as Bestor blame education professors for the problems in education and would reduce or eliminate the professional education courses taken by teacher candidates. The essentialists devote their main efforts to reexamining curricular issues, to weeding out the nonessential elements in the schools, and to attempting to promote and reinforce the authority of the teacher in the classroom.

Educational Ideas of Essentialists

What are the educational ideas associated with the essentialist position? Essentialists believe in discipline and self-discipline. Thus, "doing your own thing" is not a sufficient reason for including specific content in the educational process. They propose teacher-initiated learning and emphasize transmission of accumulated knowledge of the human race as our cultural heritage. Essentialists avoid following fads or what is "relevant" or popular at the moment in favor of emphasis on long-range goals and values. They emphasize basic skills at the elementary level and only essential subjects at the high-school level (driver's education, sex education, and many electives would be omitted from their curriculum). Essentialists promote the internal, logical organization of subject matter, rather than an organization that would make the subject easier for the student to learn. Also, they value effort and state that little is accomplished without it. Gutek (1981) made this point when he wrote:

> Learning valuable skills and knowledge requires the expenditure of time and effort. Many of the permanent and persistent interests of adult life have resulted from efforts that initially may not have been interesting or appealing to the learner. While the child's interest should not be ignored, all learning should not be based on the child's limited range of experiences. The essentialist position argues that there are many things to learn that, while they may

not be of immediate interest to the learner, can become both valuable and permanently interesting at a later time in a person's life. (pp. 17–18)

In many ways the essentialists' theories of education are in direct opposition to the life-adjustment education movement. Life adjustment advocates believe that schools should help each individual adjust himself or herself to the broader social forces in America by using current social problems as the major focus of learning and by assuming that essential learning will occur as a by-product of the study of these problems. For example, in ecology, the deterioration of the ozone layer of the atmosphere could be studied, and one assumes that skills in reading, speaking, writing, science, and math will be increased as the students are motivated to read, write, and compute in studying this topic in ecology. Life adjustment education in the early 1950s was a response to the social and economic strains of World War II. To cope with these stresses following the war, the life adjustment advocates desired to expand the issues contained in the school curriculum to include the problems faced by society as well as the economic, vocational, and personal needs of youth. Gutek (1981) assessed the essentialist opposition to this life adjustment movement in the following manner:

> The essentialist attack on incidental learning was similar to the criticism that current basic education advocates have leveled against new curricular innovations, especially those of the 1960s such as the "new mathematics," the "new social studies," and the various new approaches to science education. . . . Contemporary critics of the curricular innovations of the 1960s have charged that the "discovery method" or "inquiry method" is inefficient and causes students to "reinvent the wheel" rather than master the funded knowledge of the past in an orderly way. Contemporary critics argue that the process and method of learning has been overemphasized to the detriment of content. (p. 16)

Concerning the critics of the 1960s, Gutek (1981) continued, "While the innovators of the 1960s promised that they would teach children how to think, the critics of the 1970s and 1980s [essentialists] have argued that, in order to think, students must have something to think about. . . . They argue that the curriculum should have a content that is logically or chronologically structured" (p. 16).

A short review of the events affecting education in the 1950s, the 1960s, and the 1970s will demonstrate the influence of the essentialists and the back-to-basics movement. In 1957, the launching of *Sputnik* by the Soviet Union gave great impetus to the critics of education and to the essentialist position in favor of the back-to-basics movement in American schools. Thus, in the late 1950s the essentialist position became prominent in the United States, possibly because of *Sputnik* and possibly because of the decline of the progressive movement. Whether or not the essentialist critics of the late 1950s caused the National Defense Education Act, the emphasis on academic subject matter in teacher education programs, and the increased funding for mathematics, science, and foreign languages, the essentialists were certainly in favor of these programs. The alphabetical curriculum reforms of the early 1960s such as BSCS biology, SMSG mathematics, CHEM study in chemistry, were not strictly essentialist in nature because they proposed that students learn a subject in the same way that a scholar in that academic discipline would learn it. The inquiry approach used in these projects is not part of the essentialist doctrine, and the organizational changes in American schools in the early 1960s, such as team teaching, modular scheduling, open concept schools, and individualized instruction, were not favored by the essentialists. The essentialists fared even worse in the last half of the 1960s with the advent of the Great Society social programs and the continuing Vietnam war. Instead of essentialist programs, schools were involved in compensatory education, Project Head Start, job training, and bilingual education. Activism in social problems became the rule rather than the exception.

In the mid-1970s, the back-to-basics movement had a resurgence in the United States. However, this movement differed from the preceding essentialist periods of the 1950s and the 1960s. The "new" movement began as a grass-roots movement, founded by lay citizens and not by educators. It had a broader base of support from laypeople and parents than the previous essentialist movements. Gutek (1981) assessed the movement in these words:

> unlike other movements in educational history, the drive for basic education [in the 1970s] differed initially in that it involved few leaders of a national political or educational stature; nor were the basic education advocates enrolled in a single organization. While the back-to-basics proponents varied widely in their strategies, a common philosophical strand ran through their arguments. (p. 7)

This new essentialist movement in the 1970s was supported by grass-roots desires for accountability, minimum-competency tests, and competency-based education. Professional educators were not part of the original movement and were usually relegated to responding defensively, but they were eventually forced to become involved in identifying and testing minimum competencies. The public outcry forced several state legislatures to mandate minimum-competency tests for both students and teachers. In the 1980s, professional educators are debating what is "basic" in education, and lay citizens are still demanding basic functional literacy and mathematical skills from students graduating from high schools (Gutek, 1981).

Many criticisms of education were made by the proponents of the back-to-basics movement in the 1970s and 1980s. These essentialists deplored (social promotion) promoting a child with failing grades to keep him with his age group as well as innovations and experimentation such as electives and minicourses. The lack of emphasis on basic skills and ethical values was assailed by the essentialists. They oppose permissiveness in both the behavioral and the academic standards of the schools. The back-to-basics advocates also sounded the alarm of accountability and believed that schools were too bureaucratic and expensive. They also abhorred the lack of emphasis on competition as a form of student motivation. In addition, the essentialists criticized poorly trained teachers, the schools of education, and the special jargon used by professional educators (Gutek, 1981).

Many criticisms have been leveled at the essentialists and the back-to-basics movement. As already mentioned, determining what is basic is difficult. Are art, music, and physical education basic? What about subjects such as health and social studies? This question is more easily answered by subjects such as reading and math at the elementary-school level but becomes a quagmire at the high-school level with the diversity of courses in secondary schools. Back-to-basics proponents and essentialists often fail to agree among themselves on what is basic. Most people could agree to support the back-to-basics movement if they could define what is meant by *basic*. Gutek (1981) insisted:

> Both the friends and foes of basic education need to address the following persistent philosophical questions that have emerged in the last half century: What is a sound education? What is a school? What is the primary purpose of a school? What is the nature of the curriculum?

Table 7–1   Philosophy of Education

Traditionalist	Progressive
Subject-Centered	Pupil-Centered
Trailing edge of change	Cutting edge
Common core essential	Curriculum comes from life
Emphasis on the three Rs; spelling/achieving, and intellectual discipline	Emphasis on learning to think critically

Secondary schools should be departmentalized according to subjects:
  a. Texts are important
  b. AV is important
  c. Academic scholarship (honor roll)
	Teacher organizes, selects, directs experiments so that participation in activities will maximize the student's understanding and knowledge

Juvenile delinquency is due to the neglect of the school's role	If students are involved, they will become more responsible
Transmit values to the next generation	Moral aims should be based on civic and social experimentation, vocational and practical usefulness, and individual development. (Don't ignore both the social and the psychological education)
Authority-centered or teacher-based classrooms are the best setting	Democracy is the best setting
Active student is involved in organizing his or her notes	Active school and active student

The advocates of basic education need to ponder and answer these questions in the most coherent and comprehensive way possible so that their position is no longer based on scattered sources and conflicting opinions. Antagonists need to examine these questions in light of the historical perspective of the recurring themes of basic education. The issues raised are not fleeting ones that will go away. As they have appeared in our educational past, so they will occur in our educational future. (p. 35)

As has been seen, the ideas of the essentialists are prominent in American education today as evidenced by the influential back-to-basics movement in the United States today (see Table 7–1 on page 182).

Progressivism

The third educational philosophy examined here is progressivism, related to the pragmatism or instrumentalism of John Dewey.

What are the main ideas of progressivism as an educational philosophy? The progressives place great faith in cooperation and social learning, rather than in competition. Part of this social learning would be an emphasis on the project method or the problem-solving approach in education. The progressives, thus, believe that learning should be an active process and that students should do much more than receive information passively. Learning, they believe, can and should be related to the interests of the child. The teacher's role should be that of an adviser to the child, not a "dictator" or "director" of learning.

Progressives place more emphasis on the process (the means or the methods) of learning than on the end product (knowledge). The greatest reality for progressives, as for the reconstructionists, is change, and the progressives emphasize that the elementary student is a child, not a little adult (a concept that Rousseau believed). They insist that education is life, not a preparation for life and learning. Students do not need to store up knowledge before they can think and solve problems. In fact, knowledge comes as a part of the problem-solving process. Thus, if we want students to learn about democracy, schools should be democratic institutions. For Dewey, democracy in government and education in America were closely related.

Progressive educators would not fill the head of a student with facts as one would fill a pitcher with water, they would teach students how to learn so that they can continue to learn later on their own. For progressives, learning is the "continual reconstruction of experience." Their emphasis is on experience, not on the eternal truth cited by the idealists. Progressives think of education for the whole child and believe that education is more than subject matter alone. *Experience* and *experiment* are two key words for the progressives, as can be seen in the following statement by Kneller (1971): "It is not the absorption of previous knowledge that counts but its constant reconstruction in the light of new discoveries. Thus, problem-solving must be seen not as the search for merely functional knowledge, but as a 'perpetual grappling' with subject matter (p. 50).

John Dewey's ideas were crucial in the progressive movement. Although Dewey preferred to call his philosophy "instrumentalism" or "pragmatism," and although Dewey believed that his progressive followers distorted many of his ideas and carried them to extremes, he is still known as the leader of the progressive education movement in the United States. It is best to examine the actual writings of Dewey to ascertain his educational beliefs because both his followers and his critics tended to distort his views. Dewey eventually denounced and disassociated himself from the progressive education movement. Thus, Dewey was first an advocate and then later a critic of progressive education.

Dewey's educational philosophy was holistic and opposed to dualism such as that between theory and practice, between mind and body, between thoughts and actions, and between means and ends. Dewey especially deplored the separation of the school from life outside the school. He argued against the prevalent view that knowledge should be learned and stored up so that it can be used in subsequent thoughts and actions. However, Dewey firmly believed that learning in schools is life, not a preparation for life. Learning is living and can best occur in actual living and in solving real problems. "Real" purposes in these actual problems can best be used to integrate learning and living. Scheffler (1966) stated this point in the following way:

> This means that the whole environment of meanings surrounding the lesson is important as potentially contributing to learning. It means, for example, that the moral atmosphere of the classroom, the encouragement of curiosity and questioning, the relations among students and with the teacher are to be considered, not as irrelevant to the curriculum but as the very basis of moral and intellectual learning which goes on in the school whether we deliberately plan it or not. It means, finally, that every item of subject matter to be taught must be provided with context in the learner's perceptions. These perceptions and, indeed, the learner's whole system of motivations must be taken with the utmost seriousness by the teacher. (p. 102)

Thus, Dewey opposed any division between humanistic and vocational education, between theoretical and applied sciences, and between thought and action.

Dewey placed a great emphasis on actions and experience. For him, learning was always an active process; the brain was not a passive receiver of knowledge but an active participant in or originator of meanings through problem solving. Dewey believed that experiences are crucial to learning but that not all experiences are educational. Hook (1966) summarized Dewey's meaning of the term *experience* in these words:

Students must experiment and experience life in order to learn, according to the progressives. *(Photo used by permission of the Indianapolis Public Schools.)*

The term "experience" has many different meanings, but the sense which Dewey gives it makes it relevant to the human learning process. All education is occasioned by experience, but for Dewey not all experiences are genuinely educational. He regards only those experiences to which the individual reacts with informed awareness of the problem and challenge of his environment as truly educational. (p. 132)

My Pedagogic Creed (1897) was a booklet written by Dewey containing many of the educational beliefs on which he later elaborated. In it, he defined his five basic beliefs about education. The first is participation by the individual in the social consciousness of the race. Thus, Dewey emphasized social problems and experiences that he believed helped to shape the person from birth to death. The second point was that the school is a part of this social process. Education, thus, is the process of living, not a preparation for life. The third belief is that the social life of the child is the real subject matter of education. The fourth principle states that methods should be given form by the child's own nature, and Dewey's last belief was that education is the principal means of social progress and reform. On this final point, Dewey and the progressives would receive support from the reconstructionists as will be seen in the next section.

The Decline of Progressive Education

What were the major criticisms of progressive education that led eventually to its decline? Because the progressives were blamed for the problems of education after the Soviets launched *Sputnik* in 1957, the progressive movement, which had already been weakened by internal divisions and external criticisms, declined dramatically in the late 1950s. The authors of this text believe that schools are often used as scapegoats for society's problems and difficulties. When the Americans believed that the United States lagged behind the Soviet Union in the space race, they immediately blamed the schools and especially the child-centered methods of the progressives. Cremin (1961) cut to the heart of this decline in the following analysis of the demise of the progressive movement:

> The surprising thing about the progressive response to the assault of the fifties is not that the movement collapsed, but that it collapsed so readily. . . . But, even so, one is shocked by the rapidity of the decline. Why this abrupt and rather dismal end [in the late 1950s] of a movement that had for more than a half-century commanded the loyalty of influential segments of the American public? (p. 347)

What were the specific reasons for this decline of progressive education? First, the distortions of progressive principles by both its disciples and its critics were a major factor. Factions developed within the ranks of the progressives who never seemed to be able to agree among themselves. Negativism was another factor. Progressives appeared many times to be more certain of what they were against than of what they supported. Another possible factor was the excessive demands that progressive methods made on the teacher's time. Group work, individual projects, and learning by doing seemed to require more advanced preparation on the part of the teacher than the older methods of lecture and mental discipline. Progressivism also became a victim of its own success in changing American ideas about schooling and teaching methods. Some critics argue that progressives failed to keep pace with continuing changes in the mass media and social welfare, and most critics agree that the conservative shift in political and social thought after World War II provided, along with *Sputnik,* the final blow for progressivism. Finally, unlike the current basic education movement, the progressive movement was composed mostly of professional educators and failed to involve the lay public in its causes (Cremin, 1961).

Kneller (1971) cited additional reasons for the demise of the progressives. The progressives were criticized for allowing students to learn what they wanted to know rather than what they needed to learn. Many critics of the progressives said that the school is an artificial learning situation that can never be a real-life environment. Opponents of progressivism also doubted that self-discipline could best be developed through freedom, and these critics cited the need to use external discipline to foster self-discipline. The adversaries of the progressives also pointed out that the group decisions advocated by the progressives were not necessarily better than those made by individuals. This cooperation, the critics asserted, could result from extremes in conformity and from the tyranny of the group. The progressives, their adversaries insisted, had no monopoly on democratic principles, as the progressive movement tended to imply. Finally, Kneller (1971) cited the self-activity movement of the progressives as lacking specific goals and as being too vague to result in meaningful student activities.

The progressive movement had its beginnings after the Civil War and had gained a wide following among intellectuals by 1900. It grew and gained favor between 1900 and World War I as it was embraced by professional educators. Then, the movement became divided and fragmented in the 1920s and 1930s, finally disappearing in the late 1950s. However, the progressives made a significant impact on education in America today, especially because of the opposition movements in essentialism and back-to-basics, which the progressives spawned. Progressives did promote a belief in using education for social betterment, as did the reconstructionists, who are now examined.

Reconstructionism

The last educational philosophy to be discussed here is reconstructionism. The main goal of reconstructionists is to change society, and its main purpose is to use education as an instrument of social reform. Thus, the behavioral sciences and cultural forces are extremely important to the reconstructionists. They believe that Americans live in an age of crisis, and there is an acute sense of urgency in their exhortations. As Rosen (1968) wrote. "It [reconstructionism] is, in effect, an ideal of a utopian society. Philosophy is a tool; and as such, the reconstructionists say, should be used for more than just explaining experience. It must help build a better society" (p. 90). Major American leaders in reconstructionism have been George Counts (1889–1974), who wrote *Dare the Schools Build a New Social Order?* (1932); Harold Rugg (1886–1960), author of *Culture and Education in America* (1931); and Theodore Brameld (1904), whose major work was *Toward a Reconstructed Philosophy of Education* (1956).

How do the reconstructionists differ from other educational philosophies and the pure philosophies? Progressives and pragmatists generally supported social change but not in the same way as the reconstructionists. The progressives wanted social change but differed from the reconstructionists in that they refused to support specific reforms in society. Rosen (1968) summarized this difference when he wrote, "Reconstructionism as a philosophy of education differs from pragmatism in degree and emphasis rather than in kind. While sharing a great deal with pragmatism, it has a much more emphatic social policy" (pp. 89–90). Thus, whereas perennialism places exclusive emphasis on the past and whereas the philosophies of essentialism and progressivism place more emphasis on adjusting to the present, reconstructionism pins its hopes on the future.

The major tenets of reconstructionism can be seen in the major theses of reconstructionism as developed by Theodore Brameld (1965). There is an urgency in the cry of the reconstructionists to use education to build a new social order in order to prevent global self-destruction through atomic weapons. Like the progressives, the reconstructionists believe in democracy, and their new society must be controlled by the people. The logical end of national democracy, they say, is international democracy. The reconstructionists have an even greater social emphasis than the progressives. Society, the reconstructionists insist, makes people what they are. Thus, Brameld believed that group work should play an important part in schools. The reconstructionist teacher would not remain impartial but would have the obligation to democratically persuade students of the urgency of reconstructionism. The reconstructionists believe that the behavioral sciences are crucially important, and that both the goals and the methods of education must be modified to meet the challenging demands of the future. Thus, reconstructionists would constantly remind us that we are educating students for the future, not solely for the present.

It is difficult to be neutral toward the reconstructionists because their beliefs are both passionate and emotional. Some of their strengths and weaknesses are recounted here. On the positive side, the reconstructionists do what many other philosophies fail to do when they place their major emphasis on an education for the future. Today, reconstructionists would emphasize the necessity of a world government, the need for nuclear arms control, the importance of the postindustrial society outlined by Toffler (1970), and the widespread effect that computers are going to have on our world. On the negative side, critics cite the pluralism evident in the United States and wonder how an entire society can support a single set of goals. Whose goals will be taught, they ask? Should teachers be biased toward specific futures for their students? Are reconstructionists engaging in indoctrination, and is this compatible with a democratic society? Are the conclusions of the behavioral sciences a strong enough base on which to build a new social order? The authors of this text doubt that Americans could agree on one vision of the future to be implemented by the reconstructionists, but we see much value in their orientation toward the future and its problems.

Conclusions on Philosophy

The philosophical conclusions of this chapter are presented in three areas: the liberal versus conservative debate in educational philosophy, the advisability of an eclectic philosophy of education, and the difference that could be made by a consistent educational philosophy in U.S. schools.

American schools have always been afflicted with an "either-or" debate

TABLE 7–2 Curriculum Organization

Traditionalist	Progressive
1. Great books program: Science and math as intellectual disciplines	1. Projects such as "Why do people leave your hometown?"
2. History is good for its own sake	2. Simulate putting people on the moon
3. Spelling bees	3. Life on the Mississippi
4. Science fair	4. Helping the Public Health Service analyze streams
5. Clothing and foods	5. Making the poor aware of services available to them
6. Physical education	6. Mock zoning-board hearings
7. Sports	7. Helping minorities to get established in your school district
8. Science club	8. Designing and doing new games and teaching them to the underprivileged
9. Career day	
10. Testing (SATs, CEEBs, and PSATs)	

in the philosophy of education. Both educators and lay citizens disagree with each other and among themselves about whether the child or the subject matter is more important in schools. Should school buildings be built in an open-concept design or in an arrangement of individual classrooms? Should minicourses be offered to take advantage of students' current interests at the high-school level, or should students be channeled into basic skill courses? Should outside-of-school activities be part of the regular school curriculum or an extracurricular appendage to the school program? All of these questions revolve around the liberal versus conservative debate in education, and these two basic viewpoints are now examined in greater detail (see Table 7–2 above).

The Conservative View

The conservative view of the perennialists and the essentialists is exemplified by the conservative and essentialist views of Terrel Bell, the Secretary of Education in the Reagan Cabinet. Bell has stated that education is the acquisition of knowledge, and he has promoted the idea of a knowledge-centered school. He opposes democracy in schools, the life-adjustment curriculum, teacher–pupil planning, and the idea that learning must be enjoyable. He believes that hard work, adversity, and life's problems shape the character of students. Bell eloquently opposes emphasizing the child-centered school and basing the curriculum on the current needs and interests of students. Schools should, in his view, develop in students a lifelong thirst for intellectual knowledge, rather than accentuate their physical appetites. In Bell's (1962) own words,

> Too much time is wasted in our schools in teacher-pupil planning and committee work, and not enough is spent in vigorously seeking mastery of basic knowledge that will lead to intellectual competence and wisdom. The age in which we live is too perilous and the amount of knowledge that today's citizens must gain is too vast for us to continue to focus our attention and efforts on social adjustment processes, committee work, and setting of goals by pupils. (p. 21)

Bell does believe that the student should be active in the process of learning and also that learning should be directed toward the purpose of attaining knowledge. Bell (1962) opposes the incidental learning advocated by the progressives:

> Learning should not be activity as a process, with knowledge as an incidental by-product as the result of an activity sponsored for the sake of the activity in the name of adjustment, social interaction, and "experience getting" for its own sake. (p. 18)

He believes that this is like mistaking an effect for a cause:

> Educators who emphasize such processes as life adjustment or personality development are emphasizing results and outcomes of knowledge. This is like trying to teach a duck how to swim before it is hatched out of the egg. The duck will ultimately swim if it comes to the task or the process prepared to do so. In like manner, the child will ultimately adjust to life or develop a desired personality if he acquires knowledge. (pp. 17–18)

In much the same way, Bell (1962) made an eloquent argument for the value of the work ethic:

> There has always been more joy in work than in play. Play need only be regarded as an interval, like sleep, wherein we recoup our mental faculties and energies for more knowledge acquisition. Let our schools therefore rededicate themselves to the purpose for which they have always existed down through the ages. Knowledge-centered schools will help man to reach his ultimate destiny—which is to conquer and dominate his environment, and to place the forces of nature at the command of his will. (p. 21)

Thus, instead of adjusting people to the forces in the world, Bell would advocate gaining control of the environment through knowledge of it. Bell, it seems, is in direct opposition to the progressives in the continuing debate concerning the purposes of the schools.

The Progressive View

The progressive viewpoint is represented here by William Lauderdale and is taken from his examination (1981) of three successful progressive schools. Two of the progressive schools examined by Lauderdale are the Laboratory

School established by John Dewey in Chicago and the City and Country School founded by Caroline Pratt, another progressive, in New York City. The third progressive school, which is not examined here, was the Holtville School in Alabama. It was a famous progressive school of the 1930s and 1940s that emphasized vocational and life-adjustment education. The Holtville School was an innovative school thriving in a conservative and economically deprived rural area of Alabama. These three schools serve to delineate the three major factions within the progressive education movement: the experimental view (the Laboratory School of John Dewey); the child-centered emphasis (Caroline Pratt at the City and Country School in New York City); and the life-adjustment faction (the Holtville School in Alabama). Now, two of these progressive schools are examined as examples of the progressive movement in education.

Dewey's Laboratory School in Chicago was established in 1896, and Dewey himself ran the school until 1904. It was established to test his educational and psychological principles. Dewey emphasized a relaxed atmosphere in which children could learn cooperatively. He used field trips and believed that all learning is social in nature. Chicago, he felt, provided a wide variety of museums, factories, and businesses that should be used in educating children. As Lauderdale (1981) wrote:

> Children's interests that arose naturally from games played, stories told, or field trips taken, served as starting points for learning. However, activities that grew out of such interests were planned and shaped by the children and the teachers with an end-in-view of acquiring skills and knowledge that would provide them with greater control over their environment. (p. 16)

Problem solving was at the heart of Dewey's educational enterprise. He also placed great emphasis on consequences and experiences. He believed that thought and action are intertwined and that a thought is true only if the consequences of its actions are positive, resulting in solutions to current problems. All learning, Dewey maintained, is the result of a child's experiences. Education, for him, was the constant reconstruction of experience in the light of new experiences. Dewey insisted that individual freedom of learning could facilitate the goals of society in the long run. Lauderdale (1981) summed up Dewey's views about the needs of individuals and the requirements of the society in which they live in these words:

> Dewey found wanting that popular notion that individual freedom and independence must be curtailed in order to establish an orderly society. For him, the issue was not one of negotiating the rights of the individual with the needs of society but one of creating social arrangements in a society through which the individual can develop as an intelligent, free human being. (p. 17)

Caroline Pratt's City and Country School in New York City was child-centered. Lauderdale saw her major methods as dramatic play, "do-withs," social interaction, frequent field trips, and an emphasis on jobs. For her, the dramatic play involved Dewey's idea of the re-creation of experience and Froebel's rule that play is the work of the child. The "do-withs" were blocks used in play. These blocks were not to be formed in concrete realistic objects but were to be rough. Children were to use their imagination to make them serve as the toys of play. (The authors of this text have seen children leave fancy new toys purchased by parents to play with abandoned chips of wood or old cardboard packing crates.) The social interaction and the field trips are reminders of Dewey's ideas, and the emphasis on jobs can be traced back to Johann Heinrich Pestalozzi and others. Rousseau's influence can also be seen in Caroline Pratt's ideas, as these words of Lauderdale (1981) demonstrate:

> Children's fundamental medium for the re-creation of experience was play; and for Caroline Pratt [like Rousseau], play was a most serious subject. It was through play that children began to make sense of their world, to draw relationships among ideas, and to make cause-and-effect connections within events they experienced. (p. 33)

According to Lauderdale (1981), Caroline Pratt had an experience that helped form her child-centered, progressive philosophy of education:

> The remarkable experience occurred during a visit to the home of a friend who had a six-year-old son. There she found him at play, totally absorbed in a make-believe railroad system. Spread over the room were some toys, some blocks, and any number of household items, a few scrounged from the waste basket. The boy was re-creating a world that made sense in his terms. He was an active participant in that world, building the system, controlling the movement of the trains, and supplying the variety of sounds associated with a railroad. . . . The excitement of this boy's learning stood in sharp contrast to the dulled interest in learning she had observed among so many of her settlement house children. For her, the experience sparked an enthusiasm to find a way whereby all young people might share in the re-creation or dramatization of events, i.e., dramatic play. (pp. 30–31)

What were the similarities of these two progressive schools, which have been used as examples here? First, a vocational emphasis is to be found in all three of these progressive programs. Dewey's Laboratory School used occupations as insight into society's cultural heritage and to show how people have solved problems historically. Caroline Pratt's City and Country School found the heart of its curriculum in "jobs," and the Holtville School used work for community improvement as its central theme. Lauderdale (1981) summarized the similarities among these three progressive schools:

> Although their practices varied greatly, they stood as one in their commitment to progressive principles. Their students were free to participate in deci-

sions that affected them, to plan many of their own learning activities, and to move about freely in the performance of their work. Programs were highly individualized, and relations between teachers and students were informal and based on mutual trust. A cooperative rather than a competitive atmosphere prevailed. . . . Student evaluations were multi-dimensional and used solely as diagnostic tools rather than as instruments for rating performance. Student interests were honored and felt needs accommodated, not as ends in themselves but as springboards for learning. (pp. 58–59)

Lauderdale (1981) wrote that none of these three schools was influenced by the "cult-of-the-child" extremists, who disliked anything that restricted the freedom of the child and who gave progressive education as a whole a bad name (p. 28). The progressive educators' legacy, according to Lauderdale, was that they "set a precedent for classroom innovation by redefining the purposes of education, diversifying the curriculum, changing the roles of teachers and students and altering the very atmosphere of the school" (p. 59). The effects of the progressive education movement can be seen today in various alternative school programs, learning contracts, group work, individualized projects for learning, student councils in many high schools, and many other forms of students' participation in their own learning.

An Eclectic Philosophy

Experts in philosophy differ on the advisability of having an eclectic philosophy of education. To be "eclectic" means to take parts of various philosophies and weld them into one's own personal philosophy of education. For instance, a person could take the concept of the student as actively involved in learning from the idealists but prefer the realist view of the scientific method as the main method of gathering knowledge. One could also incorporate the pragmatic principle that values are relative and constantly changing into this eclectic philosophy. Critics of this eclectic method of developing a philosophy of education would insist that this technique does not lead to a consistent philosophy, and that one's view of reality may clash with his or her perspective on knowledge or values. In practical terms, the authors of this text believe that the philosophies of most people are, in fact, eclectic. One may believe in the scientific method of the realists but may vehemently oppose the realist view of the passive nature of the student. The most important thing is to develop one's own philosophical principles as a basis for his or her own teaching. Whether a teacher recognizes it or not, every action in the classroom is based on philosophical principles. It is crucial that teachers formulate these principles in their own minds and begin to recognize the principles on which their teaching behavior is based. If this approach means being eclectic, the authors of this text support an eclectic educational philosophy.

Can Philosophy Make a Difference?

The liberal versus conservative debate has made clear the crucial importance of a philosophy of education in practical day-to-day educational decisions. Philosophy of education can make not only *a* difference in success but *the* difference in success in teaching. It has been said many times that it is better to light one candle than to curse the darkness, and the authors of this textbook believe in this principle. Instead of decrying problems such as discipline, racial differences, lack of student motivation, or lack of sufficient funds for education, a teacher should use his or her philosophy and the resources at hand to make a difference in the world. A teacher can influence eternity and may never know where his or her influence stops. One teacher can make a difference in the life of a student, and a consistent educational philosophy can make a difference in the teaching of an individual teacher.

Summary

In this chapter the educational philosophies of perennialism, essentialism, progressivism, and reconstructionism were examined. Perennialism places its emphasis on the past and portrays truth as logical, permanent, and unchanging. The religious perennialists, such as St. Thomas Aquinas, rely on revelation as the primary way of knowing; while the lay perennialists, such as Mortimer Adler and Robert Maynard Hutchins, place their emphasis on reason as the path to truth. The mainstays of perennialist education thought are the literary classics and the mental discipline theory of learning. Like the perennialists, the essentialists look to the past for guidance; but, unlike the perennialists, the essentialists place their faith in learning basic skills instead of reading the great books. In this chapter the effect of the essentialists on the current back-to-basics movement was traced, and the apposition of the essentialists to the life adjustment movement was spotlighted. The progressive ideas on education include an emphasis on process rather than product, education as life rather than a preparation for life, and the teacher's role as advisor rather than dictator. The growth of the progressive movement in the early 1900s was highlighted, and the reasons for its decline were also examined. Reconstructionism focuses on change; and its proponents, such as George Counts and Theodore Brameld, see education as an instrument to change society for the better. Finally, the liberal versus conservative debate in educational philosophy is portrayed by contrasting the ideas of leading conservative Terrel Bell with those of Caroline Pratt, founder of the child-centered City and Country School in New York City.

Questions

1. From your own experience, take a position on whether human beings are basically good or bad. Then explain which educational philosophy would be closest to your position. Why?
2. Compare and contrast the liberal and conservative philosophies of education. With which argument do you agree and why?
3. One author said that the conservative educational philosophies were predominant until Rousseau published his educational views. In what ways did Rousseau's views change educational ideas and practices?
4. List and discuss five or more pragmatic elements that were evident in the schools that you have observed this semester. With which of these pragmatic ideas do you agree or disagree? Are you a pragmatist?
5. Assume that you are a reconstructionist. How would you change society through education? Include your ideas on what the ideal society would be like and how schools could help build such a society.
6. What kinds of support would essentialists give to the back-to-basics movement? What concerns would the progressives have about this movement?
7. Concerning the controversy over values education in schools, how would the essentialists, the progressives, the reconstructionists, and the existentialists deal with this important issue?
8. Are schools either entirely traditional or entirely progressive?
9. What is the difference between progressive education and permissive education?
10. Who needs to be the most creative—the progressive teacher or the traditional teacher?
11. Is an open-concept school a progressive school? Why or why not?
12. What are the best and the worst aspects of the activity method of teaching advocated by the progressives?
13. What method, progressive or traditional, is the most difficult and challenging to teach?
14. Why is progressive education so pragmatic?
15. Are all subjects or interest areas best taught either with the traditional or the progressive approach?
16. If you were going to be a doctor, a lawyer, a teacher, an engineer, or a homemaker, would you best be prepared through the traditional or the progressive approach?
17. When is subject matter more important than being taught to think?
18. Often, during a job interview, you are asked to state your educational philosophy. If asked such a question, what would be your response?

Activities for Unit III

1. Interview a principal, a counselor, or a classroom teacher, and summarize briefly his or her educational philosophy.

2. On a continuum of educational philosophy, with essentialism on the left end and progressivism on the right end, place a check mark on the continuum to represent your position on educational philosophy. Defend your position on this continuum by writing a two-page explanation, including supporting philosophical evidence for your position.

3. Compare your personal philosophy on discipline, evaluation, and human relations with that of the philosophy of a public-school teacher under whom you have participated or observed this semester.

4. Compare the philosophy of the school that you attended to the philosophy of the school in which you participated during this semester. Which educational philosophy and/or pure philosophy would best describe each of these schools?

5. Visit an alternative school or a school with an alternative education program, and compare the principal features of this program with the progressive principles described in this chapter. How would you evaluate this alternative education program in terms of student motivation, the depth and breadth of student learning in basic skills, students' involvement in their own learning, and teacher–student interaction?

6. Construct a model city based on your projected ideas of the twenty-first century. Based on your knowledge of his philosophy, what would be Dewey's opinion of this activity?

7. Read Phi Delta Kappa Fastback #166 on *Progressive Education: Lessons from Three Schools* (1981). In which one of the three programs described in this fastback would you feel most comfortable teaching and why? Are the same circumstances that led up to the creation of these three plans still with us today? If so, what are they?

8. Write three questions that could be posed to local boards of education whose members are predominantly liberal, conservative, or existentialist in their views. Then, divide the class into three groups, with one third of the class playing the role of board members and the other two thirds asking these prepared questions of the board members. After the liberal board has answered questions posed by the other groups, give the conservative and existentialist board members a chance to answer similar questions.

THE SCHOOL CURRICULUM

8

Teachers and the Curriculum

OBJECTIVES

After reading Chapter 8, the student will be able to:

Define the curriculum.

List some of the most important historical contributions to the curriculum.

Understand some of the basic aims of the curriculum.

Determine what some of the most important contributions have been to the present curriculum.

Assess how parents influence their child's perceptions of the curriculum.

Understand how to evaluate curriculum that is already in place.

How Should One Define the Curriculum?

It is very difficult to define something that includes so many facets of learning as does a school's curriculum. All curriculum specialists have written some definition to describe the curriculum as they see it. Three of these definitions are as follows:

1. J. Lloyd Trump (1968) wrote that the curriculum is a vital, moving complex interaction of people and things in a freewheeling setting. It includes questions to debate, forces to rationalize, goals to illuminate, programs to activate, and outcomes to evaluate (p. 12).
2. Doll (1978) noted that the curriculum of a school is the formal and informal content and process by which learners gain knowledge and understanding and develop skills, attitudes, appreciations, and values under the auspices of their school (p. 6).
3. Hass (1983) stated that the curriculum is all of the experiences that individual learners have in a program of education. The purpose is to achieve broad goals and related specific objectives, planned in terms of a framework of theory and research or past and present professional practice (p. 4).

Each of these three authors expressed himself differently, even though all were talking about the same thing. Trump wanted the curriculum to be very active and dynamic as it exists in the schools. Doll's definition seems tame compared to Trump's and it seems to cover all important bases. The definition by Hass places a lot of emphasis on research and professional practice. Whichever definition you choose to follow depends on your own personal conception of what the curriculum ought to be.

J. Lloyd Trump was a curriculum innovator in the 1960s who wanted high schools to change to flexible schedules with 30-, 20-, and 15-minute modules meeting 12, 16, or 24 periods in a day. The benefit of flexible scheduling was to schedule more time for some classes than for other classes. For example, on some days, students need more time in biology laboratory than in lecture and discussion. Trump's flexible plan was developed when many reformers were trying to make the curriculum more relevant for the learner, and some schools found his ideas helpful. A few high schools are still operating under flexible scheduling plans.

The Doll (1978) definition is broad in coverage so as to include both the formal and the informal parts of the curriculum. The formal curriculum can be planned and observed as well as evaluated and improved. The informal curriculum, sometimes known as the hidden curriculum, is not planned and is seldom evaluated. The hidden curriculum is really the students' own curriculum as they cope with the school's bureaucratic organization and arrangements and with their social relationships inside the school. It is important for teachers to be aware of as many parts of the hidden curriculum as possible.

Hass would like to see the curriculum reflect the latest research from four bases. The first base concerns *social forces,* both present and future. The teachers on the faculty of a school should know the community and the problems and concerns that exist there so that they can be in touch with their students. The second base is *human development.* Teachers need to be aware of the body of knowledge known as human growth and development so that, as they teach their lessons, they can take into consideration an individual's own nature and needs. Havighurst's "developmental tasks," (1948) Erikson's stages of "growth toward a mature personality," (1968), and Piaget's four stages of growth in intelligence through "assimilation" and "accommodation" (1952) help us to understand human growth and development better. The third base is the *nature of learning.* Knowing how learning occurs in students helps teachers to plan the curriculum. Your teaching practices might be based on stimulus–response conditioning, on the field theories, on Freudian theory, or on social learning, depending on your choice. The fourth base is the *nature of knowledge and cognition.* How you view the nature of knowledge depends on whether you view it as organized bodies of facts and concepts, as a fluid product of people's experience, or as a combination of the two.

Now that you have seen how three experts view the curriculum, perhaps you are ready to define it yourself. Your own definition will no doubt take into consideration many of the concepts presented by the experts, but in the end, it will be your own personal conception of what the curriculum ought to be.

What Are Some Historical Perspectives on the Curriculum?

So that we may shed some light on the history of curriculum development, we mention here only those happenings that still have some effect on the present and that will very likely continue into the future. In 1981, in honor of the seventy-fifth anniversary of Phi Delta Kappa, Harold Shane wrote an article for the *Kappan* entitled "Significant Writings That Have Influenced the Curriculum: 1906–81." In order to obtain data for his article, Shane wrote to 135 curriculum specialists, and 85 of them responded to an annotated list (1981) of 100 publications appearing most consistently in footnotes and in bibliographies. Shane had the specialists indicate whether they believed that a given book, article, or report had had a *major,* a *considerable,* or a *negligible* influence on curriculum theory and practice over the years 1906–1981. In order to achieve the distinction of having the most influence on the school

Keeping the Curriculum Ball Rolling

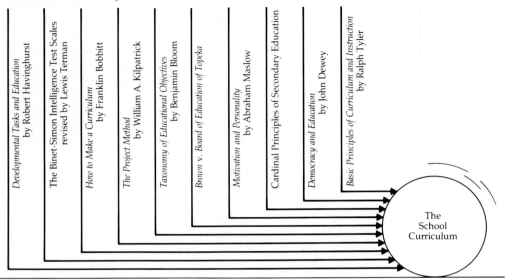

curriculum, a given publication had to be rated as having had a "major" or a "considerable" influence by at least 85 percent of the respondents. The top ten publications are listed in order below (including ties), with some comment about their contents and their contributions.

First: *Basic Principles of Curriculum and Instruction* by Ralph W. Tyler (1949)   This little book by Tyler has gone through over thirty reprints. Tyler has been one of the most noted educators in America and a noted lecturer and writer. In his book, he began by asking four simple questions:

1. What educational purposes should the school seek to attain?
2. What educational experiences can be provided that are likely to attain these purposes?
3. How can these educational experiences be effectively organized?
4. How can we determine whether these purposes are being attained? (p. 1)

The logic in those four questions sets the tone for the entire book. The book is very specific; for example, Tyler wrote that if the schoolchildren in your district suffer from either a dietary deficiency or a physical condition, then your objectives in health education should reflect these concerns. Other areas addressed in the book are equally specific.

Second: *Democracy and Education* by John Dewey (1916)   John Dewey and his impact on education have been mentioned previously. In the discussion in *Democracy and Education,* Dewey wrote that he would like to have workers see more than one side of their work. "Workers," he said, "need to see the

John Dewey emphasized work and also its relationship to society as a whole. *(Photo used by permission of the Indianapolis Public Schools.)*

technical, intellectual, and social relationships involved in what they do" (Dewey, 1916, p. 85). In the 1980s, we hear of companies' trying to make their workers more aware of the purpose of their labor beyond just making a product. Dewey's theory of teaching and learning, as in the example of workers' needs, focused on the whole person.

Dewey felt that studying history as a subject resulted in too much memorization of dates and dry facts. He wanted to see the curriculum related to social concerns in our society, such as problems with insanity, poverty, public sanitation, city planning, and conservation. He wanted to see schools incorporate social studies into their curriculum. Dewey's term *social studies* included history, economics, and politics, as well as sociology. He envisioned students' discovering real problems in their communities and attempting to solve these problems scientifically by collecting data, forming hypotheses, and testing these hypotheses. By actually being involved in solving real problems and by developing a social consciousness, students would learn in a pragmatic way what living in a democracy is all about.

Third and Fourth (Tie): Cardinal Principles of Secondary Education (1918) These seven principles are covered in more detail later in this chapter. These principles were handed down as a result of the report of the National Education Association (NEA) Commission on the Reorganization of Secondary Education. The commission was most concerned that too many electives were available to students: "Students were likely to specialize excessively or scatter their efforts over a large number of subjects having little relation to one another"

(Butts, 1955, p. 576). In order to overcome the problem of overspecialization, the commission recommended greater correlation and fusion of subject matter around the seven principles. The core curriculum emerged as that area of the curriculum to be taken by all of the students and occupying a large portion of their school time. This general education movement is still present today and is likely to continue in the near future. The so-called seven cardinal principles of secondary education are health, command of the fundamental processes, worthy home membership, a vocation, civic education, worthy use of leisure time, and ethical character. (See pages 208–210 in this chapter for more details on the cardinal principles.)

Third and Fourth (Tie): *Motivation and Personality* by Abraham Maslow (1954) Maslow wrote about the hierarchy of the basic needs and how these affect motivation and personality. The physiological needs are the most prepotent of all needs. Thus, a person who is lacking food, safety, love, and esteem would most probably hunger for food more strongly than anything else.

Maslow wrote that the higher the need, the more specifically human it is; therefore, the self-actualization need is shared with no other species. This uniquely human trait motivates us to become what we have the ability to become. An artist must paint, a poet must write, a teacher must teach, if they are to be ultimately at peace with themselves. Some other aspects of the self-actualized person are that they

> seem to have a uniformly good appetite for food; they seem to sleep well; they seem to enjoy their sexual lives without unnecessary inhibition and so on for all the relatively physiological impulses. They are able to accept themselves not only on these low levels, but at all levels as well; e.g., love, safety, belongingness, honor, self-respect. All of these are accepted without question as worth while, simply because these people are inclined to accept the work of nature rather than to argue with her for not having constructed things to a different pattern. This shows itself in a relative lack of the disgusts and aversions seen in average people and especially in neurotics, e.g., food annoyances, disgust with body products, body odors, and body functions. (Maslow, 1954, p. 207)

This book gives curriculum planners and/or teachers some new insights into motivation and personality development. The book also reinforces the importance of the development of self and the ways in which schools, through proper use of the curriculum, can help in the self-actualizing process.

Fifth and Sixth (Tie): *Brown* v. *Topeka Board of Education* (1954) What can one say about the *Brown* case that has not already been said in other chapters? Even though it first occurred in 1954, its major impact is still being felt as we try to right a lot of past wrongs. Racial equality through equal opportunity in education, in the economic arena, and in the social realm is not a fact for all Americans, but the situation is a lot better today as a result of the *Brown* decision.

Fifth and Sixth (Tie): *Taxonomy of Educational Objectives: Cognitive Domain* by Benjamin Bloom (1956) Most teachers are familiar with Bloom's taxonomy and the different levels of the cognitive domain that it identifies. One of the criticisms of the curriculum today is that teachers spend too much time asking students to recall or remember information. Facts are important to remember, but children can be challenged more by application and analysis. An illustrative test item in the application category demonstrates what is meant by applying knowledge as opposed to simply memorizing facts:

> John prepared an aquarium as follows: He carefully cleaned a ten-gallon glass tank with salt solution and put in a few inches of fine washed sand. He rooted several stalks of weed (*elodea*) taken from a pool and then filled the aquarium with tap water. After waiting a week he stocked the aquarium with ten one-inch goldfish and three snails. The aquarium was then left in a corner of the room. After a month the water had not become foul and the plants and animals were in good condition. Without moving the aquarium he sealed a glass top on it.
>
> What prediction, if any, can be made concerning the condition of the aquarium after a period of several months? If you believe a definite prediction can be made, make it and then give your reasons. If you are unable to make a prediction for *any* reason, indicate why you are unable to make a prediction (give your reasons). (Bloom, 1956, p. 131)

Perhaps one of the reasons that teaching may not be focused on the higher levels of the cognitive domain is that in traditional schools there may be too much pressure to prepare children for tests that are written on the lower levels of the cognitive domain. Bloom's taxonomy has a lot to teach us, but our schools and curricula must become more flexible and less conservative in order to implement higher-order objectives.

Seventh: *The Project Method* by William H. Kilpatrick (1918) This essay brought a little-known professor into international fame. Kilpatrick's paper was a basic attack on traditional education, and it showed how much he agreed with John Dewey. Kilpatrick elaborated on his ideas much further in *Foundations of Method* (1925).

The later book was an extension of the original essay and made very clear Kilpatrick's disdain for the separation of knowledge and skills into separate subjects such as arithmetic and geography. He felt that these separate subjects, when applied to real life, made little sense. Kilpatrick said that education should be designed to be as "lifelike" as possible.

Kilpatrick then became one of the major spokespersons for progressive education. His emphasis was teaching the child rather than the subject. It could also be said that he was helping the child to become self-actualized and was placing the child in the best position to be a continuous learner through problem solving. The example of the boy planting corn illustrates what Kilpatrick meant by teaching the child rather than the subject:

Children must be involved problem-solvers in order to truly learn, according to Kilpatrick. *(Photo used by permission of the Indianapolis Public Schools.)*

"Don't you think that the teacher should often supply the plan," asks one of the participants in Kilpatrick's dialogue. "Take a boy planting corn, for example; think of the waste of land and fertilizer and effort. Science has worked out better plans than a boy can make." Kilpatrick answers, "I think it depends on what you seek. If you wish corn, give the boy the plan. But if you wish boy rather than corn, that is, if you wish to educate the boy to think and plan for himself, then let him make his own plan." Although Kilpatrick steadfastly refused to countenance any dichotomy between "teaching subjects" and "teaching children," time and again in *Foundations of Method* he ends up choosing "boy" over "corn," with the result that his method, willy-nilly, inevitably favors the child-centered approach. (Cremin, 1961, pp. 217–218)

Kilpatrick's argument was that the teacher needs to be patient and to allow the learner to make a few mistakes. Kilpatrick and Dewey both caused curriculum planners to think more in terms of the learner.

Eighth: *How to Make a Curriculum* by Franklin Bobbitt (1924)   This publication is a basic handbook for revising a school curriculum. A whole plan is clearly outlined for those involved in curriculum building. Bobbitt wrote of "education's fundamental responsibility to prepare the child for the fifty years of adulthood, and not for the twenty years of childhood and youth" (p. 8).

Bobbitt listed the major objectives of education under nine headings. Under the heading of "Social Intercommunication" he listed such objectives as the ability to pronounce words properly and the ability to use language that is grammatically correct. Under the heading of "General Mental Efficiency," he listed the traditional subject areas like plant and animal life, as well as a study of human creations and inventions. The book provides a number of interesting ideas even for the current practitioner.

Relative to objectives, Bobbitt advocated "That nothing should be done by the schools that can be sufficiently well accomplished through the normal process of living." This comment is interesting in light of what has happened to the curriculum in the past few years. Schools are perceiving a need to incorporate more and more into the curriculum, such as sex education, peer counseling, drug education, and other courses thought unnecessary a few years ago. It is certain that Bobbitt himself would admit that what was normal living in one generation would change with time.

Ninth: The Binet-Simon Intelligence Test Scales/Revised by Lewis Terman (1912) These tests were the beginning of the American testing movement. The first wide use of group intelligence testing occurred during World War I in 1917, when the Army Alpha test was used to screen the soldiers. The intelligence-testing movement gathered more momentum during World War II. In education today, millions of standardized tests are used to measure achievement, intelligence, and aptitudes for various endeavors. The story of the proper use and misuse of tests is another side of the testing movement. Most educators who are involved in a screening process look at other measures of a child's ability besides their IQ, but test scores are still considered very important.

Tenth: *Developmental Tasks and Education* **by Robert Havighurst (1948)** Havighurst described a developmental task as

> that task which arises at or about a certain period in the life of the individual, successful achievement of which leads to his happiness and to his success with later tasks, while failure leads to unhappiness in the individual, disapproval by the society, and difficulty with later tasks. (p. 2)

The developmental tasks outlined by Havighurst extend throughout one's lifetime. These tasks are useful to educators who are attempting to state the goals and purposes of education, and they also relate to the correct timing of our educational efforts. Havighurst introduced the concept of the *teachable moment* as the best time for a task to be learned. His book has no doubt affected curriculum planning for the past thirty years and will continue to do so in the future.

The above list of publications and happenings concludes the top ten that have influenced the curriculum in the past seventy-five years. Three other significant publications appearing after 1960, but not included in the top ten, are now described.

In *Schools Without Failure* (1969), Glasser wrote that schools are set up for failure and that successful students are those who respond in ways prescribed by the teacher. His book presents suggestions for making involvement, relevance, and thinking realities in our schools. Glasser wrote, "I believe that if a child, no matter what his or her background, can succeed in school, he or she has an excellent chance for success in life" (p. 5). His book indeed gives the reader many concrete ideas for improving schools.

Alvin Toffler wrote *Future Shock* (1970) to help Americans cope with change. He described some startling bits of evidence, such as the fact that it took the human race millions of years to attain a speed of 100 miles per hour and only another fifty-eight years to reach 400 miles per hour in the air and 18,000 miles per hour in space (p. 26). The problem with change is that it can be too massive and too rapid. All of the old roots, like those grounded in religion, nation, community, family, and the professions, are shaking. Toffler suggested that we establish a future-facing education system, new social services, and new ways to regulate technology, and that we develop a strategy for capturing control of change. He ended his book on a positive note with the comment, "By making imaginative use of change to channel change, we cannot only spare ourselves the trauma of future shock, we can reach out and humanize distant tomorrows" (p. 430).

The last publication to be mentioned here that has had an impact on the curriculum is *Inequality* (1972), by Christopher Jencks. Jencks concluded that the schools themselves make only a small difference in the cognitive and noncognitive inequality among adults. The real differences, Jencks concluded, stem from the following factors: (1) the economic origins from which a person comes; (2) the differences between rich and poor children that are partly a matter of academic aptitude and partly a matter of money; and (3) cultural attitudes, values, and tastes for schooling, which play an even larger role than aptitude and money (p. 141). This book had a notable impact at the time of its publication.

As we enter the mid-1980s, many people are more concerned with educational achievement and test scores than they are with making the curriculum more relevant to the learner. This does not seem to be the decade for the more progressive forms of education; rather, it appears to be the decade of getting the most quality out of our traditional curriculum. Wider use of computer technology is sure to make the latter part of the 1980s exciting for those who are able to take advantage of this new phenomenon.

What Should the Aims of the Curriculum Be?

What should the aims of education be? This question is one of the most difficult questions for an educator to answer, and the most knowledgeable people differ on the best answer to the question. In 1918, the Commission on Reorganization of Secondary Education published a report known as the *Seven Cardinal Principles* of education. As we look over this list, we see that it is a rather complete list of goals. Some comments and questions about each of these principles may help us to realize what these aims currently mean.

The Aims of the Curriculum (the Seven Cardinal Principles—1918)

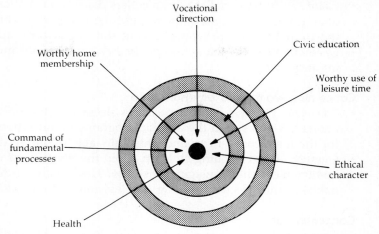

Concerning health
- *Comment:* We are taught in some health classes about the parts of the human body, the enzymes in our digestive system, the food groups, and other facts.
- *Question:* Do we teach our children enough about preventive health measures, and is health given a high enough priority in the curriculum?

Concerning command of the fundamental processes
- *Comment:* Being able to do arithmetic and to communicate by reading, writing, spelling, and speaking are considered important in American democratic society.
- *Question:* Why are some students allowed to graduate from our high schools without a command of these fundamental processes?

Concerning worthy home membership
- *Comment:* Worthy home membership no doubt includes basics such as food preparation, house cleaning, sewing, and raising a family.
- *Question:* Why are high-school courses in these areas generally taken only by students on a non-college-preparatory curriculum?

Concerning vocational direction
- *Comment:* Americans value freedom of choice, but the best career counseling in our schools occurs at the high-school level, and it relates primarily to college training.
- *Question:* Experts feel that the best career guidance plan starts at kindergarten and continues through high school, so why are many students graduating from high school with unclear or nonexistent goals?

Concerning civic education
- *Comment:* Most social studies teachers discuss our nation's history, our democratic form of government, and the manner in which the people of the United States are represented in state legislatures and the Congress.
- *Question:* Why are many voters apathetic and uninformed about the voting process?

Concerning worthy use of leisure time
- *Comment:* Physical education classes stress various sports and recreational activities, and the athletic programs in our schools stress athletics for the most competitive and physically able of our students.
- *Question:* Does teaching children about the worthy use of leisure time involve more than engaging in sports? How many students are taught habits in the selective viewing of television and movies?

Concerning ethical character
- *Comment:* Ethical character can be taught and reinforced in the classroom by the teacher.
- *Question:* What good ethical behaviors did you learn from the teachers you most admired?

Inlow (1966, p. 10) wrote that education has three major purposes: the *transmissive,* the *adaptive,* and the *developmental.* The transmissive purpose is passing on to each new generation the tried, if not necessarily the true. The adaptive purpose is fulfilled when we help students to acquire the skills, the knowledge, and the emotional adjustment needed to relate successfully to themselves and their world. We help students to meet their developmental purposes by guiding them to optimum growth at each maturational level.

So far, the aims of education have been discussed as they relate to absorbing information through the traditional school curricula. Other philosophers and thinkers see the aims of education in a more practical way. The influence of John Dewey, from the turn of the century onward, directed many modern-day thinkers more toward the practical side of the curricula.

Alfred North Whitehead (1929) wanted to see students produced who possessed both culture and expert knowledge in some special direction. Whitehead worried about teaching children inert knowledge; therefore, he stressed that *life* in all of its manifestations should be the curriculum. According to Whitehead, "The only use of a knowledge of the past is to equip us for the present" (p. 3). To illustrate what he meant, Whitehead suggested making a map of a small area using simple instruments like a surveyor's chain and compass:

> To have constructed the map of a small district, to have considered its roads, its contours, its geology, its climate, its relation to other districts, the effects on the status of its inhabitants, will teach more history and geography than any knowledge. (p. 17)

A. S. Neill, founder of the world-famous Summerhill School, saw the aim of education as creating free citizens. He believed in having children at his school learn self-government. The students at Summerhill were free to come and participate or free not to become involved. Neill prided himself on being voted down at general meetings; he really practiced freedom of will—the opposite of authority-centered schools:

> Neill believed in the inherent goodness of children, knowing full well that a hate-filled world would soon intrude and in many cases destroy their desire to live life as openly as possible. He was committed to participation and emotional equality; he wanted children to be as free as possible. (Snitzer, 1983, p.56)

The aims of education are a little different in the view of Alvin Toffler, the author of *Future Shock* (1970): "Nothing should be included in a required curriculum unless it can be strongly justified in terms of the future" (p. 363). Like some other curriculum reformers, Toffler proposed a curriculum built around themes such as childhood, adolescence, marriage, career, retirement, contemporary social problems, and many other possible alternatives. He argued that the present, obsolete curriculum imposes standardization on the elementary and secondary schools, thus giving the pupils little choice.

These are some of the aims of the curriculum. Most of them are generally stated, but they point in a definite direction. Some aims are rather matter-of-fact and others carry with them the connotation of action and excitement. These broad purposes for education give some direction for the more specific objectives that are written for local school districts.

What Should Be Included in the Curriculum?

The question of what should be included may be the most difficult question to answer because it depends so much on one's basic orientation as a curriculum advocate. Parents want what is best for their children; school board members must keep in mind the budget and what is best for all of the children; state school officers must keep in mind state guidelines; members of Congress are restrained by the U.S. Constitution and at the same time must be on guard to protect our national security as well as the equality of educational opportunity; and teachers should be aware of the implications of the textbooks they choose, the ability levels and individuality of the children they teach, and the new resources available to them.

Most parents want what is best for their children, but there are a good number who really do not care and are willing to leave educational decisions to others. Some parents have children who are particularly talented in music, art, speech, drama, athletics, or writing; these parents support or favor certain programs, often not keeping curricular balance in mind. Sometimes,

To some, fine art is an essential part of the curriculum. *(Photo used by permission of the Metropolitan School District of Lawrence Township.)*

groups of parents boost the band or the athletic teams so much that these programs get more attention and more money than the main academic offerings in the school. There are parents who fight for programs for the gifted, for Montessori method, for special education, or for numerous other special interests.

Parents also influence the curriculum by serving on textbook selection committees, and some are active lobbyists at the state level for groups such as the Parent Teachers Association and other state organizations. Still others support groups that want to censor certain books and learning materials, and some wish to restore school prayer.

School boards represent the community as a whole, as well as the parents. Most school boards listen to the needs of the school corporation through their appointed superintendent. Most superintendents enlist the help of curriculum directors, principals, and teachers before they propose curricular changes to the board. Some school boards go outside their role as policy setters and partially assume the role of administrators like the superintendents. When curriculum matters are decided unilaterally by the board and imposed by them on the school system, the best interests of the children may not be served. School board members can and do call attention to certain curricular needs, but these matters are best assigned to the superintendent for study and action.

State school officials represent an entire state, whose needs may be very diverse. In most states, there are industrial, urban, and rural interests to satisfy. Industrial areas are very concerned about vocational education; urban centers want money for equal educational opportunity; and rural communities want continued funding of vocational agriculture and home economics. State school boards can influence the curriculum in a number of ways, such as through state certification requirements. These state certification requirements regulate how teacher-training institutions train their teachers. By saying that teachers must have exposure to multicultural education, educational psychology, and a set number of credit hours in a certain academic discipline, the state influences the quality of the teachers it produces; thus, indirectly, state standards influence the curriculum in those schools for which state-licensed teachers carry out the curriculum. Some states also regulate the purchase of textbooks, which may represent a type of bias in the curriculum. With regard to money, some school districts can afford a broader and richer curriculum than others; however, the states do provide the poorer districts with more funding to help even up the financial expenditures allocated by the state for each district.

Members of the U.S. Congress also influence what is in the curriculum of our nation's schools. Through categorical grants to school districts, the federal government sets the tone for the curriculum. During the *Sputnik* era, the nation was worrying about lagging behind the Russians in math and science, so there were plenty of funds available in these areas. One of the authors was a science teacher at this time, and his department received thousands of dollars' worth of new science equipment with the help of the federal government. Government-funded curriculum-improvement projects resulted in new textbooks in math and science. Previously mentioned in other chapters was the Smith-Hughes Act in 1917 to aid vocational education, as well as the comprehensive Elementary and Secondary Education Act of 1965 to aid poor school districts and to help equalize educational opportunities. The federal government generally influences the curriculum in areas where state and local governments have failed to act. Ideally, its actions are motivated by what is best for our national interest.

Enrichment classes augment the regular curriculum. (*Photo used by permission of the Indianapolis Public Schools.*)

What should be included in the curriculum is then a multifaceted question and can be answered only by reference to all of those groups that make these important decisions. The needs of the students are sometimes at the end of the list, but they can provide valuable feedback about their own needs.

What Psychological Factors of Children Affect the Curriculum?

When curriculum planners get together, they inevitably want to plan a curriculum that is based on child psychology. They know that if the curriculum is psychologically based, the child will see the greatest relevance in what is being offered. Several researchers have given us a reasonably good idea of child psychology as it applies to certain age levels.

Intellectual Development

Jean Piaget (1896–1980) gave us significant insight into the intellectual development of the human being. He described four periods of intellectual development: sensorimotor (birth to 1½–2 years), preoperational (1½–2 to 6–7 years), concrete-operational (6–7 to 11–12 years), and formal-operational (11–12 through adulthood) (Piaget and Inhelder, 1969).

Sensory-motor Period   The characteristic of the sensory-motor period is that children solve problems by using their sensory system and their motor or muscular system rather than the symbolic processes that characterize the other three major periods. Newborn infants are capable of reflexive behavior such as the rooting reflex and the sucking reflex. Both of these reflexes have survival value, as the baby locates its mother's breast through rooting and obtains its mother's milk through sucking. During this early learning period, by using their senses, humans learn a lot about the world around them. The information that infants must learn, such as the difference between hot and cold and hard and soft, is enormous, and they use only their reflexes and sense organs to begin this process.

Preoperational Period   The most characteristic feature of this period is the development of symbolic functioning. The symbolic functioning process occurs when the child makes one thing represent a different thing that is not present. After having seen an object, children get some mental picture of the object and are then able to imitate what they observed. Also, children use symbolic play, where they treat an object as if it were something else; for example, a doll becomes a friend or a finger becomes a gun. Also during this period, children use language to describe activities of the past and to understand some reference to the future.

Concrete-Operational Period   In contrast to the previous period, children who are in the concrete-operational stage can solve a variety of tasks. The conservation tasks that Piaget asked students to perform are interesting tasks, and they demonstrate a child's progression to this period. To conserve, for example, children must recognize that differences in the size of a vessel storing liquid do not indicate changes in the mass, and that the length of an object stays the same even though its position has shifted (Ault, 1983, p. 58).

Formal-Operational Period   An adolescent in the formal-operational period can construct contrary-to-fact hypotheses and reason about their new ideas. Formal-operational thinking involves three activities: (1) generating multiple hypotheses; (2) systematically checking all possible solutions; and (3) operating on operations. In generating multiple hypotheses, children at this period

Tasks Testing for Conservation of Liquid, Mass, and Length
[(a) conservation of liquid; (b) conservation of mass; (c) conservation of length]

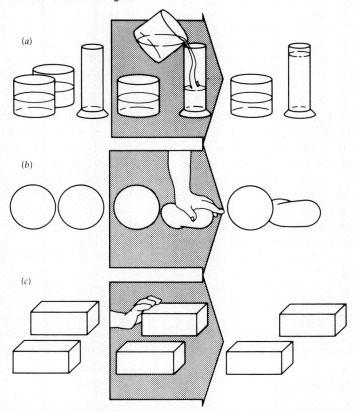

(a)

(b)

(c)

of development would not conclude that a man lying face-down on the sidewalk was drunk; instead, they would consider other options such as that he may have had a heart attack, that he may be playing a joke, or that he may even have been hit over the head by a robber. The more possible solutions to a problem there are, the greater the need for systematic solution testing. To demonstrate systematic solution testing, a type of chemistry problem can be given:

> Children are shown five colorless, odorless liquids in test tubes and are asked to discover what combination of the five will produce a yellow mixture. Concrete Operational children attempt to solve this problem through trial and error. They merely start to combine the liquids. But without an overall plan of action, one which is systematic, they soon become hopelessly lost—not remembering which combinations they have already tried and which remain to be tried. Formal Operational children proceed in a more systematic fashion, often first mixing the test tubes two at a time in a logical order (first and second, first and third, first and fourth, first and fifth, second and third, and so on). Then they try combinations of three at a time, four at a time, and all five. Moreover, if Concrete Operational children stumble upon a combination which works, they will be satisfied that the problem is solved without considering that one of the liquids may be inert and hence unnecessary. Formal Operational children will continue testing even after one solution is found, isolating the relevant factors and discarding the irrelevant. (Ault, 1983, pp. 70–71)

Finally, in operating on operations, the children begin to generate rules that are abstract enough to cover many specific instances. Roland and McGuire (1968) wrote that "The formally operational child approaches what is to Piaget the highest level of intelligence: the ability to represent, in advance of the actual problem, a full set of possibilities" (p. 50).

Therefore, Piaget gave us basic facts about the learning of the child that are useful in making intelligent curricular decisions. The ages given for the different developmental periods are meant to be rough approximations only. The child is ready for the next period when he or she has accomplished the tasks of the previous period.

Ausubel (1983) wrote about readiness as that time when an intellectual skill is at a particular stage of development. He wrote that most educators agree that there is an optimal age for learning, and that if learning experiences are delayed beyond this optimal period, valuable learning opportunities may be lost. Maturation and previous learning each contribute to one's being ready for the next level of learning, but it is very difficult to measure readiness because of its unpredictability and its lack of specificity (p. 158).

Moral Development

Lawrence Kohlberg (1973) wrote about moral education's being based on cognitive development, "cognitive" because active thinking goes on about moral issues and decisions, and "development" because it moves through certain moral stages. Using Jean Piaget's levels of intellectual development as a base, Kohlberg redefined and validated these previous studies. As Table 8-1 on the moral stages indicates, the child moves from being absolutely obedient to being an authority at the preconventional level; to being loyal to the family, the group, or the nation at the conventional level; and eventually to the point of defining her or his moral values in terms separate from the established groups' moral values at the postconventional level.

The moral stages of Kohlberg are important considerations when it comes to curriculum development. In order for children to have a chance to change from one moral stage to a higher moral stage, schools can help by engaging in moral discussions. The important conditions for these discussions appear to be

1. Exposure to the next higher stage of reasoning.
2. Exposure to situations posing problems and contradictions for the child's current moral structure, leading to dissatisfaction with his current level.
3. An atmosphere of interchange and dialogue combining the first two conditions, in which conflicting moral views are compared in an open manner. (Hass, 1983, p. 173)

Psychological Development

Goodwin Watson (1961) wrote psychological propositions about what we really know today concerning children and learning. He wrote that if educators use his fifty propositions, they will be on solid psychological ground and not on shifting sands (p. 2). The authors have used these fifty propositions on many occasions and have found them to be sound educationally. The following are two examples of Watson's (1961) propositions that have curricular implications:

Children (and adults even more) tend to select groups, reading matter, TV shows, and other influences which agree with their own opinions; they break off contact with contradictory views.

Parents want children taught what they themselves value and believe. One of the basic educational problems is to preserve minds from being closed in—surrounded by like-minded associates, like-minded commentators, and like-minded publications. (p. 9; emphasis added)

What is learned is most likely to be available for use if it is learned in a situation much like that in which it is to be used and immediately preceding the time when it is needed. Learning in childhood, then forgetting, and then relearning when need arises is not an efficient procedure.

It was once thought that childhood was the golden age for learning. We now know that adults of forty can learn better than youths of fourteen and much better than seven-year-olds. The best time to learn is when the learning can be useful. Motivation is then strongest and forgetting less of a problem. Much that is now taught children might be more effective if taught to responsible adults. (p. 10; emphasis added)

TABLE 8—1 Definition of Moral Stages

I. Preconventional Level

At this level, the child is responsive to cultural rules and labels of good and bad, right or wrong, but interprets these labels either in terms of the physical or the hedonistic consequences of action (punishment, reward, exchange of favors) or in terms of the physical power of those who enunciate the rules and labels. The level is divided into the following two stages.

Stage 1: The punishment-and-obedience orientation. The physical consequences of action determine its goodness or badness, regardless of the human meaning or value of these consequences. Avoidance of punishment and unquestioning deference to power are valued in their own right, not in terms of respect for an underlying moral order supported by punishment and authority (the latter being Stage 4).

Stage 2: The instrumental-relativist orientation. Right action consists of that which instrumentally satisfies one's own needs and occasionally the needs of others. Human relations are viewed in terms like those of the marketplace. Elements of fairness, of reciprocity, and of equal sharing are present, but they are always interpreted in a physical, pragmatic way. Reciprocity is a matter of "you scratch my back and I'll scratch yours," not of loyalty, gratitude, or justice.

II. Conventional Level

At this level, maintaining the expectations of the individual's family, group, or nation is perceived as valuable in its own right, regardless of immediate and obvious consequences. The attitude is not only one of *conformity* to personal expectations and social order, but of loyalty to it, of actively *maintaining,* supporting, and justifying the order, and of identifying with the persons or group involved in it. At this level, there are the following stages.

Stage 3: The interpersonal concordance or "good boy-nice girl" orientation. Good behavior is that which pleases or helps others and is approved by them. There is much conformity to stereotypical images of what is majority or "natural" behavior. Behavior is frequently judged by intention—"he means well" becomes important for the first time. One earns approval by being "nice."

Stage 4: The "law and order" orientation. There is orientation toward authority, fixed rules, and the maintenance of the social order. Right behavior consists of doing one's duty, showing respect for authority, and maintaining the given social order for its own sake.

III. Postconventional, Autonomous, or Principled Level

At this level, there is a clear effort to define moral values and principles that have validity and application apart from the authority of the groups or persons holding these principles and apart from the individual's own identification with these groups. This level also has two stages.

Stage 5: The social-contract, legalistic orientation, generally with utilitarian overtones. Right action tends to be defined in terms of general individual rights and standards which have been critically examined and agreed upon by the whole society. There is a clear awareness of the relativism of personal values and opinions and a corresponding emphasis upon procedural rules for reaching consensus. Aside from what is constitutionally and democratically agreed upon, the right is a matter of personal "values" and "opinion." The result is an emphasis upon the "legal point of view," but with an emphasis upon the possibility of changing law in terms of rational considerations of social utility (rather than freezing it in terms of Stage 4 "law and order"). Outside the legal realm, free agreement and contract is the binding element of obligation. This is the "official" morality of the American government and constitution.

Stage 6: The universal-ethical-principle orientation. Right is defined by the decision of conscience in accord with self-chosen *ethical principles* appealing to logical comprehensiveness, universality, and consistency. These principles are abstract and ethical (the Golden Rule, the categorical imperative); they are not concrete moral rules like the Ten Commandments. At heart, these are universal principles of *justice,* of the *reciprocity* and *equality* of human *rights,* and of respect for the dignity of human beings as *individual persons.*

Source: Kohlberg, L. (1973). The claim to moral adequacy of a highest stage of moral judgment. *Journal of Philosophy, 70,* 631–632.

Knowing these propositions may help curriculum planners to avoid training children with closed minds or teaching curriculum material that will be soon forgotten. The last proposition seems to be saying that we need to use a curriculum that leans toward teaching children self-direction in terms of how to learn rather than to give them continuous layers of subject matter.

As we plan the curriculum, we need to keep in mind the amount of attention the individual child gets in the classroom. The famous anthropologist Ashley Montagu (1983) wrote "That the most important of all basic psychological needs is the need for love" (p. 122). Montagu felt that we treat children very unequally in our classrooms. Just because children are at the same chronological age is no sign that they are at the same developmental level as well. Montagu (1983) summed up the problem very well: "The equal treatment of unequals is the most unequal way of dealing with human beings ever devised" (p. 122). The fact is that the amount of love given through special attention is diminished every time we add an additional child to a classroom.

Many scientists have written about the developmental needs of children. Two others besides Piaget and Kohlberg are Robert J. Havighurst and Erik H. Erikson, who are also human-development theorists. All four of these men

> hold that the development stages they describe have a fixed order, and that each person passes through these stages in this order. Successful achievement of each stage is necessary if the individual is to proceed with vigor and confidence to the next stage. There is a "teachable moment" or time of special sensitivity for each task or stage. (Hass, 1983, p. 118)

The curriculum, then, needs to be planned and organized with these developmental stages in mind. Although readiness for learning is difficult to determine, every effort needs to be made to individualize the learning process more closely.

What Are Some Organizational and Structural Decisions That Influence the Curriculum?

We can assume that somewhere, every significant aspect of curricular content has been presented to students in schools. Some schools may have a fine curriculum and excellent teachers, but such factors as classroom management, teaching methods, and the way in which the curriculum is organized and structured may be limiting factors. In this section, we concentrate on the organization and the structure of the curriculum.

Elementary-School Concerns

Organizational patterns for the elementary school may include self-contained classes, grade-level teams, cross-grade teams, and nongraded classes. Some schools may have a combination of these patterns, with the lower-elementary levels nongraded and the upper-elementary levels graded. In some grades, the teachers may work on the team concept while others work in the self-contained classroom. Children can be moved *vertically* from grade to grade or from level to level and *horizontally* within a grade or level. Whatever is done as far as these organizational patterns are concerned, the important thing is for the schools to be flexible. According to Wiles and Bondi (1984), "A sound approach is to organize and group according to the needs of students, abilities of teachers, and availability of facilities and resources. No single pattern fits all situations" (p. 285).

Elementary schools have done much with the grouping of students for particular purposes. The reason for grouping is to better meet the individualized needs of the children, and flexibility is the key to effective grouping. Some students may have reached a higher level of skill performance in math, yet may be lower in reading. Wiles and Bondi (1984) listed seven possible groups in which to involve students in order to best meet their needs:

1. *A class as a whole* can function as a group. Teachers sometimes have guilt feelings about whole class activities, but there are occasions when the teacher can address the whole class as a single group. New topic or unit introductions, unit summaries, and activities such as reports, dramatizations, and choral reading may be effectively conducted with the total class.
2. *Reading level groups* formed according to reading achievement levels are commonly found in classrooms. These groups are not static and must accommodate shifts of pupils from group to group as changes in individual achievement occur.
3. *Reading need groups* are formed to assist students in mastering a particular reading skill such as pronouncing a phonic element or finding the main idea in a paragraph.
4. *Interest groups* help students apply reading skills to other language arts and other content areas. Storytelling, recreational reading, writing stories and poems, and dramatization are activities that can be carried out in interest groupings.
5. *Practice or tutorial groups* are often used to allow students to practice oral reading skills, play skill games, and organize peer teaching situations.
6. *Research groups* allow for committee work, group projects, and other research activities. Learning centers in the classroom and research areas in the media center are often developed for research groups.
7. *Individualization* allows a student to work as an individual in selecting books and references for learning projects. Developmental programs provide for individual progress through a series of lessons. (pp. 270–271; emphasis added)

When we talk of groups at any level, we generally refer to them as either homogeneous or heterogeneous. Homogeneous groups are those that have some commonality among their members, such as the same reading level, the same math-comprehension level, or the same physical-performance level. Heterogeneous groups are those that contain many different levels of ability. In most schools, children perform in both kinds of groups in a single day; therefore, they can maximize their ability or talents in a special reading group or other special group and yet interact both socially and intellectually part of the day with all students.

Middle-School Concerns

About eighty years ago, only about 40 percent of the children from elementary school went on to high school under the old 8-year–4-year plan of organization. As a result, educators conceived of the junior high school, or the 6-year–3-year–3-year plan. The first of these institutions was set up in Berkeley, California, in 1910, and like others to follow, it was established to move students into high-school work sooner, and to focus on the unique needs of twelve- and thirteen-year-old students. In the eyes of many, what actually happened was that in the years to follow, junior high schools became mini-high schools with similar departments and extracurricular activities. Thus, they did not meet the unique developmental needs of the children being served (Steeves and English, 1978).

More recently, we have seen this intermediate age group housed in a school known more commonly as a *middle school* under either a 5–8-, a 6–8-, or

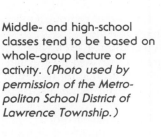

Middle- and high-school classes tend to be based on whole-group lecture or activity. *(Photo used by permission of the Metropolitan School District of Lawrence Township.)*

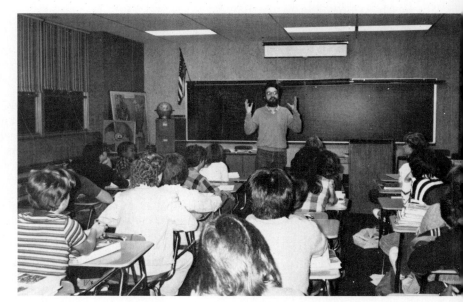

a 7–8-grade plan of organization. The most predominant organizational plan encompasses Grades 6–8 for the middle school (Steeves & English, 1978):

> Debates over the optimum school district organizational plan, whether 8-4, 6-3-3, or 4-4-4 or some other variation are largely unproductive. The choice of such plans is largely arbitrary and grounded in the dictates of local pragmatism. Research on such patterns has failed to demonstrate clearly that any one is superior to any other. (p. 29)

High-School Concerns

Flexibility is not very descriptive of the modern high school. Most high schools are departmentalized and are much more subject-centered than they are student-centered. In order to make high schools more exciting places for students to attend, most efforts have been directed toward athletics and other extracurricular areas of concentration. Some efforts in recent times toward revitalization have been in the area of alternatives, including magnet schools and vocational schools.

The high-school curriculum tends to be rigid because of the demands of society to have students achieve higher scores on college entrance examinations. Other reasons for rigidity in high schools, according to Wiles and Bondi (1984) are that for years most secondary schools have operated under the assumption that

1. The appropriate amount of time for learning a subject is the same uniform period of time, 50 to 60 minutes in length, six or seven periods a day, for 36 weeks out of the year.
2. A classroom group size of 30–35 students is the most appropriate for a wide variety of learning experiences.
3. All learners are capable of mastering the same subject matter in the same length of time. For example, we give everyone the same test on Chapter Five on Friday. We pass everyone from level one of Algebra to level two when June comes.
4. We assume that once a group is formed, the same group composition is equally appropriate for a wide variety of learning activities.
5. We assume that the same classroom is equally appropriate for a wide variety of learning activities. Conference rooms are not provided for teacher-student conferences. Large group facilities are not provided for mass dissemination of materials. Small group rooms are unavailable for discussion activities.
6. We assume that all students require the same kind of supervision.
7. We assume that the same teacher is qualified to teach all aspects of his or her subject for one year.

Operating on those assumptions, we have locked students into an educational egg-crate with thirty students to a cubicle from 8 A.M. to 3 P.M. five days a week. In short, schools operating under those assumptions have existed more for the convenience of teaching than for the facilitation of learning. (p. 334)

How can the high-school curriculum be made more flexible and more student-centered, and thus more humanistic? J. Lloyd Trump (1968) and others have suggested flexible scheduling that provides a time and place for small groups, large groups, and individualized instruction. Trump outlined a schedule with 15-, 20-, or 30-minute modules instead of the conventional 45- or 55-minute modules (p. 12). The reduced time per module would give twelve, sixteen, or twenty-four periods per day instead of the usual six- or seven-period day, but these schedules can become just as rigid if time is not used to do those things that a flexible schedule is designed to provide. William Bailey (1975) has provided us with some goals that could be implemented with a flexible schedule:

1. Variable class size.
2. Variable time allotments for classes and/or block time periods.
3. Maximum use of facilities, particularly resource centers, labs, and instructional materials centers.
4. Selected students may elect seven courses or more.
5. Multiple teaching assignments, i.e., team or cooperative teaching.
6. A weekly schedule is preferable to a routinized daily schedule that, for example, maintains the same class each afternoon during poor times for concentration.
7. Facilitate independent study and individual study courses.
8. Provide students with opportunities for individualized, continuous progress learning.
9. Maximize planning time for teacher and teaching teams—should be around 25 percent.
10. Enable band and chorus to be included in a regular school day.
11. Increase the degree to which students are responsible for their own education.
12. Provide for order in daily attendance.
13. Provide for orderly but rapid changes adaptable to pep rallies, assemblies, dismissals, and other interruptions.
14. Provide for proper sequencing of the various types of instruction, i.e., lab following demonstration, small groups following lectures, etc.
15. General flexibility.
16. In addition to the intent to accommodate the above, the schedule should make it possible to carry forward present curriculum practices that have proven successful and are crucial to progress. (pp. 154–155)

Flexible scheduling is being used today in a number of high schools. Many schools have incorporated changes, like those suggested by Wiles and Bondi, that really make the school function more smoothly. Another problem in today's schools that inhibits innovations like flexible scheduling is students' lack of maturity and the apparent inability of many students to use their independent study time efficiently. School leaders should not allow disruptive students to curtail innovations that can and will stimulate other students to greater achievements. No doubt some students may need less free time or independent study time in order to function properly.

The Nongraded Curricular Organization

The graded school concept is well entrenched in our society. The first graded school was installed at Boston in the Quincy School in 1848; the idea had been imported from Germany by Horace Mann. Most of our curriculum material is organized around the graded system of schooling, and there is a lot of resistance to changing this organizational pattern. The graded system of schooling has worked for all of these years, it is said, so why change?

There is an innate error in the established graded system of schools: there is no exact correlation between the chronological age of a child and his or her readiness for a certain grade. Inlow (1966) wrote that "grading with age as a unilateral criterion assumes falsely that children of similar ages not only have similar interests and abilities, but have had similar cultural experiences as well" (p. 308). The fact is that children who enter the first grade vary in readiness, as measured by the mental age (MA) of the child, by as much as four years. Some experts feel that by the time children reach fourth grade, the span for readiness for that grade can be measured by the number for that grade. Are we trying to fit children into the wrong places, just as a carpenter might be trying to drive a square peg into a round hole?

An obvious alternative to graded schools is nongraded schools. Whether these schools are located at the elementary-school, middle-school, or high-school levels, their goal is to allow for more flexibility and movement within the curriculum. Ideally, these nongraded schools are there to provide continuous academic challenge and growth no matter what the age of the student. In a nongraded school, the conventional grade designations are eliminated, and three or four blocks are inserted in their place. At the elementary level, where most of the experimenting has been done with nongraded schools, Grades 1, 2 and 3 are placed in a primary nongraded unit, and Grades 4, 5, and 6 are placed in an intermediate nongraded unit. Some educators envision nongraded education as being divided into five blocks from first grade through college.

The nongraded school must provide a system for identifying student needs, a delivery system for those needs in a suitable curricular package, evaluation of the degree to which those needs are being met, and allowance for the continuous progress of each student. In theory, at least, each student should start and end at a different point. Most nongraded schools use multiple criteria to choose who is to be placed in a given block. Some schools use achievement as a single criterion, but other criteria may include reading level, age, or social homogeneity, and some schools deliberately impose heterogeneity, including a mixture of ages, and social and emotional development.

Inlow (1966) listed the advantages of a nongraded school as follows:

1. Permits pupils to progress at their own individual rates.
2. Decisions on retardation of pupils are automatically delayed for three years.

3. Teachers have more flexibility in the selection of subject matter, in establishing its sequence, and assigning time allocations.
4. Pupil achievement, not time spent in school, constitutes the basis for evaluation.
5. Greater progress in reading is made under the nongraded than under the graded plan in the primary block. (pp. 316–317)

Inlow also listed the shortcomings of a nongraded school:

1. The biggest problem seems to be choosing the right vertical sequence for pupils to follow, and in what way will they follow it, as they progress through a two-, three-, or four-year nongraded curriculum.
2. After eliminating conventional grade labels, they may proceed to add others that may be no better.
3. The process of grouping children for instructional purposes is still uncertain.
4. Some incorrectly call their situation nongraded when more than one grade is represented in a typing or a Spanish class. Common ingredients of a nongraded school would be a time block longer than a year, vertical scheduling, sequential pupil progression through a given body of content, and teacher flexibility. (pp. 318–319)

A good resource on the nongraded high school is B. Frank Brown's *The Nongraded High School* (1963).

The Team-Teaching Concept

Organizing the development and the delivery of the curriculum around team teaching can be very beneficial to both the teachers and the students involved. Team teaching can be used anywhere, but it may work best at the middle-school level. When children enter the middle school, it seems like a big, impersonal organization compared to the more comfortable elementary school. According to Deibert and Walsh (1981),

> The development of the teacher team provides the school with the type of program whereby students receive the necessary individual attention and support while gaining the benefits of a large, well-staffed, well-equipped, and diversified school. (p. 169)

In Maslow's (1954) hierarchy of needs, one must progress through five levels as he or she moves through life (see the figure below). The key is that each level is built on the level below, and each must be satisfied before higher levels can be attained.

Every person has the potential to be fully self-actualized or to have a complete awareness of her or his uniqueness as a person. A self-actualized

Maslow's Hierarchy of Needs

Self-actualization

Self-esteem

Sense of belonging

Safety

Survival

Source: Data for diagram based on Maslow, A. H. (1970). A theory of human motivation. In *Motivation and personality* (2nd ed.). New York: Harper & Row. Copyright © 1970 by Abraham H. Maslow.

person is inner-directed in that her or his direction comes from the self. Many middle-school students have not realized Maslow's level of safety when they first arrive, but through the familylike team concept, these students can be given a good sense of security in which to operate. When children feel this comfortable environment, they can proceed to the next need. Deibert and Walsh (1981) wrote:

> The beauty of the team concept in a school is that it breaks down the size of the institution, increases both student and teacher acceptance in the performance of tasks, and increases a sense of belonging so that eventual self-esteem and self-actualization have a better chance of being realized. (p. 170)

Team teaching does not work in every school. The school must have an administration that fosters an open organizational climate as well as a staff that is enthusiastic and positive about what is going on. Leadership from the top by the principal is a key factor. Teachers from Ironwood School in Phoenix have worked successfully for ten years in teams. Among other things that happen at Ironwood, according to Harmon (1983), "Team decisions always take account of young adolescents' need for stability, tempered by opportunities to make choices" (p. 367). This statement tends to lend support to Maslow and others, who see need satisfaction of prime importance; thus, team teaching can be a facilitating mechanism in the success of student growth.

Other advantages of team teaching were stated by Inlow (1966):

1. *Grouping flexibility*—For example, in a team of four teachers responsible for 120 students, one teacher could do large group instruction for 90

students, while the other three could do small group instruction with 10 students each. Multiple variations are possible making the team teaching arrangement very flexible.

2. *Better use of teacher strengths*—For instance, if one elementary school teacher is more knowledgeable than his team colleagues in a single academic area, he can extend this asset, via various grouping plans, throughout the entire group.

3. *In-service education is a by-product*—As a result of the close associations most teachers have within a group, they will experience in-service growth.

4. *Provides more time for professional duties*—Often teaching teams have noncertified personnel assigned to them, who perform such tasks as paper grading, playground duty, or clerical duties; thus freeing the certified teacher to do the more strictly professional functions like lesson preparations.

Inlow also stated some disadvantages of team teaching (1966):

1. *Sustained cooperation is difficult to achieve*—To state it bluntly, certain teachers are not mature enough to work cooperatively and productively with their colleagues in a team-teaching situation. The following factors relate to this issue involving the human equation: First, it places them in a close family-like relationship wherein their paths cross hundreds of times in the course of a year. Second, the team asks that team members resolve their curriculum differences so that there will be a workable consensus. Third, team members must make collaborative decisions for unexpected occurrences. Fourth, performing under the watchful eye of colleagues is a disturbing experience for many.

2. *The curriculum problem of what should be taught*—This problem relates to what should be taught, in what way, and to what size group. It is a hard issue to resolve, but it must be resolved in order that the team may maximize effectiveness.

Team teaching, then, can enhance the curriculum if it is organized and used with the best interests of the students and the teachers in mind. Although it has some problems, it appears that its advantages far exceed its disadvantages.

The preceding pages have presented some of the factors involved in the organization of the curriculum. There are many more, but these considerations will help the prospective teacher to realize that once curricular content is decided, the organization of that content for delivery is also vital. The graded school has some inherent weaknesses, as does the nongraded school. Under the right conditions, schooling can be enhanced by the use of middle schools, nongraded blocks of time, flexible scheduling, and team teaching. The key seems to be flexibility, and the more flexible teachers are, the more they will meet the individualized needs of their students.

How Do Parents Influence Their Child's Perception of the Curriculum?

Parents have a big indirect influence on their child's perception of the curriculum. Many times, teachers strive to create an interest in a subject during the day, only to have children exposed to negative influences by their parents toward that same subject, or toward school in general, when they arrive in their home that evening. Most experienced teachers wonder often why parents and teachers cannot work together in order to maximize learning for children. The fact is that some parents and teachers do work together, and that the child is the beneficiary.

There are several areas where parents directly or subtly influence their child's perception of the curriculum. The socioeconomic circumstances that parents and children find themselves living in is no doubt one of the largest contributing factors to attitudes toward schooling. (See Chapters 1 and 2.) We all know of children who were brought up in poor neighborhoods, responded well to schooling, and made great successes of their lives. At the same time, we know of wealthy people who were not supportive of education, and neglected their child's educational development. In both cases, these circumstances tend to be exceptions rather than the common practice. Aside from the socioeconomic consideration, here are some areas in which we think parents have a big influence on their child's perception of the curriculum.

The Expectations That Parents Have

Parents who want their children to be successful work with them and help them to establish goals for themselves. A good model of parent involvement in the area of goal setting is the way in which some parents work with their children and sacrifice with them so that they can qualify for the Olympics. Many if not most of the Olympic athletes give much of the credit for their success to their parents. And most of the children who are successful in school have parents who support them and have reasonable expectations. It is very disappointing to children when their parents do not hold very high expectations for them.

As a teacher, you can possibly work with your students' parents and help them to dream along with their children to set some higher goals. Some parents have not been exposed to enough of the world, through either their educational or their life experiences, to know what is really possible. As a teacher, you can open the eyes of both students and parents to a whole new world of possibilities.

Parental attitudes strongly influence a child's school experience. (*Photo used by permission of the Indianapolis Public Schools.*)

Some parents have unrealistic expectations for their child. Often, these parents have been very successful and do not understand why their child is having trouble in school. If the child has a learning disability, teachers need to explain to the parents what the child's disability is and how, with a proper curricular program, he or she can become a school achiever. Some children may be emotionally or psychologically disturbed and may need special attention.

The Friends and Relatives of Parents

The friends and relatives of parents also have an influence on the parents and a direct and indirect influence on the children. One of the authors received his value for a higher education from close family friends. Because his parents had not gone to college, they did not see the value of a college education, as did these close family friends. Often, relatives or friends like these are as great an influence on a child as the parents.

As teachers, we need to be aware of these facts and attempt to tie them into our class discussions. Using examples in our classes of how relatives and friends have helped us understand life better is a method of reinforcing values that can enhance children's perception of the curriculum. Just as parents have friends who are positive influences, some may be negative as well. If, as teachers, we become aware of such influences on children, we can attempt to focus the children away from these influences and toward more positive thinking.

The Degree of Television Monitoring That Parents Do

As we all know, children tend to watch television for long periods of time, sometimes for as much time as they are in school. Parents who value their children's education will regulate the amount of TV watching. Television, like all media, has both good and bad offerings. Parents who only care if their child is quiet and not bothering them are often delighted if their child is preoccupied with TV, watching it no matter what the quality of the program.

Teachers can help by making parents aware of the problems that can occur when they allow their children to watch unmonitored TV. When grades are low, parents can be spoken to regarding their child's TV-watching habits. Many educational shows can be assigned to students so that they have a definite purpose in watching TV. Programs that are assigned as part of a class can be discussed the next day. Television has the potential to enhance a child's education if both parents and teachers can give proper direction to children.

Broadening a Child's Horizons

Opening up new vistas of thinking can be done in several ways, and not all of them are expensive. In the area of reading and books, a child need not have all of these resources in the home, as public libraries, college libraries, and private sources such as relatives and friends may be easily accessible. Parents who take their children to public libraries and encourage their reading and

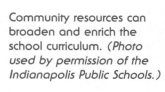

Community resources can broaden and enrich the school curriculum. *(Photo used by permission of the Indianapolis Public Schools.)*

research activities have done a lot toward promoting their children's education. Of course, a home where there is a library and where the parents do a lot of reading and sharing is a true bonus.

Another way to cause children to do some thinking is to take them on trips. If a child lives in a large metropolitan area, there are generally museums, zoos, government buildings, factories, and farms, all of which invite a family visit. Many schools organize field trips to all of these places, but family excursions to reinforce previous visits are excellent uses of family time and money. Some children are privileged to travel extensively all over the world before they even enter a college, but many never venture out of their own neighborhood or village. Family trips to different locations of interest are a wonderful chance for childen to broaden their horizons.

These two areas, reading and travel, are the types of raw materials from which children can put together their dreams for the future. As a teacher, you can encourage both of these activities. In your talks with parents, you can recommend both books and trips to them. In your classes, book reports and travel reports can be presented to the whole class. The world of experience can be tied to the academic world and vice versa through the involvement of your students' parents.

These, then, are a few ways in which parents can and do influence their child's perception of the curriculum. Negative thinking parents can become positive influences if they are involved as partners with the teacher in the education of their child. Even parents with a positive attitude toward education and toward the curriculum need some assistance in order to truly maximize what they can do for their child.

What Should Beginning Teachers Know About Learning Disabilities?

Most of the curriculum talk deals with children who can function in a "normal" classroom. Some children, no matter how much we would like for them to function normally, are not capable for several reasons. Teachers are in a position to identify these special children and to give them the type of instruction that will help them learn.

Some History on the Problem of Learning Disabilities

In 1937, Samuel Torrey Orton brought attention to the subject of the disorder of language development in children. Orton noted in his research that there is a certain location in the brain that affects reading ability, and that this location is the same as the location in adults, that, when damaged, causes them to lose

Samuel T. Orton pioneered in research on dyslexia. *(Photo used by permission of the June L. Orton Trust Fund.)*

all aspects of reading skill (Geschwind, 1982, p. 15). Through the careful work of Dr. Orton, the details of what is a dyslexic child unfolded. There is an entrenched ignorance among some educators who label these children lazy or hyperactive, or as kids who just will not try, when the root cause is a brain alteration in most cases.

There are learning disabilities other than dyslexia, though it is the most common disorder; therefore, attention must be paid to other areas as well. Research continues, and more is certain to be learned on this topic in the near future. Two sources of further information on learning disabilities are the Association for Children with Learning Disabilities, 4156 Library Road, Pittsburgh, Pennsylvania 15234, and the Orton Dyslexia Society, 724 York Road, Baltimore, Maryland 21204.

Definition of a Learning Disability

Under federal and state legislation, the child with a learning disability is referred to as having an *attention deficit disorder* (ADD). ADD children have one or more learning disabilities, many are hyperactive and/or distractible, and many develop emotional, social, and family problems. These ADD children are not mentally retarded, as they have either average or above-average intelligence. It is important to remember that in these children, if they are

232

emotionally disturbed, the disturbance is caused by the academic difficulty that they are having and not by some other family problem.

Many labels have been used to describe the difficulties of ADD children:

- *Dyslexia:* Reading difficulties.
- *Dysgraphia:* Writing problems.
- *Dyscalculia:* Math difficulty.
- *Specific learning disabilities or perceptually impaired or neurologically impaired:* Perceptual, integrative, sequencing, memory, motor, or language disabilities.

The Kinds of People Who Have Learning Disabilities

The truth is that all kinds of people from all economic and social levels have learning disabilities. Some people have been able to overcome their problems to the extent that they lead very productive lives. Such famous people as Thomas Edison, Woodrow Wilson, Albert Einstein, and Nelson Rockefeller are examples of exceptionally successful individuals who overcame a learning disability.

More often, these children lead lives of frustration and failure. Because of their inability to read, write, and calculate properly, these children tend to become underemployed or unemployed as adults. Surveys of juvenile delinquents have shown that more than half these young people may be learning-disabled. Our society depends so much on the ability to read and write that when an eighteen-year-old cannot fill out a job application, he or she is in deep trouble; thus, they may see few options open to them other than crime (Bever, 1980, p. 56). Although some people with a learning disability have become tremendously successful, there are far more who lead less fulfilling lives.

How to Diagnose Learning Disability

Because learning disabilities are of many types, and each learning disabled child is unique, it is difficult to spot this type of individual. However, if a child has a cluster of the following symptoms and they do not disappear as he or she gets older, you may suspect a learning disability:

Short attention span (restless, easily distracted).
Reverses letters and numbers (sees "b" for "d," "6" for "9").
Reads poorly, if at all (below age and grade level).
Often confused about directions and time (right-left, up-down, yesterday-tomorrow).
Personal disorganization (can't follow simple schedules).

Impulsive and inappropriate behavior (poor judgment in social situation, talks and acts before thinking).

Poor coordination (clumsy, has trouble using pencil, scissors, crayons).

Inconsistent performance (can't remember today what was learned yesterday).

Fails written tests but scores high on oral exams (or vice versa).

Speech problems (immature speech development, has trouble expressing ideas). (Bever, 1980, p. 56)

Once the child is recognized as possibly a learning-disabled person, school corporations, under new federal regulations, should provide a diagnostic team. The team approach ideally involves a learning-disabilities teacher, who gives a full battery of tests to determine if the child has learning disabilities and, if so, the types of disabilities; a psychologist, who assesses the child's level of intellectual functioning; a social worker or nurse, who meets with the family to learn more about the child's development, his or her behavior when not in school, and the family status; a speech therapist, who evaluates the child for speech, language, or hearing difficulties; and a physician, who does a complete physical examination. It is very important that the diagnosis be multidisciplinary, as most learning-disabled children have more than one problem area.

How to Treat a Learning-Disabled Child

After diagnosis, these children need to be placed in a classroom with teachers trained in learning disabilities. The style of teaching in most regular classrooms involves the use of one or two senses, but these children need a multisensory approach. For example, when a learning-disabled child is told something by the teacher, that child should be shown the same thing on the chalkboard and through the use of manipulative materials. In this way, the child is reached by auditory, visual, tactile, and kinesthetic means. Specifically, when outlining a paragraph, the student may have on her or his desk some small strips of paper on which to write the key thoughts and the supporting details of an idea. The outline is further enhanced by a strand of yarn laid across the paper to symbolize the concept of a common theme.

Percentage of Our Population with a Learning Disability

Estimates vary about how many children are actually learning-disabled, but the federal government estimates that up to 3 percent of the total population have severe learning disabilities. One major, federally funded research project found that 16 percent of all schoolchildren have learning disabilities requiring special teaching methods. Until we can more accurately identify these children, it will be very difficult to arrive at the correct total number of individual cases.

What Is the Hidden Curriculum?

One area of the curriculum that is probably as important as, or sometimes even more important than, the actual content offered for study is the so-called hidden curriculum. It is the informal part of the curriculum that you know is there, but that is difficult to see and study. Ballantine (1983) described the hidden curriculum as the part of the curriculum that refers to the three Rs—rules, regulations, and routines—to which school must adapt (p. 178). In this brief overview, we present some of these items that play an important role in influencing one's perception of the formal curriculum.

The Self-Concept Held by the Student

Children who have good self-concepts about their academic ability perform better academically. Research done by Brookover and Erickson (1975) found that changes in self-concepts about ability were followed by changes in academic achievement. Thus, it is important for teachers to encourage students to believe in themselves. If a student believes he or she can be a high achiever, this is his or her first step in trying to become one.

One of the experiments by Brookover and Erickson (1975) showed that you can raise student achievement levels by working with the parents. Parents were given a set of rules and procedures and were taught how to implement them as they worked with their children. Some of the things the parents were told to do for an entire school year as they worked with their children were (Brookover and Erickson, 1975):

- Don't reward any negative statements their children might make about their academic ability.
- Don't say things like "I was not a reader either."
- Tell children often and regularly, as subtly as possible, that they are academically able and ought to do better in school.
- Any positive statements their children made about their ability or achievement was to be rewarded with commendatory remarks, tokens, or prizes.
- Parents should expect small gains to occur, and these should be accompanied by increasingly higher demands on the student.
- Negative behavior or low achievement was to be overtly ignored. (pp. 296–297)

As a result of the above experiment the feedback to the parents was an increasing level of performance on the part of their children and a sense that they were responsible for their children's new accomplishments.

The School Value Climate

In regard to the value climate in the schools, Ballantine (1983) considered the effects of school social structure and social climate on student achievement:

Student achievement was measured by reading and writing competencies, academic self-concept, and self-reliance. The *school social structure* was measured by teacher satisfaction with the school structure, parental involvement, differentiation in student programs, principals' reports of time devoted to instruction, and student mobility in school. The *school climate* was measured by student perceptions, teacher perceptions and principal perceptions. The authors found that more than 85 percent of the variance in student attainment was explained by the combination of the above variables. In a summary of findings, which compared improving and declining schools, Brookover and colleagues found the following: The staff of improving schools place more emphasis on accomplishing basic reading and mathematics objectives; they believe *all* stu-

A championship chess team resulted from a teacher's high expectations and students' determination. (*Photo used by permission of the Indianapolis Public Schools.*)

dents can master basic objectives and they hold high expectations; they assume responsibility for learning and accept being held accountable. Principals in improving schools are instructional leaders and disciplinarians. Brookover, in short, argues that schools *do* make a difference. (Ballantine, p. 183; emphasis added)

The Brookover and Erickson study verifies the fact that a positive feeling on the part of the school staff toward learning and achievement does make a difference. What we are talking about is not a part of the regular formal curriculum, but is composed of some of those subtle things that we think about only when our attention is called to them. We have all witnessed or have known, teachers and principals who were not responsible, who held low expectations for students, and who were poor leaders, so we agree with Brookover that schools do indeed make a difference.

The Climate in the Classroom

The classroom climate can be compared to life in the "real world." Differences in people are evident in childhood as well as when they reach their adult years, but sex bias, racial prejudice, economic bias, learning bias, and many more of these human problems are less changeable in adulthood. Thus, teachers have contact with persons in their childhood years when they are more readily willing to change their behavior.

In a teacher's room, "where teacher support and involvement is at a high level, students will be more motivated toward self-improvement, academic success, and enjoyment in learning" (Ballantine, 1983, p. 188). Teachers tend to give more support to and to get more involved with children in the early grades than they do in the later school years. According to a study by Benham, Gilsen, and Oakes (1980):

> By the senior high school level, the frequency of teacher praise, encouragement, connection with guidance, and positive interaction with students had dropped by nearly 50 percent from the number of observed occurrences at the early elementary level. (p. 539)

All of this discussion points to the need to humanize the high schools and to let the students know the teacher cares about them. The tendency to teach subjects and not students is present at the high-school level, but this can all be overcome. If the students in your classes don't perceive you as a caring person, despite how much you know your subject, their academic achievement is bound to be affected.

The climate in the classroom is partially determined by the verbal and the nonverbal interactions that go on in the room. A significant study by Flanders (Amidon and Flanders, 1971) showed that student performance and learning are greatest when teacher influence is indirect. Flanders found that teacher talk, which is a direct influence, takes up 80 percent of class time. A teacher is more effective when he or she indirectly influences the class by accepting their feelings, praises or encourages them, accepts or uses ideas of students, or asks questions of students. A teacher is less effective when he or she directly influences the class by lecturing to them, gives directions, criticizes, or justifies authority. Teacher talk is not bad, but it should be used with more discretion. The Flanders scale also points out other things that teachers should be aware of pertaining to classroom interactions, such as the importance of student talk, silence, and confusion. Teachers either in service or in training can practice using Flanders's Interaction Analysis (see Table 8-2).

Table 8–2   Summary of Flanders's Categories for Interaction Analysis[a]

Teacher Talk	**Indirect Influence**	1. *Accepts feeling:* Accepts and clarifies the feeling tone of the students in a nonthreatening manner. Feelings may be positive or negative. Predicting and recalling feelings are included. 2. *Praises or encourages:* Praises or encourages student action or behavior. Jokes that release tension, not at the expense of another individual, nodding head or saying "uhhuh?" or "go on" are included. 3. *Accepts or uses ideas of student:* Clarifying, building, or developing ideas or suggestions by a student. As teacher brings more of his own ideas into play, shift to category five. 4. *Asks questions:* Asking a question about content or procedure with the intent that a student answer.
	Direct Influence	5. *Lectures:* Giving facts or opinions about content or procedure; expressing his own idea; asking rhetorical questions. 6. *Gives directions:* Directions, commands, or orders with which a student is expected to comply. 7. *Criticizes or justifies authority:* Statements intended to change student behavior from nonacceptable to acceptable pattern; bawling someone out; stating why the teacher is doing what he is doing; extreme self-reference.
Student Talk		8. *Student talk-response:* Talk by students in response to teacher. Teacher initiates the contact or solicits student statement. 9. *Student talk-initiation:* Talk by students, which they initiate. If "calling on" student is only to indicate who may talk next, observer must decide whether student wanted to talk. If he did, use this category.
		10. *Silence or confusion:* Pauses, short periods of silence, and periods of confusion in which communication cannot be understood by the observer.

[a]No scale is implied by these numbers. Each number is classificatory; it designates a particular kind of communication event. To write these numbers down during observation is to enumerate—not to judge a position on a scale.
Source: Amidon, E. J. & Flanders, N. A. (1971). *The role of the teacher in the classroom.* Minneapolis, MN: Paul S. Amidon and Associates, p. 14.

Open, flexible, and democratic classrooms stress the affective or emotional growth of students (Ballantine, 1983, p. 191). In this type of classroom, there is less chance for a child to become isolated and neglected by either the group or the teacher. When classes are run by an authority-centered teacher, the students tend to become more passive because they know that they will be listening most of the time, and they are less likely to answer questions or make decisions.

These are just a few parts of the hidden curriculum, but we have mentioned many facets of the hidden curriculum in other sections of the text. Still other parts of the hidden curriculum will be discussed in more detail in your methods classes. Some other areas that pertain to the hidden curriculum are seating arrangements for classes, the physical condition of the classrooms, the peer-group influence, the whole area of power dynamics, and the teacher's personality and background.

Why Do We Need a More Globally Based Curriculum?

Why Become More Global?

Our nation views itself as a member of the world community, but we have not learned those behaviors and attitudes that are appropriate for achieving the common goals of that community (*Global Perspective for Teacher Education*, 1983, p. 3). This section on the global curriculum relates to the short-term and long-term need to develop a curriculum that is more global in its perspective and a lot less individualistic and self-serving, as our school curriculum has been in the past. In just one area, foreign languages, we lag far behind other developed nations of the world. In 1979, the President's Commission on Foreign Language and International Studies documented Americans' scandalous incompetence in foreign languages and their widespread ignorance of other cultures (Cortés, 1983). It is not uncommon in most European countries to find young people speaking two languages besides their own native language. It would appear that a first step in any global education program would be to upgrade and accelerate the teaching of other languages.

Technology and all of its manifestations have caused the world to shrink. We are now able to circle the globe in little more than an hour in a spacecraft, and we can talk to nearly anyone in the world almost immediately. Unfortunately, our concept of human dignity and the commonality of all people has not moved along at the same rate. A sign that we are not moving toward greater understanding of human dignity is that we still hear people pass conflicts off by saying that there will always be wars, and that there will always be poor and hungry people. It appears that when people make these irrational statements, they feel relieved of the responsibility to improve the

Global awareness is essential to today's children. (*Photo by Axler.*)

situation. In the minds of the authors of this text, global education is the branch of the curriculum whose purpose it is to improve our understanding of each other throughout the world.

The AACTE

The American Association of Colleges for Teacher Education (AACTE) is very interested in global education in the training of teachers. They feel that global education ought to deal with issues and problems that affect large numbers of persons and with keeping in mind that all humans share common needs and cannot pursue their destinies in isolation (*Global Perspective for Teacher Education*, 1983, p. 2). The AACTE recommends going about global education in six different areas of study. The first is *perspective-consciousness*, in which one learns that his or her own perspective of the world may not be universally shared by others, and that all worldviews are influenced by social conditions. The second area involves the study of *planet awareness*, which includes awareness of prevailing world conditions and developments, including emergent conditions and trends, such as population growth, migrations, economic conditions, resources and physical environments, political developments, science and technology, law, health, and intranation conflicts. The third area of study is *cross-cultural awareness*, the study of how our cultural practices compare to those of other countries around the globe. A fourth area is *global dynamics*, or the global impact of local economic and social patterns beyond their effect on individuals' lives. The fifth area of study is called *awareness of emergent human goals*, or goals that transcend national cultures and ideologies. One example would be the fact that most societies now accept empirical science as a way of gathering useful knowledge and of gaining technical control. Hybrid seeds developed through empirical science are now accepted universally throughout the world. Finally, the study of *ethical problems* in the global context has to do with the increased capacities we have for sensing, predicting, and manipulating global conditions. In order to teach all of the above areas effectively, we must develop in our teachers knowledge about the world and attitudes toward diversity and common human interests consistent with global realities (*Global Perspective for Teacher Education*, 1983, p. 3).

Global and Multiethnic Education

In the past few years, multiethnic and multicultural education has been on the increase. (Chapters 1 and 2 relate to these topics in more detail.) James A. Banks (1984; see the figure on page 000) created what he called the ethno-national model, which could be a part of any global curriculum. In Banks's model for linking ethnic studies and global education, he seemed to suggest that students can benefit from studying such topics as the effect of acid rain on the world environment or the effect of food production on world hunger from the perspective of different ethnic groups from other nations around the world. According to Banks (1984), "It is important to link ethnic studies and global education because they share several important goals and because the population of the United States is constantly being changed by the infusion of ethnic and immigrant groups from beyond its borders" (p. 15). We must learn to live in an ethnically diverse world as well as in an ethnically diverse country, and as teachers, we can help our students to be enriched by this cultural challenge.

One Global Topic: Energy

There are many topics that educators can focus on to help us better understand ourselves from a global perspective. We have chosen energy as a simple illustration of how important it is for all nations to see the necessity to work together rather than independently:

> Citizens in democracies must strive to elect officials who see the interdependence of nations and who want to protect the earth for future generations. Citizens of non-democratic nations must also do everything they can to influence their governments to take a global view as well. (Murphy, 1983, p. 1)

It is strange, but also human, that we Americans start getting concerned about energy only when it affects us directly. Most of us were most concerned when we had to line up for gasoline at the filling stations, or when we had to pay a lot more money to heat our homes. These were times when our country got concerned about our use of energy, and then the government speculated about the uses of energy and the use of alternative forms of energy. New ideas in the use of solar energy, wind-produced energy, and geothermal energy were introduced. Conservation of our petroleum supply and the possibility of becoming energy self-sufficient were introduced as ways of reducing the pressure of our dependence on foreign oil imports. One thing we could do was to build up our mass transportation system in order to reduce our dependence on the automobile, but this possible solution soon died away.

In the Global 2000 Report, it was estimated that the United States uses about 29 percent of the world's energy produced in a single year (Murphy, 1983, p. 4). Other industrialized countries use another 27 percent of the world's energy. The total for these two groups is 56 percent; thus, the developed countries use over half the energy produced each year. Also, in the Global 2000 Report, it was estimated that about 40,000 pounds of new mineral materials were required annually for each U.S. citizen in 1975. The mineral consumption report in 1975 included 7,650 pounds of petroleum and 5,200 pounds of coal. The same report estimated that the industrialized nations would use a still greater percentage of the world's energy output per year into 1990. The prospect that our country and the other industrialized countries could cut down on their per capita use of energy so that there would be a more even distribution throughout the world and a saving of these resources for future generations is an inviting solution to the world problem.

Another energy concern is the fact that the world will need to shift from petroleum to other sources of energy in the coming decades. The fact is that oil and natural gas will be depleted in a few years and that this easy-to-use and easy-to-transport form of energy will need to be replaced. The time needed for this transition will be about fifty years or more, and the key to this transition will be cooperation between nations. Starting to save on our use of fossil fuels would help in the transition period. As teachers, we need to urge our students to be concerned about this problem and mindful of the steps that the world must take in the transition period. Murphy (1983) stated:

> Within nations, the public may not understand the urgency of taking measures now, even though for the short-term there are no scarcities. At the international level we must overcome real differences, or perceived differences, or self-interest between groups of nations. (p. 4)

Global education offers many opportunities to enhance the curriculum and to make it much more relevant for the coming decades. Students must learn about other cultures and must learn other languages in order to cope with our ever-changing planet. The link between multiethnic studies and global studies offers obvious possibilities for future curricula. The day has come when our American children must relate to the poor peasant children of the world in new and different ways through the globally based curriculum. Topics like the world energy supply can be used to help give students the perspective consciousness of the world hoped for by the AACTE. Other important topics can be used to fulfill the other six areas of global study suggested by the AACTE. Finally, in summarizing the importance of the global curriculum for students, Johnson and Benegar (1981) stated:

> Today's students will live most of their lives in the 21st century in an increasingly interdependent world. The very survival of "spaceship Earth," and certainly the quality of life experienced by its inhabitants, will depend on the extent to which our young people develop the ability to think, feel, and act from a perspective that is global rather than narrowly personal, national, or regional. (p. viii)

What Does John Goodlad Say About Schooling in America?

Goodlad's (1984) study of schooling in the United States was motivated by the lack of good, scientifically collected data on schools. Schooling in the United States is such a broad topic and our country is so diverse that finding and securing a representative random sample for study is almost impossible. Instead, Goodlad and his associates obtained a sample containing maximum diversity and representativeness. The eventually selected thirteen communities in seven sections of the country. Thirty-eight schools were studied, each differing from the others in several significant characteristics, such as location, size, student population characteristics, and family income. The study's data came as a result of sending twenty trained data collectors into each community, where they remained for a month to eventually produce data from 8,624 parents, 1,350 teachers, and 17,163 students. According to Goodlad, "No single study has made detailed observations of over 1,000 classrooms" (p. 18). Many of the questions asked were directed specifically toward the curriculum.

The first concern of the study is related to lack of intellectual development in the schools. Goodlad defined intellectual development as the ability to think rationally; the ability to use, evaluate, and accumulate knowledge; and a desire for further learning. The data showed little evidence that the instruction given in schools goes much beyond mere possession of information or remembering of facts. Rarely did these researchers find students trying to understand implications or exploring possible applications of the information presented. Basically, what they saw were students preoccupied at the knowledge level of Bloom's taxonomy.

Goodlad speculated that the reason children are learning at a lower cognitive level is that the precedent or model for most of the curriculum emerges from the dominant English-language arts and mathematics curricula. Our society sets a high value on mastery of English and mathematics, so how these areas are taught tends to influence how the rest of the curriculum is taught. Social studies and science classes are more often taught by teaching dry, inert facts rather than doing problem solving, visiting fields and ponds, or visiting the state legislature.

As a young man, one of the authors lived on a farm, experiencing many natural learning opportunities that most school-aged children growing up in the 1980s are not able to experience. A few of these farm experiences included caring for and selling chickens and eggs; planting, caring for, and harvesting crops; caring for animals; maintaining machinery; and solving practical problems. These experiences were very useful and stimulating to a young person; so much so, that he preferred being on the farm to being in the classroom. It appears that with modern technology such as computers, video equipment, transportation, laboratory equipment, and outside resources, today's teachers could plan more activities and problem-solving experiences under the auspices of the school.

The second concern relates to schools' not helping the individual toward personal development. At the lower elementary level, teachers appear to teach with the idea that the topics they introduce will aid personal development, but subject matter rather than the person seem to dominate as a child reaches the upper-elementary grades. Also, as students go upward in the grades teachers tend to concentrate their goals on the tests they give instead

Helping people builds self-esteem and fosters appreciation of others. *(Photo used by permission of the Indianapolis Public Schools.)*

of the personal development of the student. The "how" and "why" aspects of subject matter should be dealt with in order to help children with their personal development. As Kilpatrick recommended, we want to develop the "boy" and not the "corn" (Cremin, 1961, p. 218). Projects that cause children to think and to get actively involved in both mind and body would be good to accomplish personal development. For example, children who devise and carry out their own plan for involving senior citizens in their education are doing a lot toward developing their own character. Children who notice careless misuse of paper in their own classrooms and decide, with the help of their teacher, to save paper and encourage other classrooms to do the same have learned a valuable lesson in conservation and in acting on their own beliefs.

A third concern pertains to the best use of leisure time. Most schools provide for student participation in baseball, basketball, soccer, football, and volleyball, but when they graduate, students find themselves ill prepared for individual sports, like golf, tennis, skiing, badminton, and racketball. The Goodlad study revealed that schools have not changed much over the years, in that they neglect the physical skills needed to play individual sports. Is it possible that many schools' athletic programs influence, to a large degree, what is taught in physical education classes? No doubt, the encouragement and development of leisure-time activities is a neglected area.

A fourth concern is that schools neglect helping children with social development. In physical education classes, it appears that teamwork is fostered, but more often, the activities stress competition. Goodlad is in favor of anything designed to deliberately cultivate the values and skills of constructive social interaction and group accomplishment.

A fifth concern is the lack of development of such existential qualities as hope, courage, and love of humankind. These qualities are generally fostered through literature in myths, fairy tales, novels, drama, and poetry. The study showed that the early years of schooling appear to be shockingly devoid of fairy tales. These fairy tales have the ability to symbolize, through the use of dragons and heros, the challenges, problems, and opportunities that life presents. In the lower tracks of English courses, children did not seem to be studying poverty, disease, violence, and prejudice in some of the good literature. Most English classes were repetitively preoccupied with the mechanics of usage.

A sixth concern is that the public is blaming the schools for *not* teaching exactly the things they seem to be preoccupied *with* teaching. The big criticism of schools in the 1980s is that they are not teaching the fundamentals, but according to Goodlad's study, fundamentals are what is being emphasized, to the neglect of the other areas of the curriculum. Could it be that neglect of the lively parts of the curriculum at the higher levels of the cognitive domain are making schools and schooling in general dull and uninteresting, thus causing a loss of interest in all parts of the curriculum? We all know that the fundamentals are important (these are generally known as the 3 Rs and spelling), but maybe the most neglected fundamentals are literature, social studies, and science.

Details of the complete study by John Goodlad and his associates is found in *A Place Called School* (1984), which contains some valuable current information on the state of schooling and education in America.

How Does One Evaluate the Curriculum?

The curriculum needs to be evaluated, and changes or adjustments need to be made on a regular basis. Just as any rational person evaluates her or his own behavior, a school needs to evaluate its own curriculum. The curriculum is composed of many facets, some of which are difficult to measure, but schools must make the best effort possible to determine what successes and what failures their programs are having with their students.

Evaluation from Objectives

Probably the most used and most logical type of curriculum evaluation is one that is based on educational objectives written for the curriculum before instruction actually begins. Ralph Tyler, in *Basic Principles of Curriculum and Instruction* (1974), wrote, "The process of evaluation is essentially the process of determining to what extent the educational objectives are actually being realized by the program of curriculum and instruction" (p. 106). Tyler wrote that two important aspects of evaluation need to be examined. First, if we are actually looking for changes of behavior in individuals after they have been exposed to the curriculum, then we are looking for change not only right after students have had a particular block of instruction, but we are also interested in more long-term effects on individuals. Tyler also stated how important it is to know where a student is at the beginning of instruction so that changes due to instruction can be noted at the conclusion. In order to assess the degree of permanence of learning, the student needs to be evaluated at some time in the future. Some schools have a yearly evaluation of their students as they move through school, and schools often use follow-up studies to check on their graduates.

Using this objectives-based curriculum model puts emphasis on the proper statement of the objectives at the outset. The evaluation of the curriculum tells one how well the objectives have met the original plan and suggests modifications that are needed. One of the problems with this evaluative approach is that the test influences the objectives rather than the other way around. The pressure that college entrance examinations place on students to do well has caused and is causing adjustments in the objectives being taught. The real problem is that these new objectives, shaped by the testing services, often do not match the real needs of the students.

Evaluation Without Prespecified Objectives

A more progressive way of looking at the learning process involves getting the learner, with the assistance of the teacher, to come up with his or her own objectives. If teachers use a format like this for teaching, with no prespecified objectives, the evaluation must be handled differently from that used for teaching from prespecified objectives. Some school subjects lend themselves better to this type of evaluative format.

Teaching students about such controversial issues as peace and war, sex education, and race relations involves discussions of differing values and judgments. Teachers teaching these areas in the curriculum would be defeating their own purpose if they used prespecified objectives and expected specific outcomes. The expressive arts and the humanities, lend themselves to the kinds of objectives that develop as the course moves along. The best evaluation of this type of curriculum seems to be an ongoing monitoring of the class or the project, with a constant review of the aims so that changes can be recommended to better the curriculum. Certainly, devising specific test questions to get at certain cognitive learning would not satisfy the needs of such a curriculum. Interviews with students, the evaluation of specific projects completed, and other less formal methods of evaluation would work best.

Evaluation of a Curriculum Experiment

There are many evaluative designs that schools can use, but the true experimental design should be used whenever possible. The experimental design is generally used to measure the results of a curriculum innovation, and it is relatively free from error. Doll (1978) described how the experimental design works:

> The pupils involved in the experiment and the pupils in a control group are randomized—or randomly divided—and the teachers are selected for their similarities according to established criteria. Randomization is meant to decrease error, but it is notably difficult to achieve. After randomization, the "experimental pupils" are given the special curriculum treatment prescribed in the terms of the project while the control group receives no special treatment, continuing with the customary subject matter content and educational practices. Then, evaluation of specific learning outcomes and other outcomes is conducted for both experimental and control groups by using the same evaluation strategies and instruments for both groups. Whenever the true experimental method can be utilized, it should be selected because of its relative freedom from error and because of the confidence evaluators usually place in it. (pp. 452–453)

The experimental technique would be a good test of innovations such as new curricula in math, science, social studies, and other specific areas. The control groups would be those classes not involved in the experiment.

Standards of Achievement

When certain tests are used to evaluate individuals, the logical question is: Against what standards are they being measured? *Norm-referenced testing* is testing that measures a student against standards of achievement that have been arrived at by tests that have established national, state, or local norms. When schools want to compare their students' achievements to the achievements of other schools in the nation, the state, or locally, they use norm-referenced tests. Scores then are assigned to students on a *relative standard*, meaning that the scores are relative to the national, state, or local norms that have been established.

Another standard is the *absolute standard*, an example of which is the criterion specified by the learning objectives: "*Criterion-referenced* testing is the measure of how well each student attains the required level of comprehension and competence specified for each objective pursued" (Kemp, 1977, p. 93). It is important to keep in mind, with criterion-referenced testing, that the degree of achievement is independent of the performance of other students. Students who are measured in this way, against an absolute standard, must reach a satisfactory level of performance before they can go on to the next level of learning. The terms *criterion-referenced instruction* and *competency-based instruction* are used interchangeably. In this form of evaluation, the teachers and the schools must identify those competencies that are most desired, as well as the specific criteria for achieving them.

Mastery learning is another term that is used in connection with criterion-referenced instruction. When the criteria are set for accomplishing objectives and the students meet those criteria, they are said to have accomplished mastery learning. There is a concern about mastery learning that it places too much emphasis on minimum accomplishment. One method of getting around the minimum problem is to assign a grade of C or B to the minimum accomplishment and to leave the A grade for those who achieve more than the minimum. An example follows:

Objective: After taking biology and studying an ecology unit, the student will be able to answer correctly 8 out of 11 of the following items.

The questions are taken from Bloom's taxonomy (1956) at the application level:

After the number on the answer sheet corresponding to that preceding each of the following paired items, blacken space

A—if increase in the first of the things referred to is usually accompanied by increase in the second.

B—if increase in the first of the things referred to is usually accompanied by decrease in the second.

C—if increase in the first of the things referred to has no appreciable effect on the second.

1. Number of lemming in an Arctic habitat.
   Number of caribou in the same habitat.
2. Number of lichens in an Arctic habitat.
   Number of caribou in the same habitat.
3. Amount of carbonates dissolved in the water of a river.
   Number of clams in the river.
4. Temperature of the environment of a mammal.
   Body temperature of the mammal.
5. Compactness of the soil of a given area.
   Amount of water absorption by the soil after a heavy rain.
6. Frequency of fire in a given coniferous forest.
   Number of aspen trees in the forest.
7. Crop yield per acre of farmland cultivated in Illinois.
   Amount of soil nutrients per acre of farmland.
8. The altitude of the environment of an animal.
   Extent to which the circulating red blood cells of the animal undergo mitosis.
9. Extent of tree planting activity on forest land in the United States.
   Degree of water absorption by the soil per unit of area of the same land.
10. Amount of vegetation per square yard of soil.
    Amount of available nitrate salts in the same area of soil.
11. Amount of humus accumulated in sand during dune succession.
    Abundance of animal life in the area. (p. 134)

A student who answers 8 of the items would receive a grade of C, 9 items would be a B, and 10 or 11 items would be an A. This is an example of mastery learning.

Standards of achievement are based on *relative* standards and *absolute* standards. When schools or teachers use either type of standard, the results will give them feedback about how successful their program or teaching has been. Analysis of the test results will lead them to either change their curriculum or be satisfied with what they have now.

Evaluation of the curriculum is a difficult process because it must take into consideration all aspects of the curriculum. Testing objectives for which the criteria are spelled out works very well for math or science, but for art and humanities, another type of evaluation is needed. If you are evaluating objectives, they should be written with certain students in mind, and not to comply with an outside test. The fact is that outside tests, such as the Scholastic Apptitude Tests, often dictate the curriculum. The purpose of an evaluation of the curriculum is to check out changes in the behavior of students that result from instruction. This is the reason that objectives are sometimes referred to as *behavioral objectives*.

Summary

The curriculum is difficult to define and even experts do not agree on any one definition. Historically, many significant contributions have been made to curriculum development that are still used today. Some goals of curriculum development have been presented for review.

In considering what should be included in the curriculum, many groups have input—parents, school boards, state school officials, members of the U.S. Congress—but often fail to consider the special needs of one group: the students. Psychological factors that should be considered are the students' cognitive and moral development, and their need for love and attention. Organizing the curriculum into elementary schools, middle or junior high schools, and high schools allows each school to meet the age needs of its students. The concepts of nongraded classes and team teaching give greater emphasis to the special needs of each child. Positive parental attitudes regarding the school curriculum have a very favorable influence on the child's perception of the curriculum. The learning disabled deserve special attention in curriculum planning, and recent studies are discovering better ways to meet the needs of this group.

Teachers should be aware of the hidden curriculum in their classrooms. Each student's self-concept, the social structure of the school, the values of the staff toward education, and the interactions of teacher and student are parts of the hidden curriculum. The curriculum must become more global in outlook, and must continue to include ethnic studies. Goodlad's extensive study offers several concerns that schools' curriculum plans should address. Evaluating the curriculum must consider all aspects of the curriculum.

Questions

1. After reading the three definitions of curriculum, write your own composite definition.
2. How did the three significant publications appearing after 1960 differ from the top ten that came before 1960? What notable events may have caused this difference?
3. In the 1980s, should there be ten, fifteen, or twenty cardinal principles instead of the original seven? If so, what would your nominations be?
4. In what direction did John Dewey influence the curriculum? Give an example.
5. Why have we not changed our curriculum to conform to the ideas and teachings of A. S. Neill and Alvin Toffler?
6. Who are some other groups and people who influence the curriculum? Is all of this influence on the curriculum best for the educational growth of our children?

7. What are some of the psychological factors that affect how we build a curriculum?
8. Do you agree with Ashley Montagu, who wrote, "The equal treatment of unequals is the most unequal way of dealing with human beings ever devised"? Why?
9. Why is *flexibility* a term that is not very descriptive of modern-day high schools?
10. What is the difference between dyslexia and dysgraphia?
11. What kinds of people have learning disabilities?
12. Describe the hidden curriculum. How can you as a teacher maximize learning by keeping in mind and being knowledgeable about the hidden curriculum?
13. List five significant reasons why our curriculum should have a more global base.
14. Name five areas of curriculum concern specified by John Goodlad, and suggest five possible solutions.
15. Distinguish the differences between evaluation from objectives and evaluation without prespecified objectives.
16. What is mastery learning? How does one get around the minimum accomplishment problem?
17. Why is a teacher said to play God when he or she evaluates on an absolute standard?

Activities for Unit IV

1. Choose one of the top ten writings that have influenced the curriculum, research it in detail, and draw your own conclusions about its lasting value and contribution. Report your findings to the class.
2. The authors have raised some questions relating to the practice of the original *Seven Cardinal Principles* of education. Answer each of these questions and propose a curricular answer to each question.
3. Try Alfred North Whitehead's idea of surveying a small district and comparing it to another district. Involve the whole class in this project.
4. After observing a lesson being taught in school, analyze whether it was psychologically sound in terms of the findings of the works of Piaget, Kohlberg, or Watson?
5. Plan a minilesson in your content area, keeping in mind the developmental stage of most of the children in the class. Before presenting the lesson to the children, have three or more of your peers assess its developmental level.
6. Research the pros and cons of the homogeneous and heterogeneous grouping of students. Report your findings to the class.
7. Describe how the modern-day high school can be made more flexible to best accomplish the needs of serious students. This could be a group or

class project. Flexible scheduling, nongradedness, and team teaching may be a good place to start.

8. Read an article that relates to how parents influence the curriculum in our schools. Summarize the article and share your findings with the class.

9. Plan a lesson for a class in which you will encounter exploratory experiences, involving the positive use of TV. Assign a program for the students to watch, and plan follow-up activities for them to do the next day. TV documentaries would be good for this purpose.

10. With the permission of the principal, the teacher, and the child, do a case study of a learning-disabled child. After doing the study, make some recommendations about the best curriculum and technique to use with this child.

11. Speculate on why teachers are more effective using an indirect influence rather than a direct influence in their teaching style, according to Flanders.

12. Take the content area that you are being trained to teach and make some global objectives for your future classes. Examples for science:
    a. Make a list of the major scientific discoveries around the world and the people who made them.
    b. Examine why fewer scientific discoveries are made in undeveloped countries. What are some of the reasons behind this lack of scientific development? What would improve the situation?

13. Examine a test that has norm references. Find out how the test manufacturer arrived at the norms used in the test.

LEGAL ELEMENTS OF EDUCATION

Basic Legal Concepts for the Teacher

OBJECTIVES

After reading Chapter 9, the student will be able to:

Define written versus common law, civil versus criminal law, and key items within the law.

Distinguish between the concept of being legally right and morally right in a profession such as teaching.

Identify and delineate the functions of the various courts in the federal court system.

Understand the state court structure, the duties of state courts, and state procedures.

Articulate the legal powers of the local, state, and federal governments in regard to education.

Introduction

Our society has obviously become more law-conscious since the mid-1960s. Although this consciousness has both positive and negative aspects, members of the legal profession are overwhelmingly of the opinion that a society based on the rule of law is vastly preferable to one that is not.

The number of lawsuits involving schools and teachers has increased also. One reason is quite obvious: More and more people are becoming aware of the "law" and are more quickly turning to courts when disagreements arise.

In view of such a change, prospective teachers need some knowledge of the law: what it is, how it is made, the court system that interprets and helps make it, its relationship to ethical behavior, and how it upholds and helps to define both their rights and their responsibilities.

Because of their close contacts with and responsibility for large numbers of children, teachers have a greater chance to be involved in legal problems than most other people in society. That is not a sufficient reason to propose that prospective teachers undergo rigorous training in the study of law, however. A teacher cannot effectively act as an attorney. But it would be well for her or him to acquire enough information about the legal aspects of teaching so that she or he can develop an *awareness* of them. Without awareness, a person can do little or nothing about a developing situation until it is too late. The major purpose of this chapter on legal concepts, then, is to help prospective teachers to learn about, and thus to have the opportunity to become aware of, their rights, responsibilities, and possible liabilities.

All people, with rare exceptions, live with other people. It is virtually impossible to isolate oneself in the world today, and it will become increasingly difficult to do in the future. Thus, from birth to death, the actions of any one person affect other people. Such actions require some kind of rules that regulate the behavior of people for the purpose of achieving some measure of justice and order in society.

These rules, when accepted for a period of time by organized groups, become laws. In less sophisticated groups, they become established through long-accepted custom or tradition, or by the decree of the ruler; in more advanced cultures, they are adopted by established law-making bodies, such as legislatures, or result from the decisions handed down by law courts.

In short, law is needed to help create a society that will function on the basis of commonly accepted rules so that the needs of the majority of its members will best be served. It is the task of the legal profession, the government (especially the judicial branch), the press, the schools, and, of course, the majority of the citizens of each country to ensure the orderly operation of the laws so that the greatest amount of freedom for the individual is preserved. The United States is a society based on law, and it is hoped that one day the entire world will accept law as the basis for individual and national actions.

Sources of the Law

There are two major sources of the law in this country. The first source is called *legislative* or *written law* because it results from legislative action. The term *legislation* is frequently considered synonymous with *statute,* but in the broadest sense, legislation may include all law that originates in an official body having the power to make general rules. Thus, the written law may be of various types. There are constitutions, both state and federal; there are statutes, passed by the U.S. Congress and by each of the state legislatures; there are executive orders issued by the U.S. president and by state governors; there are rules and regulations issued by federal and state administrative officials and agencies; and finally, there are codes and ordinances of local governmental units such as cities and towns.

The second source of law, called *common* or *case law,* is the decisions handed down by law courts and administrative agencies. It is sometimes referred to as *unwritten law,* but that term is somewhat misleading because the decisions of the most important courts and agencies are written and officially published. In fact, the volumes of "unwritten" or common law far outnumber the volumes of written law.

The United States borrowed a great deal from the English, particularly in the field of common law. Those legal concepts became a part of the law in nearly every state, and many court decisions today are based, at least in part, on decisions made in English courts years ago.

Those two major sources, or forms, of law are definitely interrelated. When a legislative body passes a statute, the courts may be called on to decide whether it is constitutional, or whether it has been properly applied. With respect to the highest source of law in this country, the U.S. Constitution, the federal courts are frequently asked to interpret parts of it. The sections most closely related to education that have most frequently come up for court interpretation are the First, Fourth, and Fourteenth Amendments. The First Amendment has been involved in those cases concerned with prayer and Bible reading in public school classrooms; the Fourth Amendment involves search and seizure; and racial segregation and due process cases comprise a sizable portion of the court actions involving the Fourteenth Amendment.

On the other hand, the common law may be changed by the written law. A statute passed by a legislative body will supersede a court decision as long as the statute violates no constitutional provision. Likewise, a change in the Constitution can change the common law. The attempts to change the First Amendment to the U.S. Constitution for the purpose of nullifying the U.S.

Supreme Court decisions on prayer and Bible reading in public school class-rooms are a good example.

Thus, the law, as it operates in this country today, springs from legislative bodies, from administrative officials and agencies, and from the courts. When settling disputes between individual persons or groups, judges are called on first to interpret any written law that may be applicable to the case, and when there is no controlling legislation, the common law is then examined.

This discussion leads directly into the concept of the *precedent*. Justice requires that the parties to court trials (litigants) be treated alike when the situations are similar. Thus, in cases that deal with the saying of prayers in the public schools, a judge feels bound to follow the common law in a case previously decided by a higher court. The decisions made by the highest court, then, have become "precedents" for the lower courts to follow in cases that are similar. Adherence to precedents results in stability and predictability in the law. Sometimes, however, a lower court may refuse to follow precedents when the judge believes that the legal principle involved has no further usefulness.

The law is divided into two basic categories, called *criminal law* and *civil law*. When legal action is taken against someone who has violated a law of the state for which there is usually a prescribed penalty, the violator is charged with a crime and is prosecuted in the name of the government or the people. In other words, if the violation of a rule is against the state or society as a whole, the act is a criminal one. Thus, if one man murders another, he has violated a law of the State, and in so doing, he has committed a crime.

A civil action results from an infringement on, or attempts to enforce, the personal rights of people. Whereas criminal law refers to acts against the state or society as a whole, civil law deals with the relationships of people to each other. Most civil actions concern contract rights, or tort liability. Contracts result from agreements made between two parties, and torts result from injury or damage to one's person or property caused by another. Both contracts and torts are discussed more fully in Chapter 10.

The Law and Ethical Behavior

Teacher preparation programs today provide future teachers with more information about their legal rights and responsibilities than ever before. But such knowledge, by itself, is not enough. Teachers need to know just as much about their "ethical" rights and responsibilities. Sadly, the law has often been used as an excuse to avoid one's ethical duties. For this reason, an understanding of the relationship between legal and ethical responsibilities becomes important.

One of our American traditions is that we are, in the main, a law-abiding nation. That's a high-sounding phrase. The law, remember, refers to the level of behavior that is the minimum we can accept from each other and still survive as a community. Merely to say that a group is law-abiding is saying very little. Those claiming membership in a profession need to act at a level considerably above the legal minimum. That higher level is determined by ethical standards.

Contemporary dictionaries define *ethics* as the science that relates the actions of human beings to their moral qualities and that studies the moral obligations of individuals in society. Ethics and morals are closely related. The term *moral* pertains to character, conduct, intention, and social relations. *Black's Law Dictionary* relates it to the "general principles of right conduct" (Black, 1979, p. 909).

Teachers observe ethics through their actions toward other human beings. The rules of ethics provide the guidelines for "right action." Such guides to conduct are especially needed by teachers because they constantly come into direct contact with other persons and use predominately mental and intellectual skills rather than physical or manual ones. The problems of defining professional "right conduct" rests with the professional group. Some groups have found effective means of adopting and implementing codes of ethics, and others as yet have not.

The teaching profession, acting through the National Education Association (NEA), first adopted a code of ethics in 1929 and has amended it a number of times, the last time in 1975. This code is a clear and concise statement covering the commitments of the professional educator to his or her students, community, and profession, and to proper employment prac-

Ethical behavior or "right conduct" on the part of teachers goes beyond the legal minimum as they influence the lives of the children they teach. *(Photo by Axler.)*

tices. To perform in an ethical manner, a teacher must know the code of ethics of the profession. Without knowing it, the teacher will never be certain that he or she is acting right. (See the Appendix for the NEA "Code of Ethics" and the "Bill of Rights" of the AFT).

One facet of the relationship between the law and ethics is that the law is based to a great extent on moral and ethical considerations. The law, however, doesn't go far enough to ensure the high standards required of a profession, particularly one that is as much involved with human interrelationships as the teaching profession is. Thus, not only may teachers need to know and conform to the law to do the kind of job required of them, but they must have an adequate understanding of the ethical aspect of their actions as well.

Teachers are often "examples" to their students. A teacher who conforms to the "legal minimum" but who ignores the sometimes obvious ethical requirements expected of him or her, can expect no better from his or her students. Certainly, this is no way for a profession to contribute to the improvement of society.

The American Court System

Because the common law is derived from court decisions, and because the written law is subject to interpretation by the courts, it will help the student becoming acquainted with the law for the first time to understand the basic structure of the court system in the United States.

There are actually two separate court systems, the federal and the state. The federal courts operate in every state and territory, side by side with the courts of each individual state. But the authority of the two court systems differs. Federal courts handle only those cases that involve a federal question, that is, cases that involve the U.S. Constitution, federal statutes and administrative rules, or disputes between the states. The state courts usually hear all other cases. Because the demand by litigants to have their cases heard in a federal court is very heavy, Congress has imposed greater and greater limitations on the jurisdiction of the federal courts. For example, the great majority of civil cases that involved citizens of more than one state used to be tried in federal court. It was felt that if such cases were brought in a state court, the litigant who was also a citizen of the state in which the court was sitting would receive more favorable treatment. This theory appears to be no longer valid, so where once such cases could be brought into federal court if an amount of only $1,500 was involved, today the amount must exceed $10,000, exclusive of interest and court costs. Thus, civil cases involving parties in two or more states and less than $10,000 must usually be brought into a state court, unless a federal constitutional or statutory question is involved.

The Federal Court Structure

In its general form, the federal court system is simple to describe and understand. It is a three-tiered system. On the bottom tier is the U.S. district court. It is a court of only "original jurisdiction," or simply a trial court. *Original jurisdiction* refers to the first hearing of a dispute in court as contrasted to a second or third hearing, called an *appeal*. Appeals, of course, go to a higher court.

There are eighty-six federal district courts, covering all states and territories. The State of Georgia, for example, has three federal district courts. There may be more than one judge in a district court. From time to time, Congress authorizes additional judges for the federal district courts, but the number of districts has been left unchanged. The appointment of judges to district courts is intended to be in proportion to the caseload in each district.

In the middle of the federal court system sit the U.S. courts of appeal. When a case has been tried in the court of original jurisdiction (the federal district court), the loser has a right to appeal the case to a higher court. Except in very special cases, the appeal will be to the U.S. court of appeals of the "circuit" in which the district court is located.

There are twelve appellate circuits serving all fifty states, the District of Columbia, Puerto Rico, and the territories of Guam, the Virgin Islands, and the Canal Zone. For example, the Fifth Circuit Court of Appeals covers the states of Texas, Louisiana, Mississippi, and the Canal Zone. This means that all cases appealed from the federal district courts located within these states

Housing the nation's highest court, the Supreme Court Building is the site of many decisions affecting public education. *(Photo courtesy of the Library of Congress.)*

and the Canal Zone are usually heard by the Fifth Circuit Court of Appeals. It is important to remember that these courts are solely courts of review, or of appeals; they have no original jurisdiction.

At the very top of the federal court system stands the U.S. Supreme Court. It has both original and appellate jurisdiction, although it rarely exercises the former. Cases usually go to the Supreme Court on review. However, because it is the highest court in the land, and because one court can physically accomplish only so much, cases do not go to the Supreme Court as a matter of right. The court uses its discretion to decide which of the approximately five thousand cases that are appealed to it each year will be heard. The Court decides to hear a case only if the issue presented is of broad and general interest to the nation's welfare. As a result, the Supreme Court actually handles only about 250 cases per year and issues written opinions on only 75–100 of them. The opinions of the Supreme Court are read each Monday during its eight-month term from October to May. They are published unofficially in the *United States Law Week* magazine and some newspapers, notably the *New York Times*.

Because there is no higher court in the nation, the decisions of the U.S. Supreme Court are final. However, there are three ways by which the decisions, or the effects of them, can be changed. First, the Court may reverse itself, just as it did in the flag salute case in 1943 or in the famous "end-of-segregation" case in 1954, which reversed the "separate-but-equal" doctrine established by the Supreme Court in 1896. Second, the Constitution can be amended. There has been some dissatisfaction with the Court's decisions on the saying of prayers and the reading of Bible verses in public school classrooms. Because of the dissatisfaction, there has been some demand for a change in the wording of the First Amendment to the Constitution, which would more than likely cause the Court to interpret it differently.

Third, decisions of the Supreme Court can be changed by act of Congress. For example, when a statute has been ruled unconstitutional, or its application results in consequences different than those forseen when it was originally passed, Congress may correct the deficiencies in it and pass a new statute that will have the desired effects.

The U.S. Supreme Court has been accused of "legislating" or of "making law" through its decisions. The Constitution, however, is so vague that judges are forced to make decisions on bases other than strict constitutional law. A member of Congress, early in our history as a republic, had this to say: "We [Congress] are not the expositors of the Constitution. The Judges are the expositors of the Constitution and acts of Congress. Our exposition, therefore, would be subject to their revisal. The Judiciary may disagree with us and undo what all our efforts have labored to accomplish" ("The Supreme Court, The Limits That Create Liberty and The Liberty That Creates Limits," 1964, p. 48).

This statement implies that the Court should act as a sort of superlegislature, and Justice James C. McReynolds once declared that it had to act that

Three Ways in which U.S. Supreme Court Decisions can be Changed

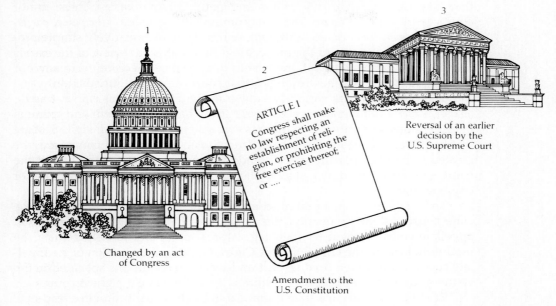

1

Changed by an act
of Congress

2

ARTICLE I
Congress shall make
no law respecting an
establishment of reli-
gion, or prohibiting the
free exercise thereof;
or ....

Amendment to the
U.S. Constitution

3

Reversal of an earlier
decision by the
U.S. Supreme Court

way. Chief Justice William Howard Taft agreed and conceived of the Court as being just that. He said that the Justices "should not live in a political vacuum. The Court should soften the impact of popular passions and restrain the impulsive desires of the majority" ("The Supreme Court . . . , 1964, p. 49).

Of the three kinds of federal courts, only the Supreme Court was established by constitutional mandate. Except for the power to change the number of justices, to approve the U.S. president's appointments, to impeach, and to set salaries, Congress has no power over the Supreme Court. However, it is up to Congress to provide for the rest of the federal court system, and this it did beginning with the Judiciary Act of 1789. The three-tiered system as we now have it was brought about by the enactment of the Judicial Code in 1911. Since 1789, numerous special courts have been established by Congress (e.g., the U.S. Court of Claims, the U.S. Customs Court, and the U.S. Court of Customs and Patent Appeals), but these will not be discussed here.

The State Court Structure

The state court systems resemble the federal system in that they, too, are at least three-tiered; that is, there are trial courts, courts of appeal, and one court of ultimate review, usually called a supreme court,* in each state. In addition

*Called the Supreme Court of Errors in Connecticut; the Supreme Judicial Court in Maine and Massachusetts; the Court of Appeals in Kentucky, Maryland, and New York; and the Civil Court of Appeals in Texas.

to the three tiers, nearly every state has a number of inferior or minor courts that take care of small civil claims and petty criminal cases. These minor courts go by various names, the most common being *justice of the peace, magistrate, municipal, small claims,* and *traffic courts.* They use relatively simple procedures and do not record the proceedings of a trial, so a review of the case is impossible. Consequently, if one wishes to appeal the decision from a minor court, there must be a new trial in a trial court of original jurisdiction.

The trial courts are variously known in the fifty states as *circuit, county, district, superior,* and *common pleas courts.* They handle both civil and criminal cases, although in the more populous centers special criminal, civil, probate (for handling the estates of deceased persons), and juvenile courts may be created to handle only the special kind of case designated by the title of the court. The area served by a state trial court is generally defined by county or city boundaries.

The losing party in a trial court may appeal to the next highest tier in the state court system. Generally, this is the appellate court. Most states had appellate courts created by their legislatures, originally to help reduce the mounting load on the U.S. Supreme Court. Usually, the decision of an appellate court is considered final, except under certain conditions specified in the statutes, when the appeal may continue up to the state's highest court.

The highest court in a state is mandated by the constitution in every state except New Hampshire, where the legislature has created one by statute. These courts have statewide jurisdiction. They generally hear cases that fall into two broad categories: (1) the hearing of appeals from lower courts on questions of the constitutionality of statutes and (2) the hearing of appeals on questions of the proper application of statutes to individual situations. The decision of this court is final when only the state constitution and state statutes are involved.

It is important to remember that each state has complete control over its own court system, and that no two states have exactly the same system. However, the preceding paragraphs should have made clear that there are enough similarities among the fifty state systems so they can be described in general terms.

Court Procedure

Whenever there is disagreement over the legal rights of two or more parties, a lawsuit can develop. As explained previously, the legal action can be either a civil or a criminal one. Because teachers are not often involved in criminal cases, a civil action is followed here from beginning to end, in very broad terms.

The injured party, the *plaintiff,* first consults an attorney to determine the strength of his or her case. If the attorney believes that court action is desirable, she or he will prepare a summons and a complaint. *Summons* is the le-

The Appeal Process Between State and Federal Courts

Federal Courts

Court
reverses itself

Amendment
to the Constitution

Act of
Congress

Decisions
changed by

U.S. Supreme Court
Original and appellate jurisdiction

Original case
(seldom occurs)

U.S. Circuit
Court of Appeals
Twelve circuits

Appeal

Appeal

U.S. District Courts (86)
Trial Courts—original jurisdiction
Cases involving federal laws or litigants
from different states

Review

Review or Appeal

Court of
Claims

Customs
Court

U.S. Court of
Customs and
Patent Appeals

State Courts

State Supreme Court

Cases:
(1) Constitutionality of statutes
(2) Application of statutes.

Appeal

Appellate Court

Appeal

Local Courts (i.e, County Circuit
Courts, Superior Courts,
City Courts, etc.)
Trial courts—original jurisdiction
Civil and criminal cases

Probate
Court

Juvenile
Court

Special-Purpose Courts—No Appeal

Justice of
the Peace

Magistrate
Court

Municipal
Court

Small
Claims
Court

Traffic
Court

gal term used to describe the writ of process used to notify the person to be sued (the *defendant*) of the nature of the charge against him or her. The court gains jurisdiction over the case when the summons and the complaint are filed with it.

In many state courts, and in the federal courts, a preliminary trial conference is held in the judge's chambers to decide what issues exist and must be tried, and whether a compromise or out-of-court settlement can be reached. If the case is not settled at this pretrial conference, it is placed on the active trial calendar to be heard at the earliest possible time.

One or both of the parties may demand a jury, which for a civil action may be composed of from three to twelve persons. Prospective jurors may be challenged by the attorney of either party, and usually, the jury as finally composed is satisfactory to all concerned. If neither party wants a jury, the judge hears the case and renders the verdict alone.

In a well-run court, the judge goes to great lengths to make things clear for the jury. *Opening statements* are made by each party's attorney, outlining the facts that she or he hopes to prove. Witnesses can be brought to testify by both the defendant and the plaintiff. A witness for the plaintiff testifies on *direct examination* to questions from the plaintiff's attorney, and on *cross-examination* to questions from the defendant's attorney. When both sides have presented, or rebutted, all the evidence they desire, *closing* or *summarizing arguments* are heard from each attorney. The judge usually makes a *charge* to the jury just before they retire to the juryroom to try to reach a verdict. The charge is an explanation of exactly what points the jury must decide. A unanimous finding by the jurors is usually required, unless the parties stipulate to a finding by a stated majority of the jurors.

After the jury's verdict is known and all legal remedies with respect to the verdict have been ruled on, the original trial case is terminated. The losing party, if dissatisfied with the outcome in trial court, may then appeal to an appellate court. He or she becomes the *plaintiff-in-error,* or the appellant. The other party, the winner in trial court, becomes the *defendant-in-error,* the appellee, or the respondent. The appellate court reviews *questions of law* only; it generally accepts the *findings of fact* of the trial court. The appeals court may then either *affirm* the decision of the lower court or *reverse* the decision and order a new trial or remand (send back) the case to the trial court with specific instructions about future proceedings.

The States' Control of Education

The American system of education is unique. It is based on the daily operation of schools being carried out in the local districts. From the legal standpoint, education is controlled by the individual states. The national, or federal, government assumes the role of junior partner to the states and the local districts. This arrangement contrasts sharply with that of other countries, where the school systems are controlled by the national government, and the states and the local communities have only a small voice in educational decision-making.

There is no reference to education in the U.S. Constitution. This does not mean that the federal government has no power at all over education. What it does mean, though, is that because of this omission, the legal control of education resides mainly with the states. What power the federal government does have with respect to education comes about indirectly through court interpretation of the U.S. Constitution and federal statutes, and through the requirements that usually accompany federal aid programs, with which local districts and states must comply.

An understanding of the concept of governmental powers is important at this point. The federal government does not possess any inherent powers. Such powers as it possesses must be delegated to it by the Constitution of the United States. Furthermore, those powers must be expressly (explicitly) enumerated in the Constitution or are to be reasonably implied from those expressly granted.

The states, on the other hand, are said to possess plenary (full, complete, or absolute) powers. The word *plenary* is somewhat misleading because state powers are limited by two distinct factors. A state legislature has the power to do anything that (1) is not delegated to the federal government or that (2) is not denied to the states by some provision of the federal Constitution. This follows directly from provisions of the Tenth Amendment to the U.S. Constitution that say: "The powers not delegated to the United States by the Constitution, nor prohibited by it to the States, are reserved to the States respectively, or to the people."

The conclusion, then, is obvious. From the legal standpoint, the states, through their legislatures, control education in the United States. The phrase "Education is a state function" is commonly used to denote that fact.

The Relationship of the Federal Government to Education

Although the states control education, in legal theory at least, the federal government does have close relationships with the schools of this country. Because federal powers are limited to those delegated, we must look to the U.S. Constitution to see what powers do exist. The Constitution does not mention education, so it can be concluded that whatever powers the federal government does have with respect to education must be implied. The powers emanating from the Constitution that affect both the state and the federal governments can be categorized as (1) positive and (2) limiting. Positive powers enable the federal government to *create* programs for education, and the limiting powers provide only for limitations on the actions of both private individuals and governmental officials and agencies. These limitations are not necessarily negative, for most of them help to protect the constitutional rights of individuals.

As far as education is concerned, one positive power is possessed by the federal government. It is derived from the "general welfare" clause, Article I, Section 8, of the U.S. Constitution, which says, in part, "The Congress shall have power to lay and collect taxes, duties, imposts and excises, to pay the debts and provide for the common defense and general welfare of the United States. . . ." The U.S. Supreme Court has interpreted that clause to include education as part of the general welfare. Thus, the federal government may give financial aid to public schools and, at the same time, may create the programs for which the aid may be given. The federal government may also simply grant money to the states and leave the programs up to them. Although federal aid to education has never exceeded 10 percent of all public elementary- and secondary-school expenses, the fifty states together receive several billion dollars in federal funds annually. Federal funding of education seems to rise and fall in relation to the political climate and to national and world events.

In addition to the positive powers given to the federal government, the Constitution of the United States places certain limitations on the powers of government, both state and federal. One of those limitations is found in Article 1, Section 10, of the U.S. Constitution, which prohibits the state or federal governments from passing legislation that would impair their legal obligations resulting from contracts. This limitation with respect to education exists particularly in the areas of teacher tenure and retirement legislation. It prevents a state that creates legislation in which the wording clearly indicates that a contractual status was intended from backing out of its obligations, particularly by passing subsequent legislation with the intent of doing so.

A second limitation placed on state powers, and on the federal government itself, is found in the First Amendment: "Congress shall make no law respecting an establishment of religion, or prohibiting the free exercise thereof." This amendment was meant to keep church and state totally separate according to Supreme Court interpretations, with the state remaining completely neutral, neither aiding or prohibiting the exercise of any religious belief.

Some of the questions that have arisen in the courts out of the First Amendment have been in the areas of (1) allowing released time for religious instruction; (2) providing transportation, textbooks, and school lunches to parochial schools at public expense; (3) providing public money to church-supported schools; (4) saying prayers, allotting time for silent meditation,

This cartoon by Thomas Nast, illustrating the separation of church and state, originally appeared in *Harper's Weekly*, February 25, 1871. (*Courtesy of the Library of Congress.*)

observing sectarian religious festivals, and reading excerpts from the Bible; and (5) allowing public-school rooms to be used for student religious activities.

The Fourth Amendment has been the focal point of some interesting cases, especially in the last fifteen years. This amendment protects people from unreasonable search and seizure by agents of the government. Because the public schools are units of government, questions of legality have been raised over the search of lockers, the personal search of students, and the search of students' automobiles in school parking lots.

Other limitations on governmental powers are found in the Fourteenth Amendment. The first of these comes out of the clause that reads: "No state shall make or enforce any law which shall abridge the privileges and immunities of citizens of the United States." The importance of this clause is that it makes the First and Fifth Amendments, which by themselves are worded so as to apply only to federal laws, applicable to the states as well.

A second clause of the Fourteenth Amendment that limits the power of government with respect to education is the one that provides that "no state shall deprive any person of life, liberty or property without due process of law." Under this clause, the U.S. Supreme Court makes the final determination of what constitutes proper exercise of police power by the states. Police power is the right, even the duty, of the state to regulate individual rights in the interest of the whole group. This means that rights of person or property may be restricted to the extent that is reasonably necessary to promote public health, safety, morals and the general welfare. Thus, if any person believes that he or she has been unreasonably or unjustly deprived of his or her liberty or property by a state exercising its police power, an appeal may be carried to the U.S. Supreme Court under this due-process-of-law clause.

A good illustration of a state law passed as an exercise of police power and then challenged on the grounds that the state exceeded the limitations placed on it by the due-process clause of the Fourteenth Amendment occurred in Oregon. The state legislature passed a law in 1922 requiring all children between the ages of eight and sixteen to attend a public school. In effect, the law abolished private schools for children between those ages. The owner of a private school, an order of Catholic nuns, challenged the constitutionality of the law, contending that it violated the due-process clause. The Supreme Court of the United States agreed, holding that the law interfered with the liberty of parents in the upbringing and education of their children, and that it also deprived private schools of property without due process of law.

A third limitation on the powers of government contained in the Fourteenth Amendment is the clause that provides that "no state may deny to any person within its jurisdiction the equal protection of the laws." This means that no state may enforce legislation or may authorize administrative agencies to enforce rules and regulations that discriminate in favor of one class of citizens over another. Acting from an interpretation of this clause, the Supreme Court in 1954 ruled that racial discrimination in the public schools is unconstitutional (*Brown* v. *Board of Education of Topeka*, 1954). (This decision reversed earlier ones that upheld separate schools for different races as long as the facilities were substantially equal.)

Charges have been frequently made that the federal government, through its right to spend money for education and through the Supreme Court's power to interpret the federal Constitution, has already exerted undue control over education, and that federal control is bound to increase in the future unless the trend is reversed. Many persons refute the charges, contending that Congress has used great restraint to limit federal control in the financial aid programs it has sponsored, and that in its decisions, the Supreme Court has been primarily concerned with the rights of people. The controversy over federal control will probably remain with us for a long time, although a clear understanding of the legal relationships that exist between the federal government and education can help to make it an argument conducted along reasonable lines.

Education and Local Government

Even though education is primarily controlled by the state and, to some extent, by the federal government through financial aid and court decisions, it is viewed by most people as being a local operation. What makes this observation a true one is the fact that schools are organized by states into local districts. Local school boards are elected or appointed to make decisions of policy and to employ a full-time professional administrator, who, in turn, oversees the day-to-day operations of the schools within the district.

But a school district, although a local governmental corporation like a city or town, operates under a different set of rules from the legal standpoint. A city or town is incorporated by the state mainly for local purposes, interests, and advantages. It is given considerable legislative and regulatory powers by the state. The school district, on the other hand, is created to execute state policy. Whereas a city or town is considered a local corporation, the school district is considered a political or civil division of the state.

School board members are therefore state and not local officials. Even though they are elected locally or are appointed by mayors or city councils, they owe no allegiance to local civil officials in the management of the schools. Generally, being agents of the state, local school boards need not even conform to local city or town ordinances that conflict with their own powers or duties, unless specifically directed to do so by state statute.

A school corporation (the terms *school district* and *school corporation* are used synonymously here) has only limited powers. Just as the federal government is limited only to those powers expressly and impliedly delegated to it by the U.S. Constitution, so local school districts are limited to those powers expressly and impliedly delegated to them by the state legislature. In many states, the powers of local school boards are listed by statute, and the only leeway given is in the form of a general statement that allows the boards to "take such action as is necessary to promote the best interests of the schools." Even this statement is not as generous as it seems, for the courts have interpreted it so as to keep local school boards within the bounds intended by the legislature.

To be legal, any action by a school board must be taken during a legal meeting, which can be held if all members of the board have been given appropriate notice of the time and place of the meeting and a majority of them appear. A legal meeting can be held without the usual notice when all members of the board are present and agree to hold the meeting.

There are two kinds of school board meetings, regular and special. A regular meeting is one set by the board, usually when it organizes, for a specific day of each week, fortnight, or month. Once set, no further notice need be given the members, and official action may include any item of business. On the other hand, a special meeting requires some kind of formal notice, and legal action can be taken only on those subjects specifically mentioned in the notice. In order to take action, a quorum, which constitutes a simple majority of the total board, must be present.

It is important to note that a school board can take official action only as a corporate entity. As individuals, school board members have no more legal power over public schools than other citizens.

Summary

Over the past several decades, the teaching profession has been increasingly affected by the law. It has become more important, therefore, that teachers learn about the law: what it is, how it originates, how it changes, and how it affects their professional lives.

The bases of the written law are the federal and state constitutions; the statutes passed by federal, state, and local legislative bodies; and the rules and regulations adopted by regulatory and administrative agencies. The common law derives mainly from court decisions as they interpret the written laws and settle disputes over matters not covered by written law.

The law is divided into two basic categories, called *civil law* and *criminal law*. Criminal law covers acts against the state or society as a whole, and civil law deals with the relationships of people to each other. Most civil rights concern contract rights or tort liability.

The relationship between ethics and law is one of degree. Both are based on moral standards or what is right and just in a given situation. Law represents the "legal minimum," whereas ethics represents the higher level of conduct that society expects, and deserves, from professionals.

Knowing the structure and procedures of the American court system is necessary if one is to clearly understand school law. There are two court systems in the United States; the federal system and the state system. The federal court system includes the federal district courts, the circuit courts of appeal, and the U.S. Supreme Court. The state courts consist of local courts, appellate courts, and (in most states) supreme courts.

Because the federal government's powers are limited only to those delegated to it by the U.S. Constitution, and education is not covered there, the states have the greatest legal control over education. Local governments exist only at the pleasure of the state; thus, local school districts are state entities and are subject to state control.

Questions

1. Differentiate between criminal and civil law. Given some examples of court cases that would fall into each category.
2. How important it is for a profession such as teaching, to have a code of ethics? What is the relationship between law and ethics?
3. What is the relationship between federal and state courts in regard to school law decisions? Give some examples of cases that would be more likely to be settled at the state or federal level.
4. Differentiate between delegated and plenary powers, and explain which level of government would have each of these powers.
5. What limitations does the First Amendment of the U.S. Constitution place on the exercise of religion and free speech in the public schools? What specific issues or cases have resulted from this amendment?
6. How has the due-process clause of the Fourteenth Amendment affected public schools?

10

Teachers' Legal Rights and Responsibilities

OBJECTIVES

After reading Chapter 10, the student will be able to:
- Understand teachers' contractual and employment rights.
- Explain teachers' rights to organize and bargain collectively and to engage in political activity.
- Comprehend teachers' roles in handling and dealing with the rights and responsibilities of pupils.
- Appreciate the rights and responsibilities of teachers in disciplining students.
- Define the tort liability of teachers and describe situations in which teachers could be legally negligent.

Introduction

Teachers, like all other citizens, have legal rights. Along with those rights, however, come certain responsibilities. Because the teaching profession is charged by society with the important task of developing the intellectual capabilities of its citizens, including its future leaders, the responsibilities are especially crucial.

This chapter will present teachers' rights and responsibilities in four basic areas: (1) certification; (2) contracts; (3) control of students; and (4) tort liability. In addition, certain miscellaneous areas deemed important for teacher candidates to know will be introduced.

Teacher Certification

For entrance into a profession, a license or certificate is usually required. One of the major reasons for certification is to ensure the public a certain standard of performance by the members. To qualify for certification and for admission to the profession, an individual must meet the required qualifications, and these are usually of such a nature as to prepare one to perform adequately. One of the reasons that certificates are required of public school teachers in all states was stated clearly by the Indiana Supreme Court as far back as 1866, when it said: "It was intended by the requirement of a certificate . . . to guard against the squandering of a sacred public fund, upon persons assuming to teach without being capable of performing a teacher's duties" (*Harrison School Township* v. *Conrad*, 1866).

The teaching certificate is not a property right; that is, it is not the result of a contract between the state and the teacher. No absolute rights, such as guaranteed employment or tenure rights, are conferred by the certificate on the holder. Rather, the teaching certificate is a personal privilege granted by the state to an individual and may not be transferred, sold, or bartered to another person. Because the state has the power to issue certificates, it also has the power to revoke them. One who holds a license to teach does so at the pleasure of the issuing agency.

States vary in the causes for which a teaching certificate can be revoked. In some states, the causes are listed by statute; in other states, the statutes say nothing. Where the statutes do list the causes, only those listed can be used to revoke a certificate; any reasons not specifically enumerated in the statute does not constitute legal grounds for revocation. Many states legislate as grounds for revocation of a teacher's certificate such things as incompetency, intentional neglect of duty, or immorality.

It is customary for state legislatures to delegate the setting of requirements for teaching certificates to the state board of education. The state department of public instruction is usually assigned the administrative task of issuing the certificates. When questions arise, particularly over whether a certificate should be issued to a particular applicant, the state board of education settles the matter.

Increasingly, state boards of education are turning to the colleges that prepare teachers for recommendations to accompany the applications of graduates for teaching certificates. The objective is to involve the teacher-training institutions, as much as possible, in the certification process.

One of the more irritating hurdles that a teacher must face when moving from state to state is getting properly certified. No two states have exactly the same requirements, and all states require their own certificates. There are three ways in which a person properly prepared to teach in one state may secure the certificate of another state:

First, he or she can meet all the requirements as listed. This is done usually when a person builds his or her college program around those specific requirements. In other words, the student knew the requirements and then aimed to meet them from the beginning.

Second, he or she can secure a certificate through reciprocity. This means that the state in which he or she wants a certificate has an agreement with the state in which he or she currently holds one to reciprocate in granting certificates to each other's licensed teachers. These are usually bilateral agreements (involving only two states). However, one state may have reciprocity agreements with as many states as it desires.

Third, he or she can graduate from a college accredited by the National Council for the Accreditation of Teacher Education (NCATE). At one time, over half the states granted teaching certificates if any one of those accredited institutions would certify that a graduate had met the requirements for certification in the state in which the accredited institution was located and

In order to be certified, every prospective teacher must fulfill the licensing requirements of the state in which she or he wishes to teach. (Photo by Axler.)

Three Considerations for Teaching Approval in Other States

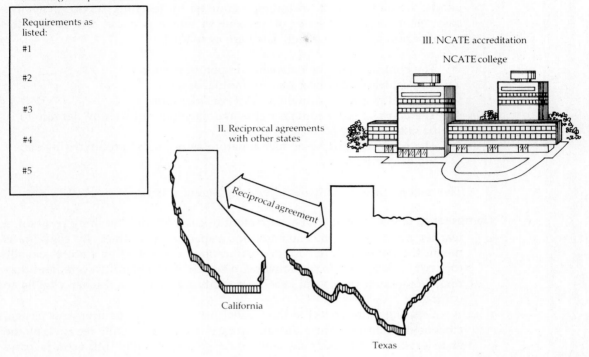

I. Meeting all requirements

Requirements as
listed:

#1

#2

#3

#4

#5

II. Reciprocal agreements
with other states

Reciprocal agreement

California

Texas

III. NCATE accreditation

NCATE college

would also recommend the graduate for the specified certificate. This seems to be a promising method for arriving at some kind of nationwide standardization of certification requirements.

Another promising method is to have a coalition of states agree to common certification requirements. In May 1984, over two thirds of the fifty states had joined the Interstate Certification Project, through which initial certification among member states is greatly simplified.

Teachers' Contracts

Nearly two million teachers are under contract in the public elementary and secondary schools each year, and each one of them represents a teacher's contract. A recent study of court cases in which teachers were litigants revealed that nearly half of them related to teachers' contracts and tenure rights. Clearly, then, the subject of teacher contracts merits serious consideration by the person preparing to teach.

To adequately understand the legal aspects of teacher contracts, it is helpful to know some essential facts about contracts in general. All contracts under the common law possess certain elements on which their validity depends. A valid contract, including a contract for teaching services, has five basic elements, the absence of any one of which is enough to render the contract null and of no effect. They are as follows:

1. The contract must be between competent parties.
2. The contract must be based on mutual assent.
3. The contract must contain a valid consideration.
4. The contract must contain rights and liabilities sufficiently definite to be enforceable.
5. The contract must be of such a nature as not to be prohibited by statute or common law.

The major concepts contained in each element follow.

Competency of the Parties To be competent to contract for a teaching position, a teacher must have both eligibility and capacity to contract. By *eligibility* is meant the possession of certain qualifications prescribed by statute, usually for certain classes of professional people such as teachers, lawyers, and doctors. Possession of a valid teaching certificate makes a teacher eligible to contract.

Capacity, with respect to the teacher, refers to such requirements as age, citizenship, marital status, and similar factors that are usually required by the state legislature. For example, a minor cannot legally enter into a contract and so would not have the capacity to do so. With respect to school boards, statutory authority to contract is, with few exceptions, vested in each of them, and this gives them the legal capacity.

Mutual Assent The negotiations leading to a contract can be categorized into *offer* and *acceptance*. For these to happen, there must exist a concurrence of assent on the part of both the offeror and the offeree about the conditions of the contract. There must be neither doubt nor difference between the parties.

Valid Consideration In the legal sense, consideration consists of the act, or the promise, of surrendering some legal right at the request of another party. It is the price that one party pays for the act or promise of another. In a teaching contract, the consideration promised by the school district is the salary and other monetary benefits; the teacher promises her or his services. Unless the contracting parties reach agreement about the consideration, there will be no contract.

Definite Rights and Liabilities It is a well-settled principle of law that a contract lacks validity when the rights and liabilities of the contracting parties are not sufficiently definite as to be enforceable. A promise to pay a teacher "good wages" is not definite enough; a specific amount of money must be offered. Other things that should be definitely stated in a teacher's contract are (1) the beginning and ending dates of employment; (2) the nature of the services to be performed by the teacher; and (3) all other things required by statute.

Not Prohibited by Law   It is logical to expect that a contract entered into in violation of a law would be invalid. Among the more common statutes barring or limiting the making of a valid contract are those concerning contracts made on Sunday, made in restraint of trade, based on gambling or usurious interest rates, or made orally when the statutes require them to be in writing.

In addition to the elements just discussed, other factors concerning contracts are worthy of consideration. State statutes, existing as well as future ones, are considered a part of all public-school contracts. When a state passes a statute requiring public school teachers to belong to and to contribute to the teachers' retirement system, that statute pertains to all teachers, even those already under contract.

State boards of education and state departments of public instruction possess explicit or implied powers to prescribe rules and regulations for the government of the public schools. Whenever these state agencies make such rules, and if the rules are reasonable and within the agency's power to make, they can be enforced even if they affect the terms of a teacher's contract.

Likewise, rules and regulations of local school boards, when not arbitrary, unreasonable, capricious, or unjust, become, by implication, an integral part of each teacher's contract. This principle pertains to rules passed *after* a contract becomes effective, as well as to those in effect when the contract is signed. Furthermore, the board must make some reasonable attempt to communicate new rules to all employees, such as a general announcement or notification by letter, before compliance can be expected.

Contracts may be terminated by mutual consent at any time. However, termination of a contract by only one of the contracting parties without the consent of the other one is called *breach of contract.* A teacher holding a valid contract with a school district may not simply abandon it by notifying the board. State statutes usually provide a procedure for resignation, which the teacher must follow to be legally discharged from the obligations of the contract. In some states, the law allows that a probationary teacher under contract may resign on twenty-one days' written notice. Other states do not make it quite so easy for teachers to get out of a contract. "Contract jumping" after a certain date in the summer, usually August 1 or 15, is the target of legislation in a number of states.

Whereas school boards are given certain safeguards against the abandonment of contracts by teachers, as just described, teachers are protected to an even greater extent against such actions on the part of school boards. Whereas state laws usually give teachers the right to resign during the term of a contract, school boards can resort to no such procedure. To release a teacher under contract against her or his will, the board must charge her or him with

Breach of contract, or "contract jumping," (symbolized by the empty chair) is a problem for school districts and a poor practice for teachers. *(Photo by Axler.)*

failure to perform the duties required. The most common charges in such cases are immorality, insubordination, neglect of duty, and incompetence. Evidence must then be supplied by the board to substantiate its charges.

Teachers not on tenure do not need to be rehired by the school board on the expiration of a contract, and the board usually need not give the reason for not rehiring a teacher. However, a number of states have what is called a *continuing-contract law,* which protects teachers from dismissal during a period of several months just before a new school year begins. The continuing-contract law requires a school board to notify all nontenured teachers by a prescribed date in the spring, usually around May 1, if they are *not* to be rehired for the following school year. The law gives teachers not so notified the right to claim a contract at their proper place on the salary schedule for the coming year.

Teachers on tenure are commonly referred to as being on *indefinite contract.* This simply means that once a teacher gains tenure, his or her contract is automatically renewed from year to year without any official action's being required by either the school board or the teacher, who, of course, continues in his or her proper place on the salary schedule. The only way a tenure teacher can be legally dismissed is by the procedure prescribed by the tenure statute in that state. Tenure and some of its implications, including dismissal, are discussed later.

Other Rights of Teachers

Teachers have both rights and responsibilities, just like anyone else. However, they must be viewed from the standpoint of the teacher, and from such a standpoint, a number of unique aspects are discernible. A discussion of teachers' rights will be followed by a look at their responsibilities.

At one time, teachers in this country were little better off than factory and mine workers were before the unions became strong enough to effect changes for the better. They were, in many instances, told what to teach, where to live, and what they could or could not do. In addition, they worked for very low salaries and few, if any, fringe benefits. To sum it all up, teachers at one time had very few rights.

As progress in other areas was noticed, teachers began to seek and to win concessions, until a sizable body of "teachers' rights" had been built. In the 1950s, teachers began to organize effectively, much as labor had been doing for several decades, and through collective bargaining, they have gained new rights and solidified their positions with respect to old ones. Some of the more important rights now legally held by teachers are discussed in the following paragraphs.

Salaries

It is a well-established principle of law that school boards have the power to fix teachers' salaries as long as no statute is violated and the boards do not act in an arbitrary and capricious manner.

In some states, the legislature determines the minimum salary that can be paid to any public-school teacher by passing a minimum-salary law. Such laws generally base minimum salaries on only two factors: training and experience. In those states, public school districts cannot pay a teacher less than the amount stipulated in the state schedule. However, most school districts adopt salary schedules that are higher than the minimums required by state schedules. When this occurs, such districts establish new minimums, and no teachers may be paid a salary lower than that called for by their local salary schedule for a person with their training and experience, except on rare occasions.

The most common reason for placing an individual teacher below his or her normal place on the salary schedule, which is approved by the courts in several states, is the failure of the teacher to improve himself or herself professionally. When the board requires the teachers of the district to complete additional college credits, or to participate in certain in-service programs, or allows approved travel to substitute for either of the first two requirements as a prerequisite to remaining in the proper place on the salary schedule, failure to do so results in a lower salary than is called for by the schedule. The Supreme Court of Missouri included membership in local, county, state, and national education associations as a factor in professional improvement, when it ruled that a teacher who refused to join them had no right to remain on the salary schedule.

There is little, if any, legal precedent to prevent a school board from increasing the salaries of teachers above their rightful place on the schedule. Should a board want to recognize outstanding performance in such a way, it can.

The salary schedule is not a contract between the teacher and the board. It is in the nature of a declaration of policy by the board and may be revised at any time. Of course, once teachers' contracts based on a certain salary schedule are signed, changing the schedule has no effect on those contracts. Once the contract period ends, however, a new salary schedule can go into effect.

Whenever factors other than training and experience are used as bases

If nonteaching duties, such as club sponsorship, are required of teachers, they should be related to the teacher's qualifications and interests. *(Photo by Axler.)*

for determining classifications in a salary schedule, great care must be taken. Of course, courts may vary in their viewpoints, but in general, it is a good rule not to use factors that distinguish between teachers as married or unmarried, as black or white, as male or female, and as having dependents or having no dependents.

A school board may require teachers to perform duties other than those required in the classroom and extending beyond regular school hours without paying them additional salary. On the other hand, a board may choose to give teachers "extra pay for extra work." Should it choose not to, the board must be careful to see that such assignments (1) are equitably distributed among all the teachers; (2) are related to teaching duties (janitorial service, police service, and school bus driving were said by a New York court not to be so related); and (3) are related to a teacher's qualifications (the science club, for example, should not be assigned to an English teacher with no science background).

Teachers are entitled to their salaries when schools are closed for reasons beyond their control. In some states, the courts have ruled that teachers do not even have to report for duty on such days though ordered to do so. It is generally conceded that days of school missed for such reasons may be made up at such times as on Saturdays and during Christmas or Easter vacation. However, it is probable that additional salary would be required if lost days were made up after the expiration date on the teachers' contracts, which is usually in late May or in June.

Retirement

All of the states have teacher retirement plans. There is a legal distinction between a *retirement* plan and a *pension*. In the latter, the teacher is not required to contribute a part of her or his salary to the plan; in the former, the teacher and usually the school district or the state both contribute. The state has no obligation to pay a pension, but it may do so if the people desire. On the other hand, a retirement plan is contractual in nature, and the state assumes an obligation to the teachers enrolled in it.

Such obligations are not absolute, however. There is no question but that the state has the obligation to pay the teachers an amount equal to their contributions, because the teachers' rights become *vested*, at least to that amount, when they are required to contribute to the plan. If the statute requires interest to be paid, that, too, becomes part of the state's contractual obligation.

The contribution of the state is not as clear-cut. When the state's share of retirement benefits is paid to a member only after she or he retires based on a formula that does not go into effect until then, a contractual relationship does not arise until retirement. This means that once a member retires and her or his benefits are computed, the state may not lower them. However, the benefit schedule may be lowered before the teacher retires.

But some states pay their share to the account of each member of the plan every year during active service, so that when a member retires, the state's share is already fully paid. In those cases, both the member's share plus interest and the state's share plus interest become a contractual obligation of the state. It should be kept in mind, however, that the member must qualify for retirement benefits under the laws of the state before he or she can claim the state's share. His or her own contributions, usually plus interest, revert to him or her whenever he or she leaves the state or leaves teaching for a stated minimum length of time.

Whenever questions about retirement arise, the teacher can turn to the retirement fund officials, to the state education association, or to the state department of public instruction for help. Providing adequately for our elderly people has become an important social responsibility; therefore, teachers should know as much as possible about their retirement rights.

Leaves of Absence

In earlier times, when a teacher was absent from his or her job for any reason, he or she often was not paid for the days missed. However, as the school year lengthened, as professional organizations became more active, and as work pressures increased, the practice of allowing teachers leaves of absence with pay became a regularly accepted practice.

At first, school boards, through local rules and regulations, took the initiative in this matter. But one by one, state legislatures have faced the issue by passing laws that guarantee teachers limited leaves of absence for specified reasons with full pay. Leaves of absence for certain other reasons can also be obtained, but without pay.

The most common type of leave with full pay is sick leave. Nearly all of the states have enacted legislation mandating sick leave in some form for regular teachers. The average number of days of sick leave per year in those states is about ten. Most of them also allow unused sick leave to accumulate, the number of such days usually being left to the local school boards. As many as 180 days have been allowed to accumulate in some districts.

In addition to allowing sick leave days to accumulate, some local districts have encouraged teachers to claim them judiciously by allowing them to be used as the basis for a form of severance pay. In other words, when a teacher retires, he or she is paid for all unused sick leave at the rate of pay of his or her last year of teaching.

It is not necessary for there to be a statute in a state for teachers to be given sick leave. Local school boards may grant sick leave as long as there is no statute forbidding the practice. In many of the states with sick-leave statutes, local boards have the authority to exceed the number of days required by the statute, and many local school districts do just that. The practice of allowing sick leave accumulated in one school district to be transferred to and used in another district in the same state is now fairly common. So far, no unused sick leave is transferrable from one state to another.

Leave for a death in the immediate family is also common. In some states, a statute requires all school boards to grant this type of leave. Where there is no statute, boards have the legal right to grant it if they wish. The usual number of days granted for this leave is from three to five, and any unused days are generally not cumulative. The "immediate family" is usually limited to spouse, children, parents, and grandparents.

Personal leave has been getting more attention since 1965. This allows teachers two or three days a year to take care of personal matters or to perform civic duties. It is usually in addition to sick leave and the leave for a death in the immediate family, and just as for those two kinds of leave, it provides for full pay for the number of days allowed by the law.

Sabbatical leave has so far not been commonly granted to public elementary- and secondary-school teachers. It is thought of mostly in connection with colleges and universities. However, there are sabbatical leave programs in some of the wealthier and/or more progressive school districts now, and the practice is certain to be expanded. A sabbatical is a leave granted to a teacher after serving a certain number of years in the district, usually six or seven. The teacher is paid while on sabbatical, but the amount varies greatly among districts. The common practice in colleges and universities is to provide the teacher with full pay for one semester and with half pay for two semesters. A few public-school districts follow this practice, but most of them grant smaller amounts.

The reasons for which sabbatical leaves may be given are usually strictly controlled. Professional improvement is the objective of most of them. Thus, further study and travel closely related to one's teaching field are the most common reasons approved by boards for sabbaticals.

Maternity leaves may be with or without pay, depending on the circumstances. Until 1974, nearly all maternity leaves were without pay and were strictly regulated by local school boards with respect to when a pregnant teacher had to begin the leave and when she could return to teaching. *Cleveland Board of Education* v. *La Fleur,* a 1974 U.S. Supreme Court decision, changed all that. At issue was a board rule requiring every pregnant teacher to take an unpaid leave of absence five months before the birth of her child and specifying a return after the child had reached three months of age.

The Court decided that the blanket five-month leave before birth, as well as the three-month return date, was arbitrary and did not consider the individual needs and capabilities of each affected teacher. It reasoned that the ability to teach effectively is an individual matter to be decided by each teacher in conjunction with her physician and the school administration.

Furthermore, in most states, pregnancy is now considered a physical condition that qualifies the teacher for sick leave. When advised by her physician to take a pregnancy leave, the teacher may apply accumulated sick leave in order to be paid for those days. Of course, once all sick leave is used, the leave reverts to being an unpaid one.

The leaves previously discussed are nearly always given with full or partial pay. Other leaves are provided by many school boards not accompanied by salary. The advantage of a leave without pay accrues mainly to the tenured teacher. By being granted a leave, a tenured teacher does not have to give up his or her tenure rights. The main advantage of a nonsalaried leave to a nontenured teacher is the implication by the board that he or she will be rehired when the leave expires, although there is no legal guarantee.

Another common reason for leave without pay is professional improvement. Although a small number of schools allow sabbatical leaves to be used for this purpose, most such leaves are nonsalaried. Service in the armed forces is still another reason. Some states make it mandatory for school boards to give a leave of absence to regular teachers going into service whether they are on tenure or not, thus guaranteeing them a job in the same district when they return.

Tenure

Teacher tenure is a much misunderstood phenomenon. Many people think of it as guaranteeing a teacher his or her job. The legal purpose of tenure, however, is to provide an orderly means for the dismissal of teachers. At one time, it was not uncommon for school boards to dismiss teachers for little or no reason. That is no longer a customary procedure because board practices today are a great deal sounder and more ethical than they were earlier in our history. The advent of negotiations between teacher groups and school boards has now created a new factor to be considered with respect to tenure, and that is the freedom with which a teacher can negotiate with his or her employer. Without tenure laws to protect him or her, the teacher would find it difficult to negotiate effectively.

To achieve tenure status, a teacher must nearly always serve a probationary period in a school district, generally three years, although state requirements vary for from two to five years. During the probationary period, the teacher serves under an annual contract, which means that the board can refuse to renew it at the end of any school year.

Tenure refers to one's status within a particular school district. Thus, probationary time served in one district is not transferred to another. When a teacher moves from one district to another, she or he must serve the required probationary period in the new district in order to achieve tenure there, even though she or he may have been on tenure in the previous district. Usually, the probationary period requirement must be met by serving those years consecutively. For example, if a state requires a three-year probationary period and a teacher serves two consecutive years, then takes a leave of absence, he or she may have to begin the probationary period over again. Service as a substitute teacher, a special teacher, a part-time teacher, or a supply teacher ordinarily does not count toward tenure status.

About four fifths of the states have tenure laws of some kind. Although they differ in detail, they all provide for two things: (1) continuing employment of the teacher who has acquired tenure status as long as the service rendered remains satisfactory and (2) a specific procedure to be followed if there is just cause for dismissal.

The procedure for dismissing a tenured teacher is set by statute. Although the specific details may vary by state, the four steps that follow summarize fairly well the procedure that is commonly followed:

1. A notice from the school board that dismissal is contemplated.
2. A statement of the charges.
3. The right to a hearing before the school board with counsel.
4. The right to appeal—either to a higher educational authority in the state and/or to the courts.

The reasons for which a tenured teacher may be dismissed must be defined by statute. The courts have consistently refused to uphold dismissals for reasons not contained in the tenure law. There is a considerable variety of reasons among the states, but among the more common ones are incompetency, immorality, insubordination, neglect of duty, and reduction of staff because of a drop in enrollment. Some states allow some leeway to local boards by including as a reason for dismissal in the tenure law the phrase "and for other just and good cause." This is not a mandate for school boards to dismiss tenured teachers for any reason whatsoever, because the courts have required the reasons under that clause to be related to the performance of a person as a teacher.

Both the school board and the tenured teacher being dismissed must follow the procedure exactly as outlined by the tenure statute. Failure to do so nearly always results in the loss of one's rights under that law. For example, if the statute requires a teacher to ask for a hearing with the board within five days of receiving a statement of charges, failure of the teacher to do so means that he or she forfeits the right to a hearing.

In contrast to the nontenured teacher, who works under an annual contract, the tenured teacher need not be reappointed annually. He or she is entitled to a succession of contracts for an indefinite period of time as long as his or her behavior does not expose him or her to dismissal for one of the reasons listed in the tenure statute. Thus, it is commonly said that a tenured teacher is on "indefinite contract." A school board need not send new contracts to its tenured teachers each year unless it wishes to change some of the conditions in the contract. As far as salary is concerned, tenured teachers receive what the salary schedule calls for whether or not they get a contract each year.

Academic Freedom

Academic freedom is a term that implies both freedom for the teacher and the responsibility necessary to maintain it. The courts have insisted that academic freedom is not an unlimited right of a teacher to speak, think, and believe as

Academic freedom allows teachers to express their opinions but not to propagandize. *(Photo by Axler.)*

she or he wishes in the classroom. Rather, the teacher has the responsibility to consider such things as the standards of the community, the laws of the state and nation, the age and capacity of her or his students, and the fact that her or his rights as a teacher are not the same as the rights of an ordinary citizen. Because a teacher believes in Christianity, for example, is not a good reason that she or he should be allowed to teach about it as the only true religion. How free should a teacher be to teach about sex? Academic freedom does not give the teacher the license to teach students that sexual intercourse between single students under eighteen is proper, because this violates certain statutes. Academic freedom does not mean academic license. It is the freedom to do good and not to teach evil. Academic freedom cannot authorize a teacher to teach that murder or treason is good.

There is no clear definition of academic freedom available. In general, the term refers to the freedom that teachers should have to discuss all aspects of a subject with their students without imposing their own viewpoints. A teacher should have the freedom to state his or her own viewpoint as one among others but should not have the right to propagandize it as the only view. When teachers believe that they are restricted by their superiors, or by the community, in their freedom to teach, they should go to the courts.

Right to Organize and Bargain Collectively

There is no doubt today that teachers have the right to organize and to join employee organizations. There was some doubt of this until the 1960s, but now most states have enacted statutes specifically permitting it.

The right to negotiate, or bargain, with school boards is not quite as clear-cut as is the right to organize. The key concept in negotiations is that school boards have the right to bargain with teachers if they wish to, but unless a state statute compels them, they are not required to bargain. It can be done, without statutory compulsion, only at the board's discretion.

One by one, the states are passing negotiation or collective-bargaining laws. These laws require school boards to negotiate with teacher organizations, and they also spell out the procedures for negotiation, as well as for settling an impasse between board and teachers. Exclusive negotiation rights have caused some problems, especially in those states without negotiations statutes. In general, though, the teacher organization with the greatest membership is given the right to bargain for all the teachers in a school district. However, minority organizations and individuals must be given the right to be heard. The statutes usually define the procedure for determining which organization shall have exclusive bargaining rights.

At the present time, public-school teachers in most states, as government employees, do not have the legal right to strike. The fact that teachers have gone on strike, and probably will in the future, does not make striking legal. The major penalty for striking is dismissal, and teachers realize that a school board will not dismiss all who have gone on strike because replacements cannot be found. There is considerable evidence today, however, indicating that public opinion is growing in support of legalizing teacher strikes. At least eight states now permit limited right-to-work stoppages, but only after certain mandatory conditions have been met.

Probably the greatest problem faced by both sides in negotiations is the impasse, which is that point where disagreement prevails and neither side will give in or compromise. Three methods are usually available. The first of these, mediation, occurs when both sides agree to employ a third party for the purpose of helping them reach an agreement. The mediator makes suggestions, persuades, cajoles, or praises in an attempt to get the negotiating parties to agree. However, nothing in this procedure is binding on either side.

Fact finding occurs when a third party (often from outside the district) is employed to conduct a study of the situation and to present a factual report, which is then usually publicized. It is then hoped that public opinion will cause one or both sides to change positions and an agreement to be reached. Again, nothing is binding on either party.

Arbitration occurs when two disputing parties engage a third party (if arbitration is compulsory, the arbiter may be appointed) to hear both sides, to study the situation, and then to make a decision. Only a few states permit binding arbitration at this time (which means that the decision of the arbiter is binding on both parties), and those states vary in how it can be used. Arbitration is not popular with either public employees or public employers and is being met with great resistance in most states. One good reason is that such a procedure takes the decision-making authority from the school board, which it has long held by statute.

Political Activity

The kind of political activity in which a teacher engages makes a difference. A teacher may engage in the normal political activities of any citizen outside the classroom. Limitations are placed on him or her only when there is some detrimental relation to his or her job as a teacher. For example, if the time required for political activities prohibits the teacher from adequately performing his or her duties, the board may require the teacher to curtail his or her political duties or risk dismissal.

Teachers have no right to impose their political views on their captive audience, the students. Academic freedom gives teachers the right to discuss politics, political parties and platforms, and candidates, but not the right to propagandize in the classroom.

The right of public school teachers to hold political office varies among the states: some allow it, others do not. Indiana allows its public school teachers to hold political office but requires them to take a leave of absence while holding public office (during the legislative session if elected to the legislature), and if campaigning for office requires a great deal of time, the local school board has the power to place them on leave for the campaign as well.

Loyalty Oaths

In the early 1960s, nearly three fourths of the states had a constitutional, statutory, or administrative requirement for a loyalty oath by teachers as a prerequisite to teaching. Many teachers oppose such a requirement, mainly because they believe that it discriminates against them as a particular class of

Sample Loyalty Oath

IMPORTANT: State law requires the loyalty affidavit to be signed and notarized on each application and requires the applicant to keep one copy.

LOYALTY AFFIDAVIT

I solemnly swear (or affirm) that I will support the Constitution of the United States of America, the Constitution of the State, and the laws of the United States and the state, and will, by precept and example, promote respect for the flag and the institutions of the United States and of the state, reverence for law and order, and undivided allegiance to the government of the United States of America.

Signed _____
(Applicant)

Subscribed and sworn to before me, a Notary Public, this _____ day of _____ 19 ___

My commission expires _____. Notary Public _____

NOT VALID WITHOUT STAMP OR SEAL OF NOTARY PUBLIC

Source: Adapted by permission from the Indiana Department of Education.

people. "Why aren't other groups or classes of people required to take a loyalty oath for employment?" they ask. State courts have consistently upheld loyalty oath laws. However, the U.S. Supreme Court has ruled some loyalty oath laws unconstitutional when it found them to be too vague for fair interpretation or to be based on the principle of "guilt by association," indicting members of certain organizations such as the Communist Party. This does not necessarily indicate that all loyalty oath laws are headed for extinction, but that some may be invalid if challenged.

Discrimination in Employment

No one has an inherent right to be employed as a teacher in the public schools. The highest of qualifications does not change this principle. On the other hand, a person may *not* be refused a position solely on the basis of race, creed, color, sex, age, handicap, or national origin. The courts have repeatedly said, in decisions since World War II, that distinctions in employment or nonemployment of persons on these bases alone are in violation of the due-process and equal-protection clauses of the Fourteenth Amendment.

To curb discriminatory practices, states have enacted "fair employment practices" and "antidiscrimination" laws. The purpose of fair-employment-practices laws is to provide opportunities for members of minority groups to secure adequate employment, and to attempt to create public attitudes that reject discriminatory practices. These laws actually extend beyond discrimination as it is commonly understood and forbid certain expressions of prejudice.

The federal government added its weight and enlarged the scope of the applicability of racial antidiscrimination in employment when it passed the Civil Rights Act of 1964. Title VII of that act contains the criteria pertinent to employment.

Since 1964, the U.S. Supreme Court has clarified Title VII through a number of decisions. The use of tests has been one of the most contentious issues related to discrimination in employment, especially when a test results in the disqualification of a disproportionate number of minority applicants. In general, a test may be used as a means of determining job qualification when there is a positive relationship between the test results and job performance, and when there is no provable attempt on the part of the employer to discriminate.

Principles of law similar to those involved in hiring are applicable when promotions and staff reductions take place. Either Title VII or the equal-protection clause of the Fourteenth Amendment is the basis for legal action when discrimination is suspected.

At times, members of a majority group feel the sting of discrimination when attempts to remedy minority discrimination are overemphasized. This is called *reverse discrimination*, and it has been addressed by the courts on several occasions. The U.S. Supreme Court has held unconditionally that the terms of Title VII "are not limited to discrimination against members of any particular race" *McDonald* v. *Santa Fe Trail Transportation Co.*, 1976). Quota systems, which prescribe definite percentages or numbers of one race or minority group, without regard to other factors, have been declared illegal by the Court.

Sex discrimination has also been the focus of federal legislation and resulting court cases. Until the 1970s, unequal treatment in employment based on sex was legally sanctioned. However, as racial minorities gained in their battle for equal rights, women began to realize that action was also needed to better their position. The legal bases for nearly all sex-discrimination cases have been the Equal Pay Act, Title VII of the Civil Rights Act of 1964, and Title IX of the Education Amendments of 1972.

The areas of greatest emphasis, in which significant gains for women have been made, are those concerning pregnancy-related policies, differential treatment of men and women in retirement programs, and sex bias in hiring, promotion, and pay.

In addition to discrimination by race and sex, considerable attention has been paid in recent years to discrimination based on age and on handicap. For additional information about those subjects, see the list of references section near the end of this book.

Duty-Free Lunch Periods

Teachers have long maintained that they should have the privilege of eating lunch during the school day entirely free from any kind of responsibility. Most schools make no such provisions for their teachers. Some states have enacted statutes giving teachers such a right. The amount of duty-free lunchtime averages about thirty minutes in those states, and the statute usually

Lunchroom duty continues to be a responsibility of teachers. *(Photo by Axler.)*

prescribes the hours during which the free time must be used. The validity of these statutes has so far not been successfully challenged in the courts.

Right to Hold Other Employment or Positions

Public-school teachers do have the right to hold employment outside the school system while under contract. It is only when such outside employment substantially interferes with the effective performance of their teaching duties, or when the outside work is of such a nature as to make teachers unfit for their positions (such as bookie or gambler or, in one case, a waitress in a "dive"), that boards have the right to dismiss them or require them to give up the outside job.

Fringe Benefits

Without express statutory permission, it is generally assumed that school boards may spend public funds for any purpose that is reasonably necessary to promote the interests of the schools. With the fierce competition for employees of the 1950s and 1960s, most school authorities adopted the philosophy that it was necessary to provide not only competitive salaries but fringe benefits as well. These have remained a vital part of teacher compensation ever since. The most common fringe benefits are prepaid hospital and medical plans, life insurance, retirement plans, leaves with pay, severance pay, and workers' compensation.

Although workers' compensation is in effect in most states by statute and has been upheld by the courts, many teachers are unaware of either its benefits or its requirements. Its benefits usually consist of payment of a weekly allowance during the period a teacher cannot work. To qualify for workers' compensation benefits, a teacher must be accidentally injured "out of" and "in the course of" his or her employment in the school. "Out of" one's employment refers to the relationship of the activity from which the injury arose to one's duties as a teacher. The question to answer here is: Did your job require you to do the act that caused the injury? "In the course of" employment refers to whether or not you were actually in the act of performing the job required of you when the injury occurred. It is interesting to note that such incidents as heart attacks and coming down with the measles have been judged by the courts to be compensable "injuries" under the meaning of workers' compensation laws.

Control of Students

Whenever people have rights, they also have responsibilities, and people who have responsibilities often incur liabilities that grow out of neglecting or forgetting them. The greatest legal responsibility that a teacher has is for the health, safety, and well-being of the students placed in her or his care. From the standpoint of the law, teachers must know what they can or cannot do with respect to their students. When they do things they shouldn't do or don't do the things they should do, teachers may incur a personal liability, usually in the form of money damages.

There are also certain things that the teacher or the school can do to control students. A school could not operate unless certain rules were established and enforced with respect to the admission, attendance, assignment, graduation, and behavior of its students. The teachers have the responsibility of carrying out such rules and regulations.

With young people in school at least half the days of the year, many of them even more, the responsibility for and thus the control of them must be lodged with the school and its personnel, at least for the time they are in school or are engaged in school-sponsored activities. The courts have come to define this relationship of the teacher standing in place of the parent as *in loco parentis*.

It should not be assumed that *in loco parentis* gives the teachers exactly the same powers over the pupils as the parents have. The teacher's authority is less broad than that of the parent because the teacher's control is limited to situations within his or her jurisdiction as a teacher. The parent, for example, controls such things as the manner and mode of religious training and the type of medical and dental treatment that the child receives. The teacher can control none of those things because they lie outside the scope of his or her authority as a teacher. It is important to note, however, that limiting the *in loco parentis* relationship to the scope of a teacher's authority does not confine that authority merely to the school premises and to school hours. Whenever the orderly operation of the school is endangered, a teacher has the right to control the actions or words of a student, whether or not on the school premises or during school hours.

As long as the teacher exercises control of pupils in a *reasonable* manner, he or she will not be denied such control. In addition, a teacher's control is sometimes limited by school board rules and by statutes. Thus, if not restricted by rule or law and if his or her demands are not unreasonable, the teacher has the common-law right to direct how and when each pupil shall attend to his or her appropriate duties, and the manner in which the pupil shall conduct himself or herself.

There are certain things pupils must do, and there are certain other things they cannot do. It is usually up to the teacher to see that those things are either done or not done, as the case may be. When the rules governing the "do's" or "don'ts" are violated, the teacher then has the right to prescribe penalties. When penalizing students, the teacher should make certain that the rule broken was a reasonable one and that the penalty is also reasonable. The paragraphs that follow discuss some of these requirements and the penalties that often go with them.

Pupil Dress and Appearance

There is no disagreement with the fact that schools have the right to regulate the dress and appearance of their students. The question that the courts are called on to answer is the *degree* of regulation that the schools can exercise. Objectors to excessive regulation contend that the student is being deprived of the First Amendment right of free expression (a form of freedom of speech).

What the court looks for in cases dealing with the regulation of pupil dress and appearance in school is evidence that the orderly operation of the school is being eroded by the dress or appearance in question. For a regulatory rule of this kind to be reasonable, there must be a logical relationship between it and the efficient operation of the school. Teachers and administrators should be careful to compile specific evidence to this effect before making or enforcing a rule regulating pupil dress and appearance.

A case dealing with pupil dress of a slightly different nature, but a fairly common occurrence nevertheless, involved a high-school girl who was suspended from school for refusal to wear a prescribed uniform in her gym class. It was contended that wearing the uniform subjected the girl to an immodest display that was in violation of her religious beliefs. A compromise was reached when the court held that the girl could be required to attend the class, but that she could not be required to wear the prescribed outfit nor to engage in exercises that would be immodest in ordinary apparel.

In another case where the school required that a certain garb be worn by students, the court looked for a relationship between the requirement and the reason for wearing the garb. A high-school senior refused to wear a cap and gown at commencement, whereupon the school board refused to give her a diploma. The court said that it could see no relation between wearing a cap and gown and the educational objectives of the school. The student could be barred from the commencement exercises, but not from receiving her diploma.

Pupil Driving

Most high schools today have huge parking lots, and most of the space is used by students who drive to school. This circumstance, of course, brings up the question of what control school authorities may exercise over student drivers. The answer is not as simple as the question, however, because the issue involved is the power of the school to regulate the use by students of public roads and streets. Those who object to the regulation of student driving by the school contend that this is a matter for the civil authorities and is not within the implied powers of school boards.

A school board may designate where students must park, and it may also prohibit student driving during school hours without permission, as long as the prohibition's primary purpose is the safety of the students and/or the orderly operation of the school. Where there is evidence to show that stu-

Schools usually regulate student driving by controlling parking and by restricting driving during school hours. *(Photo by Axler.)*

dents driving their cars on the public streets around the school endanger the safety of other students, the school may take any reasonable steps to control the practice. A common rule approved by schools is to require students to park their cars in designated areas when they arrive at school and to prohibit them from driving without written permission until they leave for home. A common penalty for rulebreakers is to deprive them of driving rights for a period of time. Of course, if the student's home location requires transportation, the school must provide it during this period.

A procedure practiced by some schools is to require student drivers to deposit their car keys in the office when they arrive at school. The reasoning is that the cars cannot be driven until the keys are given back to the drivers, and the principal can thus tightly control student driving during school hours. There are two weaknesses in this plan. The first one is that the students may have duplicate keys. The second weakness is of a legal nature. Under the law of bailments, the principal could become the bailee for all the cars for which keys are turned in. Any damage done to the cars during the time the keys are held could be charged to the principal. No case of record has been heard on that subject, but some legal experts express the opinion that it could happen that way.

Pupil Marriages

Many schools have reported problems arising as a result of students' getting married. Whether the problems are a result of the marriages themselves, or whether the reaction of the school officials to the marriages causes the problems is sometimes difficult to say. At any rate, school boards have gone to great lengths to discourage students from getting married in the first place, or to penalize married students by suspension or expulsion, or by barring them from participation in extracurricular activities.

As far as the legality of the school board efforts is concerned, much is left to be desired. The board may certainly discourage marriage by persuasion or logic, but there are no legal measures that it may effectively use to prevent student marriages.

As recently as the 1960s, many school boards adopted rules expelling students who got married on the grounds that (1) expulsion would serve as an example and thus deter pupils planning marriage from going through with it, and (2) the unmarried students associating with married ones in the schools would somehow become less moral. The courts have upheld neither point of view. In fact, a Mississippi court ruled:

> Marriage is a domestic relation highly favored by the law. When the relation is entered into with correct motives, the effect upon the husband and wife is refining and elevating, rather than demoralizing. Pupils associating in school with a child occupying such a relation, it seems, would be benefited instead of harmed. (*McLeon* v. *State ex rd. Colmer*, 1929)

Admission Requirements

Although it may be correct to say that a child has the right to attend a public school, that right is not absolute. If it were, school authorities would have a difficult time with certain children. The courts have generally said that attendance at a public school is a privilege that is granted a child, but under such terms and conditions as the lawmaking power, within constitutional limits, may see fit to impose.

Thus, a school board may, under certain conditions, deny admission to a child. One of these conditions is age. As school board may determine the age for admission to the first grade or kindergarten. It may even set a cutoff date, meaning that children reaching the age of five or six after a specified date will

Although education is a right, school authorities may set admission requirements such as age and proper immunization, which must be satisfied at the time of registration. *(Photo by Axler.)*

not be admitted to kindergarten or the first grade until the following year. The usual cutoff dates are the first of September, October, November, or December. Some states have statutes specifying admission cutoff dates. Local boards must conform to those, of course.

Another condition for admission that may be imposed by a school board is the requirement to take a physical examination or to be vaccinated. The requirement for vaccination sometimes leads to a conflict with religious beliefs. Certain religions forbid their members to receive vaccinations, blood transfusions, and other medical treatment of that sort. The reasoning of the courts in ruling on that conflict was well stated by the Supreme Court of Kentucky in 1948, when it ruled:

> Religious freedom embraces two conceptions, freedom to believe and freedom to act. The first is absolute but, in the nature of things, the second cannot be . . . the constitutional guarantee of religious freedom does not permit the practice of religious rights dangerous or detrimental to the lives, safety or health of the participants or to the public. (*Mosier* v. *Barren County Board of Health*, 1948)

Children may not only be refused admission to a public school for failure to be vaccinated but may also be expelled if they are already in attendance. State statutes that address the subject prescribe the legal procedure within their boundaries.

Attendance Requirements

All of the states have compulsory attendance laws. The constitutionality of such laws has frequently been challenged, but the courts have consistently upheld them. The courts have reasoned that an enlightened citizenry is essential for our form of government, as well as for our survival; thus, parents

Education is not optional, and all states have compulsory attendance laws. In most schools, absences must be cleared with the attendance office before students return to classes. (*Photo by Axler.*)

should be required to relinquish custody of their children to the school during certain specified years in order that minimum educational standards may be attained. Penalties are assessed against the parents if their children do not attend school while within the age of compulsory attendance, unless there is a legal reason for being absent.

Children may be placed in whatever grade or at whatever level the school officials decide on, provided there are reasonable grounds for such placement. When a child transfers from another school, for example, the public school officials may place him or her in the same grade or any other grade that a reasonable assessment of his or her abilities may indicate. Courts will not overrule a decision of this kind, which is based on professional competence, unless there is clear evidence of whim or capriciousness on the part of the board.

The school board also has a right to assign a student to any attendance unit (building) within the district. Ordinarily, pupils attend the school nearest their residence, but if a school is crowded, the board may assign pupils to another school not as conveniently located. A pupil has no legal right to attend a particular school within a district merely because he or she lives in it, or because his or her parents want the child to attend a particular school.

Since the *Brown* v. *Topeka* case in 1954 invalidated school segregation, pupil assignment has become a major factor in the integration process. Some school boards have used the discretion usually given them with respect to pupil assignment for the purpose of creating or maintaining segregation. From the many court decisions on this subject, one thing is clear: pupil assignment may not be made with racial segregation as the objective. As a matter of fact, the converse is true. Court decisions in the 1970s required pupil assignments to be made with *desegregation* the objective. Thus, the busing of children within a school district—and even between school districts—has, on occasion, been mandated by the courts.

Obviously, all children within the compulsory-attendance age limits cannot benefit from school. The various state legislatures and the courts have recognized this fact, so there are statutes and court decisions alike that set forth the circumstances under which such children are legally excused.

The most common reason for an excused absence from school is illness. No statute or court will require a child to attend school when attendance would endanger his or her health or well-being. School officials may take reasonable steps to check on students, such as requiring a signed statement from the doctor for a prolonged illness or for a student who is absent for that reason quite frequently.

Other common reasons for nonattendance are mental or physical incompetence, living a great distance from school or having to travel a dangerous route without transportation, serving as a page in the legislature, a death in the immediate family, exposure to a contagious disease, and suspension or expulsion. At one time, the courts approved the substitution of "equivalent home instruction" for attendance at a recognized school, but decisions in the 1950s and 1960s reversed this attitude. On that subject, the courts recognized that a highly qualified teacher may be secured to provide home instruction, but that even the best teacher could not provide the child with experiences in group activity and social outlook comparable to that provided in the public school. Court decisions in the 1970s and 1980s have been mixed, with some state courts approving home instruction, and others not.

The question of residence as related to the payment of tuition for attending a particular school is sometimes puzzling. Public schools are free from tuition in all states, most of them by constitutional mandate. This mandate has been interpreted to mean that tuition is free only in the school district in which the student is a resident. Generally, the residence of a student is with his or her parents or legal guardian. Whenever a student lives with someone other than his or her parents or guardian, the criterion for determining whether he or she is a resident for school purposes is the primary reason for his or her living there. If it is to provide him or her with a better home, he or she is considered a resident; if it is to take advantage of the schools, he or she has to pay tuition as a nonresident. Orphans and children on welfare are usually considered residents of the homes to which they are assigned.

Suspension and Expulsion

If attending a public school were an absolute right of an American child, suspension and expulsion would be impossible. Many teachers and administrators are thankful that such is not the case. Any student whose presence is clearly inimical to the best interests of the school, regardless of age, may be excluded. Of course, the school board must have sufficient evidence to support such charges if challenged by the student and his or her parents.

Suspension is a temporary exclusion from school, usually for several days; expulsion is more permanent, but usually only for the remainder of the term or school year. Because expulsion is a far more serious penalty, many states require the school board to make this decision, whereas suspension is often left to the discretion of the suprintendent or the principal.

Neither of these two penalties for misconduct is looked on with favor by the courts or by the teaching profession. Some incorrigible pupils violate regulations for the very purpose of being removed from school. When a pupil is denied school attendance, he or she is being deprived on an education, the one thing that he or she needs the most. There are some students, however, whose presence is extremely detrimental to the good of the school. When all else has failed, suspension or expulsion could be the only remedy.

Some states enacted "student-due-process statutes" in the 1970s. The common elements in those laws require schools to draw up a set of reasonable rules and penalties, and they prescribe the "due-process" steps that must be taken before a student can be suspended or expelled.

In-school detention is one form of discipline. *(Photo by Axler.)*

Academic Penalties for Behavioral Violations

A common practice in the schools is to penalize a student for misconduct by lowering her or his grades. Although there is very little legal precedent in this area, it is generally agreed that an obvious resort to such practice would not be upheld in a court of law. In the first place, it is poor practice because it is illogical; neither is it based on any acceptable educational theory. In the second place, the consequences to the student may be so detrimental as to cause the penalty to be out of all proportion to the offense.

For example, a bright student could be just mischievous enough to irritate some of her teachers to the point where they lowered her grades sufficiently to prevent her from securing a valuable college scholarship. Or an average student who was apt to get caught while violating school rules could be kept from graduating. This is a difficult practice to defend, especially when the misconduct is quite obviously removed from the realm of academic grades. One principal lowered the grades of a boy who would not conform to the rules on student driving. Another boy had his grades lowered because he was caught drinking alcoholic beverages at a school dance.

Where there is some reasonable relationship of the misconduct to academic grades, the practice would probably win approval. Cheating on an exam and plagiarism are examples. It could be logically argued that the grades would have been lower if the cheating or plagiarism had not occurred.

Paying for Damages

At this time, only a few states have statutes requiring parents to assume financial responsibility for acts of their children. In the majority of states, then, it would be useless to bring suit against a child to collect for any damage he or she may have caused to school property, unless the child holds assets in his or her own right. As a result, some schools have resorted to suspending or expelling students who have damaged school property until payment has been made by either the student or his or her parents. The courts have distinguished between damage caused by mischievous or careless acts and that caused willfully or maliciously. Unless a statute does make the parents liable, the school cannot require a student to pay for damage caused by negligence or carelessness, nor can the student be punished for it. However, if the damage is inflicted willfully or maliciously, recovery or punishment, or both, may well be upheld by a court.

Corporal Punishment

Once the most common method of controlling student misbehavior, corporal punishment has been declining in use for the past several decades. However, it is still used often enough so that all teachers ought to be acquainted with its legal aspects. The educational merits and demerits of corporal punishment are not discussed here.

Teachers have the right to use corporal punishment as long as a statute or a local school-board rule does not forbid it. Only New Jersey, Massachusetts, and the District of Columbia have such a statute at this time. It is safe to say, however, that most teachers in the United States have the right to administer corporal punishment, although in many school districts that do not forbid it, strict procedures are set up to regulate it.

A teacher who administers corporal punishment may be charged either with assault and battery or with breaking a local school-board rule. A battery is any intentional touching of a person, his or her eyeglasses or his or her clothing, without his or her consent, or without being privileged. An assault is causing a fear or an apprehension of a battery. An assault can be committed without also committing a battery, but a battery generally includes an assault. If an assault alone causes an injury, charges may be brought. For example, an upraised arm may cause a pupil to duck and hit his or her eye on a sharp corner or other object and thus inflict serious damage.

An assault and battery charge is upheld by a court only if the teacher inflicted immoderate punishment or caused some permanent injury and did so with malice or with wicked motives. Seldom will a criminal charge of assault and battery be brought against a teacher; most parents prefer a civil charge, in part, because damages can then be sought.

The best advice for teachers to follow might be summed up in the following points:

1. Be sure there is no statute prohibiting corporal punishment.
2. Check the local school-board regulations closely, first, to find out if corporal punishment is prohibited, and second, if it is not, to learn the proper procedures if it is prescribed.
3. Never strike a child when angry, or with malice.
4. Inflict only moderate punishment. Don't take the chance of leaving the child with a permanent injury.
5. The punishment should be suited to the age, sex, size, and physical strength of the child.
6. The punishment should be in proportion to the offense.
7. Be sure the rule being enforced with corporal punishment is a reasonable one.
8. The child punished should be under the jurisdiction of the person doing the punishing. If not, the punisher is not *in loco parentis* and is thus not privileged (see the definition of *battery* above).

Detention

Another common method of enforcing school rules and regulations is keeping the student after school. If the detention is for a reasonable time and was assigned for a good and related cause, there seems to be little objection to it from a legal standpoint. However, where detention involves a student who depends on a school bus to get home, there may be some risk of liability should the student walk, hitchhike, or ride home without someone other than his or her parents and be injured while doing so. It would be much safer to mete out some other punishment to such students.

Student Search and Seizure

The use of drugs by school-aged students became widespread in the 1970s. To combat such use in the schools, the practice of searching for illegal drugs (or tobacco or alcohol) on the persons or in the lockers or automobiles of students became fairly common. Students found with drugs in their possession turned to the Fourth Amendment of the U.S. Constitution, which protects individuals against arbitrary searches by requiring state agents to obtain a warrant based on probable cause before conducting a search. The public school, it was said, was an agent of the state.

Until 1985, the courts ruled on student search and seizure cases using one of the following three approaches: (1) the Fourth Amendment does not apply because school officials function as private citizens; (2) the Fourth Amendment does apply, but the doctrine of *in loco parentis* lowers the standard in determining the reasonableness of a search; or (3) the Fourth Amendment applies, and probable cause is required before conducting a search. It was difficult for schools to know exactly where they stood as long as the

On the grounds of "reasonable suspicion," school officials may search students' lockers for illegal or regulated substances. (*Photo by Axler.*)

courts in different state and federal jurisdictions differed in their interpretations of the situation.

Early in 1985, the U.S. Supreme Court handed down a decision that should stabilize the law and allow school officials to draw up rules that will withstand legal protests. In a case originating in New Jersey, the Court, by a 6–3 majority, declared that public schools fell under the second approach enunciated in the preceding paragraph (*New Jersey, Petitioner* v. *T.L.O.*, 1985). Although the Fourth Amendment does apply, public schools will not be held to the same standard of "probable cause" to which the police are held. School officials may search students or their purses, lockers, or automobiles parked on school property on the basis of "reasonable suspicion." A search of a student by a public school official is reasonable under the Fourth Amendment if there are reasonable grounds for suspecting that the search will reveal evidence of a student's violation of either the law or the rules of the school. The method of search must then be reasonably related to the objectives of the search and may not be excessively intrusive in light of the age and sex of the student and the nature of the infraction.

In the New Jersey case, a teacher's report that the student had been seen smoking in the lavatory in violation of school rules provided enough reasonable suspicion to justify the school officials decision to open her purse to look for cigarettes. The detection of cigarette-rolling papers in the purse gave rise to reasonable suspicion that she was carrying marijuana and justified further search of the purse for contraband.

Tort Liability of Teachers

Whenever someone has a responsibility, as teachers do, for the safety and well-being of the students assigned to them, there is a good chance that a slip-up will occur and that the responsibility will not be properly carried out. Should this happen, the teacher could incur a legal liability that would require the payment of money for any damage that may be done to the person or property of another.

Every person is legally responsible for his or her own acts or the acts of his or her legal agents. A person who negligently drives his automobile through a plate glass window, for example, commits a tort against the person who owns the window, and the courts will permit the owner to recover damages. Thus, a tort occurs when one person acts wrongfully and such an act causes real injury or damage to the person or property of another. Wrongful acts pertaining to contracts, however, are not torts.

A tort may also arise from the spoken word. One who causes injury to the reputation of another by use of the written or spoken word may be held accountable and may be made to pay damages to the injured party.

Wrongful actions that lead to a tort are called *negligence*. In other words, when a person acts negligently and causes injury to another, that is a tort. Negligence is defined as failing to do what a reasonably prudent person would have done under similar circumstances, or doing what a reasonably prudent person would not have done under similar circumstances.

It is difficult to define a reasonably prudent person. He or she is an ideal but is always of the same class of persons as the one to whom he or she is being compared. When one is trying to determine whether a teacher acted as a reasonably prudent person, for example, he or she would be measured against a reasonably prudent teacher, not an engineer or laborer. The courts try to figure out what a hypothetically reasonable and prudent teacher would have done in a similar situation, and if the accused teacher did not act in that way, he or she would be held liable for a tort.

Negligence is composed of four elements. All of them must be proved by a plaintiff to win a claim. They are as follows:

1. *Duty:* The defendant owed the plaintiff a duty of reasonable care.
2. *Breach of that duty:* The defendant failed to perform the duty in the manner of a reasonably prudent person.
3. *Causation:* The defendant's actions actually caused the injury and were proximate to it.
4. *Damage or injury:* The plaintiff must have suffered a *real* loss, not merely imaginary and usually not just financial.

If we analyze those elements from the standpoint of a teacher, it is clear that teachers have the duty to exercise reasonable care for the safety and well-being of students in their charge. As for the second element, the duty a teacher owes her or his pupils is breached when she or he fails to perform it in the manner of a reasonably prudent teacher. It is important to recognize that the standards of care vary with the ability of the students and with the type and the place of the activity they are engaged in. For example, younger children need greater care than older ones; mentally retarded children need greater care than those with normal intelligence; and the laboratory or the physical education area requires greater care than the ordinary classroom.

The element of causation requires the plaintiff to prove (1) that the event causing the injury would not have occurred *but for* the defendant's conduct, and that (2) there was an unbroken connection between the wrongful act and the injury, the sequence being such as to make it just to hold the defendant responsible. Should any other actions or factors intervene between the acts of the defendant and the injury, the responsibility for the injury may shift.

In order for there to be liability for tort, the plaintiff must, in most cases, have suffered a "real" loss or damage. A *real loss* is defined as a crippling or permanent injury to the physical person or damage to tangible property. Financial loss alone is too difficult to assess, the courts say, although in some types of libel and slander, an exception to this general rule is made.

The teacher charged with a tort has several defenses. One is to show the absence of any one of the four elements of negligence. Another defense is called *contributory negligence,* which constitutes behavior on the part of the plaintiff contributing to the injury or damage he or she has suffered, such behavior not conforming to the standard required for his or her own protection. This standard varies according to the age, intelligence, sex, physical characteristics, and training of each person. Contributory negligence is much more likely to be a factor with an older, intelligent child than with a young, retarded child. If both parties contribute to the injury, neither can recover, except in a few states where the damages are prorated according to the amount each party's acts contributed to the loss. This is called *comparative negligence*.

A third defense to which a defendant in a tort liability case may resort is called *assumption of risk*. Players and spectators alike assume the *normal* risks involved in an athletic contest, although the risks of an unsafe field or unsafe apparatus or equipment can be grounds for liability. Thus, a high-school boy voluntarily out for football is legally regarded as assuming the normal risks of injury connected with that sport and will not stand to collect damages for any injuries unless someone's negligent action, above and beyond the usual circumstances, caused them. As in contributory negligence, the age, intelligence, sex, physical characteristics, and training of each person is an important factor in determining the assumption of risk.

Supervision is the area in which most cases of tort liability originate. Teachers are responsible for the supervision of all students specifically assigned to them, as well as of other students temporarily passing in and out of their jurisdiction. For example, playground duty may involve not a specific list of students, but all the students who come and go. Hallway duty is similar.

At teacher is not expected to be everywhere at once, nor is he or she expected to foresee all possible consequences. As long as he or she is in the area he or she is assigned to supervise and remains alert to what is going on, he or she is supervising in a reasonable manner. An example of inadequate supervision would be the teacher who let his pupils out on the playground for recess but remained in his room while they played. He could see most of them from his classroom window. One of the pupils was injured because of some horseplay, but he was powerless to stop the activity before the accident occurred. Had he been on the playground, he would have been in a much better position to prevent the horseplay.

Sometimes, a supervisory assignment is unreasonable; for example, the principal may assign too many students or too large an area to one teacher. In that case, if an injury occurs because of inadequate supervision, and if the teacher makes a reasonable effort to supervise, the principal could be held liable.

Field trips often present added supervisory problems. For one thing, the standard of care that a teacher must exercise is usually higher because the conditions encountered on a field trip present more dangers than the classroom. Another problem is the permission slip sent home with the students for the parents to sign. This slip usually contains a statement to the effect that the parents will not hold the school or the teacher liable in case of an injury to their child. Many teachers rely on that signed statement as a release from all liability. There is no legal basis for the exception because parents cannot sign away their children's rights. Nevertheless, the use of permission slips is highly recommended because they show evidence of planning on the part of the teacher, they provide the parents with information about the child, and

Field trips present special responsibilities for teachers. *(Photo used by permission of the Indianapolis Public Schools.)*

they just may help to deter a parent whose child was injured on the trip from bringing suit.

A teacher should use school-provided transportation whenever available, not only for field trips but for any other activity that requires students to be transported. Unless the teacher has automobile insurance specifically covering the hauling of passengers, there will probably not be sufficient liability coverage in case of an injury to a student rider.

Sending pupils on errands may result in liability for the teacher. A "principal–agent" relationship is set up when a pupil runs an errand for the benefit of a teacher. Under this relationship, the "principal" assumes all responsibility for the acts of the "agent" as well as for the agent's safety. Thus, if a student is injured or damages someone's property while on an errand, the liability that may accrue would revert to the teacher who sent the student.

First aid and the treatment of injuries may present some problems to teachers. The courts hold that teachers are reasonably intelligent people and therefore expect them to react intelligently in an emergency. Thus, teachers are expected to render one of the common types of first aid when the situation requires it. But emergency first aid is all a teacher should administer. When an emergency no longer exists, treatment begins, and teachers have no license to practice medicine. If the condition of a student given medical treatment by a teacher worsens as a result of the treatment, liability could result. On the other hand, if an obvious emergency presents itself and a teacher does not give first aid, if a common kind is required, the teacher could also be liable if the student's condition worsens.

The one area of tort liability for which an injury to the physical person or actual damage to property is not a required element is defamation of character. A simple definition of defamation is making statements that lower or "defame" the character of another person. Written defamation is called *libel;* spoken defamation is called *slander.*

Teachers often say uncomplimentary things about some of their students. These could be defamatory and could lead to a slander suit, depending on how and to whom they were said. When a teacher makes statements, verbally or in writing, about a student to a person with a bona fide interest in that student, the statements are privileged. Privilege is a protection given to those who are required to make statements about others in the course of their daily activities, some of which may be defamatory in nature. The law of privilege recognizes that it is essential that true information be given whenever necessary to protect one's own interests, those of third parties, and certain interests of the public.

There are two kinds of privilege: absolute and qualified (or conditional). Absolute privilege covers occasions of such great importance to the public that they entitle the utterer to speak out fearlessly, knowing that she or he is immune from suit. It is usually reserved for judges in connection with judicial proceedings, lawmakers during legislative sessions, and certain executives or government employees in the discharge of their duties.

Teachers come under qualified privilege that grants immunity from liability as long as the speaker does not abuse the privilege. Abuse occurs when the speaker does not honestly believe what he or she says or has no reasonable grounds for believing it. Telling the truth is usually, but not always, a good defense against defamation. If the truth is spoken but the intent is to willfully and maliciously impugn the character of another, the speaker may be judged liable.

The important points for teachers to remember are (1) not to say anything defamatory about anyone else unless it becomes necessary; and (2) when it is necessary, to say or write it only to those who have a bona fide interest in the person. When a guidance counselor, the principal, or an adviser requests information about a student, a teacher is privileged to transmit anything she or he believes to be true, no matter how defamatory it may sound.

Immunity From Liability

Although teachers are always liable for their negligent actions as individuals, the school districts for which they work may be immune from tort liability. Most of the states are still under what is called the *immunity doctrine,* which means that the government cannot be held liable for the negligent acts of its employees, agents, and officials. A public school district is a governmental agency and is thus immune in those states. It follows, then, that where the school district cannot be successfully sued, injured parties will sue the individual whose negligence caused the injury. That's why teachers are often the defendants in tort liability cases.

There are several states, however, where statutes now permit suits in tort to be brought directly against the school district. In several others, the courts have removed the immunity doctrine (which is based on common law) with respect to governmental agencies, and in those states, school districts may now be sued for tort. Finally, several states have so-called save-harmless statutes, which do not allow the school district to be sued but do allow it to pay the damages and court costs for its employees' negligence, provided the incident occurred while the employees were performing duties connected with their jobs in the district.

In the states described in the preceeding paragraphs, the public-school teachers are protected from serious financial loss by the school district itself. In all the other states, the teachers must have insurance to protect them. School districts usually carry personal liability insurance on their employees. If the judgment against a teacher is for more than the amount covered by the insurance, the teacher is liable for the difference. In some states, the teachers' organizations carry liability policies on each member, although these policies may not give enough protection.

Summary

Teachers have certain rights, but each right is accompanied by related responsibilities. Therefore, along with the various legal rights of teachers, the professional responsibilities that accompany them should be learned.

Teachers must have certificates, issued by the states, in order to teach in public schools. Differing requirements by the states cause problems for teachers who move across state lines, but several steps are being taken by the states to reach a solution.

All states have specific statutes pertaining to teachers' contracts, which must include the five basic elements of a valid contract: (1) competent parties; (2) mutual assent; (3) valid consideration; (4) sufficient definition, and (5) legal subject matter.

Besides certification and contracts, there are other legal rights of teachers to be considered. Among these are salaries and fringe benefits; retirement plans; leaves of absence (with or without pay); tenure; academic freedom; the right to organize and bargain collectively; the right to engage in political activity and to be free from discrimination based on race, sex, age, or handicap; duty-free lunch periods; and the right to hold other employment.

The control of students is an important element of teaching. Lack of control nearly always leads to a poor learning environment for the students, and it could also lead to the reprimand or dismissal of the teacher. For these reasons, the states require the schools to control the behavior, the appearance, and the activities of students in a reasonable manner. Schools are encouraged to create reasonable rules with accompanying penalties and to enforce them with appropriate procedures that follow due-process principles. As a result, students may be legally suspended or expelled, corporally punished, detained, and searched.

All teachers are legally responsible for the safety, health, and well-being of the students under their supervision. If they breach that responsibility by doing something that a normally prudent teacher would not do, or by not doing something that a normally prudent teacher would have done in similar circumstances, they are negligent. If that negligence is the actual and proximate cause of a real injury to students under their supervision, these teachers can be held liable by a court of law and may be required to pay damages. This is called *tort liability*.

The courts, however, recognize that teachers cannot be all places at one time or see all things that go on. Consequently, the courts have emphasized the point that as long as reasonable precautions are taken by teachers to prevent injuries, they will not be held liable.

Questions

1. Explain the five basic elements that must be present in drawing up a valid teaching contract.
2. Define *tenure*. Can a tenured teacher who transfers from one school district to another still claim tenure in the new district?
3. How much freedom does a teacher have to state his or her own viewpoint on controversial issues within the classroom?
4. Explain the terms *quotas* and *discrimination*. How have these affected educational practices?
5. What is *in loco parentis?* What are the rights and restrictions that *in loco parentis* gives teachers?

6. How have the courts ruled in regard to compulsory attendance laws, and how do you personally feel about these laws?
7. Differentiate between the terms *suspension* and *expulsion*. Give some examples of each.
8. What is wrong with using grades as penalties? What are some alternatives?
9. In terms of tort liability, define *negligence* and give the four elements that must be present in order for negligence to be proved.

Activities for Unit V

1. Visit a state or federal court and report to the class what you have observed.
2. Invite a local lawyer who handles school law cases to discuss past cases.
3. Invite a professor of school law to come to your class and discuss major principles of school law.
4. Interview a superintendent or a school board member in regard to the amount of litigation that occurs yearly in the school district. Try to ascertain the magnitude of yearly legal costs in a school district.
5. Clip newspaper articles concerning school litigation to be placed on the classroom bulletin board.
6. Ask a principal what due-process procedures are employed in his or her school district. What has been the effect of due-process procedures on school discipline and special education decisions?
7. Research the *Brown* v. *Board of Education of Topeka* case (1954) and demonstrate its relationship to the Fourteenth Amendment.
8. Interview a school superintendent in regard to the procedure that he or she uses in the process of termination of a tenured and a nontenured teacher.
9. Review articles in the *Kappan* on compulsory school attendance, and summarize the pros and cons of the issue.
10. Research the topic of desegregation by investigating a case in your state.
11. Research and evaluate a Saturday school or an in-school suspension program in a school district within your area.
12. Research in a law library any case on tort liability. What significance does this case have for education?

CONTROL AND GOVERNANCE OF EDUCATION

11

Local and State Governance and Control of Education

OBJECTIVES

After reading Chapter 11, the student will be able to:

- Understand the evolution of and the current issues in state and local governance.
- Perceive the roles of state and local governments in the governance and control of education.
- Recognize the role of the various state agencies and state public officials in the governance of education.
- Be cognizant of the powers, limitations, duties, and methods of selection of local school boards.
- Become aware of the powers, duties, and responsibilities of a local school superintendent.

Introduction

Students of education and prospective teachers want to understand the "system" that they will be working in, just as new executives want to understand the corporate structure and the control of the industries in which they work. To accomplish this, it is necessary to study the control and governance of education. First, one must differentiate between governance and control. The authors of this text feel that, although the definitions of these terms have much in common, *governance* should be used for the formal system of government management of the education function of society, whereas *control* of education includes any person or group having an organized influence on education in the United States. Thus, *control* is a broader term and includes informal influences on education from special-interest groups such as parents' organizations and taxpayers' groups. Such groups do not have legal responsibilities for the running of schools and are not hired by those who do have statutory authority, but they can have a major impact on how the schools function.

Questions

Numerous questions are raised and examined in this chapter. What should be the relationship of local, state, and federal governments in governing education? What should be the role of lay citizens and professional educators in making decisions about schools? Should the primary objectives of schools be intellectual, social, personal, vocational, or a combination of these? What is the governance system for education at the state level? What are some problems that states have in controlling education, and what are some possible solutions? What are the roles of the state legislatures, the state boards of education, the state departments of education, the chief state school officers, and the state courts in governing education? At the local level, what are the duties and responsibilities of local school boards and local school superintendents in the governance of education? What problems are caused by the variation in the wealth of local districts, and what are some possible remedies for this situation? What are the roles of the U.S. Constitution, the U.S. Congress, the U.S. Department of Education, the U.S. Secretary of Education, and the federal courts in the governance of education? Who should control the public schools, and what should be the role of special-interest groups? What alternatives to public schools are available to students in the United States, and how are private schools governed?

Evolution of Governance

Before we examine the details of the system of governance of schools in the United States, it is necessary to provide a short history of the evolution of the governance and control of education in the United States.

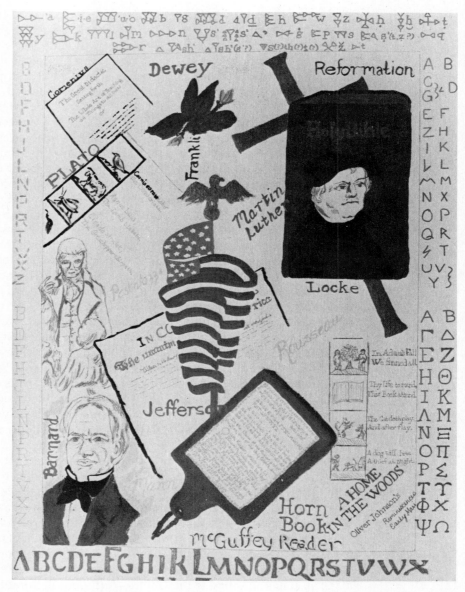

As education has evolved, so has the governance of education. *(Photo by Axler.)*

Although statutes such as the Massachusetts laws of 1642 and 1647 providing for free public schools had already been passed, the American schools were primarily private or church-related in the late 1600s and in the 1700s. The control of these early schools was concentrated in church groups or individuals. Thomas Jefferson proposed a system of free public elementary schools for Virginia, but his original proposal was defeated. The public school movement in the United States was founded on the later work of Horace Mann in Massachusetts and of Henry Barnard in Connecticut. Most of the early public schools were small one-room primary schools established by local communities, encouraged by state laws that permitted, but did not require, schools to be set up at public expense wherever a small cluster of families desired to establish them. This pattern of small, local school districts was to remain the most common configuration in the United States in the 1800s and during most of the 1900s. The county unit became the predominant pattern of organization in the South, and the town school was the most common in New England. States began to make it compulsory rather than merely permitted for local communities to establish schools supported by local taxes.

Who would govern or control these schools? Early school laws passed by the colonies contained language that would give local civil officials the power to control schools, instead of special school boards. The early state legislatures passed regulations for schools, and the local town officials provided day-to-day supervision of the local school. There was no state bureaucracy in these early days, no state board of education, nor any chief state school officer. As Campbell, Cunningham, Nystrand, Usdan (1980) wrote, "There were no separate boards of education for the first 200 years of our history" (p. 64). Schools were very simple and small during this period; and the states believed that they were to protect and encourage schools, not to establish and support them. Thus, for two hundred years, the schools were governed by the same governmental bodies as governed the towns as a whole. However, in the 1820s the Massachusetts legislature established school boards, called *town school committees,* as separate governmental bodies to run the schools, providing local governance for schools separate from the local government of cities and towns. Special governance for schools became a reality at the state level also. According to Campbell, et al., "special government for education was soon to emerge, first in the form of a chief state school officer, often called a state superintendent of public instruction, and later a state board of education" (p. 64). By 1870, thirty-six of the states had created such a position; by 1900, all states admitted to the Union—forty-four in number—had chief state school officers; all states since admitted to the Union also have such officials. Thus, a special system of governance for education has been established at both the local and the state levels in the United States.

Even though lay control and inspection of local schools were established early in American history, a necessity later arose for professional administrators to run the day-to-day operation of the public schools under policy guidelines established by lay school boards. In the local schools, these persons were called *head teachers* or *principal teachers,* and they usually also taught classes. With the growth of cities and the increased size of school districts because of the combination of smaller districts, the supervision of schools became too time-consuming for lay-school-board members who held other full-time employment; thus, the post of superintendent of schools was created in each local district. At first, the duties of both the principal and the superintendent were mostly clerical, consisting of keeping records such as enrollment and attendance figures, but soon, persons in these positions took on more substantial duties in the supervision of local schools and local school districts.

How could this evolution of governance and control of American public schools be summarized? First, the American schools are not a national system; instead, they grew from the local, grass-roots level. Second, in the United States, control of policymaking for public schools has traditionally been placed in the hands of laypeople, not professional administrators. However, the daily operation of schools and the administration of policy decisions reside in professional educational administrators, such as principals or superintendents. Meanwhile, a change from a majority of private and/or church-related schools to public and secular schools had taken place. In most places in the United States, private schools became alternatives to public schools, which enrolled the vast majority of students in the country. As Campbell et al. (1980) stated,

> The basis for state control over education was pretty well established as early as 1820 by constitutional and statutory provisions of the states which made up the union . . . 13 of the 23 states had constitutional provisions for education, seventeen had statutory provisions, and only two states—Rhode Island and Tennessee—had neither constitutional nor statutory provisions for education. (p. 64)

However, the governance of schools has continued to become more complicated as the American society has grown more complex:

> Our early schools, largely under the control of the local communities, seemed to serve a rural, homogeneous society rather well. . . . The schools of today are not only the product of forces noted above (such as secularization and egalitarianism); they also exist in a complex, largely urban, and pluralistic society. Moreover, world-wide ideologies and practices affect today's schools beyond the wildest dreams of the citizens of this nation during the last century. Under these circumstances the questions of organization and control of American schools have new meanings and require fresh analyses. (Campbell, pp. 10–11)

Although much can be learned from studying the historical background of governance and control in American schools, the modern world may require some changes in the traditional governance of schools. Citizens must learn to preserve the best and most sacred of these traditions while also fostering some modifications to adapt to changing circumstances.

State Governance of Education

Introduction

In the United States, education is primarily a function of fifty state governments. Education is controlled, legally, by state government. Teachers are state employees, school board members are state officials, and the taxes used to support schools are state and local taxes. However, the states have chosen to delegate the day-to-day operation of the schools to local school boards and the local school districts under broad state guidelines. Historically, education has been viewed as one of the powers left up to the states or "reserved to the states and to the people," as put forth in the "reserved-powers" clause of the Tenth Amendment of the U.S. Constitution:

> Although the Constitution of the United States contains no direct reference to education, most state constitutions have specific provisions which make education a legal responsibility of the state. Moreover, the statutes of most states stipulate in considerable detail how schools are to be governed. Much of this control is delegated to district boards of education and to other bodies, all of which become a part of the state system of education. In a sense, then, we have 50 systems of education in America, but in many respects these various systems are similar. (Campbell et al., 1980, p. 61)

The state has the power to establish, and to abolish, local school districts, which are legally quasi corporations created by the state. The states can also force the consolidation or the reorganization of local schools, as they have done in many states in the past three decades for purposes such as efficiency and monetary savings. Today, there are fewer school districts nationwide than there were twenty or thirty years ago because of this reorganization process. Although many residents in small rural communities have opposed this reorganization, by which they would lose a local high school in their community, the process of reorganization has continued because it has been mandated by state legislatures and state boards of education, which have the authority in these matters.

State Powers

The states can either grant local school districts broad power or, conversely, limit the powers of these local districts severely. What are the primary powers that the states exercise in their control of local schools?

Primary Powers of the State

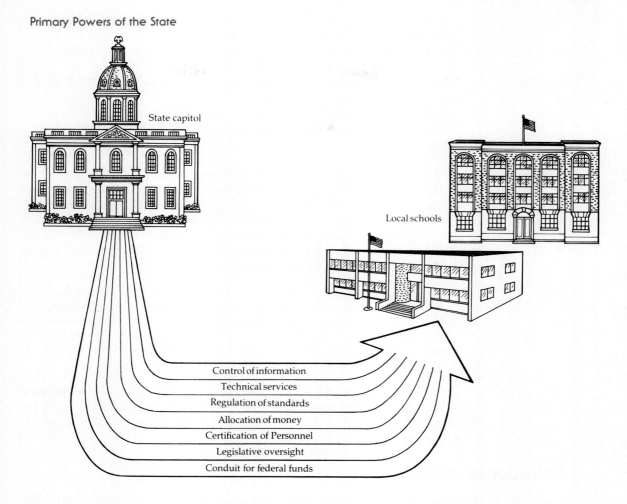

State capitol

Local schools

Control of information
Technical services
Regulation of standards
Allocation of money
Certification of Personnel
Legislative oversight
Conduit for federal funds

1. *Control of information:* The states require reports from local school districts and conduct studies of local school practices.
2. *Technical services:* The states provide technical services in areas such as curriculum and programs for both the mentally and physically handicapped and the gifted.
3. *Regulation of standards:* The states regulate standards for such things as attendance, textbooks, and fiscal records.
4. *Allocation of money:* The states appropriate and allocate money for the operation of local schools, but local schools supplement these appropriations with money raised locally.
5. *Certification of personnel:* The states now determine the nature of preservice and in-service preparation programs for teachers, but the states

are currently being challenged by universities and teachers' organizations for the control of these activities.

6. *Legislative oversight:* The states, through state departments of education, oversee and help implement legislative mandates.

7. *State legal review:* State courts settle differences in the interpretation of state laws regarding schools.

8. *Conduit for federal funds:* The states receive funds from the federal government and enforce federal regulations established for federal school programs.

Some of these state controls are exercised by the state department of education, and others are controlled directly by the governor, the state attorney general, the state auditor, the state legislature, or other state agencies concerned with building codes or health standards. The inability of many local school districts to adequately finance their schools in recent years has led to an increase in direct state involvement in education. Herman (1977) summarized the state education powers in these words:

> Individual states differ in the specifics of their control over local decision makers. Practically all of them, however, administer a wide variety of federal programs, many of them have labor relations (collective bargaining) legislation, a few have formal accountability models and all have a great proliferation of bureaucrats that write and interpret a mountain of rules and regulations to be obeyed by local school districts. (p. 154)

In the next sections of this textbook, the educational functions of the state constitutions, the state legislatures, the state boards of education, the state departments of education, and the state superintendent of schools are examined in greater detail.

State Constitutions

The states have the constitutional and statutory powers to control and regulate the schools within their borders. Each state has a constitution created by a constitutional convention. The convention delegates are elected; and thus, the state constitutions and their educational mandates ultimately reflect the will of the people of the state. The federal government has only specific powers given (or "delegated") to it by the U.S. Constitution. However, state governments have all powers except those that are prohibited to them by the U.S. Constitution or by their respective state constitutions. State constitutions deal with education explicitly, whereas the U.S. Constitution does not mention education, dealing with it only by implication. Krohne (1982) explicated further the language used in state constitutions:

> Historically, however, all state constitutions address the general concept that the legislature is responsible for providing a free public education system. A

few state constitutions make this responsibility discretionary (or optional) such as Mississippi. . . . Most, however, are written using such words as "shall," "will," or "must" instead of "may" as a clear directive of acceptance to providing educational opportunities to its citizenry. (pp. 22–23)

Let us use the state of Indiana as an example of the constitutional provisions in the states in general. In 1816, the Indiana State Constitution provided, "as soon as circumstances will permit," for the establishment of a tuition-free educational system from elementary school through the university level, but financial circumstances never permitted the state legislature to fully carry out this generous charge. The Indiana legislature did enact permissive legislation to permit property owners at the local level to levy a tax for school construction, but through the 1840s, education was basically a function of local government with little state involvement. Krohne (1982) summarized the origin of the Indiana State Superintendent and the Indiana State Board of Education:

Following the new Indiana State Constitution in 1852, which made no provisions for a state board of education but did provide for a state superintendent, a law was passed which among other things established a state board of education in Indiana. The first state board was created by section 147 of the School Law of 1852, and was made up of the state superintendent, the auditor, the treasurer, the secretary of state, and the governor. In 1855, the attorney general was added as a sixth member. The first recorded meeting was June 7–10, 1853, which appears to mark the beginning of the Indiana State Board of Education. (p. 32)

State Legislatures

The state legislatures have plenary or "full" powers to control education within their states, but this full power is limited both by pressures to provide funds for other state services and by various checks and balances in the U.S. federal system of government. The important concept to remember is that the state legislature is the "big school board" in each state and that its actions supersede those of any local school boards in the state, which are created by, and can be abolished by, the state legislature. The state superintendent and the state board of education can propose and recommend education legislation, but only the state legislature can pass laws concerning education.

The checks-and-balances limitations on the power of a state legislature in regard to education are the first type of control on the education powers of the state legislature. First, the state legislature cannot act against the contents of the federal or state constitutions regarding education. All legislation passed in the United States, including laws passed by state legislatures, is subject to the prohibitions and limitations of the U.S. Constitution. The parts of the U.S. Constitution that are most often cited by the courts in ruling on education are the First Amendment, the Fifth Amendment, the Fourteenth Amendment,

State legislatures are the major source of control over education. *(Photo courtesy of the Indiana State Department of Education.)*

and Article 1, Section 10, on obligations of contracts. (See Chapter 12 for further details on the federal role in education.) Second, the courts have ruled that state legislatures cannot be unreasonable in their use of power and that they cannot delegate their full power over education to other agencies.

Competition for funding with other state services also limits each state's ability to use the authority that it possesses in the area of education. One problem faced by state legislatures is special-interest legislation aimed narrowly at one issue, such as "creationism" versus evolution in the teaching of science. A second problem for state legislatures in the area of education is the public demand for accountability in education. As a result, state legislatures are enacting more and more specific legislation on rules concerning schools, including competency testing for both teachers and students, property tax controls, and collective bargaining.

Collective bargaining, for example, is one of the main issues in the struggle between school boards and teacher associations, with each side trying to gain power through legislative action. Collective bargaining laws are continually being modified where they already exist, and are sought in states where they have not yet been established. On one side of the issue are those, including many state legislators, who feel that too much power has been taken from local school boards and that it is time to restore local control. On the other side are teachers' associations seeking legislation to strengthen the position of their members in the collective bargaining process (Pipho, 1980, p. 38).

State legislatures find themselves caught between many competing and antagonistic forces, with their full powers over education limited in many legal, constitutional, and practical ways. In recent years, the educational problems faced by state legislatures have also been exacerbated by such general societal problems as inflation, energy costs, and the decline of the school-aged population. As you can readily see, the "big school board" of the state legislature has more problems and limitations than ever before in its history.

State Boards of Education

Although the state legislatures have full powers over education and enact legislation to set general education policy for the state, they have established state boards of education to carry out these state policy mandates. Most of these state boards of education have similar powers but vary extensively in their size, their methods of selection, their terms of office, and their relationship to the superintendent of public instruction. At first, the state boards of education were composed of state officials elected to govern the state as a whole and not elected for the specific education function. These *ex officio* members included the governor, the secretary of state, the attorney general, and the auditor, but eventually board members came to be chosen for their specific educational purpose, either by appointment by the governor or by election by the citizens of each state. According to Campbell et al. (1980), "In 1972 board members in 31 states were appointed by the governor; in thirteen states were elected by the people; and in five states they acquired office in other ways" (p. 66). Thus, most state boards of education today are made up largely of lay citizens rather than professional educators. In recent years, there has been a trend toward having the members of the state board of education elected by the citizens of the state.

State Departments of Education

Most states have established state departments of education to administer the general policies of the state boards of education and have given them a variety of functions. One of the duties of the state department of education is to regulate and enforce minimum educational standards. Another function is to operate schools for the blind and the deaf. Still another duty is to help the schools improve their operations. State departments of education provide assistance to local school districts in planning, research, and evaluation. The state departments of education perform a leadership role in improving schools in their respective states.

The divisions of a typical state department of education include administration, finance, teacher certification and licensing, instructional services, cur-

Lines of Authority in the Texas Education Agency

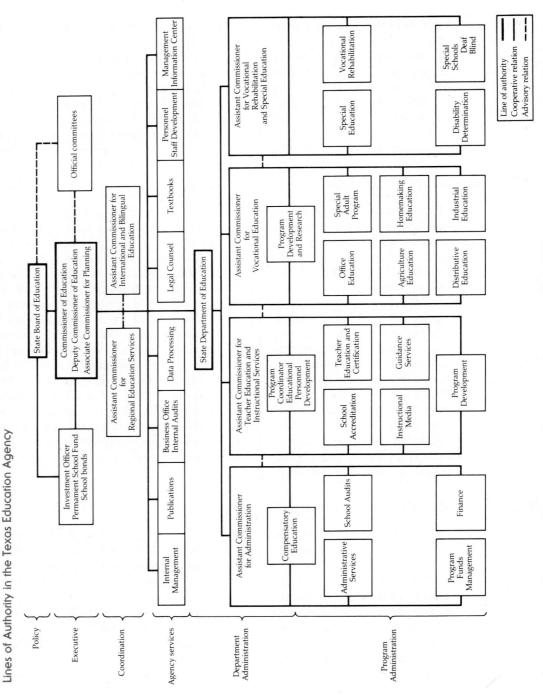

Source: Pearson, J. B. & Fuller, E. (Eds.). (1969). *Education in the States: Historical development and outlook.* Washington, DC: National Education Association of the United States, p. 1221.

riculum, vocational and adult education, vocational rehabilitation, and junior colleges. The most salient feature of state departments of education is that they act as a conduit for channeling federal funds to the local school districts. In many states, one half to two thirds of the personnel of the state department of public instruction are supported through federal money paid to the states to administer federal programs in education. In addition, the state department of education administers the state's financial contributions to education, making budget control a powerful function of the state education agencies.

State Superintendents of Education

The state superintendent of education is the top state school official in all states. He or she usually heads the state department of education and either is the chief executive officer of the state board of education or is selected independently of that group by election or appointment. In nineteen states, the state superintendent of education is elected by popular vote, and in twenty-six states, he or she is appointed by the state board of education. In five states, the state superintendent is appointed by the governor. The state superintendents who are elected by popular vote or appointed by the governors are legally state officers. Those who are appointed by state school boards, are considered employees, not officers, of their states. If we relate the method of selection of the state superintendent to that of the state board of education, fifteen states have a state superintendent and a state board of education appointed by the governor, eleven states have an elected state board of education that appoints the state superintendent, and thirteen states have an elected state superintendent but an appointed state board of education. In five states, both are appointed, and in six states both are elected. Only Wisconsin has no state board of education (Krohne, 1982, p. 28).

State Courts

The state courts also have an indirect influence on educational policy in a state because they interpret the education provisions in the state's constitution, establish common law by making decisions on educational questions brought before them, and decide whether state statutes are "constitutional" in terms of being in harmony with the state constitution. Although the state's power over education is subject to these controls, the state courts in general have been reluctant to interfere with the state's operation of the schools as long as the state acts in a reasonable and prudent manner. State school-finance plans are particularly being challenged in the state courts, and many of these courts have ruled that the unequal educational opportunities caused by inequities in school finance within a state are a violation of state constitutional provisions. These recent court decisions have encouraged school-finance-reform legislation in many states. (See Chapter 13 for more details on this reform movement.) Thus, the state courts have had a significant influence on state educational concerns.

Conclusions on State Governance

Most authorities in education are predicting an increased state role in education for a variety of reasons. First, education is legally a state function, not a local function. Even though the states have historically delegated the daily operation of the schools to the local school districts, numerous factors are currently forcing the states to become more active in education. One reason has been that local revenue sources have been inadequate. This factor, combined with inflation and local property-tax freezes, has forced the states to assume a greater role in school finance. Another reason for increased state influence is the recent demand for accountability in education, which has resulted in specific legislation on accountability in about half the states. Increasing teacher power also leads to more state jurisdiction, as seen in the fact that twenty-three states have established state-level professional-practices boards composed mostly of teachers.

A second major reason for the growth in state leadership in education has been the trend in recent years for the president to limit the federal role in education. Although both Presidents Nixon and Carter stressed the need to cut back federal involvement in education in favor of an increased state role, President Reagan has even stated that he wants to dismantle the federal education establishment and to eliminate the recently formed Cabinet-level Department of Education. Although President Reagan has not carried out these proposals, he has given impetus to state leadership in education. Merit pay and career-ladder plans in Tennessee and North Carolina show that the states are currently taking the lead in educational reform, encouraged by the president and the U.S. Department of Education. The states have increased power and authority because all federal aid is administered by the states, which act as proxies for the federal government. An additional reason for the growth in state power and influence in education is the increased number of mandates from the state legislature and the demand for more accountability in education. State education agencies are the logical choice to establish and implement legislative mandates for competency tests for both teachers and students.

What are some predictions for the role of the states in education? The role of the states in planning, evaluation, and research will increase as a result of these legislative mandates. Increasingly able personnel will be attracted to the state departments of education because of larger salaries supported primarily by federal funds. It is also predicted that state legislatures will often become "traffic cops" mediating among various state interest groups, and that special state problems of the 1980s will center on lids on taxes, inflation, and accomplishing more with fewer resources.

Additional future trends in state governance of education are foreseen by

Herman (1977, pp. 143–144). He believes that there is a trend toward spending identical amounts for the education of each student in the state regardless of the taxable wealth available at the local district level. Herman foresees a continuation of categorical aid (aid for special purposes such as special education) to stimulate innovation at the local level. The trend, in his opinion, is for the states to take away decision-making powers from the local school district level. Some state cetegorical-aid programs will be only partially funded, and some will not be worth the local effort needed to initiate and sustain them.

What are the major problems involved in the state governance of education? First, the states often mandate educational programs, such as those for special education students, but at the same time fail to provide adequate financial resources to carry out these plans, leaving the local school districts to find the necessary funds. The states often do not provide adequate financing of education in inflationary times or do not decide on fiscal allocations of funds far enough in advance to give local officials sufficient planning time to meet deadlines. Paperwork for state education agencies requires an excessive amount of local school officials' time and energy.

Educational decisions made at the state level include the scope and extent of the instructional programs, including standards, compulsory attendance, minimum length of school year, selection of textbooks, and required courses of study; certification of personnel, including approval of the programs of teacher-training institutions and the certification of school personnel; facilities standards; and financial support, which encompasses a ceiling on local-school-district taxes, stipulations for how the school budget is to be prepared and what budget categories should be used, and approval of the local-school-district budget. The execution of educational governance at the state level is performed by the governor, the chief state school officer, the state board of education, and the state department of education, with a few functions handled by other state agencies. It is important to remember that, subject to some limitations, the state legislatures have plenary or full powers over public education in their respective states because education is a power reserved to the states and the people by the U.S. Constitution and because the states must delegate any powers exercised by school districts at the local level.

Local Governance of Education

Introduction

Although the states have the legal authority to provide public education in the United States, they have delegated the day-to-day operation of public schools to local school districts in each state. These local school districts are, thus, the basic administrative unit for school organization in the United States. The states' policy of delegating authority to local school boards and the courts' practice of permitting local school boards any reasonable and prudent use of this authority have made the local school district the most important unit in American education, according to many educational experts. Campbell et al. (1980) summarized the powers delegated to the local school districts:

> In brief, the duties of school board members include the right to establish schools, to build school houses, to employ a superintendent, to establish necessary rules to manage and govern the schools, and to raise and expend money. The courts have consistently held that such delegations by the state legislature to district boards of education are appropriate. (p. 75)

The local school district is a unit of government, created by the state, with quasi-corporate powers. It is given the power to administer a public school or a public school system and is controlled by a local board of education. It has the power to tax, the power to make contracts, and the right to employ a superintendent if it chooses. Thus, these local school districts are creations or extensions of the state, which can create, destroy, or modify them, an important point to remember in studying the reorganization of local districts. The state can make these local school districts autonomous and independent, or dependent and subservient to the state control agencies.

There are some 16,000 school districts existing in the United States making them the most numerous units of local government. They vary tremendously in size (from huge metropolitan districts like Los Angeles and Chicago to small districts with a handful of schools), wealth, power, and effectiveness of operation. "Their diversity illustrates the tenaciousness with which Americans hold to these remnants of localism and grassroots expression of the public will" (Campbell et al., 1980, pp. 90–91).

Many states have established an intermediate or county unit between the local and state levels in the governance of education. Historically, the more centralized county unit of organization for education began in the South, where people were spread farther apart than in New England, where the town or township was the local unit of governance. This intermediate or county unit is another example of the state's proclivity to delegate the supervision of schools closer to the actual operation of the schools. This county unit, consisting of the county superintendent of schools and a county board of education, makes certain that local schools operate according to state legislative mandates and state-board-of-education rules. These intermediate units are more common in states having numerous small rural districts and schools, which need this additional kind of supervision:

> While the function of the intermediate unit is not always clear, the county superintendent or county board is usually charged with preparing information and making reports to the state department of education, assisting in the reorganization of school districts, registering teachers' certificates, assisting in the supervision of rural schools, assisting with in-service education of teachers,

and providing some special services in weak districts. (Campbell et al., 1980, p. 76)

Thus, these county governance units, which are found in about one half of the states, are set up to provide services that small school districts cannot provide for themselves.

Local School Boards

Local school boards, as well as local school districts, are creations of the state legislature, which also has the power to abolish or modify them if it wishes. Membership on local school boards consists of lay citizens, not professional educators. This lay control of local school boards is the salient feature of education in the United States. These local school boards are the policymakers in education, whereas the administrators and the teachers only carry out and implement those policies passed by the local board of education. Thus, two important principles to be remembered about the American governance of education are that school policy is formulated by lay school boards and then is administered by local school officials. An individual school board member has no official decision-making authority unless he or she is attending an official school-board meeting. Local school-board members should not interfere as individuals in the daily operation of the schools, just as the school administration should refrain from making school policy decisions without approval of the local school board. Local school board members are legally "agents" of the state, whereas local school administrators are "employees" of the local school district and the local school board. School boards generally have from three to seven members; and members serve terms of three, four,

Local school boards implement state school policies as well as make local policies. *(Photo used by permission of the Indianapolis Public Schools.)*

or six years. Other than some reimbursement for expenses, school board members seldom receive a salary (Campbell et al., 1980).

Powers of Local School Boards   The powers of the local school board come from the state legislature in the form of statutes interpreted by the state courts. These powers are granted by statute, fairly and necessarily implied from those powers expressly granted, and essential to accomplishing the goals set for the local schools by the state. The board, as has been said, must act as a whole and cannot delegate powers that are mandated for the boards alone to perform, such as employing teachers. The superintendent recommends candidates for teaching positions, but only the board in a duly constituted board meeting can put them under contract. In addition, the local school board has no choice but to carry out state education mandates, such as special education programs or pupil competency testing. Local boards of education have the power to establish schools, to hire administrators and teachers, to tax and to borrow money, to draw up attendance boundaries, to determine curricula, and to pass school budgets.

Limitations on Local School Boards   Many formal and informal controls and limitations exist on this wide power exercised by local school boards. The formal legal controls originate with the state legislature and the state board of education. The procedures for selecting school board members (see the next section in this chapter) and the behavior of board members after they are selected are prescribed by state statutes. These state laws govern the size of the board, the length of term of the members, the method of filling vacancies, the time and location of regular board meetings, the procedures for special board meetings, and the duties of school board members. While local school boards may have the right to raise money through local taxes, often a ceiling is set by law on the tax rate which can be levied. In addition state laws often specify specific procedures that must be followed by local boards of education in the expenditure of money. For example, new building, renovation, or major equipment purchases might by law need approval by local district referendum (Campbell et al., 1980).

An informal limitation on local school boards relates to public pressure. School boards have external and internal responsibilities. The internal duties are concerned with management responsibilities, but the external duties involve the relationship of the schools to the public that the school board serves. Especially in large, diverse school districts, many pressure groups compete for the attention of the school board. Because being a school board member is not a full-time job and pays a minimum salary, board members often feel persecuted when the public threatens, harasses, and criticizes them during public board meetings (many times concerning emotional issues over which they have little control, such as federal desegregation mandates). Campbell et al. (1980, pp. 191–192) believe that public schools often become the political arena for attempts to reconcile social controversies. As a result,

Controversy Over Local School Boards

SHOULD LOCAL SCHOOL BOARDS EXIST?	
Pros	Cons
1. Boards provide lay involvement in and control of education.	1. Boards have responsibility without funding power.
2. They promote grass-roots support.	2. They lack autonomy of action.
3. Decisions are made closest to level of implementation.	3. They lack expertise.
4. Special local knowledge is brought to decisions.	4. They lack a broad vision of education.
	5. Districts vary greatly in wealth.

HOW SHOULD MEMBERS BE SELECTED?			
Appointment		Election	
Pros	Cons	Pros	Cons
1. High-quality people are appointed. 2. Members have interests of whole community as motivation.	1. Members chosen because of "political connections."	1. It's democratic. 2. Grass-roots political support.	1. Single-issue interest. 2. Campaigning is devisive and expensive and deters many qualified candidates. 3. Members are elected because of "negative politics," i.e., being against something.

school boards often become scapegoats for public frustration on issues such as busing, prayer in schools, reduction in teaching staff, school reorganization, and school closings.

Methods of Selection How are school board members selected for American schools? The two primary methods are by appointment and by public vote. The greatest number of school boards have elected members; only 14 percent of school board members are appointed to their posts. In many communities with appointed school boards, the board members are appointed by the mayor, the city council, the county council, the county commissioners, or a combination of these. Appointive boards often have limitations on the number of members from one political party.

The advantages of appointive boards are that high-quality, capable community leaders who would not volunteer to run for an election to the school board are often selected; and that appointed board members usually have broad community interests at heart, not just specific, single interests, which often motivate individuals to seek election to a school board. A disadvantage of appointive boards is the possible political influence involved in the appointment of members by officials who are actively engaged in political parties, such as mayors or council members.

Of the school boards composed of elected members, most are selected through nonpartisan elections, either at-large in the school district or by subdistricts within the school district itself. In school districts with elected boards, the nomination procedure becomes very important. Many of these districts have umbrella grass-roots citizens' groups or planning committees that slate candidates for school board election, and others use caucuses of all eligible voters in the district or petitions to select candidates.

The advantages of elected local school boards include a democratic selection process and grass-roots political support. The disadvantages include the political campaigning necessary in an election, the single-issue politics and negative motivation "against something" that motivate many of these candidates, and the loss of many qualified candidates who are not motivated to seek political office by running in an election.

Who Serves and What Motivates Members   We now come to the questions of who serves on school boards, what the personal characteristics of school board members are, and what motivates these members to serve on school boards. About half the elected school board members have special-interest motivation for seeking election, and the other half profess broad community-oriented objectives (Campbell et al., 1980, pp. 196–197). This leaves no doubt that pressure on single issues such as busing, school finance, and closing specific schools does motivate many individuals to seek elected school-board positions. Men continue to be a majority of school board members, but the percentage of minorities on school boards is increasing. Women are usually elected, not appointed, and are a minority of school board members. The trend in school board membership is toward including both younger and older persons as members, toward higher income levels of board members, and toward higher levels of education. Many experts predict that in the future, more minorities and women will serve as school board members. The most common categories of the professions of school board members are managers and owners of businesses, professionals, farmers, and homemakers. For a few individuals, such as former President Jimmy Carter of Georgia, school board membership may lead to a political career, but for most members, service on the school board is their highest political or public-service office.

Pros and Cons of Local School Boards   The advantages of having local school boards include citizen involvement in the educational process, grass-roots support for education, decisions made closest to the level of implementation, and knowledge of the special circumstances in which each school finds itself. One of the biggest problems with local school boards today is that they have retained responsibility for local programs but have lost control of the financing power to support these programs fully because of property tax freezes and increased state aid to education. A smaller percentage of school funds is raised at the local level controlled by the school board, and yet many new mandates flow from the state to the local school each year. The local school boards seem to be caught in the middle of these pressures, as we will see in Chapter 13. Many factors seem to be encroaching on the relative autonomy that school districts enjoyed in the past, and many expect the school districts to have even less autonomy in the future. Lay school boards are chastised for lacking the expertise needed in today's society in areas such as collective bargaining and school finance. Another criticism of local school districts is their variation in wealth, especially assessed valuation, and, thus, in educational opportunity. Critics assert that a state or national system of education would be more efficient and would eliminate the disparity between the have's and the have-not's in present local school districts. In spite of these criticisms, local school districts and school board members seem to be permanent fixtures in American education.

Local School Superintendents

The local superintendent of schools is appointed to the position by the local school board and can be dismissed by this same group. (It is interesting that school administrators do not have a guarantee of tenure or automatic contract renewal after a specified number of years as a trial period. Superintendents and other school administrators may have earned tenure as teachers but cannot attain it for administrative positions.) The local superintendent of schools is the chief executive of the board of education and carries out the policies approved by this board. Many local superintendents serve small school districts and have little or no central office staff to help them carry out their duties. In populous urban areas, superintendents may have a large central office staff with differentiated duties in areas such as finance, curriculum, planning, special services, elementary education, and secondary education. Thus, the duties of a superintendent of schools can vary from the supervision of a few teachers in a small school district to the supervision of hundreds of central-office staff members and thousands of teachers.

The most important delineation of the powers and duties of the superintendent, compared to those of the local school board, is that the board formulates policy for the local school district, and the superintendent implements or carries out this board policy. When a school board member interferes in the daily operation of a school or a school district, he or she has overstepped the bounds of the sole duty of the board to make policy. The powers of a local school superintendent are given to her or him by the local board of education and include recommending teachers and administrators to be employed by the board, proposing a budget for the local school district, recommendations concerning both physical facilities and curriculum changes, and recom-

The local school superintendent serves as the chief spokesperson for the local district in the community. *(Photo used by permission of the Metropolitan School District of Lawrence Township.)*

mendations concerning purchases of materials to be made by the district. Thus, the local superintendent has both business management and curriculum and supervision functions.

Many modern school superintendents are essentially mediators among various special-interest and pressure groups. It is hoped that the superintendent will be a leader in directing the future course of the school district and the community through her or his duty to educate both the board and the local citizens on issues of concern to schools. In practice, this is not always the case, although the superintendent does wield enormous power through appointments, administration of the budget, and visibility in the community. However, it is believed by many experts on education that local school boards and superintendents have had their power eroded by encroachments from state and federal government, as will be seen in Chapter 12. Even the power of teachers' organizations and the limitations on property taxes supported by local citizens' groups have greatly decreased the actual clout of local school superintendents in many school systems.

What are the characteristics of persons who serve as local school superintendents, and what are the possibilities of superintendency as a career? The vast majority of local superintendents are males, but some females are entering the field. Finance is usually rated as the top issue by superintendents, but teacher militancy, race relations, and changing societal values are also important to superintendents (Campbell et al., 1980, pp. 224–225). The superintendency is not a very stable career for many superintendents: the median term of a superintendent in one position is four years, and the median length of a person's entire career in the superintendency is seven years. Apparently, the pluralism and pressures in American society have made this a difficult position for one person to hold for an extended period.

What conclusions can be drawn and what predictions can be made about superintendency in the future? Because of the consolidation and reorganization of local districts, the number of superintendents may decline slightly in future years. However, better selection procedures and improved preparation programs with less emphasis on academic course work and with greater emphasis on internships and field experience may improve the quality of local superintendents. A doctorate is increasingly required for superintendents in large school districts. Some education experts, such as Kirst and Garms (1980), see centralization and loss of local power as the key factor in the role of the superintendent in the future. During the recent decades superintendents and school boards saw their areas of discretionary power being eroded both from the top and the bottom. From the top, state and federal governments as well as the courts increased their roles in education, thus diminishing local control. Also private interest groups such as the Ford Foundation, the Council for Basic Education, the Education Commission of the States, and the Council for Exceptional Children raised their concerns and used their influence to shape educational policy. And from the bottom, superintendents and school boards found their powers tied to local collective bargaining contracts. There seems to be no reason to believe that this trend will be reversed in the future.

Conclusions on Local Governance

Some general conclusions and future predictions can be drawn from this discussion of local governance and control. First, although local school boards and superintendents will continue to have the legal authority to run day-to-day educational programs, several factors would seem to portend limits on this authority. Many of the problems surface at the local level, but many key decisions (especially financial decisions) are made at the state level, leaving the local board of education with the problems but without the means to deal with them. The growth of power of both teachers' organizations and special-interest groups of lay citizens also limits the effective power of the local school board. Another factor in the loss of power of local school boards has been the increase in state and federal regulations, such as rules for special education and the handicapped.

Herman (1977) summarized the variety of state and federal regulations and other pressures on school boards:

> Arbitrators tell you how to interpret master contracts with employees; individual pupil's rights provide hearings on any student disciplinary actions; MIOSHA [state occupational safety agency] inspectors levy fines and temporarily close down equipment and school plants; inspectors investigate to determine whether or not the local district is meeting affirmative action quotas; unemployment compensation is paid, with the approval of the reviewing agency, for a bus driver who quit the job—payment was made during the summer when other bus drivers were not collecting salaries; the types and quantity of food to be served students is [sic] determined by federal and state agents if the district wishes to receive reimbursement; a plan for the busing of

local students to achieve desegregation is agreed to by the courts and federal agencies; the district needs [to] establish an educational program for a month old child whose doctor has certified him as being handicapped; the local teachers' union or association threatens to strike if the provisions suggested by the state and national teachers' associations are not included in the master contract negotiated with the local board of education; and ad-infinitum. (pp. 146–147)

Thus, it seems certain that school boards will be asked to do more with fewer financial resources and increased state and federal regulations, in addition to augmented pressure from teachers' organizations and lay groups. School board members will find themselves mediating the pressures from these groups and others, too, in future years.

Summary

The most important concept for students to understand from this chapter about educational governance is that education is a state function. States, however, generally delegate the actual operation of schools to the local school district, while maintaining their powers of oversight and ultimate authority. The governance of education has evolved from early colonial laws that gave local civil authorities the permission to establish schools if they so desired, to a hierarchy of special governance for education, with a state board of education and a chief state school officer in each state. The governance issues of funding, lack of uniformity, and present economic realities have also been spotlighted in this chapter. The origin of state "reserve" powers in the U.S. Constitution was examined, as well as the authority of the state legislatures, the state boards of education, and the state superintendents of education; Indiana was used as an example of governance in a typical state. On the local level, the powers and limitations of local school boards were surveyed, including the method of selection and the possible motivation of local school board members. Finally, the duties of local school superintendents were outlined, as well as problems and solutions at the local governance level. It was found that many local school boards and superintendents feel that their authority has been eroded in recent years by court intervention, militant teachers' organizations, and state control of school finances through Proposition 13-like property-tax freezes.

Questions

1. Make a list of special-interest groups that influence your state legislature. Which ones have the most influence in your state?
2. What is the title of the person in charge of the department of education in your state, and what are his or her major responsibilities?

3. Why is there a trend toward having fewer school districts? What are the advantages and disadvantages of consolidation?
4. Why do school districts resist reorganization into larger units?
5. How does a person become a member of a school board in your state?
   a. From what socioeconomic level do most school board members come?
   b. What are the legal requirements for school board members?
   c. What are the two primary methods of selecting school board members?
   d. What are the personal motivations of persons running for the school board in your community?
   e. How has single-issue politics affected school board elections in your state?
6. Distinguish between the role of the superintendent and the role of the school board in relation to administration and policy formation. In what ways can these lines become blurred, and what problems can this blurring cause?
7. What are the general duties, as defined by law, of your state school board?
8. What are some of the ways in which the public can be involved in the selection of school board candidates?
9. What are the advantages and the disadvantages of having a lay school board?
10. List the major powers and duties of your local school board.
11. Are school board members compensated for their duties in your state? If so, how much are they paid? Do you think the compensation is adequate? Why or why not?

12

Federal Governance and Control of Education

OBJECTIVES

After reading Chapter 12, the student will be able to:
- Comprehend the provisions of the U.S. Constitution pertaining to the origins of federal involvement in education.
- Perceive the level of future involvement of the federal government in education.
- Understand the influence of special-interest groups on educational policy.
- Distinguish between the control and governance of public schools and of private and parochial schools.
- Identify the significance of the role of alternative schools in answering questions concerning problems within public schools and providing choices outside public schools.

Introduction

The third level of governance in American education is federal controls and influence on United States schools. Historically, Americans have felt that the day-to-day operation of their schools, including curriculum, qualifications of teachers, selection of textbooks, and regulation of school buildings, should be controlled at the local level. However, the federal government has had a profound influence on American schools through federal money appropriated for education, regional resource centers that support federal education programs, categorical grants that support national interests in vocational education, and federal court decisions concerning desegregation and sex discrimination.

What the the three types of powers granted to governmental units in the United States, and how do these powers affect the federal role in education in the United States? In the U.S. Constitution, delegated powers are the powers expressly granted to the national government and the U.S. Congress. In other words, the federal government has only those specific powers listed in the Constitution. In contrast, all other powers are "reserved" to the states and to the people by the Tenth Amendment to the Constitution. Some powers, such as the authority to raise money through taxation, are granted to both the federal and the state governments, however. In addition, certain powers, such as the power to conduct foreign affairs, are forbidden to the states by the federal Constitution. Education is not mentioned in the U.S. Constitution, is not delegated to the national government, and therefore is "reserved" to the states. The federal courts have ruled that the federal government has "implied" powers, which are the powers necessary to carry out the authority specifically delegated to the federal government. It is in these "implied" powers that the federal government's authority is found. If education is necessary for the national defense or the general welfare (delegated functions of the federal government), the national government has the authority to pass and implement certain education legislation. Usually, this legislation is in areas where the states have failed to act, such as vocational education. Remember, however, that the federal government has limited and implied powers in education, whereas the state powers are plenary, or full, in this area.

Historically, the federal government has been involved in public education since the land ordinances of 1785 and 1787, but the total amount of federal assistance for education was small until the Russians launched *Sputnik* in 1957. Federal aid increased after *Sputnik*, the high point being the Elementary and Secondary Education Act (ESEA) of 1965. In the 1970s and 1980s, the federal influence on education has declined, but the federal government continues to be involved in public education. In fact, the federal programs related to education are so diverse, so numerous, and so dispersed among various federal agencies that it is difficult, if not impossible, to determine how much money the federal government does spend on educational activities. Students

Education is specifically a function of the states; however, federal involvement is extensive. (*Photo courtesy of the Library of Congress.*)

of education in the United States must realize that, although education is not mentioned in the U.S. Constitution, the federal influence on education has been present and extensive from the earliest days of our nation. However, the greatest federal involvement in public elementary and secondary education came after the Russians launched *Sputnik* in 1957.

The U.S. Constitution and Education

The U.S. Constitution contains no direct mention of education for two reasons. First, when the Constitution was adopted, the federal government had only limited (or enumerated) powers, or those that were implied from the

342

enumerated powers. Second, the states did not yet have public school systems because most schools in the late 1700s were parochial and private. The framers of the Constitution conceived of the national government as limited and circumscribed. The Tenth Amendment, included as part of the Bill of Rights in order to gain ratification and approval for the Constitution, states, "The powers not delegated to the United States by the Constitution, nor prohibited by it to the states, are reserved to the states respectively, or to the people." Thus, as education was not mentioned as a federal power, it was reserved to the states. In fact, the Ninth Amendment in the Bill of Rights makes it clear that the framers of the Constitution wanted the broadest powers in the hands of the states and the people when it insisted, "The enumeration in the Constitution, of certain rights, shall not be construed to deny or disparage others retained by the people." The powers of the people and the individual were so broad that they had all powers not expressly listed in the Constitution itself.

One of the provisions of the Constitution that affects education indirectly is found in Article I, establishing the powers of Congress or the legislative branch of the federal government. Article I, Section 8, is commonly called the *general-welfare clause* because it provides for the powers of Congress in regard to the common defense, the general welfare, and the levying and collection of taxes. It states, in part, "The Congress shall have Power to levy and collect Taxes, Duties, Imports and Excises, to pay the Debts and provide for the common Defense and general Welfare of the United States." This means that the federal government has the right to levy and collect taxes to support public education because the federal courts have decreed that Congress cannot provide for the general welfare and for the national defense without being able to make certain that proper educational opportunities exist for U.S. citizens. Thus, the federal courts, and particularly the U.S. Supreme Court, have "implied" powers in the realm of education from this elastic general-welfare clause. The last paragraph in Article I is called the *elastic clause* and gives Congress the necessary and proper authority to carry out these earlier powers. It reads, "To make all Laws which shall be necessary and proper for carrying into Execution the foregoing Powers . . . ." Johns and Morphet (1975) asserted, "The General Welfare Clause has been used extensively during the past forty years to justify the expansion of old federal activities, and the addition of new activities of the federal government" (p. 364). Thus, Article I, Section 8, the general-welfare clause of the Constitution, has been used by the U.S. Supreme Court to allow expansion of the federal role in education.

Three amendments to the Constitution, the First, Fifth, and Fourteenth, have figured prominently in court cases related to the public schools. The First Amendment states, "Congress shall make no law respecting an establishment of religion, or prohibiting the free exercise thereof; or the right of the people peaceably to assemble, and to petition the Government for a redress of grievances." This amendment has been used by the U.S. Supreme Court in school-related cases in decisions involving the separation of church and state, freedom of the press, freedom of speech, and freedom to assemble. The Fifth

Amendment states in part that no person shall be deprived of life, liberty, or property without due process of law and that private property should not be taken for public use without proper compensation to the owners. This "due-process" clause has been used by the federal courts in cases involving students' rights and teachers' rights, especially in discipline and punishment cases. The Fourteenth Amendment, which was passed after the Civil War, guarantees the rights and privileges of U.S. citizens to residents of all the states in these words:

> No State shall make or enforce any law which shall abridge the privileges or immunities of citizens of the United States; nor shall any State deprive any person of life, liberty, or property, without due process of law; nor deny to any person within its jurisdiction the equal protection of the laws.

This clause, commonly called the *equal-protection clause,* extends the federal due process to the state level. (See Unit V for more information on these topics.)

The U.S. Congress and Education

The legislation passed by the U.S. Congress has been influential in public education since the United States was founded and even preceding the present U.S. Constitution. The involvement of the U.S. Congress in public education began with the Land Ordinance of 1785 and included the Morrill Act of 1862 for land-grant colleges, the Smith-Hughes Act of 1917 for vocational education, the aid for federally impacted areas passed in 1941, the National Defense Education Act of 1958, and the Elementary and Secondary Education Act of 1965.

As has been shown, the Congress has been granted wide powers in education by the U.S. Supreme Court's interpretation of implied powers, the general-welfare clause, and the elastic clause in the U.S. Constitution. The first federal legislation concerning education was passed by Congress under the Articles of Confederation and consisted of land grants in federal territories for the purpose of establishing and supporting public elementary schools. These were included in legislation establishing methods of surveying and dividing up the western lands. Later in the 1860s, federal lands were given for the establishment of land-grant colleges in each state by the Morrill Act. In 1917, Congress passed the Smith-Hughes Act, establishing the federal role in stimulating vocational education through categorical grants for specific purposes with requirements for matching state funds. Congress was providing stimulation for needed changes in public education from a total college-preparatory emphasis to an additional concern for vocational education caused partly by World War I.

The legislation passed by Congress for relief during the Great Depression of the 1930s and World War II in the 1940s accelerated this trend toward more federal involvement in education. Again, Congress, spurred on by national emergencies and defense requirements, stepped in to correct omissions at the state level in educational programs. Two of the relief measures passed by Congress were the Civilian Conservative Corps (CCC), related to the conservation of natural resources to provide jobs for young people who were unemployed during the Great Depression, and the National Youth Administration (NYA), which provided funds for students to attend school during the Depression. In 1941, Congress passed the Lanham Act for national defense reasons. This law aided local governments, which were overwhelmed by a large influx of students in areas where war industries or military installations for World War II were located.

The 1950s and 1960s saw a greatly increased involvement of Congress in education. The major legislation passed by Congress during this twenty-year period included extensions of the original "G.I. Bill of Rights" benefits for veterans; the National Science Foundation, which was established in 1950 to promote education in the sciences; the National Defense Education Act (NDEA) of 1958; the Vocational Education Act passed in 1963; and the Elementary and Secondary Education Act of 1965, which supported the education of children of low-income families. It seemed as if Americans believed that every social, political, and economic problem in the United States could be solved by education legislation passed by Congress. Inevitably, these high expectations were followed by a period of doubt that federal education programs could accomplish these herculean tasks. As Campbell, Cunningham, Nystrand, and Usdan (1980) state, "The boom in federal influence began to slow down about 1970. The seventies were a time of reappraisal, retrenchment, and redirection in federal involvement in education" (p. 35). Campbell et al. also believe that research studies in the 1970s and 1980s have cast doubt on the ability of educational programs to make a difference in solving society's problems and deficiencies.

Despite this general retrenchment of education in the 1970s, at least one major piece of legislation affecting education was passed during this period. In 1975, Congress passed Public Law 94-142 concerning the education of handicapped children. As a result of Public Law 94-142 and state regulations governing handicapped students, local school districts were required to prepare individual educational plans (IEPs) for every handicapped student, to provide a "least restrictive" education environment with mainstreaming where it is appropriate, and to provide medical support services such as occupational therapy and physical therapy for such students. The cost of implementing these requirements is a tremendous burden to local school districts because the federal government pays only a fraction of these expenses.

What has been the impact of Public Law 94-142 on local school districts, other than its cost? The positive impact of Public Law 94-142 on local school districts has been fourfold. It has increased cooperation between parents, schools, and other agencies serving the needs of handicapped children. It has increased the knowledge of all concerned about the education of these special children. New priorities have been established for the use of resources and funds, and special education has also come to be considered as a legitimate part of the total school program (Atkin, Allen, and Wachter, 1980, pp. 120–121). Perhaps the greatest effect of Public Law 94-142 has been the influence it has exerted on the regular school programs. The regular school students have been put in closer contact with these special students through mainstreaming and have been exposed to their similarities and differences. Hopefully, these regular students will learn that they are more similar to than different from these special-education pupils. Because of the IEPs required through special education legislation, the public is beginning to demand that individualized educational plans be drawn up for regular students as well. Special education programs have served as models for implementing competency testing and for developing remedial programs for regular school students. Greater cooperation has resulted between teachers in the regular school program and special education teachers, because of mainstreaming, and the work of resource teachers who serve as bridges between the two programs. The authors of this text have also observed that special education students behave differently and often in a more positive way when mainstreamed with regular school students than when they are attending special education classes. "Every decision regarding handicapped children will somehow affect the total program for all students" (Atkin, et al., 1980, p. 120). Thus, the terms *mainstreaming, least restrictive environment,* and *due process* for special education students have become common terms in the language of education since 1975.

The 1980s seemed to continue the retrenchment in federal legislation on education. With enrollments down and money tight, the federal government has attempted to place the burden for education back on the states. However, there is no doubt that Congress has had an impact on education throughout American history, especially since the 1950s through categorical grants for specific purposes perceived as both urgently needed for national priorities (such as for defense or for economic development) and consistently neglected at the local and state levels.

The U.S. Department of Education and the U.S. Secretary of Education

Throughout U.S. history, programs of education have been administered by numerous cabinet-level departments and other agencies of the federal government. For example, the schools abroad for military dependents are ad-

President Ronald Reagan speaks before the National Forum on Excellence in Education. *(Photo used by permission of the Indiana State Teachers Association.)*

ministered by the U.S. Department of Defense, and schools on Indian reservations in the United States are run by the Bureau of Indian Affairs in the U.S. Department of the Interior. So many federal agencies have been involved in administering federal educational activities that even an overview of federal activities in education is difficult, but the most visible national education agency was the U.S. Office of Education in the federal Department of Health, Education, and Welfare.

The National Education Association (NEA) had been lobbying for many years for the creation of a Cabinet-level department of education, to be separated from the Department of Health, Education, and Welfare and to replace the Office of Education in this Cabinet-level department. The NEA representatives argued that establishing such a high-level education department headed by a Cabinet-level secretary of education would enhance the prestige of both American public-school teachers and American education in general. Although many opponents view this idea as an example of special-interest

Former Education Secretary Terrel H. Bell was a motivator of state reforms in education. *(Photo used by permission of the Indiana State Teachers Association.)*

legislation for the sole advancement of teachers, the bill that established this Cabinet-level department was passed in Congress during President Jimmy Carter's administration. In spite of extensive lobbying by the NEA, it passed by only four votes in the House of Representatives, certainly not the mandate for the new department that the NEA had sought. During his campaign for the presidency, Ronald Reagan, who succeeded Carter as president, called for abolishing the Department of Education as a Cabinet-level position, but he eventually appointed Terrel Bell to succeed Shirley Hufstedler as the second U.S. Secretary of Education. Bell, a conservative from the West, operated under and shared President Reagan's philosophy of a limited federal role in education. He attempted to motivate educational improvements by the various states, and the programs that he supported encompassed merit pay and master-teacher or career-ladder plans in several states, including Tennessee and North Carolina. Bell was succeeded in 1985 by William J. Bennett, who continued the conservative thrust of this office.

What are the implications of the establishment of the Department of Education to replace the former Office of Education in the Department of Health, Education, and Welfare? First, this department is only an administrative agency, carrying out the will of Congress. It cannot make education laws but only policies to carry them out. Second, the new department had mostly a public-relations advantage; it took over the functions of the old Office of Education and some education functions that had been conducted by other Cabinet-level departments. It made education more visible and gave the Secretary of Education more access to the president. Savage (1980) believes that the new Department of Education is just an administrator, not a policymaker, in education and concluded:

> In all but foreign policy, Congress calls the shots. In education, Congress creates a new program, says how much money it will get, says exactly how it will be distributed, who will get it, and what they can and cannot spend it for. The Office of Education or the Department of Education simply sends out the checks. (p. 117)

Although the Department of Education may have more influence than Savage believes, it is true that almost all of the federal programs in education are for specific purposes, such as vocational education, and that this categorical aid is established by Congress, not the Department of Education. Congress also has a proclivity to pass laws expanding existing educational programs and creating new programs rather than cutting back or eliminating existing programs. Therefore, Congress, rather than the U.S. Department of Education, seems to wield the real power over education in the United States.

Quattlebaum's report (1951) concerning the U.S. Office of Education and the administration of federal education activities (which seem to be appropriate to describe the U.S. Department of Education as well) led Campbell to conclude:

> One, these activities were extensive and widespread. Two, the money appropriated for such activities was appreciable. Three, the United States Office of Education had meager influence and even less control over this vast program, Four, there was apparently little, if any, coordination of the programs of the several federal agencies. (p. 30)

Thus, the federal education programs are splintered among numerous federal agencies, and the Department of Education has little control over them. Students of education should remember that the federal government administers its aid to public schools not directly, but always through state education agencies, and that the Cabinet rank of education is threatened by the conservative views of President Reagan and others.

The Federal Courts' Influence on Education

The federal courts rule on cases involving the interpretation of laws passed by Congress, and the U.S. Supreme Court has the power of "judicial review" and can decide which powers are "implied" as "necessary and proper" for both the states and the federal government. The power of judicial review was established by John Marshall, the first Chief Justice of the U.S. Supreme Court. Under this power, the Court can rule on the constitutionality of laws passed by the Congress and, if necessary, declare them unconstitutional (or null and void). Constitutional issues such as public aid to private schools, the separation of church and state, due process in students' and teachers' rights, and integration of schools have been addressed by the federal courts over the years.

Campbell et al. (1980) synthesized the variety of educational issues on which the state and federal courts have ruled:

> Let us summarize these legal milestones as they pertain to the public schools. In response to social, economic, and political development in this country, there was first the establishment of public schools by constitutional and statutory provisions. As time went on, attendance of pupils in school and payment of taxes for school purposes were required. In the latter half of the nineteenth century the public school program was extended to include the secondary level. Convictions about the importance of public schools, however, were not sufficient to eliminate the nonpublic school. While the doctrine of separation of church and state still pertains, it does not rule out the use of some public money for the benefit of pupils (not the schools themselves) in nonpublic schools, nor does it prohibit a limited amount of cooperation between school and religious bodies. Finally, the obligation of the public school to serve all children without regard to race or color has been given rigorous interpretation by our highest court. (p. 15)

(See Chapter 11 for more detailed information on these court decisions.)

Because educational and social issues seem to be intertwined, education has often been the battleground—and sometimes the scapegoat—for society's social issues. Schools are shaped by society to accomplish its purposes, whether they be education of the handicapped or integration of the races. In fact, federal court decisions have often mandated actions that were unpopular in some sections of the United States, such as racial integration of the public schools. The federal courts have ruled on the confidentiality of student records based on the Family Educational Rights and Privacy Act of 1974 and on the equal treatment of female employees and students under Title IX of the Educational Amendments of 1972. However, the implementation of these federal court rulings depends on the respect that the majority of Americans have for their laws, as seen by the thirty-plus years of struggle to fully implement the desegregation ruling in the 1954 *Brown* decision of the U.S. Supreme Court. Education and the federal courts are likely to continue to be in the center of social conflict and often to be blamed by society for its unsolved problems.

Who Should Control the Public Schools?

The debate continues in the 1980s concerning who should control the public schools. Should the control be at the local, state, or national level of government? How much control should school administrators have in education? Should the state governors, state school boards, or state superintendents of public instruction be in complete charge of education in their states? What should be the role of parents and local community leaders in educational policy? What is the role of local school-board members in the education process? Should teachers' organizations and unions be able to dictate conditions of employment and other policies to local school boards? What role should university professors and teacher-training institutions play in the education process? Should public school students, the consumers of education, have a role in contributing to educational policy decisions?

Concerning the role of school administrators in school decisions, many superintendents see an erosion of authority and power at the local district level with more local responsibility than ever but with less power to solve educational problems locally. Principals see the need for power to run their schools at the local building level and cite numerous studies showing the local building principal to be the key to teacher morale and educational excellence at the local level. Robert Schain, the principal of Wingate High School in Brooklyn, New York, said, "We don't need structural changes in the ways schools are governed so much as we need a new attitude on the part of both professionals and the public" ("How Should Schools Be Ruled?" 1980, p. 104). He believes that education must become a top priority if the current problems in governance of education are to be surmounted. He feels that the public is simply not committed to excellence in education. For while many speak of the need for good public schools, budgets are cut, so that resources are not available for needed programs. Salaries and status accorded educators are also low, keeping capable people from entering or staying in the field, and the media feature negative stories about the schools, belying the claim that first rate schools are a top priority for Americans.

John Prasch, a superintendent, cited the social climate that opposes both shared values and consensus. He accused us of being suspicious of our own institutions, leading citizens to cut off the resources needed for public schools. He castigated our inadequate decision-making processes and concluded, "The best evidence of our inability to reach decisions efficiently is how frequently we turn to the courts" ("How Should Schools Be Ruled?" 1980, p. 105). He criticized legislatures for their procrastination in making important education decisions—making many just before they adjourn—instead of using an orderly decision-making process. It is easy from these examples to see that school administrators at all levels are increasingly frustrated by their role in the governance of education.

What is the feeling of government officials at the local, state, and federal levels concerning their roles in the governance of education? A governor cited problems such as increasing demands for accountability in education, the era of scarcity and limits, the decline in the school-aged population, economic recessions decreasing funds for all state services, and taxpayer revolts against further education spending. A member of the Virginia State Board of Education foresaw a greater state role in education, citing the increasing financial problems of local school districts and the taxpayer concerns about the increasing federal bureaucracy ("How Should Schools Be Ruled?" 1980, p. 106). Anne Campbell, Commissioner of Education in Nebraska, also emphasized the "strings" attached to federal aid to education:

> Except for issues involving a clear national interest, educational policy is a
> state responsibility—and most states delegate a great deal of authority to local
> districts. But prescriptive federal legislation and regulations are increasingly
> limiting the latitude within which states and local districts can work. In areas
> such as vocational education, education of the handicapped, and bilingual
> education, there is far too much specificity in federal directions. ("How Should
> Schools Be Ruled?" 1980, p. 103)

Campbell said that most local citizens may agree with the federal goals but resent the increased financial burdens placed on local taxpayers to carry them out.

Carl Perkins, a member of the U.S. House of Representatives from Kentucky, admitted that the role of the federal government in education has expanded recently but counteracted the myth that the federal government's share of education funding has increased. He cited statistics do show that because of inflation and increasing education costs, the federal government's share of funding for schools has remained at an almost constant 8 percent. He admitted that the public perceives a greater control of education by the federal government through its regulations, but claimed that Congress has attempted to reduce the burdensome paperwork connected with federal education programs. He emphasized that federal education aid has always been, and will continue to be, categorical in nature for very specific programs and purposes related to the national interests, not a general or block-grant aid to education

("How Should Schools Be Ruled?" 1980, p. 109). Thus, from the viewpoint of Congress, the perception of increased federal control of educational governance is exaggerated and incorrect.

How do local community leaders, teachers' organizations, and professors in university teacher-preparation programs view the governance–control issues and their roles? Many local community leaders believe that improvement of education should begin at the local school with shared decision-making involving parents, students, and other citizens, who they feel have been left out of the decision-making process. Carl Marlburger, a parent advocate, believes that if students and parents are not included in the governance of education through shared decision-making, the existence of public schools will be threatened in future years. He sees teachers' organizations as gaining more power in the present governance structure ("How Should Schools Be Ruled?" 1980, p. 108).

Yet, one teachers' organization official sees the erosion of local decision-making power as the current trend. Norman Goldman, Director of Instruction for the New Jersey Education Association, cited the implementation of statewide competency testing programs for students as "governance by testing" and believes that this emphasis on testing will lead to less local control of education in the future ("How Should Schools Be Ruled?" 1980, p. 103). Albert Shanker, President of the American Federation of Teachers, agreed that local power over education is decreasing, but he worried that this power is being fragmented instead of being concentrated in one source, where it can be used effectively to promote education. He believes that future educational leaders will need to be more informed about both finance and politics because financial and political considerations seem to be controlling education to a greater degree now than in the past ("How Should Schools Be Ruled?" 1980, p. 105).

Schools of education in American universities have been blamed by the public, the state legislatures, and other public officials for the perceived "failures" of the present educational system. Although university professors of education have been used as scapegoats by the public during educational crises, they, too, see the same erosion of local power mentioned by other reference groups. Michael Kirst, Professor of Education at Stanford University and President of the California State Board of Education, put the problem in these words:

> Over the last two decades public education in the United States has been legalized, centralized, and bureaucratized at an increasing rate. The discretionary zone of local superintendents and boards has been squeezed progressively into a smaller and smaller area, especially during the last decade.
>
> It is simplistic, however, to call this change "centralization"; there is no central control-point but rather a fragmented oligopoly. Local school boards are subject to pressures from higher authorities—federal and state legislatures, agencies, and courts; and from outside interests like Educational Testing Service and the Council for Exceptional Children. Moreover, the shift of influence

to higher levels has not resulted in a commensurate loss of pressure from local sources. ("How Should Schools Be Ruled?" 1980, pp. 103–104)

What conclusions can be drawn from this discussion of who should control education? The era of extreme local control seems to be at an end, but most experts do not wish to put the control of schools at the federal level of government. A trend can be discerned toward increased direct involvement of the states in education, particularly in the financing of schools and in the reform of education. Most experts see the local school board as having increased pressures but less real power than in previous years. Most advocate shared decision making in education but caution against the fragmentation of the political clout of education groups. Alvin Toffler, the author of *Future Shock* and *The Third Wave*, summarized the problems and possible solutions:

> Some problems cannot be solved on a local level. Others cannot be solved on a national level. Some require action at many levels simultaneously. Moreover, the appropriate place to solve a problem doesn't stay put. It changes over time.
>   To cure today's decision logjam resulting from institutional overload, we need to divide up the decisions and reallocate them—sharing them more widely and switching the site of decision-making as the problems themselves require. . . .
>   The issue is not "either/or" in character. It is not decentralization in some absolute sense. The issue is rational reallocation of decision-making in a system that has overstressed centralization to the point at which new information flows are swamping the central decision makers. ("How Should Schools Be Ruled?" 1980, pp. 102–103)

Thus, although Toffler was discussing the problems of government in general, his solutions seem relevant to educational governance as well.

The Influence of Special-Interest Groups on Educational Governance

In addition to the formal legal controls of local school boards, state legislatures, the U.S. Congress, and the courts, numerous informal controls on education are exercised by various special-interest groups.

Types of Special-Interest Groups

What types of groups attempt to influence education by lobbying in state legislatures or in the U.S. Congress on educational issues? The first and most important of the special-interest groups are the local, state, and national organizations of teachers, administrators, and school board members. Some of the teachers' organizations consider themselves professional organizations, and others are known as unions. (See Chapter 15 on education organizations for more detailed information.)

A second type of special-interest group lobbying on education legislation is taxpayer groups that are concerned about the cost of education. In this category are included business groups, such as the state chamber of commerce or the National Association of Manufacturers; farm organizations, such as the Farm Bureau; and taxpayers' associations, such as those that supported Proposition 13 in California. In many agricultural states, the Farm Bureau opposes additional educational expenditures, whereas labor organizations, such as the AFL-CIO, have generally supported educational spending, which usually benefits their members' children.

A third category of special-interest groups includes school-related groups, such as the special education organizations, the groups promoting education for the gifted, and the National Congress of Parents and Teachers. A fourth type of special-interest group includes ethnic minorities, such as blacks and Hispanics, who desire a better education for members of their group.

A final type of special-interest group includes right-wing religious organizations, such as the Moral Majority, which has been influential in educational debates in the 1980s. These organizations seem to be afraid that the schools are undermining the moral character of U.S. youth by not allowing prayer in public schools and by a lack of emphasis on values in public schools. It seems clear that a multitude of groups are attempting to influence education legislation for their own specific purposes.

Effect of Special-Interest Groups

What influence do these special-interest groups have on education? One of the problems in passing education lelgislation is that the various education groups do not speak with one voice. Many state legislators often complain that lobbyists related to education cannot agree on what is best for education. For example, teachers' groups often lack agreement with superintendents' groups or organizations of school board members on issues such as school finance or collective-bargaining legislation. State legislators are often confused by these conflicting demands of education's special-interest groups, and as a result, education legislation suffers. Another problem influencing the effectiveness of education groups is related to the increasing militancy of teachers. Because of teachers' attitudes and collective-bargaining legislation, teachers' organizations have excluded principals and other administrators who formerly were members of these groups. This same teacher militancy has led to an estrangement between teachers and lay citizens in many communities, making confrontation, instead of conciliation and collaboration, the modus operandi. As has been explained, the growth of special-interest groups has been one of the reasons for the decline in power at the local-school-district level of education.

Whereas most authorities see teachers' organizations as very influential in education legislation, Donmoyer (1980) found in his research that the impact of professional educators on decision making is lessening even as they participate more fully in the political process. Earlier findings seemed to indicate that educational interest groups played a significant role in legislative policymaking. But Donmoyer concentrated on curriculum legislation rather than on funding legislation, as had been done earlier, and found that professional educators' groups played only a minor supporting role in the legislative process. Thus, it seems that organizations of professional educators have been relegated to responding to initiatives of others in areas such as competency testing and professional standards, although they have more influence on school finance legislation in many states.

What does this influence of special-interest groups in education mean for the future? It would seem that the control of education will be more divided and splintered in the years ahead, so that it will be necessary for special-interest groups to form coalitions to implement common objectives in state and national legislatures. Kirst and Garms (1980), suggested that more money and effort on the part of teachers' organizations should be used at the state level rather than at the national level if these organizations want to increase their effectiveness in lobbying for educational legislation. The trend toward a multiplicity of special-interest groups also means that administrators must be trained to mediate conflict between these groups and that no one voice will speak for education in future years.

Governance and Control of Private or Parochial Schools

How are private and parochial schools governed, and how does this process differ from the governance of public schools? Attendance at private or parochial schools does satisfy the states' compulsory attendance laws, but the states do have the right to make private or parochial schools meet certain standards, such as public health, safety, building requirements, and zoning laws. It is generally agreed that the states also have the authority to regulate and to inspect private schools to determine if they state standards for curriculum and teacher training. State requirements for citizenship training, particularly teaching about the electoral process, must be met by private and parochial schools as well as public schools. However, the states differ widely in the strictness of their regulation of and their enforcement of regulations in private or parochial schools. The percentage of the total student population in attendance at nonpublic schools varies significantly from state to state and from region to region in the United States. States such as Rhode Island, Connecticut, Pennsylvania, Massachusetts, New York, and New Jersey have higher enrollment of pupils in private schools, whereas southern states, such as North Carolina, West Virginia, and Georgia, and western states, such as Wyoming, Utah, and Oklahoma, have small nonpublic enrollments. Historically, the enrollments in nonpublic schools, which are not supported by public taxes, had shown a steady increase until the 1970s. Because of financial pressures, many private or parochial schools have closed since the mid-1970s, and there has been a 10 percent decline in the number of pupils enrolled in nonpublic schools during this period.

Church-Related Private Schools

Nonpublic schools can be divided into two types: church-related and non-church-related. The vast majority of these schools have a religious affiliation, and only 15 percent of the total is made up of non-church-related schools. Over half the church-related schools are Roman Catholic, followed by Lutheran and Seventh Day Adventist. Even the religious schools vary in their governance and control: some are controlled by groups of parents, whereas others are under direct church control. For example, some Roman Catholic schools are under the direct control of the parish, and others are run by religious orders or private Roman Catholic groups.

The diocese is the equivalent to the local public-school district in the governance of Roman Catholic schools. The bishop oversees Roman Catholic schools in the diocese, and the priest has jurisdiction over the schools in his parish. Because of the burden created by these schools on church officials, a superintendent of schools and a board of education have been created in each diocese to relieve the burden on the bishop. The Roman Catholics have expanded the percentage of lay members on these diocesan school boards to over 40 percent. In corresponding fashion, most parishes in the Roman Catholic church also have parish boards of education. The parish Roman Catholic schools are financed by parish contributions and by tuition paid by the parents of the students. However, only about one half of Roman Catholic elementary-aged pupils attend Roman Catholic schools, and about one third of Roman Catholic high-school-aged students attend Catholic high schools. Increased financial costs because of inflation and the decline of membership in the religious teaching orders have forced the closing of many Roman Catholic schools in the last decade.

The Roman Catholic schools remove a great financial burden from the public schools by educating millions of American youth. Three fourths of the non-public-school enrollment is in these Roman Catholic schools. If all Catholic schools were closed, the increase in the cost of educating the students in the public schools would be catastrophic. It should also be noted that private and parochial school parents also pay taxes to support public schools as well as pay tuition to nonpublic schools. Thus, the effect of nonpublic schools on public education is potentially tremendous. In addition, Roman Catholic schools and other nonpublic schools provide an alternative to public schools and have often stimulated innovation in education and sparked changes in the public schools.

Non-Church Related Private Schools

The second type of nonpublic school is not related to churches or religious groups. These nonchurch or nonsectarian schools comprise only 10–15 percent of the total enrollment in nonpublic schools in the United States. They range from small store-front schools to prestigious college-preparatory schools. These schools have many problems in common with church-related schools. Many face uncertain enrollments, unstable finances, and the pressure of inflation. Some of these prep schools also have the image of snobbishness to overcome, whether they deserve this reputation or not. According to Campbell, Cunningham, Nystrand, Usdan (1980) "In general the quality of independent school education is sufficiently high that states need not be concerned unduly about supervising them" (p. 9). However, the states have the same authority to supervise nonsectarian or non-church-related schools as they have over church-related schools.

Campbell et al. (1980) summarized the importance of these nonpublic schools as follows:

> to understand the schools of America one must look at the public and the nonpublic schools. The presence of the nonpublic school affects in many ways the organization and control of public schools. Also, events in some public school systems have given impetus to nonpublic alternatives. (p. 9)

Conclusions About Governance and Control

What general conclusions can be drawn in the area of governance and control of education in the United States? The conditions in public education have changed drastically in the late 1970s and in the 1980s compared to the 1950s and 1960s:

> The decade of the 1970s was marked by paradox. Many school districts accustomed to rapid and sustained growth since World War II, faced decline for the first time. Increasing enrollments, new facilities, and program extensions gave way to retrenchment, reductions in (work) force, and program cutbacks. The pronounced nature of these changes coupled with school finance uncertainties and the impact of the courts on the schools placed new stresses on the governance and management of education. The future of local school districts appears to be caught up in the question of whether or not our political system, functioning through the mechanisms of local districts, states and federal centers of responsibility can carry its burdens. (Campbell et al., 1980, p. 113)

Critics of the increase in federal rules and regulations pertaining to education in the last two decades see a loss of local freedom in the governance and control of U.S. schools. Not all educators agree with this view. Some feel that centralization of the process of financial support for schools is possible without centralization of administration and operational control (Johns and Morphet, 1975).

Education students must decide for themselves whether centralization or decentralization is better for the future of governance in education. Those who favor decentralization believe that it encourages local citizens' interest and participation in the governance of schools, whereas those who support more centralization in school governance stress the improvement in school financing that is possible under a more centralized governance. Some of the control and finance questions that education students need to examine were listed by Herman (1977):

1. How much of the financial resources of the federal, state, and local units of government should be placed into the education of the children and youth of this country?

2. Should the unit of government mandating that specific educational and social programs be conducted at the local school district level be required to provide the funding for the mandated programs?

3. Should every child be provided with an equal educational opportunity regardless of the degree of wealth that exists within the locality of his parents' residence? . . .

4. If collective bargaining is permitted by public employees, should the state take over this function in order to balance the resources brought to the task by a local Board of Education and by a unified national, state, and local teachers' union or association?

5. What agency or group is to have final decision-making authority about the multitudes of programs and functions carried on at the local school district level? Also, how much responsibility and control is to be given to the local level and its agents, the state level and its agents and the federal level and its agents? (p. 162)

Summary

In our examination of the U.S. Constitution, it was found that education is not mentioned directly in this document but that education is a power reserved to the states and to the people by the Tenth Amendment. However, the federal involvement in education has been justified by the "implied" powers of Article I, Section 8 (the general-welfare clause), and by three amendments to the Constitution, the First, the Fifth, and the Fourteenth Amendments. The role of the U.S. Congress in passing educational legislation was surveyed, with highlights on key federal legislation from the Morrill Act in the 1860s through Public Law 94-142 and the federal retrenchment in educational funding in recent years.

The evolution of the Office of Education into the Cabinet-level U.S. Department of Education was traced in this chapter, including the implications of this change for the prestige of education in general. The federal courts were also found to have exerted a great influence on education in the United States, sometimes making education the scapegoat for severe national problems.

Finally, several specific issues concerning governance and control in general were addressed. First, future trends in the governance of education were discussed, as well as the issue of who should control the public schools. Then, the influence of special-interest groups at all levels of government was scrutinized, as well as the governance of private and parochial schools in the United States.

In Chapter 13, we examine in greater detail school finance, a topic closely related to the questions of control and governance.

Questions

1. What is the significance of each of the following parts of the U.S. Constitution?
   a. First Amendment.
   b. Tenth Amendment.
   c. Fourteenth Amendment.
   d. General-welfare clause (Article I, Section 8).
2. What was the significance of the establishment of the U.S. Department of Education? What benefits have accrued to education as a result of this event?
3. In what ways has federal assistance improved the state departments of education?
4. What is the relationship between the state departments of education and federal aid to education?
5. Give five examples of how the federal government is involved in education. Is it important for the federal government to be involved in each of these areas? Why or why not?
6. Of the three levels of control of education in the United States (local, state, and federal), which one has the primary responsibility for control of education, and what are the functions of the other two levels in education?

Activities for Unit VI

1. Plan an individual visit to your state legislature. Interview a lobbyist, and talk with a conservative and a liberal state legislator. Summarize your findings.

2. Interview a member of the state board of education in your state. Find out about his or her duties and about the amount of influence he or she has on education in the state.
3. Ask your U.S. Representative what have been the differences in the function of the current U.S. Department of Education compared with the old Office of Education. Has this change been an improvement?
4. Contact a state legislator and inquire about the function of the state department of education. In what ways has this department been effective, and in what ways does it need to be improved?
5. Interview a person from another country. Compare the local control of education used in the United States with the national control of education found in France, Japan, or another country.

FINANCING EDUCATION

13

Local and State Financing of Education

OBJECTIVES

After reading Chapter 13, the student will be able to:
- Delineate the primary state and local taxes used to support education.
- Understand the role of the "foundation program" in state financing of education.
- Explain possible reforms and solutions to state and local problems in financing schools.
- Differentiate between a progressive and a regressive tax.
- Perceive the advantages and disadvantages of the property tax as a primary source of educational funding.

Introduction

Why should students of education study educational finance? First of all, the "bottom line" in any endeavor or organization is usually money. Members of any group wonder, "What can we accomplish with the resources at our disposal?" Because resources are scarce and limited by nature, the question becomes one of priorities: "What is most important for us to do, given these limited financial resources?" The 1970s and early 1980s have been an era of limits, and as a result, questions of educational finance have taken center stage. Whereas the schools received much financial support in the 1950s and 1960s, the public mood turned toward taxpayer revolts and refusal to support bond issues for education in many states in the 1970s and the early 1980s. Coupled with this public mood in these two decades were inflation, the energy crunch, and a decline in the school-aged population. In addition, financial pressures on local, state, and national governments forced education to compete fiercely with other needs, such as defense spending and police officers' pensions for tax dollars. Economic recessions in the late 1970s and the early 1980s exacerbated this problem, making educational finance one of the top two issues, along with discipline, in most polls of teachers and administrators in the 1980s. Another reason for the study of educational finance by students of education and by all citizens is that education is one of the biggest business enterprises, in terms of dollars spent, in the entire nation. In many states, the expenditures for education make it the biggest "business" in the state, and many times, education, from kindergarten through the university, consumes more than half the state's budget. A third reason to study school finance is that the salaries of teachers and administrators are closely related to financial conditions in the local school system. Because concern about adequate salaries is uppermost in the minds of many teachers and prospective teachers, the financing of education is an important topic. Attracting high-quality people into teaching may depend on educational finance and higher salaries for teachers.

Many important educational questions are discussed in Unit VII. How well do states fund education? What are the primary state taxes used to raise money for education? What problems exist in using these taxes, and can the states move toward full state funding for education in the future? What local taxes are earmarked for education, and what are the strengths and deficiencies of these taxes? What are some possible solutions to inequities in the local property tax? What percentage of school revenues comes from local, state, and federal sources? What is the history of federal aid, and has it increased or decreased in recent years? What is the difference between "categorical aid" and "block grants," and what effect does each have on education? What are the major specific federal programs in education, and what is the purpose of each? What problems do critics see in federal aid, and are there any possible solutions to these difficulties? What are the current trends in federal aid, and how will they influence education? What is the budgeting process, including the major divisions of funds in educational accounting and in the planning, programing, budgeting system, a system for linking financial resources to educational outcomes? How may vouchers, tax credits, performance contracting, and accountability contribute to solutions to educational finance problems? What conclusions can be drawn regarding educational finance, and what future trends can be discerned?

What personal characteristics influence a citizen's viewpoint on educational finance, and what variables affect a local community's spending for education? Campbell, Cunningham, Nystrand, Usdan (1980) found that the two most important personal factors that influence a citizen's financial support of education are occupation and the number of years of schooling the person has had. To a lesser degree, they found that age, race, and religion can help to predict a person's financial support of education, but that income, sex, and type of community were variables not closely associated with support of education by citizens. The three variables that influence the expenditures of a local community for education include the wealth of the local district, variations in government access and control, and differentials in the educational aspirations of the district. Thus, the assessed valuation of the school district and the educational aspirations that parents have for their children affect the financial resources available for education in that community.

In the following sections of this chapter, state, local, and federal financial support of education is examined.

State Support

Introduction

The percentage of total public school revenues coming from state sources has been increasing in recent years. According to the National Center for Education Statistics [NCES] (1982), in the 1969–1970 school year 52.9 percent of public elementary- and secondary-school revenues nationwide came from local sources, and only 38.6 percent came from state sources. However, in 1981–1982, 47.7 percent came from the states and only 43.4 percent could be traced to local sources. Thus, it can be seen that the local share of revenue for public elementary and secondary education, formerly over 50 percent, is declining and that the state share is increasing, approaching the 50 percent level. (See Table 13–1.) (It is interesting to note that during this twelve-year period between 1969–1970 and 1981–1982, the federal share remained more stable, rising from 8.2 percent in 1969–1970 to a high of 9.3 percent in 1979–1980 but reverting back to the 8.6 percent level in 1981–1982.) This same source (NCES, 1982) shows that the percentage of the gross national product spent on public and private education at the elementary, secondary, and

TABLE 13–1 Estimated Expenditures of Educational Institutions, by Source of Funds: United States, 1969–1970 to 1981–1982 (amounts in billions of dollars)

Source of Funds (by level of institution and type of control)	1969–1970		1975–1976		1977–1978		1979–1980		1981–1982	
	Amount	Percentage	Amount	Percentage	Amount	Percentage	Amount	Percentage	Amount	Percentage
Elementary and secondary schools:										
Total public	$41.0	100.0%	$70.9	100.0%	$81.2	100.0%	$96.4	100.0%	$112.4	100.0%
Federal	3.4	8.2	6.3	8.9	7.7	9.5	9.5	9.8	9.7	8.6
State	15.8	38.6	31.6	44.6	36.0	44.3	45.1	46.8	53.6	47.7
Local	21.7	52.9	32.9	46.4	37.3	45.9	41.5	43.1	48.8	43.4
All other	0.1	0.3	0.1	0.1	0.2	0.3	0.3	0.3	0.3	0.3

Source: Adapted from the National Center for Education Statistics (1982).

university levels increased from 3.1 percent in 1929 to a high of 8 percent in 1975, and then declined to 6.8 percent in 1981. (See Table 13–2.) Clearly, until the last few years, the nation was spending a greater percentage of its resources on education at all levels, and the states have assumed a greater role in financing public elementary and secondary education.

One of the major problems with state support of education is the enormous variation in the financial ability of the states to support public elementary and secondary education. In 1976, the personal income per capita varied from less than $5,000 in Mississippi and Arkansas to over $7,300 in New Jersey, Connecticut, and Illinois, the U.S. average being $6,399. Similar variations exist in expenditures per pupil in average daily attendance (ADA) in public elementary and secondary schools in the individual states. Whereas the national average is $2,494 per pupil, Alabama spends $1,741 per pupil, and Alaska spends $5,146 per pupil. The six states in addition to Alaska that spend over $3,000 per pupil in ADA are Delaware, New Jersey, New York, Oregon, Washington, and Wyoming, as well as the District of Columbia (NCES, 1982). (See Table 13–3.) From these figures, it can be easily determined that wealthy states can spend almost twice as much per pupil in ADA in public elementary and secondary schools than can the poorest states.

Several terms in school finance should be defined before the topic of school funding is examined in more detail. These terms are *foundation programs*, *average daily attendance* (ADA), *average daily membership* (ADM), and *assessed valuation*. Garms, Guthrie, and Pierce (1978) defined the *foundation* or *flat grant program* as "a certain amount of 'basic' education that should be provided on an equal basis to all. Any amount beyond that provided by the flat grant or foundation guarantee is a local luxury, not to be aided by the state" (pp. 79–80).

TABLE 13–2   Gross National Product Related to Total Expenditures for Education:
United States, 1929–1930 to 1981–1982

Calendar Year	Gross National Product (in millions)	School Year	Expenditures for Education[a]	
			Total (in thousands)	As a Percentage of Gross National Product
1	2	3	4	5
1929	$ 103,400	1929–30	$ 3,233,601	3.1
1931	76,100	1931–32	2,966,464	3.9
1933	55,800	1933–34	2,294,896	4.1
1935	72,500	1935–36	2,649,914	3.7
1937	90,700	1937–38	3,014,074	3.3
1939	90,800	1939–40	3,199,593	3.5
1941	124,900	1941–42	3,203,548	2.6
1943	192,000	1943–44	3,522,007	1.8
1945	212,300	1945–46	4,167,597	2.0
1947	232,757	1947–48	6,574,379	2.8
1949	258,023	1949–50	8,795,638	3.4
1951	330,183	1951–52	11,312,446	3.4
1953	366,129	1953–54	13,949,876	3.8
1955	399,266	1955–56	16,811,651	4.2
1957	442,755	1957–58	21,119,565	4.8
1959	486,465	1959–60	24,722,464	5.1
1961	523,292	1961–62	29,366,305	5.6
1963	594,738	1963–64	36,010,210	6.1
1965	688,110	1965–66	45,397,713	6.6
1967	796,312	1967–68	57,213,374	7.2
1969	935,541	1969–70	70,400,980	7.5
1971	1,063,436	1971–72	82,999,062	7.8
1973	1,306,554	1973–74	98,019,434	7.5
1975	1,528,833	1975–76	121,603,841	8.0
1977	1,899,508	1977–78	140,367,563	7.4
1979	2,413,900[b]	1979–80	169,615,149[b]	7.0
1981	2,925,500[b]	1981–82	199,800,000[c]	6.8

[a]Includes expenditures of public and private schools at all levels of education (elementary, secondary, and higher).
[b]Preliminary data.
[c]Estimated.
Source: National Center for Education Statistics (1982).

TABLE 13–3   Expenditure per Pupil in Average Daily Attendance in Public Elementary and Secondary Schools, by State: 1979–1980

State	Total[a]	Current[b]	Capital Outlay	Interest on School Debt
1	2	3	4	5
United States	$2,494	$2,275	$170	$ 49
Alabama	1,741	1,612	115	14
Alaska	5,146	4,728	151	267
Arizona	2,433	1,971	398	64
Arkansas	1,839	1,574	224	41
California	2,376	2,268	89	19
Colorado	2,826	2,421	330	75
Connecticut	2,520	2,425	47	48
Delaware	3,019	2,868	55	96
District of Columbia	3,265	3,259	6	0
Florida	2,082	1,889	160	33
Georgia	1,833	1,625	181	26
Hawaii	2,528	2,322	204	2
Idaho	1,914	1,659	215	40
Illinois	2,778	2,587	140	51
Indiana	2,166	1,910	248	7
Iowa	2,552	2,340	177	35
Kansas	2,422	2,205	175	42
Kentucky	1,847	1,701	91	55
Louisiana	2,017	1,794	172	52
Maine	1,947	1,824	82	41
Maryland	2,843	2,598	204	41
Massachusetts	2,952	2,819	54	79
Michigan	2,873	2,640	151	82
Minnesota	2,686	2,457	221	9
Mississippi	1,788	1,664	124	1
Missouri	2,071	1,936	98	37
Montana	2,882	2,476	363	43
Nebraska	2,403	2,150	199	54

Nationwide state support for school funding averages about 40 percent of total school revenues, and most is distributed under a foundation funding plan (Benson, 1975). To understand foundation funding, let us examine three hypothetical school districts within a single state, each having 1,000 students (see the illustration on page 372). The purpose of foundation funding is to provide an adequate education to every child in a state. To this end, the state government estimates an annual cost per pupil for basic education. Generally, this is a single value, but sometimes states set higher amounts for secondary than for elementary pupils (Benson, 1975). This figure per pupil times the number of students in a district determines the total foundation program

TABLE 13—3 (*continued*)

State	Total[a]	Current[b]	Capital Outlay	Interest on School Debt
1	2	3	4	5
Nevada	2,553	2,088	356	108
New Hampshire	2,069	1,917	115	37
New Jersey	3,379	3,191	116	72
New Mexico	2,396	2,034	339	23
New York	3,681	3,462	134	85
North Carolina	1,871	1,754	104	313
North Dakota	2,071	1,927	121	23
Ohio	2,208	2,075	94	39
Oklahoma	2,176	1,926	229	21
Oregon	3,104	2,692	355	58
Pennsylvania	2,742	2,535	101	106
Rhode Island	2,670	2,601	17	52
South Carolina	1,996	1,752	209	35
South Dakota	1,932	1,911	1	19
Tennessee	1,825	1,635	175	14
Texas	2,309	1,916	316	77
Utah	2,208	1,657	491	60
Vermont	2,240	2,049	137	55
Virginia	2,211	1,970	191	51
Washington	3,073	2,568	446	58
West Virginia	2,160	1,920	219	21
Wisconsin	2,693	2,495	145	53
Wyoming	3,326	2,527	698	101

[a]Includes current expenditures for day schools, capital outlay, and interest on school debt.
[b]Includes expenditures for day schools only; excludes adult education, community colleges, and community services.

Note: Because of rounding, details may not add to totals.

Source: U.S. Department of Education, National Center for Education Statistics. (1982). Preliminary data from the Common Core of Data survey.

cost per district. For the purpose of this example, the state sets a figure of $1,500 per pupil, which results in a foundation program cost of $1.5 million for each of our three districts ($1500 × 1000 pupils = $1.5 million).

State governments do not ordinarily provide the entire amount of the foundation cost but require local districts to make what Benson (1975) called a "fair local contribution." The fair-local-contribution amount is generally raised by the state's requiring local districts to levy a property tax at a rate determined by the state, say, 5 percent. Looking at District A of our example, suppose the assessed value of property in the district is $12 million, or $12,000

Foundation Funding

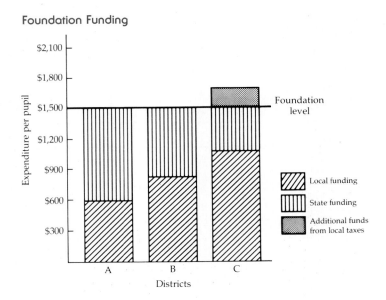

per pupil. A property tax levy for schools of 5 percent would therefore raise $600,000, or $600 per pupil. The state would then provide the balance of the foundation funding, or $900,000 for the district, $900 per pupil in District A. The state is providing 60 percent of this district's foundation budget for education, a higher percentage than the national average because of the lower-than-average property values of the district. District B, on the other hand, has property whose assessed value is $17 million, or $17,000 per pupil. With a 5 percent property tax levy this district can raise $850,000 ($850 of the needed $1,500 per pupil), with the state contributing $650,000, or 43 percent of the budget. District B falls nearer the national average. District C may be a district with a larger commercial base, for its assessed property value is $22 million. It raises $1.1 million with the 5 percent property tax, thereby costing the state only $400,000, or 27 percent of the total foundation budget.

If a local school district desires to spend more money per student than the state's foundation program provides, it can attempt to raise the additional money through a higher local-property-tax rate—unless the local district is under a state property-tax freeze or Proposition 13–like state legislation. Should District C residents decide that they wish to improve their schools beyond the programs provided by the state's foundation amount, they could raise their property tax rate to, say, 6 percent. By so doing they could now raise $1,320,000 locally, $1,100,000 of which would fall under the foundation program. The state would still provide $400,000, and the district would have an additional $220,000, or $220 per pupil, to expand their programs.

Average daily attendance (ADA) is based on the number of students actually in attendance at a school, not just on the rollbooks. It is calculated from a tally of the number of students in attendance and those legally excused for the school year; then this total is divided by the number of days in the school year. In contrast, the average daily membership (ADM) is based on the total number of students enrolled in school each day, whether or not they are actually in attendance. In other words, the ADM is tied to enrollment, not to attendance. In school systems with large numbers of absent or missing students, this difference between the ADA and the ADM is significant.

Assessed valuation is the official estimate of the value of property for the purpose of taxation and is usually much less than the market value of the property, many times only one third of the market value. The tax rate is then set as so many cents per hundred dollars of assessed valuation, not of the market value. For example, a house with a market value of $100,000 may be assessed for tax purposes at $33,000 (assessed valuation). If the tax rate for schools is set at 10 cents per hundred dollars of assessed valuation, this hypothetical home owner would pay $33 in taxes per year to support the schools. The actual rates and amounts would be much higher, and it should be remembered that the financing of other units of local government besides schools would also be included in the final tax rate.

What is the general process used in establishing the budget of a local school district, if we use Indiana as a typical example? First, the local school budget is the conversion of the educational program of a school district into the dollars and cents needed to operate such a program. The budget is for a specific period of time, usually the calendar year (January 1 through December 31) or the fiscal year (July 1 through June 31). The school board is charged with approving the budget for the school district, but the preparation of the budget is usually delegated to the superintendent and her or his assistants.

In Indiana, the final approval of the district's budget is accomplished on the last Thursday in August after a public hearing held not later than seven days before the final action on the budget. Indiana law requires that the time and place of this budget hearing be properly announced as a part of the publication of the budget in two local newspapers at specific times set by law. The entire budget is planned and expressed as dollars to be expended during the budget cycle. In Indiana, all miscellaneous revenues, such as license excise taxes, bank taxes, and state support, are subtracted from the total expenditure planned. The remaining amount of money must be raised by a local-property-tax levy.

The state usually provides a process of review for the local school budget before it becomes final. In Indiana, for example, the county tax-adjustment board reviews all budgets within the county on the second Monday in September and may recommend reductions, but not increases, in the local-property-tax rates. Indiana law also provides for a final review of all school budgets of local districts in the state by the State Tax Board of Tax Commissioners, which has the authority to make further adjustments in levies and may restore reductions made by the county tax-adjustment board.

In addition, because Indiana is one of many states operating under a

Divisions of local school district budgets: transportation, operating expenses, capital expenses, and debt service. (*Photos by Axler.*)

property tax freeze, Indiana law also provides for a State School Property Tax Control Board, which hears appeals on budget matters from financially troubled school corporations. This board can authorize loans of state funds to these school districts or may permit the transfer of money from the Cumulative Building Fund to the General (Operating) Fund for use in paying for the current operation of the schools. In addition, this board reviews all new school construction that would increase the debt of the school district and any changes in the cumulative building fund for a local school district. This Control Board can also recommend an excessive levy (above the legal tax-freeze limits) for a school district, but this increase must be approved by a referendum of voters in that district. A school corporation that is granted special financial relief by this Control Board becomes a "controlled" school district and must have the approval of the Control Board for most major financial decisions for that year, including its budget. Thus, it can be easily seen that local-school-district budget approval is a complicated process with many mandatory reviews at the county and state levels.

What are the various divisions or "funds" into which the local school district budget is divided? These funds can be thought of as separate accounts, and it should be remembered that money from one fund (account) cannot be transferred to another without special state approval. Thus, money from the cumulative building fund cannot ordinarily be used to pay teachers' salaries, which are an operating expense. In Indiana, for example, state law provides for four funds: a general fund for current operating expenses, such as utility costs and teachers' salaries; a debt service fund to pay interest on district borrowing; a cumulative building fund for capital expenditures such as those for buildings and equipment; and a transportation fund to pay for the costs of transporting students, except for the purchase of school buses. All of these "funds" have separate tax levies in Indiana, and money from one fund may not be transferred to another fund without special state approval. Almost every state limits the borrowing capacity of schools for capital outlay purposes, such as school buildings, equipment, and buses. This limit is usually expressed as a percentage of assessed valuation, and beyond this limit, bonds may not be authorized even by a vote of the residents of the district. Many states require a referendum of the voters in the local school district to approve bond issues, but Indiana has no such provision.

A recent development in the budgeting process has been the use by several states of the planning, programing, budgeting system (PPBS). This is a system for linking educational objectives to the financial costs of accomplishing these objectives, forcing local school districts to examine the cost of a program in its planning and to weigh carefully the benefits obtained from each dollar spent in the local district. Although the results of this system have been mixed in the various states that have used it, the trend seems to be toward accountability by establishing priorities and linking costs to the benefits received by the students in the local school districts.

How much responsibility should the states have to finance public elementary and secondary education? The trend is clearly toward the states' funding an increasing percentage of education costs, but state legislators must weigh the money required for public education with the demands of other public services, such as prisons, mental health facilities, welfare, and highways. This question also involves issues such as the scope of state responsibilities, local control, property tax relief, and equalization. Because almost all public school revenue comes directly or indirectly from taxes, the next sections of this chapter examine the two major state taxes: the state sales tax and the state individual and corporate income taxes.

State Sales Tax

In 1979, thirty-one states had a statewide sales tax to raise revenue. What are the advantages and disadvantages of this tax, and what trends can be discerned in its use? First, the state sales tax is a relatively painless way to collect tax revenue because the majority of this money is paid in small amounts as purchases are made. Second, the burden is placed on citizens who spend money, not on those who save it. One disadvantage is that the impact of the sales tax falls more heavily on citizens who are poor and are forced to spend most of their money on the necessities. It should be noted, however, that many states exempt necessities such as food and medicine from the sales tax to alleviate this problem. Another disadvantage is that because revenues from the sales tax are based on the purchase of goods, the amount of money

The state sales tax is one of the chief sources of state revenue, but its pros and cons as a fair tax are a matter of debate. (Photo by Axler.)

collected can decrease rapidly during a recession or a depression, when fewer purchases are made. The sales tax is relatively elastic, however, and it brings in an abundance of revenue in more prosperous times.

What are the trends in state sales tax use, rates, coverage, and exemptions? The sales tax is a significant source of state revenues: thirteen states receive 40 percent or more of their income from this tax. Though no new states have added a sales tax since 1969, the states currently levying sales taxes have tended to increase the rates very slowly over the years. The state sales tax rates usually range from two cents to seven cents on each dollar spent, and many states exempt food (but not restaurant meals) and prescription medicine. The most common rate is currently 3 or 4 percent, although it is likely to rise because of the pressures of inflation (Due, 1982). The state sales tax and the state individual income tax (to be discussed in the next section) are by far the most-used sources of state revenues.

State Income Taxes

After the sales tax, individual and corporate income taxes combined are used by more states than any other major source of revenue. (See Table 13–4.) In fact, together, these two income taxes form the major source of state revenue. Forty-five of the fifty states have one or both of these taxes. The rates have generally remained constant for many years, with little or no tendency to raise them. The state income taxes are generally simpler and more easily calculated than the federal income tax, having fewer exemptions and deductibles. There has been a trend, however, to add and to liberalize exemptions in the state individual income tax in recent years. The corporate income tax rates

TABLE 13–4   Number of States Using Various Taxes as Major Sources of Income for Selected Years, 1927–1979

Tax	1979	1975	1970	1960	1950	1940	1927
State sales tax	31	31	30	24	21	15	0
State individual income tax	26	24	19	12	9	6	4
State corporate income tax	10	8	8	7	7	5	6
State motor fuel and vehicle license	12	15	19	27	29	37	35
State tobacco	3	4	5	5	5	3	—
State liquor	2	3	3	4	5	6	—
State property tax	2	2	2	2	2	3	7
Other state taxes	11	11	12	16	18	17	25

Sources: Advisory Commission on Intergovernmental Relations. (1977). *Significant features of fiscal federalism, 1976–77,* p. 29; U.S. Bureau of the Census. (1980). *State government tax collections in 1980,* p. 5.

are generally kept low by the competition between states to attract businesses and industries to locate in their areas, but forty-five states have some form of the corporate income tax (Due, 1982).

What are the advantages and disadvantages of the individual personal income tax? First, it is based on the "ability-to-pay" principle, and citizens with larger incomes pay a larger total tax bill. It should be noted, however, that some state individual income taxes are not progressive; that is, the wealthier citizens do not pay a higher rate than the poorer citizens. The same rate applies to all citizens (unlike the federal income tax, which is progressive), although the total amount of money paid by the higher-income citizens may be higher. Second, the revenue from this tax may increase or decrease according to economic conditions in the state, in contrast to the local property tax, which can be levied on property whether people are working or spending money or not.

State Finance Problems and Possible Solutions

What are the major problems of the states in school finance, and what solutions are proposed to alleviate these difficulties? First, the history of these school finance problems and reforms is reviewed.

During the 1950s and 1960s, enrollments in the U.S. public schools grew rapidly, and increased funds were spent to build new buildings and to hire new teachers. However, in the late 1970s, public school enrollments peaked, and the period of rapid growth in education came to an end, caused by the decline in enrollments coupled with the increased opposition of taxpayers to school revenue increases. When funds became tight, the inequalities in the financing of education became more prominent.

As major funding for schools comes from property taxes, property-poor districts often need tax rates two or three times those of property-rich districts to raise the same amount of capital per pupil for education. (For example, in the figure on page 372, District A would need a property tax rate of 9 percent

Inequality between districts is one of the major problems in school funding. Property-rich districts can provide many extras, such as this performing-arts center, while property-poor districts struggle for necessities. (Photo by Axler.)

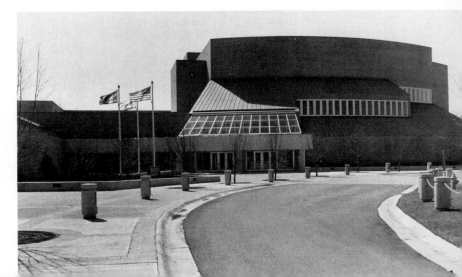

to raise the same amount of money for schools as District C, with a 5 percent levy.) The courts have ruled in California, Minnesota, Texas, New Jersey, Wyoming, Kansas, Connecticut, and Idaho that education or equal-protection clauses in the state constitutions were violated by existing methods of funding schools. Yet, the job of finding solutions to the problem fell to state legislators, as the courts offered no remedies. The legislators found themselves facing the need to control or cut back spending on education and at the same time to guarantee that the quality of each child's education was not unduly dependent on the wealth of his or her local school district (Garms, Guthrie, & Pierce, 1978, pp. 339–340).

Thus, the forces demanding retrenchment in educational spending and those forcing reform in educational finances hit state legislators simultaneously in the early 1970s. This process culminated in the *Serrano* decision of the U.S. Supreme Court in 1971, which declared that public-school finance laws that made the quality of a student's education dependent on the wealth of a local school district were unconstitutional:

> Equalizing educational resources would not have been so difficult had additional state dollars been available to increase spending in poor districts nor would budget tightening have been so difficult if everyone's budget were squeezed by the same amount. Combining reform and retrenchment was politically explosive, however. These became the underlying themes of what has come to be known as the school finance movement. (Garms et al., 1978, p. 340)

One of the problems for educators was that they were not in control of this school-finance-reform movement. Legislators and governors, not educators, made the decisions on school reform in the 1970s. Add to this the role of the state and federal courts, and it can be easily seen that educators were not in control of the school finance reforms during this period. In addition, the old educational coalition of teachers and administrators was splintering, partly because of differences on how tight money should be spent and how limited resources should be allocated. Teacher-militancy, collective-bargaining, and accountability issues resulted from the breakup of this education coalition.

The major state educational finance program before the 1970s was the foundation or flat grant per pupil, which was explained earlier in this chapter. What were the criticisms leveled by reformers at this program?

First, poorer school districts that had much less than wealthier districts in assessed valuation of property had to use higher school tax rates to raise the money needed for an adequate education program. Often, even after suffering higher tax rates on their property, these poorer districts were not able to offer adequate educational programs to their students.

A second criticism of the foundation school-finance plans was that a flat grant per pupil failed to take into consideration that education costs more per pupil in urban areas than in rural areas of the United States. Whereas large cities receive the state support per pupil, their costs, including teachers' salaries, are significantly higher than in most rural areas. One reason for this situation is that high local taxes for other government services prevent large cities from raising local taxes for schools.

A third criticism of the old school-finance plans was that many poor districts had an inordinate number of special education students, who were more costly to educate than the average public-school student. The foundation or flat-grant program of the states provided the same number of dollars to a school district for each student, regardless of the cost of educating that student. The states, in addition, often passed laws requiring more special classes and special services for these special students, without appropriating the state money to fund these requirements, forcing local school districts to take money from other parts of the school budget to meet these needs.

In summarizing the criticisms of the state foundation programs, Benson (1975) hypothesized the conditions under which such a foundation program would work:

> Under certain circumstances, the foundation program could (would) work quite well. First, there should be no major differences in prices that school districts pay for teachers' services, instructional materials, school houses, maintenance, etc., as one moved from one part of the state to the other. Second, districts would need to be large enough to include more or less equal proportions of children who are costly to educate, or some action would be required to see that even small districts had no more than their proper share of costly children—children requiring say, bilingual teachers. Third, the local taxable resources per student would need to be more or less uniform among the districts of the state. (pp. 80–81)

Regarding Benson's third point, you will remember the examples from the figure on page 372, in which the wealthiest district, District C, was able to raise $1,000 per pupil of the foundation amount of $1,500 from the 5 percent local property tax. Yet, some school districts have much greater property value than District C. Consider a fourth district, District D, which is heavily industrial, having an assessed valuation per student of $60,000. With the basic property tax rate of 5 percent, District D raises $3,000 per pupil for education with no more sacrifice than the other districts must make to get the minimal state-funding level of $1,500 per pupil.

Another problem leading to school finance reforms in the 1970s was taxpayer revolts and property tax limitations or freezes, which were often part of the reforms passed by state legislatures (Pipho, 1981):

> Taxpayer revolts, slashed budgets, and now federal cutbacks—many states are facing the strictest spending limits of the decade. Ever since California voters approved Proposition 13 in the summer of 1978, the mood of the country has moved steadily toward lower spending for education. To date, 17 states have

Economic recession and the closing down of important industries adversely affect education. *(Photo by Axler.)*

adopted either constitutional or statutory limits on taxation or spending. Some states have been harder hit than others. Although comparing states is difficult, the industrial states of the North appear hardest hit by legislated spending limits combined with inflation-driven cost increases, declining enrollments, and a recession-triggered drop in tax receipts. (p. 722)

Thus, the poor fiscal condition of the states has increased the pressure for school finance reforms. Nearly all states were experiencing a deterioration in their financial condition in the early 1980s, caused by a decrease in federal aid, changes in the corporation and individual income taxes, and a severe national economic recession. Clearly, the industrial states of the North and the Northeast are most affected, losing population because of declines in the automobile and steel industries due to foreign competition and lack of modernization. The southern and western states, in contrast, are generally gaining in population, wealth, and industries. School finance in these latter areas is less a problem because of increased population, industrialization, and wealth in the South and the West. For example, the governor of Michigan, hard hit by the decline in the automobile industry, ordered a 25 percent reduction in state expenditures in 1981, including a 50 percent cut in property taxes, an increase in the sales tax from 4 to 5.5 percent, and a limit on increases in taxes to 6 percent a year unless citizens vote for a larger increase. In Indiana, the 5 percent increase in school funding in 1981 was the lowest in ten years, and educators in this state worried that the school revenue increases would fail to keep up with the inflation rate (Pipho, 1981). Because the states estimate their revenues in advance in order to prepare their budgets, high estimates often lead to cuts in proposed spending, whereas low estimates result in budget surpluses. As Pipho (1981) wrote, "Either way, states walk a fiscal tightrope" (p. 722).

Reforms and Solutions   What reforms have been proposed as solutions to these problems in state educational finances? First, the state reforms in the 1970s are examined. Then, a study of reforms in five states are studied. Next, this

381

section investigates the obstacles to state school-finance reform and the accomplishments of these state reforms. Finally, conclusions and predictions for the future are summarized.

What were the school finance reforms of the 1970s? About half the states enacted public-school-finance reforms in the 1970s, most of these in the early 1970s before the enrollment declines, recessions, and fiscal crunch of the late 1970s and the early 1980s. These reform movements used the citizens' growing resistance to increases in local property taxes to demonstrate how state taxes could replace school revenue from the property taxes. By the mid 1970s, an economic recession had caused further concern about government spending and had made significant reforms more difficult to execute. Also, by the late 1970s, declining public-school enrollments made it difficult to convince state legislators that more and more funds were necessary to educate fewer and fewer students. These reforms usually included statutory or constitutional limits on taxation or spending for education, or both. The issues in this reform movement included "accommodation between wealthy districts and poor districts, urban-rural tensions, conflicts between taking care of special needs and supporting the basic program" (Fuhrman, 1980, p. 123).

Stephen Carroll (1982, pp. 255–256) studied the school finance reforms passed in 1972, 1973, and 1974 in five states: California, Florida, Kansas, Michigan, and New Mexico. He found that the reforms resulted in growth in school district revenues in all five states and that the property tax rates declined in four of the five states. Thus, the reforms increased spending for education while reducing the school-property-tax rates in most of these states. Another outcome of the reforms in these five states was only limited progress toward a more equal distribution of revenues per student. In fact, the tax rates in the poor school districts in these five states tended to increase more than those in the wealthier school districts. Carroll believes that result was caused by too many conflicting objectives of these reforms and the exemptions or adjustments enacted with the reform proposals. Finally, he found that the states' attempts to use block grants and matching grants to stimulate local spending for education were not very successful.

Next, what are the obstacles to public-school finance reform, and what were the accomplishments of these reforms in the 1970s? One of the obstacles was the failure of the federal government to adequately support state public-school finance reforms. Only the federal Title I program of compensatory education channels more funds to poor school districts than to the wealthy systems and greater aid to financially hard-pressed urban districts than to more affluent suburban districts. A small number of federal block (general) grants for education have also given states more flexibility in putting funds where they are most needed at the local level, but most federal aid is still categorical (that is, for specific purposes, such as vocational education). Callahan and Wilken (1976) concluded, "At this point, the federal government seems to be interested in supporting state equalization efforts only if it costs very little money" (pp. 9–10).

The positive accomplishments of these public-school finance programs have been numerous. First, the local-school-property taxes have been reduced or at least have been prevented from increasing. Second, in some states, property taxes have been made more equitable and fair. Third, the debate in state legislatures sparked by school-tax-reform legislation has raised the public consciousness on issues in education. Fourth, disadvantaged students and less wealthy taxpayers have benefited from these finance reforms. Greater equity between poor and wealthy districts has resulted, but this improvement has been spotty and uneven at best.

What conclusions can be drawn from this school-finance reform movement in the 1970s? Callahan and Wilken (1976) stated it best when they wrote:

> The record of the four years following the Serrano case demonstrates the states' desire to work toward fiscal equity in school finance systems. School property taxes have been reduced. Expenditures in poorer districts have often been increased. More state funds have been alloted to children with costly learning problems. Tax and expenditure controls have been established to produce more local fiscal discipline, and new aid programs have been developed to meet the extraordinary school finance needs of urban and rural areas. In short, poor taxpayers and educationally disadvantaged children have been the main beneficiaries of reform. Any shortcomings in state school finance reform are overshadowed by these achievements. (pp. 10–11)

Here are predictions for the 1980s in school finance reform. User fees to finance education will be utilized more fully, especially for nonrequired courses such as drivers' education or other electives. Parents will increasingly directly pay a greater share of their children's educational costs through tuition and fees for summer schools and special courses. The pressure to accomplish more with fewer resources seems to be the slogan for the 1980s. Fuhrman (1980, pp. 123–124) sees the possibilities of school finance reform as troubled in the 1980s. She cited factors such as tight state budgets, decreased federal aid, suspicions about government in general, declining enrollments, and competition with public higher-education institutions for state funds as negative trends. The courts, she believes, will exert the most consistent pressure for public educational finance reform in the 1980s. Fuhrman also believes that there will be less equalizing of school revenues between poor and wealthy school districts in each state in the 1980s. In addition, she believes that all education constituencies, such as teachers, administrators, school-board members, and parents, must again re-form the splintered education coalition and agree on the reforms needed if progress in educational finance is to be made in the 1980s. She sees accountability and competency-testing for both teachers and students as the wave of the future, predicting that these will force state legislatures to appropriate more money for remediation for students who fail these tests. Doyle (1982) agreed and further suggested that education will be forced to consider "productivity" as a major goal for both teachers and students by emphasizing time-on-task, mastery learning, ability grouping, and giving priorities to objectives. Many states will continue to increase their share of the cost of public elementary and secondary education; a few states may adopt full state funding, with governance decisions still being made at the local level.

Indiana: An Example of State School Finance   Indiana is a good example of a typical public-school finance program. Indiana's three major sources of state revenue—the state sales tax, the individual income tax, and the corporate income tax—are also the primary revenue sources for the other states in the United States. Together, these sources comprise 85 percent of the state's general fund revenue. In Indiana, state support for local school districts consists of a basic grant (based on enrollment, teacher education and experience, and the maximum tax levy for the school district); a flat grant per pupil in average daily attendance (ADA) in the school district; and transportation aid for pupils transported more than one mile.

The Digest of Public School Finance in Indiana (1981) explained the complicated calculations necessary to figure the basic grant for a school district in these words:

> The Basic Grant is a composite of potentially three separate calculations. Data necessary to the calculations include the Teacher Ratio, Average Daily Membership (A.D.M.), Additional Pupil Count (A.P.C.) for handicapped and vocational pupils, Maximum Normal Tax Levies (M.N.T.L.), and the prior calendar year Basic Grant (less handicapped and vocational education monies for that year). (p. 11)

The teacher ratio is computed by division of the corporation teacher factor (based on a computation involving the districts' teachers' education and experience) by a state factor computed on the basis of teachers' education and experience for the entire state. In other words, school corporations receive more state funds in Indiana if their teachers have more education and teaching experience. As previously explained in this chapter, average daily membership (ADM) is the number of students enrolled in Grades K through 12 in the district, not just those present or in attendance. The additional pupil count (APC) is the number of students participating in handicapped and vocational programs in the school district. Both ADM and APC totals are taken on one day near the beginning of the school year. The maximum normal tax levy (MNTL) is the maximum number of dollars a local school corporation is allowed to raise by Indiana law. The MNTL, then, is the tax ceiling for the local school district.

How is the basic grant figured from all of these calculations? In the words of the Digest (1981),

> The prior year net basic grant and prior year maximum normal tax levy are added: this total state and local revenue is adjusted upward or downward by multiplying by an A.D.M. adjustment to compensate for increases or decreases

Calculation of Basic Grant

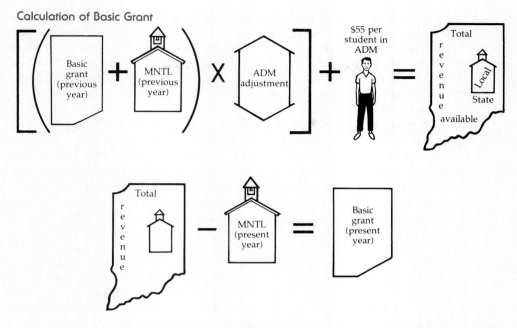

in enrollment from the previous year. . . . To this sum is added a flat grant of $55 per student in A.D.M. . . . The sum of these calculations represents the total revenue available for 1982 from state tuition support and local property tax sources. When the local share (defined as the 1982 or ensuing year's maximum normal tax levy) is subtracted, the residual becomes the 1982 regular program tuition support to be paid by the state. (p. 13)

As one can easily see, this is a complicated procedure, to say the least. In other words, Indiana computes the basic grant by using enrollment, not attendance, figures and subtracting the maximum amount that can be raised by local property taxes. The previous year's basic grant and the money raised locally are added, multiplied by a factor to compensate for increased or decreased enrollment, and augmented by a flat grant per pupil. Then, from this amount is subtracted the money that can be raised by the local property tax, and the remaining sum is the basic grant that the state pays the local school district for the current year.

The two additional components of state public-school aid in Indiana are a flat grant and transportation aid. The flat grant is simply $40 per pupil in average daily attendance (ADA), which is based on the number of students present at school and not on those on the rollbooks. The transportation aid is computed by a complicated formula, but basically, it partially reimburses the local school district for transportation costs for K–12 pupils who are transported more than one mile by school buses. A set amount per pupil is multiplied by the number of eligible pupils, but the local district is required to pay part of this amount by a property tax with a 15-cent tax rate on the assessed valuation of the school district's property. In transportation aid, as well as the basic grant, the local school district receives additional funds for special education and vocational students, for which the educational and transportation costs are likely to be greater than for other students. The basic grant provided 91 percent of state funds distributed to school corporations in Indiana, and the flat grants and transportation aid accounted for only 3–4 percent of the total funds.

Like many other states, Indiana is currently operating under a property tax freeze. In 1973, the Indiana General Assembly (or state legislature) froze at 1973 levels the amounts (not the rate) that could be collected by local school districts. The only way that a specific school corporation can increase this amount is to appeal to the State Property Tax Control Board, which can grant an increase based on an unusual situation (such as the opening and operation of a new school building) or can recommend that a school corporation be allowed to conduct a referendum of its citizens to see whether a higher base levy or dollar amount should be established for that school corporation. Increases in this base levy (amount of money) are also allowed for school districts that have had an increase in pupils in ADA, that have lost federal aid to impacted areas, or that have registered an increase in their assessed valuation. Also, the state legislature has granted a few percentage increases in this base amount to take inflation into account, although in general the increases had fallen far short of the inflation rate. Thus, in Indiana, there is a ceiling on the amount of money (not the rate) that can be collected from the property tax by each school district, based on 1972–1973 amounts, with some adjustments for special conditions and inflation. This freeze has caused hardships in many school corporations in Indiana. Since the 1972–1973 school year, inflation has seen school costs mount; yet, school districts have not been able to increase their property tax amounts. If the assessed valuation increases in the school district, the actual tax rate may decrease because the amount of money (levy) that can be raised is frozen instead of the tax rate. Yet, the school district would be forced to use existing revenues to educate any new students added to the district rolls. Wealthier school districts are also prevented from raising additional dollars to support additional educational programs in their corporations.

The state school revenue in Indiana is divided into four funds: the general fund, the cumulative building fund, the debt service fund, and the transportation fund. The general fund has already been discussed, and the cumulative building fund is for the construction and equipping of new school buildings. The debt service fund is used to raise money to pay interest charges, and the transportation fund includes money for school buses, bus drivers, and related expenses. There is a tax or rate limit on the cumulative building fund, but there is no limit on the transportation fund.

The state of Indiana also has a property-tax-replacement fund that provides to local school districts 20 percent of the amount that was formerly raised through local property taxes. Approximately 55 percent of the total revenues of local school districts is provided by regular- and property-tax-replacement funds in Indiana. The major sources of revenue for the state of Indiana are a 5 percent retail sales tax, an adjusted gross income tax of 2 percent, and a corporate gross income tax.

Indiana, then, is a typical example of the complicated nature of state public-school finances, illustrating the property tax freeze and the definition of the many terms used in state public-school finance.

Local public school finances are now examined in more detail.

Local Support

Introduction

Local support for education comes primarily from the local property tax. This tax is among the most criticized and controversial of all the taxes used to support public schools. The property tax can be defined as a tax on real property (land and improvements such as building) and personal property, such as household furnishings. As Benson (1975) explained:

> Local revenues are drawn primarily from property taxation. For the most part, property tax yields are obtained from levies on "real property": owner-occupied houses, apartment houses, hotels, factories, warehouses, stores of all kinds, and land. The property tax rate can conveniently be thought of as a percentage levy, for example, a "$4.00 per $100" property tax rate means that taxes in the current year are 4 percent of the *assessed value* of the property. Assessed value is presumed to bear a relationship to the sale value of the property in the market, and by conventional practices properties are assessed at some fraction of their presumed true or sale value. A house, for example, may be assessed at 25 percent of its market value, so a "$4.00 per $100" school tax rate is actually a tax rate equal to 1 percent of market value. Assessment ratios are supposed to be the same for different pieces of property, at least those in the same class (e.g., houses vs. factories), and those situated in a given taxing jurisdiction. (p. 79)

The property tax for the support of education is truly "local" because it varies from school district to school district in each state. Thus, a suburban school district could have a school tax rate that varies from a nearby urban system and from other suburban systems as well. The advantages of this tax are its dependability and stability. Whereas fluctuations in retail sales may cause variations in state-sales-tax collections, and whereas economic recessions can cause decreases in the revenue from state personal or corporate income tax, personal property always exists in each school district and can be taxed to fund public schools. In this section, the following topics are addressed: other local taxes besides the property tax, problems and inequities in local-

Many local school systems are setting up foundations to provide for needs unmet by tax revenues, such as providing this special physical training equipment for special education students. (*Photo by Axler.*)

property-tax assessment, the "regressive" nature of the property tax, the increased choices provided for the wealthy by the property tax, the lack of flexibility in the property tax, the effect of population shifts on property tax revenue, and the failure of state aid to equalize local support of public schools. In addition, the effects of the "taxpayer revolt" on the property tax and possible solutions to property tax problems are examined.

Before discussing the local property tax in more detail, it is necessary to explain the other local taxes briefly. If we use Indiana as an example, most of local revenue for schools is raised by the property tax, but Indiana, as well as most other states, does collect local revenue from other sources. Indiana has an excise tax on automobiles, light trucks, and airplanes, which varies from $12 to $400, depending on the age and value of the vehicle. This excise tax is paid when license plates are purchased for the vehicle. Indiana also has an intangibles tax of 25 cents on each $100 of value in the capital stock of building-and-loan associations. In addition, Indiana counties can adopt a local-option income tax on citizens who live or work in the county. Local school districts also have a few nontax sources of income from transfer tuitions, money from the sale of school property, and gifts or contributions. In regard to the latter, in these times of economic crunch, many local school systems are setting up foundations to actively seek contributions from private citizens and groups to support public school programs for which tax revenue is insufficient. In Indiana, all tax levies for school purposes are subject to review and approval by the county tax-adjustment boards in each county and by the State Board of Tax Commissioners. In many states, a local referendum is required to increase state or local taxes for schools, but in Indiana, citizens do not have to vote on local tax increases for schools, except an excessive levy above the property-tax-freeze limits.

Local Property Taxes

Is the property tax a good tax? What are its problems and inequities, and should it be used more or less extensively to support local public schools? The next part of this section examines this issue in detail.

The first problem of the local property tax concerns the assessment inequities of its application. The usual practice in most states is to have the county or township assessor, usually elected, assess the property in his or her jurisdiction once every five or ten years. Several difficulties are associated with this system. First, the assessors are usually politicians who lack formal training in proper assessment procedures. Second, in the past, some of these officials have been politically corrupt, accepting bribes to lower assessments on commercial, industrial, or private property. Third, because individual assessors assess the property in each county or taxing unit, the assessment on identical property varies from jurisdiction to jurisdiction because of a lack of common standards and procedures. A fourth problem with this system is the difficulty of keeping up with changes in property values when full assessments are usually carried out only every five or ten years. For example, in the late 1970s and the early 1980s when the nation experienced rampant inflation, the assessed valuation of property did not always reflect this increase in property values because of inflation.

A second area of difficulty with the local property tax is that it is a regressive tax. A *regressive tax* is defined as a tax that takes a greater percentage (not amount, but percentage) from those who have the least ability to pay. In other words, the citizens who have the least wealth and resources pay a greater percentage of the property tax than people at the upper end of the scale. For example, a widow who owns her home but who has very little income must pay property taxes on the same basis as everyone else. Also, a local resident could own much property but have little cash on hand to pay the taxes on this property. A *progressive tax,* on the other hand, would take a greater percentage of tax revenue from those people who have the greatest ability to pay. Wealthier people usually pay a greater "amount" in taxes, but who pays a larger "percentage" of her or his resources in taxes is the issue here. The state sales tax is also criticized by some as regressive, but this would partially depend on whether food, medicine, and other necessities were exempted from the sales tax.

The best example of a progressive tax is the federal income tax, with its many exemptions and deductions. Many state income taxes are not as progressive as the federal income tax because these state income taxes are gross taxes with few exemptions and deductions. The local property tax may be made less regressive if homestead exemptions and "circuit breakers" are used in conjunction with it.

Homestead exemptions are used to help low-income owners of single-family residences by exempting a portion of the assessed value of their property before the property taxes are levied (see the figure below). For example, in Florida, Georgia, Louisiana, and Mississippi, the first $5,000 of assessed value of family residences is not considered in the determination of property taxes. Some states allow additional deductions from assessed value for senior citizens and veterans (Johns and Morphet, 1975).

"Circuit-breaker" relief programs are more complex (see the illustration on page 391). The purpose of the circuit-breaker program is to better match the burden of taxes to the cash flow of a household and particularly to help the elderly, who may own property but may have little disposable income. Under this program, a state agency examines income tax and property tax information and determines the amount of rebate due or the deduction on taxable income to be given to eligible citizens (Johns and Morphet, 1975). A few states allow a credit to tenants for rent paid, arguing that renters deserve credit for the portion of their rent a landlord uses to pay property taxes, if a credit is allowed to home owners for the same purpose.

Other criticisms of the use of a local property tax for the support of public schools are that this tax gives the wealthy more choice of which and what

Homestead Exemption

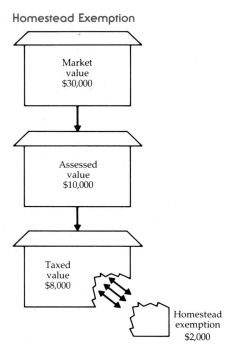

Circuit-Breaker Tax Relief

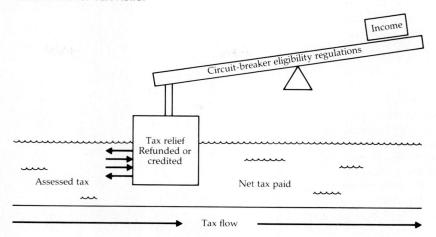

kind of schools their children attend, and that population shifts have made this tax inadequate for financing urban education. Although wealthy families have always had more choice in educating their children than poor families because the wealthy could afford to send their offspring to private schools, upper-income families have more choice even within the public schools. By buying houses in suburbs having schools that can spend more money per pupil on the education of their youth or in sections of large cities having superior schools, high-income families can "purchase" a good education for their children, whereas poor families are more place-bound and cannot usually afford to change their place of residence in order to escape poor schools.

A second related problem is the population shifts from central-city urban areas to the suburban and rural areas of many states. The more affluent citizens flee to the suburbs along with business and industry, leaving a greatly reduced assessed valuation for the support of public schools in central-city areas. In addition, the pupils who remain in these areas include a high percentage of pupils with problems that make them more expensive to educate, such as minorities or the handicapped. Urban areas also often suffer most from inflation and the high costs of teachers' salaries. Pinkney (1980) insisted that all Americans will suffer if this trend continues. Failing to take this "flight" from central-city areas and the high cost of educating inner-city students into consideration, Pinkney believes, is sabotaging the next generations of American youth, and he believes that, in the long run, this sabotage will create a problem for all Americans, not just those in inner-city areas.

Additional criticisms of the use of the property tax to finance public schools are the lack of flexibility inherent in this tax and the failure of state aid to equalize local support. The criticism of lack of flexibility concerning the property taxes involves the recent controls that have been placed on these taxes in most states. Placing lids or caps on total property tax levies or rates

Inner-city schools often educate more students with special and costly needs, and yet these schools have less money available to provide for these needs. (*Photo by Axler.*)

does not allow school districts to deal with inflation or with changes in local conditions, such as an influx of new students or the loss of tax revenues from a major industry. Also, the so-called equity or equalizing features of state aid formulas have, in general, failed to make up for differences in ability to raise revenue for schools at the local level. Although Indiana has had some increases and modifications in its initial property-tax freeze, the overall effect has been to increase school revenues at a rate much less than the rate of inflation in the years since 1973, while at the same time mandating schools to do more in expensive areas such as special education.

Taxpayer Revolt A taxpayer revolt beginning with Proposition 13 in California in 1978 has exacerbated the problems of the local property tax. It should be remembered that in many states, citizens of local school districts must approve increases in school funding or borrowing in a referendum. In turning down increases in these local taxes, citizens have been demonstrating their dissatisfaction with the spending for government in general and for schools in particular. Public elementary and secondary schools were shut down for brief periods in Ohio and other states when voters failed to approve the funds needed to operate them. Statewide limits on local taxes, such as Proposition 13 in California, have often been accompanied by increases in state funding, but not always.

What have been the causes of this revolt of American taxpayers in the years after Proposition 13 in 1978? Sharp increases in taxes have been suggested as a possible cause of this revolt. However, John Due (1982) found that state and local expenditures as a percentage of the gross national product (GNP) had remained fairly constant since 1972, and that the local property tax as a percentage of the GNP increased slowly up to 1971–1972 and then declined. Thus, although taxes have risen, state and local taxes as a percentage of the GNP have not increased significantly. Inflation has also been cited by some people as a cause of the property tax revolt. John Due (1982) however, asserted, "Most of the population clearly is not adversely affected; incomes have kept up with the cost of living and values of typical assets have risen even more rapidly than inflation" (p. 278). It should be remembered, however, that older citizens on fixed incomes have been adversely affected by the rampant inflation of the late 1970s and the early 1980s.

Instead of either inflation or sharply increasing taxes, the real causes of the taxpayer revolt would seem to be emotional. Because of the Watergate scandal and other factors, there seems to be a widespread feeling that government is inefficient and corrupt, that inflation is caused by excess government spending, and that schools are offering too many "frills." The public sees verbal SAT (Scholastic Aptitude Test) scores declining and public school enrollment decreasing at the same time that expenditures for schools are on the increase. Many voters are aghast at the pressure of unions for salary increases for government employees, including teachers, and at skyrocketing welfare costs in large urban areas of the United States. At the same time, these citizens are bombarded with distasteful government regulations, such as speed limits of fifty-five miles per hour, mandatory motorcycle helmet laws, pollution controls, and occupational health and safety regulations. Although the purpose of these laws is to help and protect citizens, many people see them as government meddling in their lives and taking away their freedoms. The general populace has also been reacting to minority rights legislation with a backlash against quotas and other government rules. At the same time, inflation is rising and pushing citizens into higher federal-income-tax brackets without any increase in their real income. Many of these reasons are emotional and simplistic, but they caused citizens to lash out at their government. Where can citizens quickly and directly "get back at" the government? The easiest place is in referendums for school revenue at the local level. As John Due (1982) concluded, "much of the anti-tax sentiment has little to do with taxes per se. The votes are votes against inflation and irritating regulations and government actions, not just against taxes" (p. 281). Thus, the "taxpayer revolt" centers on emotional issues, and the schools are used as scapegoats for the general condition of society. One of the greatest dangers of this movement is the tendency to make important educational decisions in an irrational manner and thus to harm future generations of young people in the United States.

What conclusions can be drawn from this taxpayer revolt movement? Hartley (1981) listed eight specific trends resulting from this movement? It will result in more centralized state governance and control of education, causing a major shift from local to state financing of public education. Educators will be forced to form new coalitions to offset the taxpayers in revolt. Statewide collective bargaining for teachers' salaries and an increase in user fees for education will be legacies of this movement. In addition, Hartley believes that less variation within states in spending for education, changes in school budgeting procedures, and more pressure to justify supervisory positions in schools will result from this revolt. He even foresees a voucher plan and a possible constitutional amendment to require a balanced budget as results at the federal level. Others even predict the abolition of local school districts and local boards of education as an outcome of the taxpayers' revolt. Not all of these trends and predictions will come true, but they are warning signs for the educational community of serious problems for public schools in the years ahead. John Due (1982) concluded:

> The hazards of the tax revolt expenditure limitation movement for education as well as for other basic state and local government functions are obvious. How serious they will prove to be remains to be seen. The bandwagon was rolling at full tilt in 1981, with politicians leaping on at each opportunity. But the bandwagon appears to be slowing down—as the consequences of drastic tax reduction and federal budget cuts become apparent. Services that people want must be reduced, and competent personnel must be let go. California voters in 1980 rejected a proposal to cut state income taxes in half, and most of the proposals in 1980 and 1981 were defeated at the polls. (p. 284)

Possible Solutions to Local-Property-Tax Problems   What are some of the solutions proposed to solve or alleviate these problems with the local property tax? Common sense should lead Americans to believe that the wealthiest nation on earth must reexamine its spending priorities. Education, not automobiles, microwave ovens, and videotape recorders, should be America's first priority. Certainly, a paradox exists when in such a wealthy country, the beginning of a new school year recently found over a million children on the streets because of lack of funds for their schools. Additional money may not guarantee better education, but without more adequate funding the very survival of some public school systems is at risk. As Pinkney (1980) stated:

> Those citizens who seemingly fail to care about the survival of public education in urban areas fail to realize that the real destiny of all Americans is tied together. The destiny of all school systems (urban, suburban and private) is

tied together; we all must share the concerns and blame and put the rhetoric into concrete action.

The possible solutions include full state funding of education, as exists in Hawaii now. The U.S. Constitution clearly makes education a state responsibility by failing to mention it as a federal power and therefore delegating it, by omission, to the states. Increased federal aid is another alternative, but this is not likely because the federal percentage of public school revenue has remained fairly constant for many years, and because the purpose of federal aid has been to stimulate reform in education, not to provide general support for schools. Also, many citizens fear that increased federal aid will lead to a loss of local control of education. Others refute this argument by insisting that local control is a myth, as schools are legally a state, not a local, responsibility. They assert that local governance and control can exist even if the majority of public school revenues comes from federal or state sources. Another possible solution to the financial problems of schools is to hold teachers more accountable for the "products" they produce by testing student performance periodically. Many business people prod schools to be more "cost-effective," in business terms. A more practical solution to the property tax problems may be to use circuit breakers and exemptions to eliminate the hardships caused for the poor by this tax. As Benson (1975) suggested, "the property tax is too productive of revenue to be abandoned in the short run" (p. 91). Rather, he suggested that the administration of the property tax be moved to the state level to eliminate some of the abuses in the assessment and the administration of this tax. All in all, the property tax is too dependable a source of revenue to be abandoned. Instead, it should be improved by the elimination of abuses wherever possible.

Summary

This chapter on the local and state financing of education has focused on how adequately state and local governments are now financing public education, showing that states and local school districts vary widely in their expenditures per pupil for education. Several important terms in educational finance were defined, such as a *foundation program, flat grant,* and *average daily attendance.* Illustrative examples of both a foundation program and the budget process in a typical state were delineated, as well as the two primary state taxes used for education: the state sales tax and the state income tax. In addition, present state school-finance problems were surveyed, culminating in the school-finance reform programs of the 1970s and 1980s. As an example, a typical state school-finance system was examined, including the basic grant formula of a foundation program and a property tax freeze currently in effect in the state. The main feature of local support for education was found to be the local property tax, which varies for each school district. This tax is regressive, not progressive, and has many disadvantages. However, because the local property tax is a stable source of revenue, it is likely to continue to be used to finance schools in the future, but perhaps with circuit breakers and homestead exemptions added to ameliorate its regressive nature. The advantages and disadvantages of the local property tax were discussed, as well as taxpayer revolts against such taxes in recent years.

Questions

1. What are the primary local and state taxes used to support education in your community? Explain whether each is regressive, proportionate, or progressive.
2. List several advantages and disadvantages of the use of the local property tax for the support of education.
3. What is your favorite tax for educational support? Why?
4. If a school district adheres strictly to the planning, programming, budgeting system, what important learning could be overlooked or omitted?
5. Explain the statement, "Education is big business."
6. What are the pros and cons of accountability for the schools?
7. In what ways have states reformed their financial support for education in recent years? Which of these reforms would you support? Why?
8. Describe the importance of the assessed valuation of a school district in its ability to adequately fund an educational program.
9. Describe how one private school in your community is financed. What limitations are placed on this school by its funding sources?
10. As an individual taxpayer, would you rather live in an industrial or a residential area? Why?

14

Federal Support of Education

OBJECTIVES

After reading Chapter 14, the student will be able to:
- Explain the differences between categorical grants and block-general grants in the federal support of education.
- Explain the pros and cons of federal involvement in the financing of education.
- Identify the significance of *Serrano* v. *Priest* and other federal and state court decisions on public school finance.
- Comprehend the role of tuition tax credits and voucher plans as possible solutions to school finance problems.
- Recognize three future trends in federal support of educational opportunity.

Federal Aid to Schools

> Moses came down from the Mountain to address the assembled multitude. In his arms he bore two Tablets. He said, "I have some good news and some bad news. First the good news. There are only Ten Laws to be obeyed and they are inscribed on these two Tablets. The bad news is that one hundred strong men must accompany me up the Mountain to carry down the regulations." (Wise, 1981, p. 484)

This quotation illustrates the reaction of many citizens and educators to the federal role in education, but in reality, the federal government provides less than 10 percent of the total expenditures for public elementary and secondary education. In 1975–1976, federal aid for these schools was 8 percent, and the rate has remained fairly constant in recent decades. In fact, the federal government provides only 10 percent of the funds for public and private educational institutions at all levels from preprimary through graduate school. Although federal aid as a percentage of total public education funds has not changed in recent years, in actual dollars federal aid increased by an average annual rate of over 10 percent in the six years before 1981–1982; it dropped by over 3 percent in the 1981–1982 school year. Thus, federal aid to K–12 education may have started to decline in actual dollar amounts under President Ronald Reagan's education policies.

This trend sets the scene for the era of limits that has begun for both government and education. Words such as *retrenchment, scarcity,* and *priorities* seem to occur more frequently in the literature on education.

World War II was followed by a decade of economic growth and expansion in America, but the New Federalism now demands that priorities be set and limits be maintained in all areas, including education. Doyle (1982) addressed school board members in the following words:

> You are on the firing line, because you are in the undesirable position of dealing with scarcity. In political and financial terms, you are now playing a zero-sum game. Each slice of pie dished up for education means that much less for some other sector. And within the education enterprise itself, each slice for one education program means that much less for another. (p. 23)

In other words, education is not going to receive automatic increases in funds in the 1980s, and it must compete with other government services, such as police and fire protection, welfare, mental health, and highways, for the revenue it does receive. Various education programs will even be competing with each other for funds and survival itself. The New Federalism of President Reagan seeks to place more of the responsibility for improving education back in the hands of state and local officials, diminishing the federal role in education. According to Doyle (1982, p. 25), although the conservative federal government is the most easily identifiable cause of diminishing federal aid, it

Estimated Expenditures of Educational
Institutions, by Source of Funds: United
States, 1981—1982

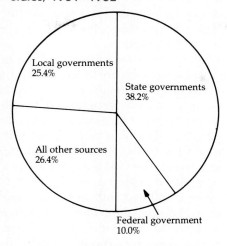

Local governments
25.4%

State governments
38.2%

All other sources
26.4%

Federal government
10.0%

Total expenditures = $199.8 billion

Source: U.S. Department of Education,
National Center for Education Statistics (estimates).

is actually a reflection of the times. Lack of economic expansion coupled with
the increased demand for social programs for an aging population forces
schools to compete head-to-head for the available resources. Doyle believes
that school districts must reorder their priorities, spending more funds on
reading and the three Rs, rather than on courses such as drivers' education.
He sees the most obvious solution as statewide funding of public education
and stated that Proposition 13-type legislation promoted such a remedy. He
predicted a continued but modest federal presence in education but emphasized that the real battles of educational finance will be fought at the state, not
the local or federal, level.

In the late 1970s and the early 1980s, the trend in state government was to
regain initiative and control over programs from the federal government.
During the 1960s, increasing numbers of federal dollars were transmitted
through state governments to local public-school districts. The states, in turn,
used the federal funds granted to them to administer the various federal
programs to augment their own contingent of consultants and supervisors.
At first, these staff additions were just icing on the cake, and the basic cake
itself was provided with state funds. However, by 1979, Pipho (1981, p. 125)
stated that 20–30 percent of state education budgets came from federal funds.
Thus, the state education agencies have become dependent on federal support, and many state legislatures spent the late 1970s and the early 1980s

attempting to regain control over the 20–30 percent of state-education-department revenue that came from federal sources.

The states do seem to be seizing the initiative as education becomes an important political issue in state politics. Instead of simply serving as a conduit for federal aid, the states are increasingly seeking to control the direction of educational policy within their borders.

Besides the modest federal role in education and the new era of limits, it is necessary for the student of education to understand the nature of the federal aid itself. Federal aid has traditionally been "categorical"—that is, for specific programs and purposes—not general aid to education. In other words, federal money cannot be spent for any current needs in public schools but must be used for specific programs to help the poor, the disadvantaged, the handicapped, the minorities, or the vocational education student. "Block grants," on the other hand, would provide more flexibility to the states and to local school districts in the use of federal money, and in 1981, thirty federal educational programs were combined into one block grant for the states, demonstrating a trend toward more federal block grants in the future, according to Kirst (1982, p. 72). However, it is important to realize that most current federal aid is designated for specific purposes. Among these purposes are improving reading effectiveness, vocational education, guidance and counseling, school social work, school health, and special education. It remains to be seen whether more federal block grants will replace the present categorical aid in the future.

What are the real and perceived problems connected with federal aid to education? One of the problems is related to the categorical grants already

A federally funded breakfast program starts off these children's school day. (*Photo by Axler.*)

discussed, which critics contend give no discretionary power to officials at the local and state levels on how federal funds are to be spent. In addition, some federal programs require matching funds from the state and the local levels, further reducing the money available to finance other educational programs. The biggest problem, however, is the mandates and regulations associated with federal aid to education. Often, the mandates accompanying federal aid cost more than the federal funds provide for these programs, especially regulations regarding special education and the handicapped. Also, although federal aid would seem to be an appropriate vehicle for reducing the disparity between the states in their ability to support public schools, federal aid does not seem to be accomplishing this purpose. In fact, federal aid seems to equalize these differences among states only slightly, and although Title I of the Elementary and Secondary Education Act (ESEA) provides more aid to poorer school districts, many federal programs seem to help wealthy districts more than poor districts (Campbell, Cunningham, Nystrand, and Usdan, 1980, pp. 383–384).

What are some possible solutions to these problems associated with federal aid to education? Block grants to replace categorical aid would give local and state leaders more flexibility in meeting needs at these levels, but some argue that block grants would diminish the federal government's role as an innovator in promoting change in education at the state and local levels.

Federal aid provides funds for special educational programs, but not for general programs for all children. (Photo used by permission of the Metropolitan School District of Lawrence Township.)

Reducing the number of federal mandates and regulations would also be a possible remedy, but few experts foresee this development in the future. The states, however, do seem to be seizing more initiative in controlling their educational programs, and the New Federalism of the Reagan administration is encouraging state efforts to solve educational problems. It would appear that the modest percentage of school revenues coming from the federal government will not be sufficient to equalize the disparities between the states in their ability to finance public schools. More will be said about this problem when solutions to school finance issues are discussed later in this chapter.

What are the future trends in regard to federal aid to education? First, the federal presence in education will continue to be modest, and the dollar amounts of this aid may actually decrease in future years. Second, general aid in the form of block grants is unlikely to replace federal categorical aid for specific purposes, such as vocational education, in spite of recent emphasis on revenue sharing and the consolidation of categorical grants into a few block grants. Third, the major purpose of federal aid to education will continue to be the stimulation of state and local officials to put more resources into programs that are in the national interest but that have been slighted at the state and local levels, such as programs for the handicapped and the disadvantaged. As Doyle (1982) concluded, "This, I say, is the reality of the '80's: a substantially diminished federal role in education no matter who occupies the White House." He believes that the era of limits is here to stay and has not simply been caused by the conservative policy of the Reagan administration. Recessions, inflation, tax revolts, decreases in the school-aged population, and pressure to fund other government services are the real causes of the era of limits, and they guarantee that scarcity, retrenchment, and priorities will be significant in the future of federal aid to education.

In the next section, the influence of federal and state courts on educational finance is examined.

The Courts and Educational Finance

Introduction

The federal and state courts have had a significant impact on educational finance, especially in recent years. Increasingly, educational policy is determined by the courts, from desegregation decisions to rulings on school finance, because of the greater use of litigation by society in general. On the issue of school finance, Benson (1978) asserted:

> Enter the courts on the issue of education finance. As is well known, the courts in a number of states have ruled that the existing system of education finance discriminates against poor people or—at the best—distributes educa-

tional resources in an irrational fashion. The general order or remedy is for state governments to play a more active role in educational resource allocations (though some of the more popular reform schemes would leave considerable discretionary powers over spending at the local level, as long as the state acts to equalize local taxing power). (p. 78)

In fact, increasingly, the finances are controlling the schools, not the schools shaping their finances. Federal and state court decisions have forced state legislatures to restructure their entire system of financing schools at a time when the states must do more with less money because of state and federal pressures for increased aid to the handicapped and minorities. Thus, every dollar used to equalize educational opportunity must result in a dollar-for-dollar decrease in educational spending in another area.

In the next sections the background of the school-finance-reform movement and the *Serrano* v. *Priest* (1971) decision, its results, its significance, and its possible negative consequences are examined.

Background of the School-Finance-Reform Movement

Arthur E. Wise, John E. Coons, William Cane, and Stephan Sugarman were the pioneers in the movement for public-school finance reform. They suggested that the quality of education within any state should not depend on the wealth of the local school district. They suggested that the state collect

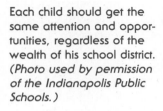

Each child should get the same attention and opportunities, regardless of the wealth of his school district. *(Photo used by permission of the Indianapolis Public Schools.)*

and distribute all revenue to local public-school districts and that the states attempt to equalize the tax bases of local school districts by revising equalization formulas and by redrawing local district boundary lines.

Arthur Wise (1981) has been generally credited with being the father of this movement, which led to numerous state court decisions on school finance. Although Wise advocated full state financing of education, he believed that it was still possible to have local operation of these districts and that local operation was preferable to state operation of schools. He believed that the main problem concerned the distribution of state school funds, not how these funds were raised at the state level. Wise emphasized that the then-current inequality in the ability of local school districts to finance education within a state ought to be illegal. Wise became interested in school finance reform when he wrote a term paper for a graduate course in school law. This paper was later published in the *Administrator's Notebook* (1965) and led to a general reexamination of school financing at the state level. His ideas resulted in lawsuits on public school finance in several states.

Serrano v. *Priest* and Related Cases

The landmark state court decision on school finance reform is the *Serrano* v. *Priest* decision of the California Supreme Court in 1971: "The Serrano criterion merely requires that the quality of education (usually defined as amount spent per child) shall not be a function of community wealth, but only of the wealth of the state as a whole" (Garms, Guthrie, & Pierce, 1978, p. 218). This decision seemed to eliminate local flat-grant or foundation programs, which allowed local school districts to spend more per child if they wished, but it did not outlaw the state or local property tax to finance education if the funds were distributed equally among the school districts in the state. In fact, the *Serrano* decision did not specify a particular school finance program, although it did provide that district spending should not be related to the taxable wealth of that school district. It declared the school finance system in the state of California at that time unconstitutional, arguing that this system violated the guarantees of equal protection in both the state and the federal Constitutions. Benson (1978) summarized the background of this decision:

> On August 23, 1968, a suit was filed by school children and their taxpaying parents of a number of Los Angeles school districts. The case, *Serrano* v. *Priest*, listed the state treasurer, the state superintendent of public instruction, and several other state and local officials as defendants. Plaintiffs claimed that there were disparities in educational provision among the districts of California; that these disparities arose primarily as a result of differences in taxable wealth per student; and that educational opportunities in low-wealth districts were substantially inferior to those available to children attending schools in high-wealth districts. (p. 339)

Public-school-finance lawsuits followed in several other states. In *Rodriguez* v. *San Antonio* (1971), a state court ruled that the Texas educational finance system was unconstitutional because it violated the equal-protection clause of the Fourteenth Amendment to the U.S. Constitution. In 1973, this case was appealed to the U.S. Supreme Court, which reversed the decision of the Texas court and thus prevented a nationwide uniform solution to the inequities in school finance. In other words, the Supreme Court ruled that equalization of school finance was not a federal problem and should be decided at the state level. After this decision, the action took place in various state courts in Alaska, Connecticut, Florida, Georgia, Kansas, Maine, Missouri, New Jersey, New York, Ohio, Oregon, and West Virginia.

Results and Significance of *Serrano* v. *Priest*

What have been the results of the *Serrano* and related decisions? The most important result of these state court decisions has been to put pressure on state legislatures to reform their school finance programs. These decisions established the concept of *fiscal neutrality* in school finance. This term means that a child's education may not be determined by the wealth of a local school district. Another effect was the domino effect, which caused challenges to school finance plans to be filed in the courts of numerous other states. In addition, these cases placed in jeopardy the school finance systems in every state except Hawaii, which has statewide public-school financing. Thus, state legislatures were forced to consider major revisions of their school finance programs to avoid further litigation. Thus, the *Serrano* and related state court decisions have made a permanent impact on public school finance in the various states, both through what the decisions stated and through what they did not say.

Possible Solutions to Problems in School Finance

What are possible solutions to the problems of school finance that were accentuated by the *Serrano* case and other state-school-finance court decisions? The possible and suggested solutions include power equalizing, full state funding, tuition tax credits, vouchers, and private grants to public education. In addition, an increase in federal funds, restructuring educational priorities, mandating the same expenditure for each pupil nationwide, accountability, performance contracting, and school consolidation have been proposed as possible solutions to the school finance problems in the United States. Each of these suggested remedies is examined briefly in this section, and the likelihood of the use of each is assessed.

Two of the most prominent of these solutions are power equalizing and full state funding of public education. Power equalizing equalizes the ability to raise dollars per pupil at the same tax rates but does not mandate the rate or the expenditure level that results. Under power equalizing a variety of levels of educational quality would be available in a school system; and a family could choose the level of quality it prefers, realizing that taxes would vary according to the level of quality chosen. Full state funding would result if all local-public-school revenues were raised through state taxes and were then distributed to the local school districts. Hawaii has had full state funding of K–12 public education for many years, and recently Florida also adopted a full-state-funding plan.

Many people argue that because education is legally a state function, it should be supported entirely by state funds. It is further asserted that state taxes are more equitable than local taxes, such as the local property tax. However, even statewide funding of education would not solve the financial problems in the nation because states, too, vary greatly in their ability to support schools. Less wealthy states would have to greatly increase their tax rates to raise the same revenue provided by lower rates in wealthier states. Full state funding is an acceptable solution under the *Serrano* decision because the money spent per pupil would be a function of state wealth, not of the wealth of the local school district. Full state funding would not mandate that an equal number of dollars be spent on educating each child in the state but would require that state money be allocated to local districts based on the learning requirements of its children and the local costs of educating them. Under full state funding, local districts would lose only their power to tax but not their powers to hire, fire, and promote teachers. This plan retains the advantages of local control but provides statewide financing for all districts in the state. Several states seem to be moving toward a combination of power equalizing and full state funding to finance education in their states.

Other major solutions that have been suggested include tuition tax credits and vouchers to finance education. Both of these plans would further the interests of private and parochial schools by allowing parents to choose which schools their children would attend. Critics of these plans assert that they would foreshadow the demise of public schools as we now know them and would increase the educational disparity between poor and wealthy students. Proponents claim that these plans would introduce free enterprise and competition to revitalize education in the United States. Even if weak schools fail to go out of business, they say, the schools in general will be stronger and more progressive. The Reagan administration favors tuition tax credits for parents who send their children to private schools, allowing these parents to deduct a portion of the tuition that they pay from the income on which they must pay federal income taxes. Leonard (1982) assessed the results of tuition tax credits:

The allowance of tuition tax credits or the use of vouchers would help the private and parochial schools. The question arises whether this type of funding would subsequently hurt the public schools. *(Photo by Axler.)*

If tuition tax credits are approved by the Congress, they may change elementary and secondary education in important ways. First, the Administration estimates that such credits would cost the federal government $2.7 billion in fiscal year 1982, the cost rising to nearly $7 billion by fiscal year 1986. The government would have to recoup this loss of revenue somehow—most likely through future cuts in federal education spending. Another round of budget cuts could well wipe out some programs and leave others at subsistence level. Second, some observers believe that tuition tax credits will bring a jump in private school enrollments, compounding the problems that public schools already face because of enrollment declines. Proponents of tuition tax credits argue that such credits should not affect public school enrollments adversely; public schools will merely be forced to improve the quality of their programs in order to compete for students who will now be able to afford private schools, they say. (p. 601)

Thus, Leonard anticipated less money for public schools and a decline in public school enrollments if tuition-tax-credit legislation is passed by Congress.

The voucher plan, in contrast to tuition tax credits, was originally proposed in 1955 by Milton Friedman, an economist at the University of Chicago. Under Friedman's plan, governments would guarantee each child a minimum level of education by giving parents vouchers each year redeemable for a certain sum of money toward tuition at any "approved" school. Schools participating, both public and private, would have to meet minimum government standards in their educational programs in order to be "approved" and to be eligible to receive payment for their vouchers. Parents would be free to

The Voucher System

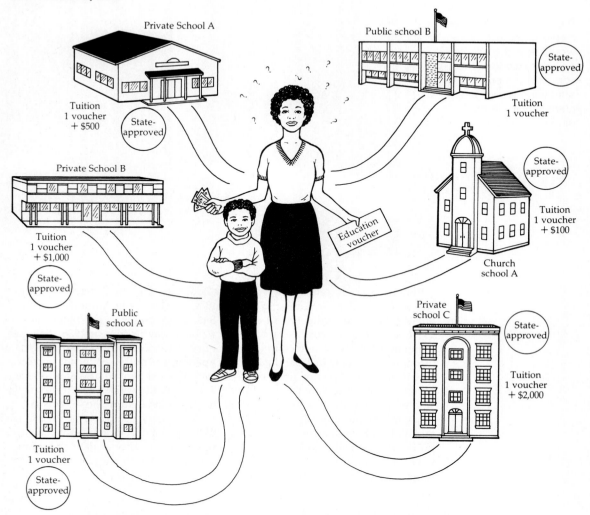

Private School A

Tuition
1 voucher
+ $500

State-approved

Public school B

State-approved

Tuition
1 voucher

State-approved

Private School B

Tuition
1 voucher
+ $1,000

State-approved

Church
school A

Tuition
1 voucher
+ $100

Education
voucher

Public
school A

Tuition
1 voucher

State-approved

Private
school C

State-approved

Tuition
1 voucher
+ $2,000

chose the school best suited to their child's needs and to supplement the voucher amount with additional money if they so desire.

Because the original Friedman voucher proposal would permit parents to supplement the government voucher with additional funds of their own, it would not meet the criteria set down in the *Serrano* decision unless the Friedman plan were modified to eliminate this problem.

There are both pros and cons to such a voucher system. On the positive side, parents would have expanded choices in providing for their children's education and would not be forced to use one school or teacher about which they have no particular enthusiasm. Also, theoretically, the presence of competition for students would improve both the quality and the variety of educational programs. Teachers' salaries, proponents contend, would become more responsive to the fluctuations of the economy and would presumably be forced upward by the pressure of competition. On the negative side is the contention that such a plan would increase class and racial distinctions and would segregate rather than integrate the population. Additionally, it is argued that some rural areas would not have alternatives to public schools; that the values instilled by schools of various religious groups would vary, breaking down the common core of values necessary to perpetuate our society; and that it would be difficult for parents to judge the quality of the various school alternatives. Opponents of this voucher plan assert that the greatness of the United States has resulted from the public schools and that this plan would weaken them by making them a dumping ground for only the poor and disadvantaged students.

To answer some of these criticisms, Friedman suggested modifications to his original proposal. Under this revised voucher plan, parents who want to send their children to nonpublic schools would receive a voucher or payment equal to the cost of educating each child in the local public school. Thus, under this revised plan, the size of the grants or vouchers would be determined mainly by per pupil educational expenses at the local level.

Another voucher plan is Family Power Equalizing (FPE), proposed by Coons and Sugarman (1978) in 1971. This plan attempts to avoid the criticism of accentuating social stratification leveled at other voucher plans by specifying that schools must be financed solely by money received from vouchers without the use of endowment or additional funds "added on" by parents to supplement the vouchers. The FPE plan would abolish school tuition and substitute a "price-of-education" tax on families with children. This household tax would be determined both by the expenditure level of the school chosen and by the level of income of the family. Whenever more students elect a school than the school can accommodate, the students would be selected on a random basis to prevent elitism. In other words, under FPE, the family can choose the level of education it desires and is taxed according to this decision and the family income.

Although the Reagan administration favors some form of voucher plan for public school finance, none has been enacted by Congress thus far.

What other possible remedies have been proposed for the present problems in school finance? First, some suggest contributions from foundations and corporations to replace the loss of funds, especially federal funds, for public education. However, 95 percent of these monies go to higher education, not to public elementary and secondary schools. Thus, private sources would seem to be unlikely to replace any loss of public revenue for K–12 schools, even though some public school districts are forming private foundations to seek contributions for their schools. Private charitable foundations do not have sufficient resources to make up for the loss of public funds to education. Related to this solution would be the increased emphasis on "user fees," under which students would pay a portion of their own costs for education, especially for electives such as drivers' education classes.

Other suggested solutions are numerous and varied. One is an increase in federal aid to education, but the trend seems to be toward less, rather than more, federal aid for public elementary and secondary schools, with the percentage of funds from federal aid remaining fairly constant over the long run. Another proposed solution is to use the shortage of public school funds to restructure the priorities in American education and to place more emphasis on basics such as reading and mathematics. The authors of this book believe that the restructuring of priorities must take place in the society as a whole, not just in education. They castigate American society for placing its spending priorities on entertainment and automobiles rather than on the education of its children. Yet another remedy suggested by the *Serrano* case would equalize all educational expenditures in a state by mandating that the same number of dollars be spent on each child in the state while allowing the funds to be raised by taxes at the local level.

Still other solutions that have been proposed for the problems of public school finance are performance contracting, greater use of accountability, and more emphasis on the consolidation of smaller schools. Performance contracting was tried in Gary, Indiana, and other cities in the 1960s as a way of using the economies of the free enterprise system and competition to improve education. Under the Gary plan, a private firm was hired to take over a Gary elementary school in an inner-city area. The firm could hire noncertified teachers to educate the pupils and would be paid if previously set levels of reading and math scores were attained by a set percentage of the pupils in this school. This approach led to an emphasis on only certain subjects, and other areas were omitted, such as social studies, health, physical education, and the fine arts. In some school districts using performance contracting, teaching to the test was also a problem because the schools knew in advance what the test questions would be and taught only this material.

The emphasis on performance contracting has declined in the 1970s and the 1980s, yielding to a greater emphasis on solutions such as accountability and consolidation of schools with smaller enrollments. Garms et al. (1978) believe, "Rapidly rising school expenditures with little or no improvement in performance have led taxpayers and their legislative representatives to demand demonstrable results in return for additional educational funding" (p. 349). They also assert that these demands for greater accountability are a direct challenge to the local control of education by placing increased power at the state level. Benson (1978) believes that consolidation of school districts could also save enough funds to relieve some of the financial burden on local school districts by introducing economies of size. Although many states with large populations do have excessive numbers of local school districts, state legislatures are unlikely, in the opinion of the authors of this textbook, to willingly tackle the emotion-laden issue of consolidating these schools in the near future.

Thus, although many solutions to school finance problems have been proposed, no one solution can be seen as the answer at this time, although increased state funding seems to be the most likely course in most states.

Conclusions and Future Trends in School Finance

What conclusions and future trends can be discerned from this discussion of public school finance? First, several conclusions can be identified. In general, the prospects for funding public education in the United States in the 1980s are not bright for a variety of reasons. As Pinkney (1980) wrote, our priorities in America fail to put education first:

> We often boast and brag about our nation's wealth, our highly industrialized society, our world leadership, and even our concern and services to mankind; yet we have failed to give priority to education with adequate funds. In spite of our bragging, evidence is mounting that urban school systems are deteriorating in many instances because there's a lack of funds. Some writers have even said that the financial problems are cancerous. In most cases, the current system of financing public education remains "unjust and unequal" and if we are really concerned about the future, the urgency now exists for us to put our priorities in rank order. (pp. 72–73)

Another problem in financing schools in the 1980s is the current political conservatism in the United States. The inflation rate, which was in double digits in the United States in the early 1980s, has declined to modest levels, but spending for schools in the 1980s will still have difficulty keeping up with inflation.

The present problems in public school financing are becoming political questions of: Who should pay? How much? For what services? Difficulties also result from the categorical nature of federal aid and from the high cost of educating pupils in the inner-city urban areas of the United States. There is growing evidence of the disenchantment of citizens with the government, including schools as government agencies. In addition, single-issue politics leads to public support for portions of the public school program, such as vocational education, but not for the educational program as a whole. Also, declining enrollment means that a smaller percentage of citizens now have sons or daughters in the public schools, a situation that may lead to a decrease in political support for public school programs. To further complicate the situation, declining standardized test scores and the tax revolt at the grassroots level put public school financing in jeopardy. The possibility of tax credit and/or vouchers also clouds the future of public school funding.

Another conspicuous concern in the future of educational finance is the property tax, considered regressive by many experts because it falls most heavily on those with the least ability to pay. Table 14.1 shows that real-estate property taxes take a larger percentage of the income in low-income families and a smaller percentage in high-income families. Of the three major taxes for school support (the individual and corporate income tax, the sales and excise taxes, and the property tax), the income tax is progressive, whereas the sales and property taxes are regressive, the property tax being the most regressive of all. Remember that a tax is progressive if the amount of money collected from a wealthy family represents a larger share of family income than that collected from a poor family. Conversely, a tax is regressive when the tax represents a larger share of family income for a poor family than for a wealthy family. Property tax relief will remain an educational finance issue in the 1980s, and the prospects for full state funding of education are not encouraging because this would require large increases in present state taxes or the addition of new state taxes. Thus, the property tax is likely to remain the mainstay of public school finance in the foreseeable future.

TABLE 14–1   Real Estate Taxes as a Percentage of Family Income, Owner-Occupied Single-Family Homes, by Income Class and Region, 1970

Family Income[a]	U.S. Total	North-east	North Central	South	West	Home Owners No. (000)	% Dist.[b]
Less than $2,000	16.6	30.8	18.0	8.2	22.9	1,718.8	5.5
$ 2,000–2,999	9.7	15.7	9.8	5.2	12.5	1,288.7	9.7
3,000–3,999	7.7	13.1	7.7	4.3	8.7	1,397.8	14.1
4,000–4,999	6.4	9.8	6.7	3.4	8.0	1,342.8	18.5
5,000–5,999	5.5	9.3	5.7	2.9	6.5	1,365.1	22.8
6,000–6,999	4.7	7.1	4.9	2.5	5.9	1,530.1	27.8
7,000–9,999	4.2	6.2	4.2	2.2	5.0	5,377.4	45.0
10,000–14,999	3.7	5.3	3.6	2.0	4.0	8,910.3	73.6
15,000–24,999	3.3	4.6	3.1	2.0	3.4	6,365.6	94.0
25,000 or more	2.9	3.9	2.7	1.7	2.9	1,876.9	100.0
All incomes						31,144.7	
Arithmetic mean	4.9	6.9	5.1	2.9	5.4		
Median	3.4	5.0	3.5	2.0	3.9		

[a]Census definition of income (from all sources). Income reported received in 1970.
[b]Cumulated from lowest income class.
Source: U.S. Bureau of the Census, *Residential Finance Survey, 1970* (conducted in 1971), special tabulations prepared for the Advisory Commission on Intergovernmental Relations (ACIR). Real-estate tax data were compiled for properties acquired before 1970 and represent taxes paid during 1970. Medians were computed by ACIR staff. Reproduced from Advisory Commission on Intergovernmental Relations (1977), p. 143.

The property tax is a regressive tax, hitting hardest those citizens with limited or fixed incomes. *(Photo by Axler.)*

What possible solutions and future trends can be discerned from present data on educational finance? First, a shift in the funding balance from local to state can be seen, as well as shifts within state funding itself. The trend from less local to more state funding of public schools has been pronounced in the last four decades. At present, the local and state shares of public school revenues are about equal, at approximately 40 percent for each level, but many experts in educational finance predict that state funding at the 50 percent level will be a reality by the end of the 1980s. Within the state tax structure, the revenues from state personal and corporate income taxes are rising rapidly, and for the first time, their combined yield will probably exceed the yield of the state sales taxes. On the other hand, the declining consumption of energy, the increased costs of energy, and fuel-efficient auto-

413

mobiles have resulted in less state revenue from taxes on gasoline and motor fuels. Other trends include the fact that the federal share of educational finance will very likely remain at a constant level or may possibly decrease slightly.

A continuing problem in educational finance is likely to be the so-called taxpayers' revolt of Proposition 13-type state legislation. In Hartley's (1981) words,

> Proposition 13 and its progeny have raised American tax consciousness to a high level that is not inconsistent with the 200-year tradition of distrust of public officials and taxes that gave rise to the Boston Tea Party and rebellion against monarchy. . . . Despite confusing evidence that Americans support tax cuts in principle but resist limiting government expenditures when specific programs are threatened, there is a rather steady tone to the tax revolt messages that form the basis for the education scenario for the next decade: reduce the tax burden; reduce government waste and unresponsiveness; control the growth of government spending; and develop better social policy that improves efficiency in the delivery of human services and programs in areas such as education. (p. 39)

The reliance on the property tax is by no means uniform in all states, and the southern states show the least reliance on local-property-tax revenue. Even though the shift from local to state financing has resulted in less reliance on the property tax, areas of the country with a large proportion of senior citizens still face the prospect of property tax revolts and protests.

Although the 1970s were a generally good period for educational finance, the omens for the 1980s are not as bright. In the 1970s, public education expenditures as a percentage of the gross national product and as a percentage of personal income remained constant, and the expenditures per pupil had increased 173.7 percent from $657 per pupil in 1970 to $1,798 per pupil by the end of the decade (Odden & Augenblick, 1981, p. 13). However, Adams (1982) found that in the fiscal year 1981–1982, the growth of state revenues for K–12 public schools had grown at the 6 percent level, whereas local revenues had increased at the higher rate of 12 percent. Thus, the trend toward a greater share of education funds' coming from state tax sources may slow down or reverse itself in the future.

A survey (Odden and Augenblick, 1981) of state education policymakers in 1981 revealed that the major school-finance issues of the 1980s would continue to be a concern about school finance reform, coupled with an emphasis on reducing local property taxes. Hartley (1981) concluded:

> Clearly the 1980s will be a decade of limits, with Americans challenged to set realistic goals based on reduced resources, from global energy to individual purchasing power. The "politics of less" and retrenchment management are part of an evolving pattern of change in American expectations. Traditionally a nation optimistic about the future, America is turning pessimistic. In his sur-

vey of public attitudes, Yankelovich observed: "Now a majority of Americans not only believe that the past was a better time for the country than the present, they anticipate that the present, however bad it may be, is more likely to be better than the future" (p. 39)

Thus, the prospects for the future of educational finance in the 1980s appear bleak, especially when compared with public school funding in previous decades. It is possible, however, that some continued progress will be made in school finance reform in the next decade.

Summary

This chapter began by emphasizing the stability of the percentage of the K–12 public-school revenues coming from the federal government, which has remained steady at about 8 percent in recent years with little prospect of getting larger in the foreseeable future. The problems associated with federal aid were examined, and possible solutions to these problems were suggested. The realities of the 1980s seem to be a diminished federal presence in education and an increased state initiative by means of school finance reforms and career ladder programs. Significant terms in federal aid, such as *categorical* and *block grants*, were defined; and their influence on education was examined. This chapter also traced the background of the school-finance-reform movement and surveyed its future prospects, including the influence of *Serrano* v. *Priest* and related court cases. The possible solutions to these school finance problems suggested in this chapter were family power equalizing, full state funding, the voucher plan, and tuition tax credits. The advantages and disadvantages of each of these solutions were discussed, along with future trends in school finance.

Questions

1. Define categorical support for education. What are the advantages and disadvantages of this approach?
2. Summarize the views of both the advocates and the opponents of federal aid to education.
3. Which state probably would receive the greatest amount of federal aid? Why?
4. Identify five future trends for educational finance in the United States. Be certain to relate these trends to local, state, and federal support of education.
5. What are the dangers and rewards to public education of implementing a voucher plan for financing the education of youth? How do you feel personally on this issue?

Activities for Unit VII

1. Pick two school districts in your state and demonstrate the inequality between them of financial support for education.
2. Of the expenditure per pupil for education in your school district, how much is paid by the state and how much comes from local taxes? What does the federal government contribute per pupil?
3. Find two or three periodical articles in the *Education Index* dealing with the pros and cons of the proposed voucher plans for education. How do you feel personally about this issue?
4. Invent and describe your ideal plan for financing public schools. Demonstrate how it would be equitable to all groups involved.
5. Research the funding per pupil in average daily attendance (ADA) in the top five states and the lowest five states in the United States. What conclusions about school finance can you draw from these data?
6. How is the local tax rate for a school district determined in your state? What steps or controls are involved in this process?
7. If the support per pupil in ADA were magically doubled in your state, how would you spend the additional funds?

EDUCATIONAL ORGANIZATIONS

15

Educational Organizations

OBJECTIVES

After reading Chapter 15, the student will be able to:
- Gain a historical perspective of the role of teachers' organizations in American education.
- Realize the importance of teachers' organizations in the supporting role they play in representing the teacher.
- Compare the policies and goals of the American Federation of Teachers (AFT) and the National Education Association (NEA).
- Determine the role that teachers' organizations play in the collective-bargaining process.
- Select other organizations that will help her or him in professional development.

419

The Purpose of Teachers' Organizations

The primary purpose of teachers' organizations—or unions, as some people prefer to call them—is to provide a forum in which teachers can unify to prepare their case for presentation to the school board, the state legislature, and the U.S. Congress. Teachers normally present the school board with a contract proposal that is dealt with through the collective-bargaining process. Teachers are often affiliated with state teachers' organizations that have certain employees registered as lobbyists during each state's legislative sessions. Legislators, many times, rely on teacher lobbyists for valuable information and for help in writing education bills. At the federal level, teachers are represented by lobbyists from the large parent organizations for teachers—the National Educational Association (NEA) and the American Federation of Teachers (AFT).

Why Belong to a Teachers' Organization?

Primarily, individual teachers choose to belong to teachers' organizations to support the unified voice of teachers. Teachers are cognizant of the power and influence that come from unifying into one group. Second, teachers like to belong because of member benefits such as insurance plans, travel-agency and car-rental agreements, book clubs, educational journals, newsletters, and legal assistance. Third, some teachers enjoy taking an active role in organizations and rising to leadership within them. A fourth reason is that membership may help a teacher to feel more involved in the educational process. On the negative side, a few teachers may join because of a feeling of coercion from colleagues. Some dedicated teachers' organization members feel that those who fail to join and pay their fair share are "freeloaders." Frequently, some teachers do not belong because the organizations support one issue with which they disagree or because of personal dislike of an officer or a member.

How Effective Are Teachers' Organizations?

The effectiveness of teachers' organizations in achieving their goals depends on the issue in question and on whether one is referring to implications at the local, state, or federal levels of government. An impressive show of power and influence was seen during the 1980 presidential elections, when we saw more teacher delegates at the Democratic National Convention than from any

Teachers' organizations increase the power of individual professional educators through collective action. *(Photo used by permission of the Indiana State Teachers Association.)*

other organized group. The NEA teachers were pleased with President Carter for his leadership in changing the U.S. Office of Education to the Cabinet-level Department of Education, and they came in force to nominate him for a second term. Teachers were able to celebrate a victory for Carter at the convention but were not able to elect him in November. The AFT did not have the same interest in getting a U.S. Department of Education as did the NEA, but the AFT does support the department now that it has been established.

The effectiveness of teachers' organizations in representing teachers at the bargaining table and in grievance procedures seems to be improving. An increasing number of issues, both monetary and nonmonetary, are now included in the bargaining process. Administrators, who were once in a very authoritative position, are now almost afraid to say or do anything for fear of teacher grievances or a lawsuit. Teachers' organization power in relation to collective bargaining and teachers' grievances may be a sign of effectiveness in influencing school administration and school boards, but this shift may be only temporary until the power struggle levels off. Most administrators are still in control of their buildings and their school systems, but some administrators are not aware of, nor do they have the time for, exercising all their legal rights and responsibilities. Probably, a true measure of effectiveness will come when both administrators and teachers can work harmoniously as a team for the benefit of the students.

A Brief History of Two Major Teachers' Organizations

In the early days of schooling in America, there were only a few examples of individual teachers registering their complaints. Two of these isolated examples are cited in the following:

> In 1766 Ezekiel Cheever, who had established a "Town Free School" in Charlestown, Massachusetts, found himself in unusually tight financial straits. His pittance of a salary had not been paid on schedule, schools in nearby towns had lured away some of his pupils, and his schoolhouse was falling apart. Cheever spoke up at a town council meeting and by his audacity persuaded the selectmen to promise that they would "take care the schoolhouse be speedily amended because it is much out of repair" and see to it that his yearly salary was paid (the constables, he told them, being "much behind him"). Cheever also won their promise that no other schoolmaster would "be suffered or set up in the town."
>
> Another instance of "militancy" took place during the 1790s elsewhere in Massachusetts. Schoolmaster Caleb Bingham was a modest and, usually, a timid man. But the town fathers had not paid him or the other teachers for months. Instead, they were handed a paper certifying that the town owed them a certain sum. These certificates or "town orders" could then be sold at the bank for a considerable discount. Bingham decided he had had enough. When he received his next certificate, he advertised it for sale in the town newspaper, in effect publicizing the fiscal state of the community. This public insult led to a town meeting, to which Bingham was summoned by a constable. Called on for his apology, Bingham gave a brief account of his frustrations. "I have a family and need the money," he explained. "I have done my part of the engagement faithfully, and have no apology to make to those who have failed to do theirs. All I can do is to promise that if the town will punctually pay my salary in the future, I will never advertise their orders for sale again." Reportedly the town treasurer slapped him on the shoulder and said, "Bingham, you are a good fellow; call at my office after the meeting and I will give you the cash." Presumably, Bingham had no further trouble collecting what was due him. (Donley, 1976, p. 4)

Most of the early teachers were not like Cheever and Bingham, and they did what was expected of them with few complaints. Teachers were expected to teach and to do numerous other chores, and to keep quiet. Because teachers were of a rather passive nature, teachers' organizations were slow in emerging as a powerful force in education. Some old-time teachers would not recognize the profession today.

The first teachers' association, the Society of Associated Teachers of New York City, was established in 1794. Later, county and city teachers' organizations were set up across the country, and thirty state teachers' associations were formed between 1840 and 1861. From the beginning, teachers have been torn between emphasizing society's needs for good education and emphasizing their own economic benefits. On the side of emphasizing society's needs were those who wanted to protect the welfare of our country by being very service-oriented. Historically, teachers have remained service-oriented, but they have become less reticent about protecting their own economic benefits.

Differences and Similarities Between the AFT and the NEA

The leading similarities and differences between the American Federation of Teachers and the National Education Association are outlined in Table 15–1. There are additional similarities and differences, but those that are listed

TABLE 15—1   Leading Similarities and Differences Between the AFT and NEA

Similarities	Differences
1. Both are for the betterment of teacher welfare.	1. Ages: NEA—1857 AFT—1917.
2. Both participate in the collective-bargaining process by assisting bargaining teams at the local level.	2. The AFT is affiliated with the American Federation of Labor and the Congress of Industrial Organizations (AFL-CIO).
3. Both favor the strike as a last resort when agreements cannot be reached.	3. The AFT believes in voice votes, whereas the NEA believes in the secret ballot for major offices.
4. Both provide supplemental services for teachers such as insurance, car rental, and travel.	4. Size (approximately): NEA 1,700,000 AFT 450,000
5. Both are big lobbying organizations for education at the state and federal levels. Both use the efforts of political action committees (PACs).[a]	5. The AFT is most active in our largest metropolitan areas.
6. State and local affiliations are integral parts of both of the national organizations.	6. The NEA makes extensive field and research services available to teachers.
7. Both use unified dues to unite local, state, and national organizations financially.	7. The NEA provides uniserve directors to help local affiliates.[b]
8. Both strongly support public education.	8. NEA dues are higher than AFT dues.

[a] Historically, the NEA promoted education from both the teachers' and the administrators' sides, but since collective bargaining, they primarily aid the teachers.

[b] A uniserve director is a full-time NEA employee who helps with the collective-bargaining process and other matters relating to teachers' welfare.

stand out as the most important ones. Most of the listed items in Table 15–1 are described in greater detail later in the chapter.

History of the NEA

The first of the two major teachers' organizations was formed in Philadelphia in 1857 by forty-three educators. Called the National Teachers' Association, it later became known as the National Education Association (NEA) and has now grown to 1.7 million members from every state in the nation. Dual purposes were proposed for the National Teachers' Association: to elevate the character and advance the interests of the profession of teaching, and to promote the cause of popular education in the United States. Most of the early discussions centered on promoting the need for public education in America, and it is still one of the prime interests of the NEA.

Resolutions passed by the NEA give us an idea of what the organization stood for during those early years. The following historical resolutions reveal something of the social and educational philosophy of the members of the NEA:

1876. Resolved, next to liberty, education has been the great cause of the marvelous prosperity of the Republic in the first century of its history, and is the sure and only hope of its future.

Meeting in state assemblies, NEA affiliates decide issues. (Photo used by permission of the Indiana State Teachers Association.)

1889. Universal suffrage without universal education is a national peril. The aim of the school is not training of the mind alone, but the training of the man.

1894. Education is the inalienable right of every child of our Republic.

1915. The people of each and every nation need to sink their nationalism in a larger internationalism. . . .

1932. No nation can afford to entrust its children to incompetent teachers.

1944. Education should prepare each generation to meet the social, economic, and political problems of an ever changing world. (Wesley, 1957, pp. 369–370)

In 1892 and in 1910, firm resolutions are made in support of the public schools. The 1915 resolution in support of internationalism is not very different from the present NEA support of multicultural education.

Not until 1925 did the classroom teacher become a full-fledged participant in NEA activity. Before this time, school administrators did all of the policymaking in the association. In two democratizing moves by the NEA in the 1920s and 1930s, classroom teachers became full members, and a National Representative Assembly of Delegates was established. Teachers could then have a voice in the National Representative Assembly. Still, there was no evidence of great militancy during this period.

Throughout the years, the NEA had accumulated over thirty departments. These departments are listed here in four categories (Wesley, 1957):

Departments of the NEA

1. *Administration*
   a. American Association of School Administrators, 1870.
   b. Department of Elementary School Principals, 1921.
   c. National Association of Women Deans and Counselors, 1918.
   d. National Association of Secondary-School Principals, 1927.
   e. National Council of Administrative Women in Education, 1932.

2. *Curriculum Areas*
   a. American Association for Health, Physical Education, and Recreation, 1937.
   b. American Industrial Arts Association, 1939.
   c. Association for Supervision and Curriculum Development, 1929.
   d. Department of Home Economics, 1930.
   e. Department of Vocational Education, 1875.
   f. Music Educators National Conference, 1940.
   g. National Art Education Association, 1933.
   h. National Association of Journalism Directors, 1939.
   i. National Council for the Social Studies, 1925.
   j. National Council of Teachers of Mathematics, 1950.

Terry Herndon, past executive secretary of the National Education Association. *(Photo used by permission of the Indiana State Teachers Association.)*

k. National Science Teachers Association, 1895.
l. Speech Association of America, 1939.
m. United Business Education Association, 1892.

3. *Instruction of Selected Groups or Classes*
    a. American Association of Colleges for Teacher Education, 1948.
    b. Association for Higher Education, 1942.
    c. Department of Kindergarten-Primary Education, 1884.

Profile of Terry Herndon

Terry Herndon, who was the Executive Secretary of the NEA from 1973 to 1983, believes that the greatest accomplishment during his administration was facilitating congressional acceptance of the Department of Education. Other important issues were unemployment compensation for teachers, more money for handicapped children, Title IX grants for women and girls, creation of federally funded teacher centers, and opposition to federally funded aid to private schools. He says his greatest pleasure was to see the development of teachers as a political force.

Herndon feels that his greatest disappointment was not achieving passage of general federal aid to education. All federal aid at the present time is categorical; thus, Congress specifies exactly what the money should be used for in the schools. The NEA has long thought that federal aid should be about one third of the cost of public education, but federal aid is now only 8 percent of the total, or less. General aid would be assistance for general school programs rather than for specifics. Another disappointment was the lack of congressional passage of a federal collective-bargaining bill. Herndon believes that it is wrong for negotiations to take place in the presence of fear that one may be jailed for striking. Confiscatory fines are sometimes imposed on striking teachers.

Looking forward, Herndon sees little hope for an NEA-AFT merger in the near future. He believes that the two organizations are very stable and that there is not likely to be movement toward merger. Herndon's attitude toward merger was changed from optimism to pessimism in the years when he was Executive Secretary. He says that most of the leaders believe the existence of the two separate organizations is productive rather than counterproductive (West, 1980, p. 255).

Writing about the NEA's new image since 1973 when Herndon began his tenure, West (1980) listed five developments cited by Herndon:

1. The NEA is unified which means the local, state and national units have been tied together. Prior to unification, a teacher could join one unit without joining the other. Now with one dues payment the whole NEA team works more together and there is little duplication of services.
2. The goals of the organization are clearly defined, programs and strategies are understood, and there is broad participation by members in program implementation.
3. The Association's decision-making machinery and the service delivery system have been made more efficient. Much was accomplished to simplify decision-making by the adoption of a new constitution. A staff reorganization in 1979–80 provided for the delivery of a coordinated program of services through six regional NEA offices.
4. In the past decade Association services for the protection of its members, students, and schools have increased greatly.
5. Herndon feels that the elected and staff leadership is of high quality. This leadership team has provided for the infusion of fresh ideas from the rotating terms of the elected presidents and continuity of leadership through the appointed executive secretary and staff. (p. 252)

d.   Department of Rural Education, 1907.
e.   International Council for Exceptional Children, 1941.
f.   National Association of Public School Adult Educators, 1955.

4.   *Service*
a.   American Educational Research Association, 1930.
b.   Department of Audio-Visual Instruction, 1923.
c.   Department of Classroom Teachers, 1913.
d.   National Association of Educational Secretaries, 1946.
e.   National Retired Teachers Association, 1951.
f.   National School Public Relations Association, 1950.

By 1976, because of disaffiliations of these departments, there were only four left with the NEA. The underlying cause of the dissatisfaction was the adversary relationship inherent in the collective-bargaining process (West, 1980, p. 84). The NEA had decided to promote the cause of collective bargaining in the 1960s, and this decision led administrators who had been strong leaders of the NEA to disaffiliate with the association. The nonadministrator affiliates, however, were probably influenced by other factors as well (West, 1980, p. 85). There is now a continuing relationship with these disaffiliated organizations, and the NEA has simplified its organizational structure and clarified its public image. On pp. 437–445, collective bargaining is discussed in detail, and it should become clearer to the reader why most of these disaffiliations took place.

The NEA has a long history of promoting civil rights in our country. One example was the Prince Edward County, Virginia, Free School Association, which was supported by the NEA. Prince Edward County closed its public schools rather than comply with the *Brown* decision in 1954 to integrate their schools. The NEA assisted by asking its membership to donate money to keep the Free School Association going during this tense period: "The superintendent of the Free School Association later told the NEA staff the schools could not have opened without the NEA's prompt assistance" (West, 1980, p. 104).

There had been both black and white affiliates of the NEA in the South, and in another case, the NEA issued four suspensions of state affiliates in 1969. The goal was to gain mergers of the two separate state affiliates in these states. By 1977, unification was completed when the two associations in Louisiana merged. John Ryor, then president of the NEA, declared, "The doctrine of separate but equal has no place in the teaching profession" (West, 1980, p. 122). The 1954 *Brown* decision of the U.S. Supreme Court regarding "separate but equal" as being inherently unequal was the power behind both of these actions by the NEA.

Policymaking decisions are made by the NEA in the following manner. Any teacher member can submit resolutions to the Resolution Committee for a hearing. Resolutions are voted on by the committee, and before each delegate assembly, the proposed resolutions are printed for the delegates to con-

Mary Hatwood Futrell speaks out on the issues as president of the National Education Association. *(Photo used by permission of the Indiana State Teachers Association.)*

sider before voting. At the delegate assembly, the 7,165 delegates have an opportunity to debate and vote on the proposed resolutions. The representative assembly meets annually, and in 1984, they passed 214 resolutions, which then became part of the policy of the association. Resolution A-2 on public education is presented here:

Public Education

The National Education Association believes that the priceless heritage of free public educational opportunities for every American must be preserved and strengthened. Members of the Association are encouraged to show their support of public education by sending their children to public schools.

Free public schools are the cornerstone of our social, economic, and political structure and are of utmost significance in the development of our moral, ethical, spiritual, and cultural values. Consequently, the survival of democracy requires that every state maintain a system of free public education that prepares its citizens to—

a. Use the English language properly in written and oral communications
b. Compute effectively enough to ensure their ability to procure and/or dispense services and materials necessary to their health and general well-being
c. Exercise attitudes of good citizenship, societal productivity, and global awareness
d. Appreciate the aesthetic and moral qualities of life
e. Formulate values for their lives that will lead to continual growth and self-fulfillment
f. Recognize and appreciate the cultural diversity of this nation
g. Recognize the cultural, social, political, and religious differences found throughout the world
h. Use leisure time effectively and develop sound physical health habits.

The Association urges its state and local affiliates to intensify efforts to maintain and strengthen comprehensive programs of education that aspire to these goals. (*NEA Handbook,* 1984–1985, pp. 191–192)

The NEA also sets policy by passing new business items during the representative assembly. Two of these new business items passed during the 1984 assembly were as follows:

Testing of Teachers and Teaching Candidates

The NEA opposes all testing of practicing teachers and must continue to monitor the development, implementation, and impact of testing on teaching candidates in order to ensure equity for all prospective teachers. The results of this monitoring shall be a report to the 1985 Representative Assembly. (*NEA Handbook,* 1984–1985, p. 263)

Rehabilitation Centers for Juvenile Substance Abusers

The National Education Association supports the establishment of substance abuse rehabilitation centers specifically designed to help juvenile substance abusers and their families. The Association urges its state affiliates to support actively legislation which will lead to the creation of such juvenile substance abuse rehabilitation centers, and/or which mandates the referral to such centers/programs of all juveniles found guilty by the courts of use or possession of a controlled substance. (*NEA Handbook,* 1984–1985, p. 268)

The policies of the NEA are administered by the 117-member Board of Directors and the 9-member Executive Committee. The president is a member of the Executive Committee, and he or she directs the administration of policy. Priorities among the multitude of resolutions and new business items are sorted out by the Board of Directors and the Executive Committee. The president also consults with the executive director, whose main function is to implement the policies of the NEA. The accompanying schematic outline depicts the NEA working structure and lists the important committees of the association.

The Executive Secretary of the NEA presides over a staff of 600 people. It is the responsibility of the Executive Secretary to take the policy developed by the representative assembly and turn it into action. The highest elected officer in the NEA is the president, who presides over the representative assembly and the executive board. These two positions have separate functions, and it is important that the incumbents understand each other's role.

NEA Structure

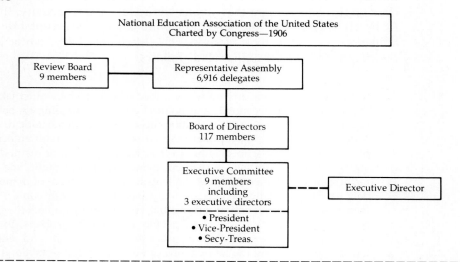

Standing Committees of the Representative Assembly	Standing Committees related to Program	Special committees
• Constitution, Bylaws, and Rules • Program and Budget • Resolutions • Credentials • Elections	• Affiliate Relationships • Benefits • Civil Rights • Higher Education • Human Relations • Instruction and Professional Development • Legislative and Financial Support for Public Education • National Public Relations • Peace and International Relations • Student Members	• Minority Affairs (1975–1985) • Educational Support Personnel (1982–1985) • Vocational, Technical, and Practical Arts Educators (1978–1986) • Women's Concerns (1980–1986)

Note: The chart does not include ad hoc internal committee of the Board of Directors and Executive Committee.

Source: *NEA Handbook.* (1984–1985). Washington, DC: National Education Association, p. 10.

History of the AFT

Unlike the NEA, which has preferred the term *teachers' association*, the American Federation of Teachers (AFT), from the beginning, used the term *union* to describe itself. The first teachers' union was formed in 1897 in Chicago and became known as the Chicago Teachers Federation (CTF). Even in those early days, low salaries and job security were the highest priorities to be dealt with by the young union.

In 1902, Jane Addams, the social settlement reformer in Chicago, encouraged the teachers to affiliate with the American Federation of Labor. John Dewey, the famous educational philosopher, actively urged all instructors to join in common cause with the laborer. Dewey once said that he cherished his union card second only to his teaching certificate. In fact, he held AFT card number 1 (Braun, 1972, p. 48). As most teachers came from lower-middle-class origins and thought that unions were a lower-class activity, they needed to be convinced that the affiliation with labor was acceptable. After the affiliation with labor took place in 1902, Margaret Haley, editor of the *CTF Bulletin*, explained the affiliation as follows:

> Not only has the time arrived when public school teachers must take a position on the serious economic and political questions pressing for solution. . . . but the public school as an institution must be either democratic or autocratic. A democratic form of government cannot be maintained with autocratic principles controlling the schools either in their administration or methods of teaching. The labor interests lie in popular, democratic government, and in the maintenance of democracy. It is the largest organized force of democracy. The only people you can depend upon to act permanently with you are those whose interests are identical with yours. We expect by affiliation with labor to arouse the workers and the whole people, through the workers, to the dangers confronting the public schools from the same interests and tendencies that are undermining the foundations of our democratic republic. It is necessary to make labor a constructive force in society, or it will be a destructive force. If the educational question could be understood by the labor men, and the labor question by the educators, both soon would see they are working to the same end, and should work together.

No wonder Jane Addams was interested in the CTF: the organization supported many reform movements such as women's suffrage, municipal ownership of public utilities, and direct primaries. The CTF was the force behind the successful passage of the Illinois Child Labor Law in 1903, and it supported the proposal to have an elected schoolboard in Chicago. A greater spread of democracy throughout our republic, particularly concerning education, was a dominant theme of the teachers' union. During the 1930s, prominent advocates of progressive education were active in the union, and George Counts became the president of the AFT. The progressives, according to the

John Dewey model, wanted to see the schools become the agent for a democratic society (Eaton, 1975, p. 74).

One of the reasons that the CTF became so popular with the teachers in Chicago was the failure of the NEA to relate to the classroom teacher during this period. Most of the leadership of the NEA was then composed of college presidents and school district superintendents, who relegated the classroom teacher to the role of listener. In the early 1900s, the CTF was composed entirely of grade-school or elementary teachers, mostly female, who wanted a voice in the American education movement.

The American Federation of Teachers (AFT) was started in Chicago in 1916. The AFT was formed from four local unions, including the CTF. Among the goals that the union supported were free schools, free textbooks, and compulsory education. In these early days, members of the AFT perceived themselves as simply a more radical group working within the structure of the NEA (Eaton, 1975, p. 18). It wasn't until 1921 that the AFT considered itself a competitor of the NEA rather than a part of the NEA.

During the period of 1916–1929, the AFT adopted a social platform that remained consistent through the 1960s. The major points for which the AFT fought were the following:

1. Greater pay and better working conditions for all teachers.
2. Equal pay for teachers regardless of race, creed, or sex.
3. Tenure provisions for teachers.
4. The granting of sabbatical leaves for teachers.
5. Equalizing the pay and benefits between elementary and secondary teachers.
6. The political freedom of teachers to belong to organized parties, participate in political activities, and espouse political candidates outside of their teaching duties.
7. The inclusion of teachers on boards of education.
8. Academic freedom for teachers to discuss national and international issues in the classroom setting.
9. Protection of women teachers from unfair hiring practices, dismissals due to marriage, and the failure of boards of education to provide maternal leaves.
10. Recognition of the special education plight of the black American and his teacher. Promotion of equal pay and school facilities and recognition of the need to publicize the inequities of Negro education.
11. Gaining a role for the teacher in the process of school administration especially in matters pertaining to the profession or in the instruction of children.
12. The inclusion of laboring-class peoples on boards of education.
13. Condemnation of plans that would separate vocational programs of education from regular school settings.
14. Resistance to those groups who sought to use the schools to indoctrinate children, such as the National Association of Manufacturers, U.S. Chamber of Commerce, American Legion, and others.

Profile of Albert Shanker

Albert Shanker was born in New York City in 1928, the son of Polish immigrants. Both of his parents were active in trade unionism and in the Roosevelt New Deal. As a child he marched in parades to honor Franklin D. Roosevelt. Always an excellent student, Shanker earned a bachelor's degree from the University of Illinois and a master's degree in philosophy and mathematics from Columbia University.

As a youngster, he lived in the Ravenswood area of Queens, a Jew in a primarily Irish area. It was here, as an eight-year-old boy, that Shanker experienced an incident of ethnic discrimination that nearly took his life. He was hung by a rope from a tree by a gang of boys who accused him of killing Jesus, but he was saved by a woman who ran to his aid. Later, at the University of Illinois at Urbana, he found that the only living quarters offered to Jewish students were located six miles from campus. It was no doubt incidents like these that caused Albert Shanker to become committed to the civil rights movement. His New York union contributed large sums of money to Martin Luther King's voter registration drive in Alabama.

After some teaching experience in Harlem and Queens, Shanker slowly, but surely, rose in union leadership to become president of the AFT and vice-president of the AFL-CIO. In 1984, he was elected to a sixth two-year term as president of the AFT. Donley (1976) wrote, "Albert Shanker's rise to leadership in the AFT began when the New York City teachers chose his local union as their representative in 1961. Later he directed a merger of the AFT and the NEA teachers in New York State. He then emerged as one of the most powerful teacher leaders in the nation (p. 124).

As a union leader, Shanker believes in union solidarity. He insists on helping other unions associated with the AFL-CIO in their labor disputes. Teachers' union pickets have appeared in support of department-store, hospital, and sanitation employees. In 1966, during a strike at St. John's University, Shanker was able to prevent student teachers from that university from student teaching in New York City schools.

Shanker believes that if teaching is to be a profession, teachers, through their unions, must have some determining authority about where nonsalary education funds are to go. Albert Shanker and David Sheldon, former president of the AFT, envision union power extending to the administration of education; therefore, they say that education programs must be administered by the union and that personnel policies and control of the distribution and content of teaching materials must be vested within the profession and the organization that controls the profession. If the union were to obtain power over these administrative matters in education, teaching would become a true profession according to Shanker and Sheldon (Braun, 1972, p. 159). These statements were made in the 1960s, but few, if any, major administrative matters are controlled directly by the union at the present time.

Mr. Shanker is no doubt one of the most colorful teachers' union leaders in our nation's history. He tends to be on the cutting edge of social change; therefore, he is active on the national political scene. In 1980, he supported Senator Ted Kennedy for the democratic presidential nomination over President Carter, although later, his union endorsed Carter. He strongly supports the public school system and is opposed to tax credits, school voucher proposals, and state and local tax-cut movements.

15. Opposition to secondary school ROTC and military training courses.
16. Support for the workers' education movement.
17. Federal aid to education.
18. The establishment of a cabinet-level Department of Education. (Eaton, 1975, pp. 168–69)

By 1947 the AFT had grown to 86 chartered locals, which included groups in twenty-four of the twenty-five U.S. cities of more than 100,000 population (Donley, 1976, p. 4). In 1961, after a rough campaign, the United Federation of Teachers (UFT), an AFT affiliate, won from their rival, the Teachers' Bargaining Organization (TBO), an NEA affiliate, the right to represent all New York City teachers at the bargaining table. "The union (UFT) victory in New York City was probably the biggest single success in the history of teacher organizing in the United States" (Donley, 1976, p. 49). The AFT victory in New York increased AFT membership and motivated teachers in the larger cities to new and greater efforts. At the time of the New York victory, AFT membership was 60,715 teachers, whereas the NEA membership was 1,300,000 teachers. The NEA then started concentrating on better service to teachers in the larger urban areas, which had been long neglected by them.

The AFT had an illustrious beginning, John Dewey being one of its chief advocates. Its greatest successes have been in the largest cities of our country, where there is an established union tradition. Its commitment to civil rights and the laborer is well established. Where the AFT establishes itself in the next ten years will depend largely on Albert Shanker, its president, and one of the most influential leaders in the entire labor movement.

Merger Talks

David Sheldon won the presidency of the AFT in 1968 with a pledge to open merger negotiations with the NEA. By that time, the AFT had won bargaining rights in nearly every major city, including New York, Boston, Philadelphia, Detroit, Chicago, Cleveland, and Gary. The AFT had only 200,000 members, but it represented nearly a half million teachers at the bargaining table. Sheldon was able to convince antimerger forces within his own organization that the strength of the AFT in the larger cities was enough to keep it from being swallowed up by the larger NEA forces. A merger of the Flint, Michigan, union with a much larger NEA affiliate in 1968 was cause for hope that at long last there might be a merger of the two national organizations. Both David Sheldon and Albert Shanker had dreamed of and planned for the day when there could be a national merger of the two unions. The goal, after merger, would be nationwide teacher strikes to elicit massive federal aid to education.

There were too many roadblocks to merger in the late 1960s, some that Sheldon did not foresee. Many rank-and-file members of the AFT were former NEA members, and they knew full well that some NEA representatives had made deals with school boards to help eliminate the union. There were black teachers in the South who knew that the NEA had backed off on de-

Merger Issues

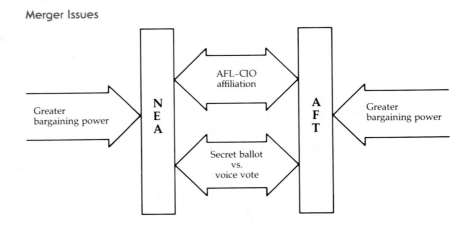

segregation measures. Probably, most of all, as far as the AFT was concerned, there was too much dissension within their own staff. Sheldon's leadership ability was being questioned, and as a result, he gave up the merger issue.

In 1969, NEA President Elizabeth D. Koontz made informal inquiries directed to David Sheldon about merger talks, but by 1970, the NEA had officially banned merger talks. Still, there were unofficial merger talks at the NEA conventions. One of the big problems preventing merger, as far as the NEA was concerned, was the AFT affiliation with the AFL-CIO (Eaton, 1975, p. 197). Sheldon had been willing to consider merger talks without the AFL-CIO affiliation, but Shanker insisted on AFL-CIO membership. Albert Shanker was himself a block to merger talks because of his strong AFL-CIO stand.

Whatever the historical happenings have been between the NEA and the AFT regarding a possible merger, the current positions of both organizations are as follows:

A Single National Organization of Educators

The 1976 Representative Assembly reaffirms the Association's policy concerning a single national organization of educators as follows:

The Representative Assembly reaffirms the NEA's desire to unite all educators in a single national organization. The Representative Assembly further recognizes that a merger with the AFT, the AAUP, and other appropriate organizations could contribute to that end. The NEA believes, however, that if a merger is to produce true "unity," the resulting organization must embody the following basic concepts: (a) no affiliation with the AFL-CIO and no obligation to the institutional positions and objectives of the AFL-CIO; (b) guaranteed minority group participation in the governance and operation of the new organization; (c) the use of the secret ballot to elect the officers and change the governing documents of the new organization.

The Representative Assembly authorizes the NEA president to enter into discussions regarding the possible establishment of a single national organization embodying the foregoing concepts if and when the president, in conjunction with the Executive Committee, believes that such discussions will be productive. (*NEA Handbook*, 1984–1985, pp. 278–279)

The AFT Official Policy on Merger

The official AFT policy on merger, established in 1972, includes the following provisions:

Before any AFT local or state federation may engage in unity talks with another organization, it shall receive approval of two-thirds vote of the AFT executive council. Before any agreement between an AFT local or state federation and another organization shall become final it must be approved by two-thirds vote of the AFT executive council and by a majority vote in a membership referendum of the AFT local or state federation involved. (Dashiell, 1982, pp. 5–6)

Although the AFL-CIO issue is a big problem blocking merger, the secret ballot is another difficult issue to settle. The NEA simply believes that its delegate assembly would be undemocratic without the secret ballot. In 1982, the AFT reaffirmed a commitment to voice vote, although some members of the AFT are trying to change this rule. If the two organizations ever do merge, the voice of teachers will be more powerful than ever before.

The Collective-Bargaining Process

The authors once heard a story of a township trustee whose wife enjoyed insulting teachers on payday by having them line up behind the family sedan. The wife of the trustee would then use the trunk lid as a desk and proceed to distribute the salaries. The humiliated teachers wanted to keep their jobs, so they lined up and did not overtly complain. Now, most teachers negotiate for their salaries through the collective-bargaining process, and they receive their money in a dignified manner.

At the present time, there is no federal law governing the collective-bargaining process. In the absence of such a law, fifteen states have written laws that deal with the question in a comprehensive way. Another fifteen states have laws requiring school boards to "meet and confer" with teacher representatives, but the rights of teachers in these states are limited. The remaining twenty states have no bargaining laws at all, but in most cases, teachers are allowed to discuss working conditions with school boards (Dashiell, 1982, p. 6).

Elections

In states where there are laws governing negotiations, an election is generally held to enable one organization to gain sole bargaining rights for all the teachers in a school system. Teachers are represented at the bargaining table by either the NEA or AFT local affiliates or by other teachers' representation groups, so that the negotiation process can be simplified. When a teachers' organization wins an election over rival groups, it gains exclusive bargaining rights with the school board in that district. These elections are supervised by the Public Employee Relations Board (PERB) set up in many states to administer the public-employee collective-bargaining law.

Once a union has gained exclusive bargaining rights, it must represent fairly all persons in that bargaining unit. The bargaining unit generally contains members of rival unions and nonmembers, as well as members of the majority teacher organization in that district. Two cases, one in Michigan and one in Rhode Island, are presented here to indicate what a delicate issue fairness is to the bargaining unit.

> The first case again involves the Detroit Federation of Teachers, which agreed to a two-year contract that raised regular teachers' salaries in both years but raised the pay of emergency substitute teachers in the second year only. An emergency substitute filed suit alleging that this disparate treatment constituted a breach of the union's duty of fair representation. A Michigan court upheld the contract. It noted that a union must have *broad discretion in considering proposals and in recommending a combination of contract provisions that in its judgment represents the best total agreement.* Accordingly, to avoid utter chaos in labor relations and to keep the interventions of the courts to a minimum, a breach of the duty of fair representation is proved only when there is "showing of bad faith, arbitrary or discriminatory action, or fraud." (*McGrail* v. *Detroit Federation of Teachers* (1973)

The Rhode Island Supreme Court reached a somewhat different result in a very interesting and widely discussed case involving a union's duty of fair representation while handling teachers' grievances.

> In the summer of 1972 the Warwick, Rhode Island, school board posted a vacancy notice for the position of chairman of the high school business department. The vacancy was a *"promotional position"* that, according to the union/board contract, was to be filled on the basis of qualifications; but if the qualifications of two or more candidates were considered equal, the job would go to the person with the most seniority in the Warwick school system. After reviewing the qualifications of the four applicants for the position, the school board appointed Richard Belanger. An unsuccessful applicant, Arthur Matteson, who had more Warwick seniority than Belanger, filed a grievance with the union. The union pressed Matteson's grievance all the way to binding arbitration, where a panel of three arbitrators held that Matteson should have

been selected for the position. After a year as department chairman, Belanger was demoted to classroom teacher and Matteson assumed the chairmanship.

Belanger then wrote the union, requesting that a grievance be pursued on his behalf. The union refused on the ground that to do so would be inconsistent with its earlier advocacy of Matteson's grievance and with the union/board agreement that binding arbitration would be the final step in grievance proceedings. Belanger filed suit alleging in part that the union breached its duty of fair representation when it agreed to press Matteson's grievance. A lower court agreed with Belanger and ordered him reinstated as department chairman. Matteson and the union appealed.

The Rhode Island Supreme Court found that the union failed to represent fairly all members of the bargaining unit when it agreed to pursue Matteson's grievance without ever contacting Belanger or considering his qualifications for the position. The court termed as "simplistic" the union's defense that Matteson was the only member of the bargaining grieving the selection of Belanger. The court stated: "It should have been apparent to the union that Matteson's grievance, although theoretically against the School Committee, was in reality against Belanger." Because Belanger was also a member of the union's bargaining unit, the union had an obligation to ascertain Belanger's qualifications before determining that the seniority clause should control the selection. The court stated that it would have been sufficient to investigate "in an informal manner. . . . so long as its procedure affords the two employees the ability to place all the relevant information before the union." Even though the court could find no evidence of bad faith on the part of the union, it held that the arbitrary refusal to consider Belanger's qualifications before championing Matteson's cause was "a clear breach of the duty of fair representation."

Despite this holding, the Rhode Island Supreme Court refused to reinstate Belanger to the chairmanship. Even though Belanger's right to fair representation was breached by the union's advocacy of Matteson's grievance, the qualifications of both men were fully and fairly considered by the arbitration panel. The school board "forcefully" argued Belanger's suitability for the job, yet the arbitrators ruled for Matteson. This led the court to conclude that even if the union had considered Belanger's qualifications, it still would have elected to press Matteson's grievance and the identical result would have ensued. Accordingly, Belanger could not demonstrate that he was actually harmed by the union's breach of the duty of fair representation.

Taken together, the Michigan and Rhode Island cases confirm that a *duty of fair representation attaches to both bargaining and grievance proceedings.* The duty compels neither neutrality by the union in disputes between its members nor equality of results. What is required, however, is a broad consideration of the interests of all members of the bargaining unit. Although states will differ in their application of the duty of fair representation, the principles articulated by the Michigan and Rhode Island courts are likely to be important considerations in any such case.

In order that the exclusive bargaining agent not abuse its privileges, most states have built-in safeguards to protect the other groups. Whenever sufficient dissatisfaction builds up against the exclusive bargaining representative, an election can be called to reestablish which agent will be the exclusive bargaining representative. Also, in most states, before the contract is made law, members of the entire group, including rival unions and nonunion members, are given an opportunity to ratify the contract. Flygare (1977) summarized this important point:

> Even though the exclusive bargaining representative may have the privilege of sitting at the bargaining table without interference from rival teachers' organizations, it still must perform in accordance with the wishes of its whole constituency. If not, it may suffer the embarrassment of having the agreements it hammered out with the school board rejected by the teachers or, worse yet, it may lose its status as exclusive bargaining representative at the next election. (p. 20)

The Scope

The scope of bargaining that teachers enter into with school boards varies greatly from state to state and from school district to school district. Some of the topics that are commonly included are salaries, insurance, sabbaticals, student discipline, the curriculum, tenure, emergency leave, and a host of other topics and issues. Some items that cannot be bargained for are those that violate constitutional principles; those that are already clearly determined by state law, such as tenure provisions; those that are subject to accrued contractual rights, such as sick leave; and in some states, those topics that are considered the exclusive prerogative of management. The scope of what teachers bargain for is very important because, without much breadth allowed, the law is shallow, and bargaining may become a waste of time for all concerned (Flygare, 1977, p. 25).

The Scope of Bargaining

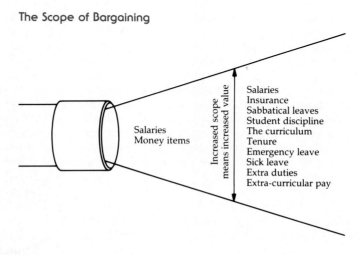

Salaries
Money items

Increased scope
means increased value

Salaries
Insurance
Sabbatical leaves
Student discipline
The curriculum
Tenure
Emergency leave
Sick leave
Extra duties
Extra-curricular pay

The Process Itself

The bargaining process is generally started by the selection of a bargaining team from the faculty and the recruitment of someone to represent the board of education. The spokespeople for the teachers are frequently bargaining specialists from the teachers' organization or officers of the teachers' organization, whereas the school board is more often represented by a professional negotiator, who is often an attorney. Bargaining works best when one person speaks for each side. The teachers begin by presenting their contract proposals to the board. The board members consider the teachers' proposals and then come forward with counterproposals. The first round of proposals on both sides represent lavish demands from the teachers and sparse offers from the board. Negotiations continue from counterproposal to counterproposal until either a contract is agreed on or an impasse has been reached.

Most states with collective-bargaining laws have set down orderly ways of resolving impasses between the two parties. Mediation is the first step taken, and it involves having the state Public Employees Relations Board

Collective bargaining between school districts and teachers' organizations is often complex and lengthy. (Photo used by permission of the Indiana State Teachers Association.)

(PERB) select a labor mediator. The mediator remains impartial and tries to narrow down the issues, to improve communication, and to make specific recommendations to the parties that are not binding on either party. A mediator's recommendations are usually not made public. Mediators are often able to prevent a work stoppage by improving communication between the groups. Because mediators have little power, relying primarily on personal dynamics, some say that mediation is a waste of time, but it appears to be a necessary part of an orderly process.

Fact finding is the next step in the process of impasse resolution after mediation. Many of the same techniques are used by the fact finder as were used by the mediator, but his or her recommendations are made public. Making certain facts a part of the public record puts a great deal of pressure on both the teachers and the school board to come forward with reasonable proposals. One disadvantage of fact finding is that there is a widespread belief among teachers' unions that if they hold out until fact finding, they will gain more in the ultimate settlement. Whatever disadvantages there may be, fact finding is another method of getting both parties to come to a voluntary solution of their differences.

Finally, arbitration is used to settle disputes that go beyond fact finding. It is commonly known as *binding arbitration* because both parties agree to let the arbitrator decide what is fair for both sides. Many arbitrators try to divide the settlement down the middle so as not to be unfair, but neither side generally likes the results. The results of arbitration settlements have caused boards to be very careful about their final offer, as that one is used to make the "split-the-difference" award.

Because of the problems with arbitration settlements, a new system called *final-offer arbitration* has been devised. In this case, both parties are asked to make their final offer, and the arbitrator chooses one or the other of the proposals. This system causes both sides to carefully consider their final offer and provides some incentive for voluntary settlement. Table 15–2 summarizes the bargaining process.

Strikes

Both the NEA and the AFT were opposed to strikes at one time, but both organizations now approve of strikes. The AFT affiliates were the first to call for strikes. The 1963 strike threat in New York City by the UFT caused the following reactions from William B. Carr, the Executive Secretary of the NEA, who said:

> The tactics used in New York City before the opening of schools do not represent values that can be taught to American public school children—disturbing extremes were reached when some of their leaders openly called on all

TABLE 15–2   Major Steps in the Process of Collective Bargaining

Depending on the state, the following are the usual steps:

 First: Selection of the bargaining teams for both sides (school board and teachers).
 Second: Presentation of the teachers' contract proposal to the board of education.
 Third: Presentation of the board's counterproposal.

(At this point there may be several proposals and counterproposals before both sides decide that they are at an impasse.)

 Fourth: Either an *agreement* or an *impasse* is reached. If an *impasse* is reached, the following occurs:
 Fifth: *Mediation* leading to an *agreement* or an *impasse*. If an *impasse* is reached, the following occurs:
 Sixth: *Fact finding*. In most states this is the final step, and the two groups must continue bargaining until they reach an *agreement*.

However, in a few states, the following occur:

 Seventh: *Arbitration*. This means that the dispute between the board of education and the teachers will be determined by a mutually agreed-to-arbitrator. Often an agreed-to settlement by an arbitrator is binding on both parties.
 Eighth: In most states, *strikes* are not permitted, but in a few cases, the teachers can strike if they have followed all of the collective-bargaining steps and no agreement has been reached. Several states list penalties for striking.

teachers to defy both the statutes and court injunction. (Donley, 1976, pp. 52–53)

Charles Cogen, President of the UFT, responded by saying:

Teachers are setting a good example. Civic courage and idealism should be practiced by those who teach it. I am confident that our strikes have enhanced the respect which students have for their teachers. (Donley, 1976, p. 52)

Carr was referring to the Condon-Wadlin Law in New York, which provided penalties for striking civil employees. Public-school teachers have felt for years that it is unfair that they are prevented from striking whereas teachers in private schools can legally engage in strike activity. Teachers are often linked with police and firefighters as civil employees, but they believe that they should not be associated in this manner because their occupation does not involve the health and safety of the public as is the case with the other two groups.

When Carr spoke for the NEA in the 1960s, the NEA was a different kind of organization, dominated by administrators. By 1980, over ten years after Carr's departure from the association, attitudes toward strikes and teacher militancy had changed so that they were very much in line with the thinking of the AFT. The NEA strike policy as of 1984 is as follows:

E-11. Strikes

The National Education Association denounces the practice of keeping schools open during a strike. It believes that when a picket line is established by the authorized bargaining unit, crossing it is strikebreaking. This unprofessional act jeopardizes the welfare of school employees and the educational process.

The Association also believes that the chances of reaching voluntary agreement in good faith are reduced when one party to the negotiation process possesses the power to use the courts unilaterally against the other party.

The Association recommends several procedures to be used in resolution of impasse—such as mediation, factfinding, binding arbitration, political action, and strike—if conditions make it impossible to provide quality education. In event of a strike by school employees, extracurricular and cocurricular activities must cease. Appropriate teacher training institutions should be notified that a strike is being conducted and urged not to cooperate in emergency certification or placement practices that constitute strikebreaking.

The Association condemns the use of ex parte injunction, jailing, setting excessive bail, fines, firing of members, decertification of an organization as the bargaining agent, loss of association rights, and revocation or suspension of tenure, certification, and retirement benefits in school work stoppages. The Association also condemns denial of credits to students who have honored a work stoppage. The Association urges state and federal governments to enact, where they do not exist, statutes guaranteeing school employees due process of law when a work stoppage occurs, including the right to present their case to the state or courts, before back-to-work orders are issued.

The Association urges all local and state affiliates to provide financial assistance to NEA affiliates engaged in a sanctioned strike. (*NEA Handbook,* 1984–1985, pp. 226–227)

Not only has the NEA approved of strikes, but it has become very specific about how its striking rights are to be guarded. Both the AFT and the NEA now believe that the strike is the ultimate way to resolve an impasse during the collective-bargaining process.

There are a few states that permit strikes by teachers. Until better collective-bargaining laws are passed by the states that do legally allow teachers to withhold their services, teachers will remain frustrated by the system. The system of collective bargaining is an orderly process for resolving contract disputes between the teachers' organizations and the school boards. Before the collective-bargaining laws, teachers had to work with their administrators and school boards to produce a contract, and often, the decision was an arbitrary one made by the board. The teachers had no legal right to argue for their point of view. Some say that now that teachers, as far as collective bargaining is concerned, are on an equal basis with administrators, an adversarial rather than a congenial relationship has resulted. Adversarial relationships between administrators and teachers, many say, are the reason that we have an erosion of public support of education. Others point out that

Strikes when they occur affect teachers, parents, children, and communities. (Photo used by permission of the Indiana State Teachers Association.)

if the public is upset by adversarial conflicts between teachers and administrators, it is because the public does not understand the collective-bargaining process and that it is up to the teachers, the administrators, the school boards, and the media to tell the true story. One fact is that adversarial relationships of the collective-bargaining type are not allowed in totalitarian countries. Flygare (1977) expressed the hope of many when he wrote:

> After all has been said about statutes, court rulings, and the like, the hope remains that teachers and school boards can settle their differences of opinion with civility and with eyes focused on the quality of education. (p. 49)

Agency Shop

One of the most controversial items concerning teachers and union membership is the so-called agency shop provision. Unions or teachers' organizations believe that the exclusive representative organization ought to be paid dues by all members of a teaching staff whether they belong to that union or not. Unions assert that bargaining costs a lot of money and takes a lot of time, and that all members of a teaching staff receive equal benefits whether they are members of the bargaining unit, are members of a rival union, or are not members of any union. Union members sometimes refer to these nonpaying members of a teaching staff as free riders or free loaders. The nonpayers consider themselves independent thinkers who want to preserve their freedom of choice.

There are obviously strong arguments to support both sides of this controversial issue: the union needs financial support for the work that it has been elected to do, and nonmembers want freedom of choice. Some say that a possible compromise would be to have all members of a teaching staff pay a reasonable fee, but not one that is equal to the full union membership dues that regular members must pay. This solution would eliminate the objection that some nonmembers have to being required to support the broader causes of the AFT and the NEA when their views differ. The difficulty here is figuring out what a fair assessment would be in relation to the real cost of collective bargaining. In order to protect those who are already members of the school corporation from being forced to belong, it could be decided that the "agency fee" would be assessed only from all new teachers entering the school system, who will have the opportunity to accept or reject the "agency fee" provision at the time of hiring.

Members of competing minority unions object to having to pay full membership fees in two unions, only one of which represents their views. Some say that for competing minority unions, a proportionate cost of the bargaining process that is conducted by the majority union should be all that the minority union members are asked to pay. Minority unions need to support themselves financially and in other ways so that they can continue to put adequate pressure on the majority union to do the job it has been elected to do.

The agency shop provision is not a resolved issue. A group called Concerned Educators Against Forced Unionism, a division of the National Right to Work Committee, has been formed simply to fight the agency shop. Whether a compromise can be worked out to settle this dispute will be interesting to observe.

The Political Action Committee (PAC)

Teachers' organizations have been supporting political candidates for years, but these efforts have increased since the 1970s. During the 1974 congressional campaign, the NEA and the AFT spent about $3.5 million to elect "friends of education." The Carter–Mondale ticket was heavily supported by the teachers in 1976 and in 1980. Their political clout has been growing because their organizations have grown in numbers and their political action committees have become more effective. Besides helping to elect Jimmy Carter in 1976, NEA-backed candidates in congressional races won in large numbers. Albert Shanker's AFT was also very effective in the larger cities.

The NEA's political action committee, known as NEA-PAC, was begun in 1972. Today, it is one of about 2,500 PACs in the country, which spent a grand total of $130 million on the 1980 elections. The NEA's determination to influence national elections through political action was demonstrated in a forceful speech by the president of the NEA in 1973. In her concluding speech to the 1973 representative assembly, President Helen Wise said:

> The NEA has indeed awakened and we are on our way. Our first major objective, politically and legislatively, will be to reverse the national leadership in Washington and put a friend of education in the White House and more friends of education in Congress.
>
> We will initiate a grass roots campaign that will bring about the victories that we must have in 1976, and if that means building a war chest to get friends of education elected—then we need to keep the old lid open and continue to plunk in the money.
>
> One thing is certain—the NEA will never again sit out a national election.
>
> In fact, we will build NEA's political force over the next two years to the point where the Presidential candidates will seek NEA endorsement. (West, 1980, p. 194)

Wise was blowing the bugle for events to come. The assistance that NEA members gave the Carter–Mondale ticket, both in 1976 and in 1980, was considerable. Concerning the 1976 election, Carter's campaign manager, Hamilton Jordan, said, "The mass support from teachers was critical to our winning this very close election. All over the nation, we turned to NEA for assistance. We asked for help and they delivered" (Elam, 1981, p. 170). President Carter then kept his promise for greater financial support for education and for the establishment of a U.S. Department of Education, which became a reality during his term.

How successful the NEA-PAC effort has been can be measured by the number of candidates it has endorsed who have won elections. West (1980) stated:

> In 1972 the NEA-PAC endorsed 32 candidates. Twenty-six were elected—80% of those endorsed.
>
> In 1974, 229 candidates for the House were elected of 282 endorsed, and 21 Senatorial candidates were elected from 28 endorsed—another 80% record. . . .
>
> The 1978 elections produced a 77% success ratio, with 197 out of 247 endorsed candidates winning election to the House and 13 out of 24 winning their Senate races. . . .
>
> One of the gratifying developments of the more aggressive political action policy, according to NEA leaders, is that more and more candidates are consulting with them prior to the election on the association's legislative goals and priorities. (p. 200)

In the 1980 elections, the NEA-backed candidates won in 209 of the 278 House races, a drop to a 75 percent level from a 77 percent success ratio in 1978 (Elam, 1981, p. 171). Part of the cause for the 1980 drop was that PAC groups from the far right wing, such as the National Concerned Citizen's PAC, put a big effort into defeating liberal candidates in 1978. For example, the National Concerned Citizen's PAC spent more on anti–Birch Bayh and anti–George McGovern campaigns than the NEA-PAC was able to raise for 309 of its endorsed candidates combined (Elam, 1981, pp. 171–172). Birch Bayh and George McGovern were two of the best friends that education had in the U.S. Senate.

Elam (1981) compared the PAC effort made by the American Medical Association (AMA) to that of the NEA-PAC in the 1980 elections. The average U.S. physician earned $68,000 annually from private practice, compared to the average teacher's income of $17,264 in 1980. The AMA has 230,000 members (out of a potential 394,000), and the NEA has 1,680,566 members (out of a potential 3,000,000). The AMA member contributed $250 for national dues, and the NEA member paid $48 nationally for dues. Of the AMA members, 35 percent contributed $12.75 annually to their PAC, whereas about 20 percent of the NEA members made PAC contributions, averaging less than $1 per contributor. In the 1980 national elections, the AMA-PAC contributed $1,405,000, compared to only $337,000 spent by the NEA-PAC. Of the AMA-endorsed candidates, 81 percent won in 1980, compared to less than 75 percent of the NEA-endorsed candidates (p. 172). It would appear that if teachers want to improve their potential for helping to elect national candidates, their effort in both amount and number of givers to the NEA-PAC must improve. The NEA has an average of 6,000 members in every congressional district; their potential for political contacts is enormous. Chapman (1980) said, "Most teachers are bright, articulate, and reasonably well-informed, making them naturals for political activism" (p. 10).

Some feel that if teachers can ever unify in the belief that friends of education elected to local, state, and national offices do make a difference, teaching and the field of education will have taken a giant step. Teachers will need to shed completely the age-old belief that politics is a dirty business in which teachers ought not involve themselves. Many teacher leaders say that teachers need to take the time and provide the dollars to elect public officials who will speak up for the true merits of maintaining the kind of public schools that have made our country great.

Special Professional Organizations

This chapter on educational organizations would not be complete without a mention of a few special professional organizations associated with selected fields of preparation. Becoming acquainted with professional journals printed by these organizations in your major and/or minor fields will cause you to ask probing questions that will lead to answers earlier rather than later in your career. Students often find exciting new ideas in these journals to use in early field experiences or later during student teaching.

Some organizations, like Phi Delta Kappa, deal with education in general and not with any specific discipline or branch of study. People who belong to Phi Delta Kappa are known as Kappans, and they are very proud of their professional journal known as *The Kappan. The Kappan* is published ten times a year, and it is sent all over the world to nearly 125,000 members. One feature of *The Kappan* is that the September issue generally contains the "Annual Gallup Poll of the Public's Attitudes Toward the Public Schools." The main purpose of Phi Delta Kappa is to promote quality education, particularly public education, as being essential to the democratic way of life. If one needs some in-depth information on a topic, the organization publishes minibooks, called *fastbacks*, which now list nearly two hundred titles.

Another example of an educational organization that has a wide appeal is the Association for Supervision and Curriculum Development (ASCD). Classroom teachers, curriculum coordinators, supervisors, professors of education, and many other professionals involved in education are included in its membership. The primary purpose of the ASCD is the improvement of education at both the elementary and the secondary levels. *Educational Leadership*, the ASCD's professional journal, usually covers many timely educational topics. The ASCD yearbook focuses on one current topic of interest to educators, such as humaneness or lifelong learning. This is an organization to be involved in if you are interested either in keeping up with or making curricular changes yourself.

For a complete listing of all educational organizations, consult a current copy of Volume 1 of *The Encyclopedia of Associations* (Akey, 1983). A few examples taken from *The Encyclopedia of Associations* are presented in the Appendix.

Summary

The main intention of this chapter has been to acquaint the beginning teacher with the two partisan teacher organizations in the United States. No matter whether the teacher belongs to one of these organizations or not, they will become a factor in most teachers' careers in the public schools. The purposes of these organizations were examined, along with why one might want to become a member. The degree of their effectiveness depends a lot on how they function locally at the bargaining table, how they lobby in the state legislatures, and what effect they have on the U.S. President and the Congress.

The collective-bargaining process was presented to give the reader a view of the way in which it is set up, the scope that it covers, and the process that it entails. Some general comments were made, but in the absence of a federal collective-bargaining law, each state is somewhat different. Strikes, which are illegal in most states, are backed as a last resort by both the NEA and the AFT. The agency shop is still another controversial issue for teachers to resolve, and at this time, it appears to be mostly a local issue. Political action comittees, or PACs, have been increasingly active, particularly on the national scene. The AFT and the NEA certainly put a lot of money and effort behind the last four presidential elections, and there is no sign that this effort will diminish with time.

Questions

1. In what ways are the NEA and the AFT getting closer together?
2. What are some comparisons between union leaders like Albert Shanker and Terry Herndon?
3. Is a merger between the NEA and the AFT a real possibility? Discuss the pros and cons of such an outcome.
4. The collective-bargaining process causes an advocacy position to be developed by both the teachers and the school administration. Discuss the pros and cons of this situation.
5. Why do teachers' organizations take such a strong stand against tuition tax credits?
6. Besides being tied together financially, what are some other benefits of the local, state, and national teachers' organizations?
7. How would you feel about being a member of a militant teachers' organization?
8. Suppose you are or have been a strong Republican, yet the NEA and the AFT endorse mainly Democratic liberals. What will you do? How do you rationalize your views?
9. What will your fellow workers think if you don't join and take part in a teachers' organization? Will you accept the benefits along with those who pay the dues and work within the organization?
10. Make a list of the differences and the similarities between the NEA and the AFT. Why are the two organizations so different and yet so similar?
11. What is the present status of the U.S. Department of Education? Why did the NEA want the department so much?
12. What is the controversy surrounding the "agency shop" provision in many teachers' contracts?
13. What is a uniserve director, and what are his or her duties?
14. Why is political action on the part of the teacher an accepted part of her or his function as a teacher?
15. Why do teachers sometimes strike, and what risks do they take? What is your state law on teachers' strikes?

Activities for Unit VIII

1. Do a simulation game in collective bargaining. A game is available called *A Collective Bargaining Simulation in Public Education,* by Marcus H. Sandver and Harry R. Blame. The simulation game can be purchased from Grid Inc., 4666 Indianola Avenue, Columbus, Ohio 43214.

2. Analyze the problems that caused a teachers' strike in your state. What alternatives were open to the teachers, and what solutions were finally arrived at?

3. Invite members of the AFT, the NEA, and other teachers' groups to debate the pros and cons of their points of view before your class.

4. Attend a conference or a workshop sponsored by a teachers' organization in your local area. Report to the class concerning the general value of such a workshop or conference.

5. Invite a school administrator and/or a mediator to talk to you in regard to how he or she feels about working with teachers' organizations during contract negotiations.

6. Go on a field trip to a labor union office with some prewritten questions about unions; then, draw some comparisons on your own between the union philosophy and the NEA philosophy.

7. Play a videotape, if one is available, of the collective-bargaining process. After seeing the tape, write down questions you have about collective bargaining, and then discuss the questions in class.

8. Invite a uniserve director to your class to discuss her or his function in the NEA structure.

9. Write for or collect the legislative proposals of the state NEA, the state AFT, and the state school boards' association. How are they similar, and how are they different from each other?

10. Invite a state legislator to talk about pending education bills. What are some differences between the role of a legislator and the role of a union lobbyist?

11. Who are the real leaders in your state in the promotion of education? Make a list of these people and debate in class the merits of their stands on educational issues.

12. Simulate in your own class various leadership roles in teachers' organizations. By rotating roles throughout a quarter or a semester, one can really experience what being a member of a union is like. Examples of roles are building representative, chief lobbyist, and president of the union.

13. Get yourself invited to a local teachers' organization meeting. Summarize the deliberations at the meeting and be prepared to discuss the meeting with the class.

14. Ask your state legislative representative if you can act as a page for him or her during the legislative assembly.

15. Find out if there are any local alternatives to either the state NEA or AFT affiliates for teachers to join. If there are some alternative organizations, report on these to the class.

ORIENTATION TO TEACHING

16

Planning for Teaching

OBJECTIVES

After reading Chapter 16, the student will be able to:
* Determine what it means to study the discipline of teaching.
* Answer why he or she wants to become a teacher.
* List many traits of the ideal teacher.
* Realize some of the important concerns that teachers must be aware of in order to teach.
* Be aware of special opportunities and challenges of the first year of teaching.
* Have an approximate idea of the salaries and fringe benefits paid to teachers.
* Project, for the near future, the supply-and-demand probabilities for certain positions within the teaching profession.

Introduction

It is the purpose of this chapter to address several topics of particular interest to students in teacher-training programs. Most of these topics have not been covered elsewhere in this book, and they are very important for anyone to consider who wishes to become a teacher.

After reading this chapter, you will hopefully be better able to state why you want to become a teacher. The characteristics of the ideal teacher are discussed here, not to make you as a prospective teacher feel inadequate, but as a standard for comparison. Knowing where the potential problems lie ahead of time, may allow you as a teacher to recognize what is happening to you and to take corrective action. Teaching is a discipline and beginners should know why it is so and should treat what they are learning about teaching with great respect. No one can anticipate all of the new experiences that you will have in your first year of teaching, but some concerns or ideas are given to assist you as you make the transition from student to teacher. The financial rewards and fringe benefits that a teacher is likely to receive are presented honestly, and finally, predictions are made concerning the supply and demand of teachers.

Why Become a Teacher?

Many motives are involved in choosing a career in teaching. The one we have all heard many times is that a teacher must love "kids." Liking children is definitely a major reason that people choose teaching, especially in elementary education. Research indicates (Lasley, 1980), however, that simply liking children is not enough.

Teaching is really a combination of an art and a science. Teaching as an art is reflected in first grade teachers who, despite unorthodox methods and unusual techniques, consistently enable all of the students in their classes to read, and teaching as a science is exemplified when a teacher uses known principles of learning (Lasley, 1980). Someone who likes children but can neither identify basic instructional principles nor weave those principles together to form coherent lessons will have difficulty accomplishing learning goals. Liking children is a definite asset, but teachers must possess more specific skills to go along with their love.

Many students entering teaching comment that they like a specific subject, such as science, history, mathematics, or music. It is very common for secondary students to want to teach a subject because they have done well in that subject in both high school and college. Love of a subject is a good reason to want to teach, but it has to be joined with other desires, such as a love of kids. The authors have noted several education majors who have relied too heavily on their subject-matter interest and not enough on other aspects of motivation for teaching; thus, student teaching did not turn out to be a pleasant experience for them.

Being of service to others is a good reason to want to go into teaching as teaching is really a service occupation. Helping a student to learn is not very much different, from a service point of view, from nursing a patient back to good health, putting out fires, policing a city, or making laws to protect others. For some people, there is an almost missionary zeal in teaching a child how to read, helping her or him learn a trade, or assisting her or him in finding a career. Being of service to others has traditionally been a primary reason for most teachers to teach. Priests and nuns often dedicate their entire lives to education and to teaching. The Jesuit Order has a worldwide reputation for its high standards of education. Many young men and women enter teaching because they like to coach. Coaching is teaching with a greater emphasis on developing psychomotor skills. Most coaches like kids; therefore, there is a compatible combination for their success.

Other reasons for teaching are not verbalized as much but may be as important to many people. The list would include ego satisfaction, teaching as a status position, lifestyle, the unique vacation schedule of teachers, the powerful position that the teacher has to influence others, and a love of learning. Whatever your reasons are for teaching, you will need a magic combination of the aforementioned motivational factors in order to be highly successful as a teacher.

What Are the Characteristics of the Ideal Teacher?

In using the term *ideal,* the authors mean "as close to perfection" as one can come. Becoming an ideal teacher is a process that good students of education and practicing teachers should strive for during their careers. Theoretically, no teacher will ever become totally ideal. Becoming totally ideal would mean that the teacher has reached such a level of perfection that he or she no longer needs further effort toward improvement; thus, growth would stop. Personal and academic growth in one's chosen career are essential to staying fresh and interesting as a teacher; therefore, one must always reach for something better. The followng list of ideal teachers' characteristics is presented to give you an ultimate goal to strive for.

Being Knowledgeable

Being knowledgeable is possessing knowledge or understanding. When teachers begin to practice what they have learned in the college classroom, they are expected to be knowledgeable. Being knowledgeable also carries

A teacher must be knowledgeable, yet must always be willing to learn and to expand in knowledge and outlook. *(Photo used by permission of the Indianapolis Public Schools.)*

with it a feeling of self-confidence without arrogance. The main reason for going to college is to gain knowledge and understanding in one's chosen field. Just as you expect your professors to be knowledgeable about their subjects, your students will expect you to know the content of the subjects you teach. No teacher knows all of the answers to the questions pupils ask, but you should know of ready references where you can send them for further information. Connected with this teaching ideal is the fact that truly exceptional teachers are scholars and are constantly reading and upgrading themselves in their subjects.

Being Humorous

Being humorous is the faculty of perceiving, appreciating, or expressing what is amusing or comical. This part of teaching must be done in good taste or it will become a negative feature rather than a positive one. On the positive side, teachers must be able to laugh at themselves when things go wrong in the classroom. A young science teacher hurriedly moved a mobile laboratory into a classroom to demonstrate some experiments. The drain in the portable laboratory went into a small bucket. As the students and the teacher got involved in the experiments and more and more water was used, the bucket filled up and began emptying on the floor. None of the students said anything until the pool of water had reached the rear of the classroom. When the teacher finally discovered the problem, there was at first a big gasp, followed closely by laughter. Her eighth-grade science class enjoyed the joke they had played on the teacher, and they appreciated the ability of the teacher to laugh at herself.

Another teacher enjoyed making jokes about the cute girl in the front row. In the beginning, the jokes were funny to the rest of the class, but later in the school year, his jokes became stale. Eventually, the rest of the class began to perceive that this girl was receiving special treatment. The teacher was unaware that the rapport he had had with his class had slipped; therefore, he was unable to correct the problem.

In the first example, the teacher was able to turn a negative situation into a positive one with an appropriate humorous response. In the second example, the teacher used bad judgment in his use of humor and lost his class rapport. The appropriate use of humor is a personal matter, and it demands the use of good common sense. As you work on your sense of classroom humor, think about the teachers you most admired and how they used humor. Also, examine the humor you have used in the past and contemplate how it could be adapted for future use in the classroom. Be cautious, but be humorous.

Being Flexible

Being flexible means being susceptible to modification or adaptation. Teachers need to be flexible because some days the best lesson plan will not work. We hear teachers say, "I couldn't do anything with my classes today." Being flexible is being able to talk about problems that have arisen in the classroom and eventually to get back to the lesson. For example, suppose the television series *Roots* has been shown the previous night, and the children have questions about the series involving serious racial and ethical considerations. Even though you are ready to go on with the lesson for the day, you will need to take some time to deal with this important matter.

After the *Roots* situation has been resolved, you may notice that you have gained greater attention from your class, and the class can now focus more intensely on the lesson. In not recognizing important learning opportunities as they occur in the classroom, on the playground, on television, or wherever they may happen, the teacher misses learning moments that may not naturally arise again. Flexibility during classes and elsewhere in the career of teaching is a definite asset.

Being Upbeat

Upbeat is a term borrowed from the field of music that has come to mean a positive spirit and demeanor. An upbeat person genuinely likes kids and enjoys the task of teaching. Teaching is not just a job for these people; it is a source of great pleasure, and they show it in their facial expression and in their positive attitude around the school. Upbeat people always seem to have time to talk to a colleague or to do something extra for the school or the staff. One key to being upbeat is having a good self-concept.

Being Honest

Being honest or having the highest integrity is a very important trait for anyone, particularly a teacher. Teachers of high integrity tell their class what to expect and then deliver on those promises. We have all had teachers who promised things to us but never followed through on their promises. For example, when a teacher gives an exam, it is understood that the results of that exam should be back in a reasonable length of time so that the student will benefit from the feedback. Basically, the student ought to be able always to trust what the teacher says and does.

Being Clear and Concise

Being clear and concise relates to both oral and written expression in the classroom. One of the main goals of education is to help students become clear and concise communicators; therefore, we must be good models of this learning goal. Feedback from our classes will indicate how well we are getting our points across. The questions asked by students, the examination answers received, and certain nonverbal cues should give teachers an adequate understanding of how well they are communicating with their students. The process of communication can be aided by such audiovisual devices as overhead projectors, chalkboards, film projectors, duplicated papers, textbooks, posters, and artifacts.

Being Open

Willingness to share a part of yourself is another way of saying that you are open as a person. Teachers who share happenings about their own lives to illustrate a point or share how they feel about a given situation often help learners to relate to situations in more meaningful ways. Young people continue to undergo new emotional experiences as they grow up, and it is helpful to them to know that teachers have experienced these same emotions. As you share yourself with your class, you will feel a greater rapport developing between you and your students.

Being Patient

Being patient is often expressed as being persevering or diligent. Few people have enough of this quality, and teachers need an especially large amount. Learners will come to you in every state of being: slow and gifted, dyslexic, emotionally disturbed, and so on. Parents and the general public will expect you to produce outstanding results with the students you receive. Researchers and practitioners have uncovered hundreds of teaching–learning techniques to use with the diverse group of learners you will receive. You may be frustrated by large classes and your lack of ability to reach all students. Pa-

Clear expectations are characteristic of a good teacher. *(Photo used by permission of the Indiana State Teachers Association.)*

tience is required as you carefully decide what teaching–learning technique is best for each learner in your class, and as you learn to see bits of progress day-to-day rather than expecting dramatic results immediately.

Being a Role Model

The teacher should be an excellent role model. Young children and young adults need and seek role models to guide their lives. But many children pattern their lives on less desirable role models seen on television or in movies or on other kids in the neighborhood. Some of the models seen in the media may be good, but many roles portrayed are very negative. Children who do not have loving parents, grandparents, uncles, and aunts and positive teacher models are operating at a disadvantage as they make critical decisions about who they are going to be. Being a good role model to all the children you teach is one of the greatest contributions you can make to society.

Being Able to Relate Theory to Practice

It is often very difficult to relate the theories advocated in college classes to actual practice in the schools. Throughout this text, in the activity sections of each unit, there are suggestions for doing things individually or as a group to enhance your interest and motivation in teaching. Most states and teachers' education colleges are attempting to provide field experiences while you are in training to tie in with the theories presented in the college classroom. For example, many states stipulate that laboratory or field experiences shall be initiated as soon as possible and continued throughout the student's program of preparation.

Simulation games and role-playing exercises can be very important in teacher training. Cruickshank and Broadbent (1968) found the actual teaching problems to be less numerous for students receiving simulation training. They also found simulation experiences to be at least as effective as an equal amount of student teaching. The more you get involved with actual classroom situations and ask questions of experienced teachers, administrators, school board members, teachers' organization personnel, parents, and students, the sooner you will experience the reality of what the career of teaching is all about. Don't be like those college students who will later look back on their student life and be sorry that they didn't take advantage of every learning opportunity. Many opportunities will be provided to help you relate theory to practice.

Being Self-Confident

We have all noticed those individuals who seemingly know themselves very well. Chances are these people feel self-confident. The best way to become self-confident as you orient yourself to teaching is to test yourself and to develop confidence in as many experiences relating to teaching as possible. Students who have taught church school classes, have been counselors in summer camps, have been senior scouts, or have been in any other youth-related experiences generally feel more confident about teaching.

Receiving positive comments for work well done goes a long way in enhancing one's self-confidence. Successful athletes exude confidence, and so do successful students of education. As we receive and feel good about the positive comments given by others for our work, we need to remember to give positive feedback to the pupils or students we work with in the classroom. If we are models of self-confidence, not egomaniacs, our students will want to model themselves after us.

Being Diversified in Your Preparation

Most successful schoolteachers do not have a single concentration. They major in certain areas such as elementary education or history at the secondary level, but if they are wise, they also choose a minor. A minor certification, such as special-education endorsements in elementary education or another subject area in secondary education, gives prospective teachers a better opportunity for employment and gives them more latitude on the job. In the 1980s, there will continue to be a demand for science and math teachers. With the sudden rise in women's athletics, coaching ability for women will also help as one enters the employment arena.

Being diversified also means having outside interests or hobbies in music, chess, bridge, minor sports, or travel. Outside interests are attractive to potential employers because of one's ability to sponsor activities and to be a more interesting staff member. The curriculum today includes such a multitude of offerings that administrators are often hard-pressed to find someone to fill all the needed spots.

Being Well Groomed and Having Good Personal Hygiene

An expensive designer wardrobe is not a necessity in the teaching field. It is important, however, to be clean and neat and to wear the type of clothing that is acceptable in the school building in which you teach. Some school staffs seem to prefer casual clothing and others seem to favor more formal attire. Teachers' clothing is nearly always different from and more formal than student clothing. This contrast is a good one because it sets the teacher apart as an adult model for the students.

The personal hygiene of a teacher can become a problem. Unpleasant odors or an unkempt appearance can be a distracting problem when one is working with students. The ideal teacher needs to be a model to look up to, and this includes maintaining her or his body in a very hygienic manner. Excellent body hygiene will pay off for the teacher in both better health and a better rapport with students.

As in all exercises of this type, there are some dangers in identifying the ideal teacher. There is always the unique person who is far from fulfilling the criteria but who has other qualities that cause her or him to excel at teaching. We must be open to these types of people because they often act as needed change agents in our schools. As we strive to become more ideal, there is a chance that we may become more conservative and less likely to take any chances. The latter problem may be avoided by reevaluating our ideal teacher list.

Items That Cause Teachers Stress

Teaching is a challenging career, and some of these challenges and problems are discussed in this section. In one study, four hundred kindergarten through twelfth-grade teachers in a middle-sized midwestern community were asked to rank eleven stressful conditions in teaching. Table 16–1 is a tabulation of the results of this Midwest study.

Disruptive Students

Disruptive students seem to emerge close to or at the top of about everyone's list. All public-school teachers and administrators are confronted with the problems of a disturbed society and must deal daily with the symptoms of the sociological problems of their communities. As was discussed in Chapters 1 and 2, symptoms manifest themselves in the form of drug and alcohol problems, teacher assaults, vandalism to the school, verbal abuse of teachers and administrators, pregnancies, dropouts, decline in test scores, increased student apathy, and many more. The schools alone cannot hope to solve the deep-seated causes of these problems, yet schools are often the scapegoats for society's problems. Educators can only hope that religious institutions, government agencies, community organizations, and the home will unite with them in an effort to solve the real problems. In the meantime, preservice

TABLE 16–1   Rank Order and Male/Female Rankings of Items that Cause Stress

	Overall Ranking	Male Ranking	Female Ranking
1.	Disruptive students	Disruptive students	Lack of time
2.	Lack of time	Student apathy	Disruptive students
3.	Student apathy	Financial pressure	Nonteaching duties
4.	Nonteaching duties	Lack of support from parents/community	Student apathy
5.	Financial pressure	Lack of positive feedback from administrators	Lack of support from parents/community
6.	Lack of support from parents/community	Lack of time	Financial pressure
7.	Dealing with multiability students	Nonteaching duties	Dealing with multiability students
8.	Lack of positive feedback from administrators	Dealing with multiability students	Lack of positive feedback from administrators
9.	Lack of input into curricular/administrative decisions	Lack of input into curricular/administrative decisions	Lack of input into curricular/administrative decisions
10.	Lack of recognition for teaching excellence	Lack of recognition for teaching excellence	Lack of recognition for teaching excellence
11.	Lack of colleague support	Lack of colleague support	Lack of colleague support

Source: Dedrick, C. V., Hawkes, R. R., & Smith, J. K. (1981). Teacher stress: A descriptive study of the concerns. *National Association of Secondary School Principals Bulletin, 65,* 32.

teachers need to study deviant behavior and to learn a multitude of ways to minimize its effect on them and on the students they teach.

Lack of Time

Lack of time also rates very high on all three lists in the midwestern study. As a teacher, you will be asked to do many things that take up your time. You may be asked to do lunchroom duty, playground duty, study hall supervision, ticket taking, bus-loading supervision, and so on, none of which are actual teaching responsibilities. Because of strained education budgets, you may have to deal with large class sizes, requiring more time to be spent in paper grading and on class preparation. Lack of time correlates strongly with the dislike of nonteaching tasks.

Student Apathy

Student apathy also rates high as a stressful part of teaching. There are probably many factors causing student apathy in our schools today. Slow or learning-disabled students sometimes give up trying to participate in school after experiencing frustration and failure. Many young people see the subject matter taught in school as irrelevant to their lives. Students may be turned off by schools and learning because of the influence of television. Many students watch television more hours per week than they go to school, and the shows they observe are far more exciting than an orderly, disciplined classroom. The threat of nuclear war, often discussed on television, also has an effect on our children. Some actually feel that there is no sense in getting an education because they will be killed by the bomb anyway. Apathy may also arise in certain subcultures of students who are out of the mainstream of events because of heavy use of alcohol and drugs. Whatever the reasons for apathy, teachers have to expend far more energy to motivate and teach apathetic students.

Nonteaching Duties

Nonteaching duties are probably the least publicized and the most misunderstood problem of teachers. Most of the American public visualizes teachers in the act of teaching and not as curriculum planners, paper graders, ballgame-ticket takers, hall duty monitors, lunchroom overseers, activity sponsors, playground supervisors and so on. Nearly all teachers are on task not only during the school day, but also after school hours, in the evenings, on weekends, and in the summers. These nonteaching expectations, when added to the problems of disruptive students and excessive class size, can and often do produce additional stress for dedicated teachers.

Educators are often expected to perform duties not connected with classroom teaching. *(Photo used by permission of the Metropolitan School District of Lawrence Township.)*

Financial Pressure

The financial pressures on families and on individuals today are tremendous. Teachers are intelligent individuals who are leaders in our communities, and they may be dissatisfied when they compare themselves to other professionals in the community who reap giant financial rewards for their services.

Lack of Support from Parents/Community

Lack of support from parents and the community also rated high as a source of stress in the midwestern study. Again, as a teacher, you must learn to cope with this problem and know that its causes are deeply rooted in society. Most elementary teachers get a reasonable amount of support from parents, but at the secondary levels, parent support drops off considerably. On parent nights, many junior-high or middle schools and high schools are fortunate to greet one fourth of their parents. The following guidelines offer some positive first steps toward working more effectively with parents (Bordeaux, 1982):

1. Make home visits so that the parent(s) can remain on familiar territory. (Though teachers may be ill at ease in a setting out of their control, benefits accrue in development of trust and better understanding of children.)
2. Write letters of welcome to children and parents, including brief information about your aspirations for the children and invite the support of parent and child.

3. Organize several group planning meetings for parents at different times to accommodate work schedules, with follow-up telephone calls or personal contact to reaffirm that parents are needed to help plan for their children.

4. Organize a corner, table or bulletin board for parents, making available announcements, schedules, brochures and books appropriate to parent interests.

5. Design a one-page memo to parents for regular distribution, including class highlights, films viewed, projects initiated or completed, trips planned, etc.

6. Develop an open-door policy for parents to visit the classroom whenever they can, teaching children to greet, introduce and see to the comfort of parents visiting the classroom during instruction.

7. Survey parents for topics or problems they would like to discuss or have considered.

8. Contact parents with words of caring when circumstances warrant.

9. Develop lists of seasonal activities and places to visit with children on weekends and holidays.

10. Write letters of appreciation or arrange for other recognition of parents who participate in the instructional program or commit time to special projects.

11. Help children plan an afternoon, evening or weekend reception for parents so they may meet one another and get acquainted.

12. Help children get acquainted through classroom activities that highlight strengths of each child.

Although the list may seem to be best suited to elementary teachers, many of these guidelines are as well suited to secondary teachers. Common sense and the literature tell us that home visits can be very productive in eliminating most of the problems that students are having in school. The most important single ingredient of a home visit is establishing a common understanding between you and the parents on how to work with that child in a more constructive and consistent manner. Getting on the same wavelength with parents is absolutely essential to making real progress with a problem learner and is nearly as essential with other students.

When going to students' homes, each teacher will want to gather different information, but most will want answers to the following questions (Bordeaux, 1982):

1. Do you think your child likes school?
2. What activities interest your child at school?
3. What does your child enjoy doing at home? (This is needed so that teachers and parents can get together and withhold activities from either home or school, when children misbehave.)
4. What is your child's favorite subject at school? (This is necessary so that

teachers can check with each other to find out if the child's behavior is
consistent in every class; and if not, why not?)

5. Do you have any concerns about your child with which the school can
help? (p. 276)

In your preservice training you may wish to go on a few home visits to gain
some practical experience in this challenging area.

The members of the community must also be a part of the educational
establishment; they are the ones who, acting through legislators, fund our
schools. As a new teacher, you will be too busy to be concerned unduly with
community understanding, but there are some ways you can help. Teachers
should assist citizens by:

1. Showing courtesy and genuine pleasure toward all visitors.
2. Actively participating in parent-teacher organizations and other community affairs.
3. Seeking, through invitation, use of the community's human resources
   both in curriculum planning and in instruction.
4. Emphasizing the unique value of citizen contributions. ("The School's Role
   in Community Life," 1982, p. 125)

Getting to know your community better, especially if you are a newcomer, is
an exciting part of living. Many people in your community can enhance your
curriculum with valuable expert knowledge on many subjects, and they will
be flattered to be asked to speak to your classes.

Dealing with Multiability Students

Teachers are confronted with the problem of individual differences in students. Even in very homogeneous classes, the ability of individuals may vary
considerably. Meeting these individual needs is not easy even for the most
experienced teachers. It is often frustrating to teach a concept to your class
and have only about half the students grasp the meaning the first time. Even
after the third time, there will be a few who will need some individual tutoring. The nongraded type of school mentioned in Chapter 8 is an administrative setup intended to meet this need.

Lack of Input into Curricular/Administrative Decisions

Teachers generally enjoy being a part of the curricular decision-making process, but too often, their curricular ideas are not sought. Administrators,
pressured to facilitate things, make decisions about the curriculum or important school policy with little or no input from classroom teachers. Teachers,
then, who must abide by these decisions, are angered as they must implement these same policies. Many teachers suffer stress as a result of the frus-

Being able to deal with students of widely ranging abilities is a problem for all teachers. *(Photo used by permission of the Indianapolis Public Schools.)*

tration that comes from their having little or no input into the decisions that affect them.

Lack of Positive Feedback and Support

Positive feedback and support depend on your administrators, your colleagues, and the students you teach. Lack of positive feedback from school administrators is an additional cause of stress on teachers. It appears that many administrators are so concerned with the daily tasks that keep a school running that they overlook the internal human-relations aspect of their jobs. Teachers may seldom get positive comments on the work that they are doing—only negative comments when things go wrong. Feedback, especially positive feedback, from administrators means a great deal to the teacher. In fairness to the administrators, they themselves seldom get positive feedback from the public they are trying to serve; they actually receive more negative feedback from the public than do teachers.

It is always great to receive support from those you work with on the job, but often, we get too busy to be concerned about others as we go about our daily concerns. Frequently, in teaching, we let envy or jealousy creep in as a deterrent to real dialogue with our fellow teachers. Colleague support among the members of a department or a school group is very rehabilitative. It results in much greater productivity, and the students are the greatest beneficiaries. In addition, teachers want to be and deserve to be recognized for teaching excellence, but often, it goes unnoticed. In the military, there are awards for about every type of excellence one can imagine, but teachers must rely on their students to praise them. If the students remember to go back to their teachers and thank them, they will eventually be praised, but teachers need more immediate recognition for excellence.

The Discipline of Teaching

The authors believe that becoming a good teacher is as much a learning experience as becoming proficient in one's chosen subject or subjects. Neither of these learning endeavors begin in college, and neither ends in college; for the professional teacher, they are continuous processes of growth. A physician may say that he or she has learned all that is necessary about physiology, and a teacher may say that he or she knows all that is necessary about child psychology and the elementary subjects; both of them will be grossly mistaken. The truth is that there are physicians and teachers who have stopped learning and growing in their profession soon after their formal schooling has ended. Whatever one does to learn to be a professional, she or he must learn the subject matter and the ways and means of practicing the profession, too. We want our physicians to understand us as people and to know how to heal our physical wounds, and we want our teachers to understand our growth levels and to be able to focus learning where we, as students, can maximize our intellectual potential.

Is it easier to become a teacher or a physician? I hope your answer was that neither profession is easier than the other if one wants to accomplish the degree of excellence that we hope all future teachers will strive to attain. The pay and the professional status that physicians enjoy may mistakenly lead one to believe that being a teacher is easier, but there is really no difference when we are talking about excellence in performance. Both are disciplines, in which certain facts and skills must be learned. A physician must be a careful and precise diagnostician, an informed prescriber of medicine, and often a skilled surgeon; teachers must test and analyze a student's abilities, must devise a teaching style or a learning method that will meet a certain child's needs, and must be able to use various techniques to meet individual children's learning patterns.

The traditional foundations-of-education subjects presented in this text (history, sociology, and philosophy) are all very important in understanding how to become a fully disciplined teacher. Other subjects mentioned in this text and other teachers' education subjects are important as well. To illustrate the point that studying and learning the foundations of education are a real part of studying about pedagogy as a discipline, we would like to present two illustrations:

One-on-one teaching is one of the best ways to determine a child's strengths, weaknesses, and interests. *(Photo used by permission of the Metropolitan School District of Lawrence Township.)*

Illustration 1

- *Situation:* A student has failed biology exams repeatedly.
- *Reactor A* is a teacher who mainly thinks of teaching in the narrow sense of teaching a subject.
- *Reactor A* says that the only answer for some students is to fail the class; thus, it is inevitable that some students will fail. Academic standards must be upheld in this school.
- *Reactor B* is a teacher who has become well informed about the whole child and her or his needs. This teacher studies his or her teaching technique as much as the subject matter area and is a scholar in the foundations area of education.
- *Reactor B* says that it would be a good idea to look into the family background of the child, his or her academic potential, the classes he or she is placed in, whether he or she is taking the class for the first or second

time, and whether good rapport with the child has been established through meaningful dialogue. Further examination of the child's background may show a need for additional testing, a family conference, and the establishment of a definite plan to facilitate the child's study habits. The child is *not* written off by *Reactor B*.

Illustration 2

- *Situation:* Teachers are bombarded with some new idea every year, such as the back-to-basics movement.
- *Reactor A* tends to see these media trends as fads and feels that if one waits long enough, they will go away. There probably will be no noticeable teaching adjustment in this teacher's class, although the curriculum that he or she teaches may be affected eventually by outside forces.
- *Reactor B* accepts new ways of doing things as another challenge. Although he or she may wish that some new fads had not appeared, he or she accepts these adjustments as part of teaching. Reactor B knows that historically, education has gone through both liberal and conservative trends, and that neither is a bad omen. He or she feels that any new idea offers a chance to look at and evaluate one's approach to teaching and education. Big publicity items, like the back-to-basics movement, will lead to more money for education, changes in textbooks, special conferences, and reforms in teachers' education.

Students in teacher education classes who understand the foundations sequence and the purpose behind it will become better teachers. These foundation-enlightened students will become teachers who not only read about how to improve their subject, but who also keep informed about current trends in education, as they read such journals as the *Kappan* and the *Saturday Review*. These teachers know that *how* they present subject matter to young people is as important as *what* they present.

The First Year

Getting through the first year of teaching is a tremendous challenge. Any occupation presents more difficulties in the first year than in the years following, but teaching has so many facets that it is especially demanding. Many of the challenges are of a practical nature, such as learning to get along with colleagues, learning whom to trust and whom not to trust, getting to know your supervisors, learning the school's accepted disciplinary procedures, and following school policy. Also, the first-year teacher is challenged by the academic responsibility of providing a workable lesson plan for each day.

Many articles have been written about how to induct a new teacher into a school and into a system. Myers (1981) wrote that beginning teachers gener-

In-service orientation is valuable for beginning teachers. *(Photo used by permission of the Indianapolis Public Schools.)*

ally identify the following six items as being most significant in helping them to adjust to teaching:

1. Achieving status with peers or co-workers.
2. Gaining the attention and concern of the principal.
3. Having ample opportunity to know and understand the local situation with emphasis on general school policies, school facilities, and school routines.
4. Opportunities to make unique and personal contributions to the school.
5. Opportunities to grow and progress personally and professionally.
6. Opportunities to associate socially with peers. (pp. 71–72)

Myers commented on all the items in this list from the principal's point of view, and he discussed many excellent suggestions for the principal and the new teacher. One of the most meaningful comments by Myers (1981) is one made in connection with opportunities to make personal contributions to the school. He wrote that if

> beginning teachers are convinced that they are at liberty to be themselves, to implement their own techniques, to exercise their own personalities, what a tremendous boost it is to their morale! Most beginning teachers have come to recognize that teaching is so much more a personal affair that there can be no one way of teaching. Rather, each teacher must be permitted to discover his optimum efficiency in a climate that not only permits but encourages experimentation and self-expression. It would be argued that this attitude on the

part of the principal is by far the most significant contribution he can make to the development of the beginning teacher. (pp. 73–74)

This statement will be very meaningful to you as you begin to teach. For some of you, that first year may seem far away, but it is closer than you think. Although the comment by Myers is directed to the principal, it is an ideal that you can help to facilitate for yourself. The latitude you have as a teacher, within your classroom, to be yourself and to direct your own unique style of learning is a powerful responsibility.

The Financial Rewards for Teachers

Salaries

Financial pressure rates high on all lists of items that concern teachers. As a preservice teacher, you deserve to know more about the financial standing of teachers. Although the information given here is not the worst news, it is not what teachers think their financial situation ought to be.

Teachers' beginning salaries vary slightly by geographic region in the United States. Table 16–2 indicates that the Southwest region has the highest average beginning salaries, and that the lowest average beginning salaries are found in New England. The mean average beginning salary for all regions is $15,394. To help you think ahead about your economic security, the same table lists maximum salaries of teachers for the same geographic regions in the United States. You should keep in mind that some districts pay at the maximum level after fifteen years of experience, whereas other districts may not pay their maximum salary for twenty years or more. The average maximum salaries paid as listed in Table 16–2 reflect, in most cases, additional training beyond the bachelor's degree. Table 16–2 also includes minimum salaries offered for other professional positions in education. Principals and superintendents usually must have several years of classroom experience, as well as additional classroom credits, to be eligible for promotion to those positions. Many districts also mandate that their superintendents have a doctorate.

Ornstein (1980) documented what the cost-of-living increase has done to teachers' purchasing power in Table 16–3. As seen in this table, the average salaries for teachers increased 6.3 percent per year, compounded and based on the 1969–1970 average salary of $8,635, but the consumer price index increased by 8 percent per year (also compounded) in this same period. The net loss in purchasing power to teachers amounted to 1.7 percent per year or −17 percent from 1969–1970 to 1979–1980. The estimated loss in 1969 dollars between 1969–1970 and 1979–1980, as far as purchasing power was concerned, was $1,468, (determined by the subtraction of $7,167 from $8,635).

TABLE 16—2 Mean of Minimum Scheduled Salaries for Personnel in Selected Professional Positions in Reporting School Systems, by Geographic Region, 1984—85 (maximum scheduled salaries for classroom teachers are included for the same school year)

Position 1	New England 2	Mid-east 3	South-east 4	Great Lakes 5	Plains 6	South-west 7	Rocky Mountains 8	Far West 9	Total All Regions 10
Supts. (contract salary)	50,830	58,490	56,316	53,350	52,450	63,765	58,536	59,586	56,954
Elementary-school principals	33,026	31,473	27,148	32,045	31,059	29,066	30,365	34,294	30,950
Senior-high-school principals	38,235	36,458	31,702	38,112	35,721	35,097	34,891	39,561	35,085
Classroom teachers (minimum)	14,188	15,249	14,903	15,038	14,710	16,468	15,515	16,420	15,394
Classroom teachers (maximum)	28,254	32,756	26,846	30,326	27,660	29,630	31,805	31,715	29,904
Counselors	16,001	15,998	16,401	16,129	15,816	18,461	17,056	19,248	16,950
Librarians	14,376	15,314	15,310	15,393	15,086	17,084	16,026	17,004	15,770
School nurses	12,187	14,246	12,511	14,516	13,042	16,024	14,942	16,805	14,657

States included in geographic regions. New England: CT,ME, MA, NH, RI, VT; Mideast: DE, DC, MD, NJ, NY, PA; Southeast: AL, AR, FL, GA, KY, LA, MS,NC, SC, TN, VA, WV; Great Lakes: IL, IN, MI, OH, WI; Plains: IA, KS, MN, MO, NE, ND, SD; Southwest: AZ, NM, OK, TX; Rocky Mountains: CO, ID, MT, UT, WY; Far West: AK, CA, HI, NV, OR, WA.

Note: The data in this table may be subject to considerable sampling and response variation and should be used only as general, not precise indicators of current relationships among categories; data are not appropriate for year-to-year trends.

Source: Educational Research Service, Inc., *Scheduled salaries for professional personnel in public schools, 1984—85, Part 1: National survey of salaries and wages in public schools.* Arlington, VA: ERS, pp. 16, 17.

TABLE 16—3 Average Salary of Public Classroom Teachers, 1969—1970 and 1979—1980[a]

	1969—1970	1979—1980	Percent Increase Over 1969—1970	Purchasing Power in 1969 Dollars[b]
Average salary of classroom teachers	$8,635	$16,001	6.3%	$7,167
Elementary	8,412	15,661		
Secondary	8,891	16,387		

[a]Differences in salary between elementary and secondary teachers reflect the fact that the latter group has more experience and education.

[b]Author's estimate.

Sources: Adapted from National Education Association, *Estimates of School Statistics, 1970—71* (Washington, DC, 1970), Table 7, p. 32; National Education Association, *Estimates of School Statistics, 1979—80* (Washington, DC, 1979), Table 7, p. 32.

This is an alarming statistic when one considers the massive effort that teachers' organizations and other groups mounted to raise the economic status of teachers during that same time period. Although the purchasing power of the teachers has improved since 1980, teachers have not recovered the losses they incurred during the decade of the 1970s.

Table 16–4 is a comparison of average beginning salaries of teachers compared to the beginning salaries of other professionals between the 1971–1972 and 1981–1982 school years. In no case did salary increases match the cost-of-living increases during this time period. Engineering and math statistics came the closest, with increases of 117 and 115 percent, respectively. Average starting salaries for teachers increased $5,435, or 77 percent, during the 1971–1972 to 1981–1982 time period. Teachers' beginning salaries are lower than those of other professional groups because of their 9½–10-month working schedule, compared to the 12-month working schedule of the other professional groups, but the issue here is cost of living, which the teachers have not maintained as well as most other professional groups. Teachers have actually done better with the cost of living at the beginning level than they have at the average salary level, but they are behind in both instances.

Whether teachers' beginning salaries and average-and-above salaries will catch up with the cost of living is a big guess at this point. Teachers' organizations argue that salaries, at least at the beginning level, must be raised to attract the best people into the profession. In the technical fields, as we have pointed out before, teacher recruiters are in stiff competition with industry recruiters. Higher beginning salaries to attract the math and science teachers

TABLE 16–4 Comparison of the Changes in the Average Starting Salaries of Teachers and Other Professionals from 1971–1972 to 1981–1982

Group	Average Starting Salaries (school year)		Percent Increase
	1971–1972	1981–1982	
Beginning teachers with Bachelor's degree (men and women)	$ 7,061	$12,496	77%
Graduates with Bachelor's degree			
Engineering	$10,500	$22,836	117
Accounting	10,260	17,148	67
Sales, marketing	8,736	17,544	101
Business administration	8,424	16,440	95
Liberal Arts	8,292	14,700	77
Chemistry	9,720	19,464	100
Mathematics, statistics	9,192	19,776	115
Economics, finance	9,216	16,320	77

Source: National Education Association, *Rankings of the States, 1982*, NEA Research Memo, 1201 Sixteenth Street, N.W., Washington, DC 20036.

will be a cry in years to come, and the other areas of teaching will continue to demand equal consideration. As we approach the 1990s, we hear more about tightening the belt on all educational expenditures. It appears that, for the time being, increases are going to become tougher rather than easier to negotiate. The best thing that could happen concerning the economic situation of teachers would be for the cost of living to go down.

Part-time Employment

Because teachers have not kept up with increases in the cost of living, many teachers find part-time employment to help sustain them. The practice of moonlighting is not new for teachers, but it is now more commonly accepted as a way of life. Men, in particular, have traditionally painted houses, played in bands, taught driver's education, sold insurance, and followed other similar lines of employment during the summer break or during the school year. At present, both men and women teachers work at a variety of jobs part time, and waiting on tables at a restaurant seems to be very common. Although the trend is toward moonlighting, and the economic situation seems to demand extra work, the best plan for the teacher is to concentrate on only one occupation. As we have pointed out before, teaching as an occupation demands the use of large amounts of physical, mental, and emotional energy. On the plus side for working at extra jobs, some say that they are a good diversion from teaching. Others feel that the jobs keep them in touch with the "real world," and still others feel that the job experience directly enhances what they do in the classroom.

Fringe Benefits for Teachers

Fringe benefits for teachers are extensive, and they vary from region to region and by school district. In most school districts, fringe benefits are bargained for through the collective-bargaining process.

Teachers receive many and varied fringe benefits in addition to their contracted salary. Although your interest in fringe benefits may not be great at this stage in your preparation for teaching, we have included a comprehensive list of items that you should consider when seeking a job. Most school corporations provide all or some of the fringe benefits found in Table 16–5, which give the teacher an underlying sense of security. Table 16–5 lists the major fringe benefits offered teachers in eight geographic regions in the United States. The survey questionnaire used to obtain the data in Table 16–5 was sent to 1,808 school systems enrolling 300 or more pupils.

Sick leave is offered almost universally across the country, and it is designed to protect the teacher against loss of compensation because of illness. Most school systems provide ten to twelve days of sick leave per year, which can accumulate to an unlimited number of days. The majority of systems reporting allowed no sick leave credit toward retirement benefits; however, a

TABLE 16—5 Summary of Selected Fringe Benefits for Teachers in Reporting School Systems, by Geographic Region, 1983—1984

Position 1	New England 2	Mid-east 3	South-east 4	Great Lakes 5	Plains 6	South-west 7	Rocky Mountains 8	Far West 9	Total All Regions 10
							Geographic Region		
Total responding	58	180	181	236	108	104	49	148	1064
Percentage providing sick leave	98.3	99.4	98.9	98.7	99.1	98.1	100.0	100.0	99.1
Specified no. days per yr.[a]	100.0	99.4	100.0	97.0	99.1	100.0	93.9	100.0	98.9
Provided as needed[a]	—	0.6	1.1	3.0	0.9	—	6.1	0.7	1.4
Sick leave counts toward retirement service[a]	19.3	14.5	31.3	31.8	9.3	24.5	8.2	82.4	31.1
Percentage providing personal/ emergency leave	96.6	96.1	95.6	96.6	96.3	96.2	100.0	95.9	96.3
Charged in whole or part to sick leave[a]	10.7	12.1	49.7	19.3	42.3	54.0	22.4	71.8	35.9
Percentage providing sabbatical leave	91.4	78.9	40.9	69.9	58.3	43.	73.5	76.4	64.9
Sick leave									
Days credited per year	15	12	11	12	13	10	10	11	12
Maximum accumulation	152	187	95	158	110	95	114	150	136
Personal/emergency leave									
Days allowed per year	4	3	3	3	3	4	3	5	4
Percentage providing insurance									
Group hospitalization	96.6	98.3	95.0	98.3	96.3	91.3	100.0	96.6	96.6
Single coverage[a]	96.4	94.9	85.5	96.1	80.8	85.3	91.8	74.1	88.3
Fully paid[a]	96.4	94.4	73.8	94.0	75.0	73.7	91.8	72.7	83.9
Family coverage[a]	96.4	94.9	79.7	94.0	74.0	72.6	89.8	73.4	84.8
Fully paid[a]	32.1	61.6	6.4	45.3	15.4	.0	36.7	54.4	34.2
Medical/surgical	94.8	97.2	89.5	97.0	93.5	90.4	100.0	97.3	94.8
Single coverage[a]	96.4	94.3	85.2	96.1	82.2	85.1	91.8	73.6	88.2
Fully paid[a]	96.4	93.7	72.8	93.9	76.2	73.4	91.8	72.2	83.7
Family coverage[a]	96.4	94.3	79.6	93.9	75.2	72.3	89.8	72.2	84.6
Fully paid[a]	32.7	59.4	6.2	45.4	15.8	.0	36.7	51.4	34.1
Major medical	94.8	98.9	92.3	98.3	92.6	90.4	98.0	98.6	95.9
Single coverage[a]	96.4	93.8	83.8	96.1	84.0	83.0	91.7	74.0	87.9
Fully paid[a]	96.4	93.3	71.3	94.0	79.0	70.2	91.7	72.6	83.4
Family coverage[a]	96.4	93.8	78.4	94.0	77.0	70.2	89.6	72.6	84.4
Fully paid[a]	34.5	59.6	4.8	46.1	15.0	0.0	35.4	51.4	34.0
Dental	51.7	89.4	28.2	74.2	52.8	42.3	67.3	98.0	65.4
Single coverage[a]	96.7	88.8	82.4	96.0	80.7	95.5	90.9	75.9	87.6
Fully paid[a]	96.7	87.6	80.4	94.3	71.9	81.8	87.9	75.2	84.9
Family coverage[a]	90.0	77.0	70.6	91.4	64.9	86.4	84.8	66.9	78.6
Fully paid[a]	53.3	42.9	15.7	53.7	14.0	2.3	24.2	51.0	39.9
Vision care	17.2	28.9	10.5	22.9	10.2	12.5	20.4	69.6	25.6
Single coverage[a]	90.0	98.1	94.7	96.3	54.5	76.9	90.0	80.6	87.5
Fully paid[a]	90.0	96.2	84.2	92.6	45.5	69.2	80.0	80.6	84.6
Family coverage[a]	80.0	71.2	78.9	92.6	45.5	53.8	80.0	63.1	71.7
Fully paid[a]	60.0	40.4	21.1	64.8	0.0	0.0	30.0	49.5	44.1
Prescription drugs	46.6	54.4	47.0	65.3	45.4	62.5	71.4	72.3	58.3
Single coverage[a]	96.3	93.9	81.2	96.8	85.7	83.1	88.6	76.6	87.9
Fully paid[a]	96.3	92.9	70.6	95.5	79.6	72.3	88.6	76.1	84.4
Family coverage[a]	92.6	86.7	74.1	94.2	81.6	75.4	88.6	71.0	82.9
Fully paid[a]	33.3	50.0	1.2	53.2	18.4	1.5	31.4	50.5	34.8
Mean percentage of insurance premium paid if less than full									
Hospitalization									
Single coverage	70.3	84.5	70.9	87.6	73.9	62.3	75.3	82.2	76.5
Family coverage	69.9	81.9	45.0	79.5	63.9	41.6	65.7	68.7	68.0

TABLE 16-5 (continued)

Position 1	Geographic Region								
	New England 2	Mid-east 3	South-east 4	Great Lakes 5	Plains 6	South-west 7	Rocky Mountains 8	Far West 9	Total All Regions 10
Medical/surgical									
Single coverage	70.3	84.4	71.8	87.3	71.6	62.4	75.3	82.2	76.8
Family coverage	69.9	82.0	46.4	79.1	63.9	41.6	65.7	69.9	68.7
Major medical									
Single coverage	69.5	80.8	72.4	87.5	72.3	62.3	75.3	81.0	76.3
Family coverage	69.1	79.5	47.2	78.0	63.4	42.8	65.7	70.2	67.9
Dental									
Single coverage	87.0	78.2	64.3	88.9	75.6	67.9	65.0	77.7	78.9
Family coverage	82.4	75.9	50.2	81.3	61.9	45.9	55.2	63.2	71.1
Vision care									
Single coverage	70.3	79.0	60.5	75.3	80.0	—	57.0	74.3	73.9
Family coverage	65.5	76.2	50.0	74.2	80.0	—	62.5	67.3	71.6
Prescription drugs									
Single coverage	79.3	85.6	71.8	87.3	69.2	62.7	76.0	86.5	77.3
Family coverage	76.5	83.3	51.8	77.7	68.7	43.7	60.3	64.8	69.1
Percentage providing income protection insurance	10.3	17.8	20.4	34.3	41.7	22.1	44.9	20.3	25.9
Mean salary coverage	68%	55%	64%	67%	63%	63%	68%	66%	65%
	10.3	11.7	17.1	29.7	37.0	13.5	36.7	15.5	21.0
Mean monthly benefit/limit	$ 1,625	$ 1,230	$ 1,455	$ 2,537	$ 1,971	$ 1,540	$ 1,856	$ 1,580	$ 1,900
	6.9	11.7	9.9	21.6	29.6	15.4	32.7	10.8	16.4
Percentage providing group life insurance	77.6	62.2	59.7	85.2	63.9	65.4	89.8	56.8	68.7
Fully paid[a]	53.3	75.0	65.7	77.6	75.4	69.1	79.5	75.0	72.8
Mean percentage of premium paid if less than full	63%	65%	43%	70%	62%	73%	62%	—	62%
	24.1	7.2	7.2	10.6	2.8	2.9	10.2	.0	7.1
Mean face value/maximum value of policy	$12,111	$20,154	$20,879	$19,763	$22,482	$12,369	$33,512	$26,699,	$20,479
Percentage providing professional liability insurance	63.3	65.6	74.0	69.1	78.7	63.5	73.5	54.7	67.5
Percentage with retirement plans									
State retirement system	94.8	96.7	96.7	97.5	98.1	96.2	91.8	97.3	96.7
Local retirement system	1.7	1.7	5.5	2.1	3.7	2.9	2.0	—	2.5
Social security coverage	22.4	88.9	79.6	44.9	63.9	39.4	51.0	25.0	55.9
Tax-sheltered annuity plan	63.9	77.8	84.0	78.0	72.2	83.7	73.5	65.5	76.2
Early retirement option	51.7	36.7	30.4	53.4	44.4	30.8	67.3	56.1	44.5
Percentage providing severance pay	43.1	52.2	31.5	62.3	33.3	33.7	49.0	9.5	40.6
Percentage with tuition reimbursement provisions	58.6	60.6	29.3	31.8	15.7	26.0	8.2	9.5	31.3
Percentage paying all or part of teacher org. membership dues	12.1	4.4	0.6	2.5	2.8	1.0	2.0	1.4	2.7
Percentage with collective negotiations agreements	96.6	97.2	24.9	92.4	72.2	29.9	77.6	94.6	73.2

[a]Percentages based on only those respondents providing the benefit specified above.

Note: Tabulations of single and family group insurance coverage do not include school systems that provide such coverage under "cafeteria plan" arrangements.

States included in geographic regions. New England: CT, ME, MA, NH, RI, VT; Mideast: DE, DC, MD, NJ, NY, PA; Southeast: AL, AR, FL, GA, KY, LA, MS, NC, SC, TN, VA, WV; Great Lakes: IL, IN, MI, OH, WI; Plains: IA, KS, MN, MO, NE, ND, SD; Southwest: AZ, NM, OK, TX; Rocky Mountains: CO, ID,MT, UT, WY; Far West: AK, CA, HI, NV, OR, WA.

Source: Educational Research Service, Inc., (1984). *Fringe Benefits for Teachers in Public Schools, 1983–84,* Part 3. Arlington, VA: ERS, pp. 38–40.

growing number of systems are allowing full or partial credit for unused sick leave days toward retirement. Sick leave days normally cannot be transferred from one district to another.

Personal and emergency leave days generally fall between one and six days per year and are to be used for personal business, civic affairs, and severe illness or accident to a member of the immediate family of the teacher. Three days is the most common number of days granted by school systems. A few school systems agree to an "unlimited/as needed" phraseology. Over half the systems do not allow unused emergency or personal leave days to be charged to sick leave, but over 30 percent of the school systems charge all or some unused days to sick leave.

Sabbatical leaves, paid or unpaid, are provided in 65 percent of the school systems for the purpose of doing advanced study. In a typical school system, one must teach seven years before becoming eligible for a sabbatical leave. A few systems allow a sabbatical leave after one year of employment. Monetary compensation for sabbatical leaves varies from no salary to full salary. Seventy-two percent of the school systems pay a certain percentage of the teacher's salary during her or his leave.

Group health insurance is provided by most school corporations. Both single and family coverage are provided. Most health-insurance plans are very generous and include hospitalization, medical/surgical, and major medical coverage. Many of these comprehensive plans are fully or nearly fully paid for by the school corporation. Dental coverage is increasing in importance as part of the teacher's health-care package. Many systems have provisions for orthodontic work. Vision care is provided by only 25 percent of the school corporations reporting, but prescription drugs are provided by 58 percent of the corporations.

Income protection and group life insurance are also offered by many school corporations. Twenty-six percent of the corporations provide income protection insurance for their teachers. The average salary percentage covered is 65 percent, and the mean monthly benefit (limit) is $1,900. Sixty-nine percent of the corporations reporting provide group life insurance with a face value averaging about $20,500.

Other fringe benefits include professional liability insurance, provided by 68 percent of the school corporations; retirement plans, generally state-supported, but supplemented by local school corporations; severance pay; and tuition reimbursement provisions.

Teacher Supply and Demand

The question of the supply of and the demand for teachers is very important in the minds of most educators today. In a recent survey of 775 superintendents in the western states concerning teacher supply and demand, eighteen

Demand for teachers varies by subject area and region of the country. *(Photo used by permission of the Metropolitan School District of Lawrence Township.)*

subject areas were researched. The figure on page 482 contains the results of the western study, which compares the percentage of superintendents who cite shortages of teachers to the percentage who cite surpluses of teachers.

The superintendents in the western states clearly listed mathematics, physical sciences, reading, vocational education, special education, and music as areas of need, and English, social science, health and physical education, elementary, and administration as areas of surplus. (De Roche & Kujawa, 1982). Generally speaking, the more technical the area, the more demand there is for that teaching expertise. The demand for technically trained personnel in the private sector generally causes a shortage of teachers in those corresponding subject areas.

Related to this whole area of supply and demand is the number of new teachers graduated. There has been a drastic decline of new graduates in the Northeast since the early 1970s (DeRoche & Kujawa, 1982). In New York alone, there were 38,716 graduating teachers in 1972, compared to 16,801 in 1979. There has not been as much of a decline in other regions of the country, but most states show substantial declines in graduating teachers.

Elementary-school enrollments have been on the decline since 1967 because of fewer births in the 1960s. In 1967, elementary enrollment peaked at 32 million, and there was a steady decline until 1983, when enrollments leveled off at 27 million. According to the National Center for Educational Statistics, enrollments will increase to 32 million by 1990. The figure on page 483 indicates the elementary projection and the secondary projection through 1990 (National Center for Education Statistics and Bureau of Labor Statistics, 1980–1981).

A Comparison of Superintendents Who Cite Teacher Shortages and Surpluses in Certain Teaching Areas

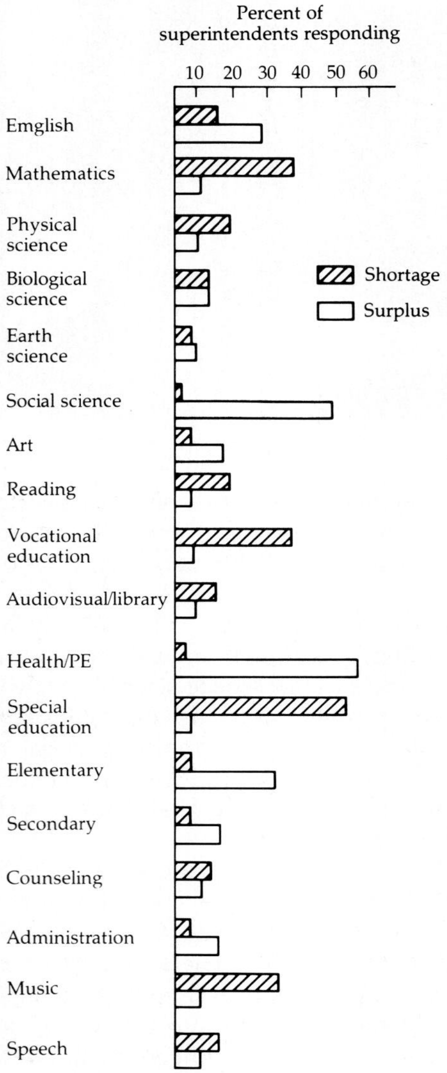

Percent of
superintendents responding

10 20 30 40 50 60

Emglish

Mathematics

Physical
science

Biological
science

Earth
science

Social science

Art

Reading

Vocational
education

Audiovisual/library

Health/PE

Special
education

Elementary

Secondary

Counseling

Administration

Music

Speech

Shortage

Surplus

Source: DeRoche, E. F., & Kujawa, E. (1982). A survey of teacher supply and demand in the West. *Phi Delta Kappan, 4,* 566. Adapted by permission of the publisher and the authors.

Changing Enrollment Levels Will Be the Primary Factor Affecting the Employment of Teachers

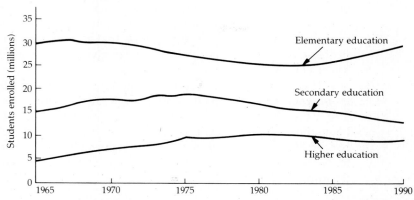

Source: National Center for Education Statistics. (1980–1981). Teaching occupations. In *Occupational outlook handbook and Bureau of Labor Statistics.* Washington, DC: U.S. Government Printing Office, pp. 175–182.

Pupil enrollment is the primary factor affecting the demand for teachers; to a lesser extent, demand is affected by teachers who retire, die, or leave the profession for other reasons. Ideally, there should be a demand for more teachers to improve the pupil–teacher ratio, but a growing conservative, budget-cutting era has caused school systems to raise their pupil–teacher ratio in the 1980s.

Whatever your interest area in teaching is, you would be wise to keep in touch with your college's placement office and/or the department of education's placement office for current trends in employment in teaching.

Summary

In this chapter, you have read of several reasons that one would choose teaching and education as a career. Being a teacher involves more than enjoying a subject or liking children, although these are important. Some characteristics of the ideal teacher were presented to help you focus on what the teacher is really capable of doing. Other chapters have related to important considerations about becoming a teacher, and it is hoped that you will take every opportunity during the remainder of your teachers' training to relate theory to the actual practice of teaching in the classroom.

It would be unwise for us to be dishonest about some of the causes of teacher stress—and, in some cases, teacher burnout—but all of these can be found in other occupations as well. We think that you should know from the beginning what to expect from the occupation you are about to enter, so that you can better prepare yourself to handle some of the difficulties that we all encounter. It is, indeed, a worthy occupation to serve our fellow human beings and to help, as others have said, make the world a better place to live.

You have learned that teaching is both a discipline and a profession just as is the practice of medicine or, for that matter, any of the other learned professions. Also, we hope that we have given you some constructive ideas to assist you in your first year of teaching.

The whole area of salaries, fringe benefits, and teacher supply and demand was presented to give you a rough idea of what to expect in these areas. The economic rewards for teaching may suddenly escalate, but that has not been the trend in recent years. As far as teacher supply and demand is concerned, keep in tune with local, state, and national trends. This area of teachers' welfare is very important, but consider the entire picture before deciding on teaching.

Questions

1. Teachers, like everyone else, have pressures placed on them as they practice their occupation. Discuss some of the pressures alluded to in the chapter and how you might overcome these pressures.
2. Teaching is both an art and a science. Why are both of these aspects important to being a successful teacher?
3. Discuss why the motivation to be an elementary teacher differs from the motivation to be a secondary teacher. Why should these motivating reasons for becoming a teacher be closer together than so far apart for both elementary and secondary teachers?
4. Why are the theories presented in the college classroom often remote from actual practical application? How can you as a student, with the instructor's assistance, overcome this disadvantage?
5. Who was the greatest and most influential role model in your life? Discuss the importance of this favorite role model with other students in the class.
6. Who are some teachers you know who are models of self-confidence? Why are these teachers self-confident?
7. Of the list of stress-producing items on Table 16–1, which one would you currently choose as potentially most stress-producing? Discuss your choice with other members of the class.
8. Myers alludes to the teachers' being at liberty to be himself or herself. How can you best prepare yourself for this challenge?
9. How can one justify being a teacher, considering the current monetary problems? What are greater reasons, other than monetary considerations, for entering the teaching profession?

Activities for Unit IX

1. Being a teacher is a service occupation. Write down as many reasons as you can about why teaching is service-oriented. Similarly, write down the service aspects of another occupation in private industry. Compare the two occupations, and write down three generalizations about your findings.

2. Make a list of ten components that go into the making of an ideal teacher. Be prepared to present to the rest of the class your rationale for choosing the components on your list.

3. When you observe classes, identify as many types of deviant behavior as possible. Write down what you think is the best answer to these deviant behaviors and discuss them with other members of your class.

4. Interview a teacher about what he or she thinks are the benefits of being a teacher. How does he or she feel teachers have been treated monetarily in relation to private-sector fields, and what does he or she think is more important than money? Discuss your interview with the rest of the class.

5. Interview some experienced teachers about the pressures or disappointments they have had in teaching. Ask them how they handled these problems.

6. Arrange with a teacher in the public schools to help plan a home visit, and go on a home visit with her or him. If the home visit cannot be arranged, plan to simulate a visit before the class.

7. Invite outstanding teachers to your class for a panel discussion. Have them share some of their accomplishments as teachers, and then open the discussion up for questions and answers.

References

Adams, E. K. (1982). The fiscal condition of the states. *Phi Delta Kappan, 63,* 598–600.

Advisory Commission on Intergovernmental Relations. (1977). *Significant features of fiscal federalism, 1976–77.* Washington, DC: U.S. Government Printing Office.

Akey, D. S. (Ed.). (1983). *Encyclopedia of Associations,* Vol. 1, (17th ed.). Detroit: Gale Research Company, Book Tower.

Akin, R., Allen, C. I., & Wachter, H. H. (1980). PL94-142 and local district governance. *Educational Leadership, 38,* 120–121.

Amidon, E. J., & Flanders, N. A. (1971). *The role of the teacher in the classroom,* Minneapolis: Paul S. Amidon and Associates, Inc.

Anderson, L. F. (1931). *Pestalozzi.* New York: McGraw-Hill.

Archambault, R. D. (Ed.). (1966). *Dewey on education: Appraisals.* New York: Random House.

Ault, R. L. (1983). *Children's cognitive development.* New York: Oxford University Press.

Ausubel, D. P. (1983). Viewpoints from related disciplines: Human growth and development. In Glenn Hass (Ed.), *Curriculum planning: A new approach,* (pp. 155–163). Boston: Allyn and Bacon.

Bacon, F. (1901). *Novum organum.* New York: Collier and Son. (Originally published in 1620.)

Bailey, W. J. (1975). *Managing self-renewal in secondary education.* Englewood Cliffs, NJ: Educational Technology Publications.

Ballantine, J. H. (1983). *The sociology of education.* Englewood Cliffs, NJ: Prentice-Hall.

Banerjee, S. (Feb.–March 1983). Use and misuse of the media. *World Health,* pp. 18–20.

Banks, J. (1977). *Multiethnic education: Practices and promises.* New York: Longman.

Banks, J. A. (1984). *Teaching strategies for ethnic studies* (3rd ed.). Newton, MA: Allyn and Bacon.

Bash, J. H. (1973). *Effective teaching in the desegregated school.* Fastback No. 32. Bloomington, IN: Phi Delta Kappa Educational Foundation.

Bell, C. A., Casto, G., Daniels, D. S. (1983). Ameliorating the impact of teenage pregnancy on parent and child. *Child Welfare, 62,* 167–173.

Bell, T. H. (1962). *A philosophy of education for the space age.* New York: Exposition Press.

Benham, B. J., Gilsen, P., & Oakes, J. (1980). A study of schooling: Students' experiences in schools. *Phi Delta Kappan, 61,* 337–340.

Bennett, C. (1979). Interracial acceptance in desegregated schools. *Phi Delta Kappan, 60*-(5), 683.

Benson, C. S. (1975). *Educational finance in the coming decade.* Bloomington, IN: Phi Delta Kappa Educational Foundation.

Benson, C. S. (1978). *The economics of public education* (3rd ed.). Boston: Houghton Mifflin.

Bever, S. (1980). *Building a child's self image.* St. Paul: Minnesota Association for Children and Adults with Learning Disabilities.

Black, H. C. (1979). *Black's law dictionary,* (5th ed.). St. Paul: West Publishing Company.

Blau, J., & Blau, P. (1983). The cost of inequality: Metropolitan structure and violent crime. *American Sociological Review, 47,* 114–129.

Bloom, B. S., Engelhart, M. D., Furst, E. J., Hill, W. H., Krathwohl, D. R. (1956). *Taxonomy of educational objectives: Cognitive domain.* New York: Longman.

Bobbitt, F. (1924). *How to make a curriculum.* New York: Houghton Mifflin.

Bordeaux, D. B. (1982). How to get kids to do what's expected of them in the classroom. *Clearing House, 55,* 273–278.

Boyd, W. (1963). *The educational theory of Jean Jacques Rousseau.* New York: Russell and Russell.

Brameld, T. (1965). *Education for the emerging age.* New York: Harper and Row.

Brameld, T. (1956). *Toward a reconstructed philosophy of education.* New York: Dryden Press.

Braun, R.J. (1972). *Teachers and power.* New York: Simon and Schuster.

Brickman, W. (1966). *John Dewey: Master educator.* New York: Atherton Press.

Brodinsky, B. (1976). Twelve major events that shaped America's schools. *Phi Delta Kappan, 58*(1), 68–77.

Brookover, W. B., & Erickson, E. L. (1975). *Sociology of education.* Homewood, IL: Dorsey Press.

Brown v. *Board of Education of Topeka,* 347 U.S. 483 (1954).

Brown, B. F. (1963). *The nongraded high school.* Englewood Cliffs, NJ: Prentice-Hall.

Brown, B. F. (1980). A study of the school needs of children from one-parent families. *Phi Delta Kappan, 61,* 537.

Bullock, C. S., III, & Rogers, H. R., Jr. (1975). *Racial equality in America.* Pacific Palisades, CA: Goodyear Publishing.

Butler, J. D. (1968). *Four philosophies and their practice in education and religion.* New York: Harper and Row.

Butts, R. F. (1955). *A cultural history of Western education.* New York: McGraw-Hill.

Butts, R. F. (1978). *Public education in the United States.* New York: Holt, Rinehart and Winston.

Callahan, J. J. & Wilken, W. H. (1976). State school finance reform in the 1970s. In J. J. Callahan & W. H. Wilkens (Eds.), *School finance reform: A legislators' handbook* (pp. 1–11). Washington, DC: National Conference of State Legislatures.

Callahan, J. J., & Wilken, W. H. (Eds.). (1976). *School finance reform: A legislators' handbook.* Washington, DC: National Conference of State Legislatures.

Campbell, R. F., Cunningham, L. L., Nystrand, R. O., & Usdan, M. D. (1980). *The organization and control of American schools* (4th ed.). Columbus: Charles E. Merrill.

Carroll, S. (1982). The search for equity in school finance. In W. W. McMahon & T. G.

Geske (Eds.), *Financing education: Overcoming inefficiency and inequity* (pp. 237–266). Urbana: University of Illinois Press.

Chapman, S. (1980). NEA seizes power: The teachers' coup. *The New Republic, 183*(15), 9–11.

Child Abuse and Neglect, U.S. Department of Health, Education, and Welfare, Publication No. (OHD) 75-30073, Vol. 1. Washington, DC: Superintendent of Documents, U.S. Government Printing Office.

Cleveland Board of Education v. *LaFleur,* 414 U.S. 632 (1974).

Commager, H. S. (1976). *The people and their schools.* Fastback No. 79. Bloomington, IN: Phi Delta Kappa Educational Foundation.

Coons, J. E. & Sugarman, S. D. (1978). *Education by choice.* Berkeley: University of California Press.

Coorsch, R. (1982). The low down on alcoholism. *Consumer's Research Magazine, 65* (Oct.), 4.

Cortés, C. E. (1983). Multiethnic and global education: Partners for the eighties? *Phi Delta Kappan, 64,* 568–571.

Counts, G. (1932). *Dare the school build a new social order?* New York: John Day.

Cremin, L. A. (1961). *The transformation of the school.* New York: Random House.

Cremin, L. (1970). *American education: The colonial experience, 1607–1783.* New York: Harper.

Cruickshank, D. R., & Broadbent, F. W. (1968). *The simulation and analysis of problems of beginning teachers.* Brockport, NY: New York State University.

Cubberley, E. P. (1934). *Public education in the United States.* New York: Houghton Mifflin.

Dashiell, R. (1982). *Report on the 66th Annual Convention of the American Federation of Teachers.* Washington, DC: National Education Association.

Dedrick, C. V., Hawkes, R. R., & Smith, J. K. (1981). Teacher stress: A descriptive study of the concerns. *National Association of Secondary School Principals Bulletin, 65,* 31–35.

Deibert, J. P., & Walsh, K. J. (1981). Maslow and team organization. *Clearing House, 55,* 169–170.

DeRoche, E. F., & Kujawa, E. (1982). A survey of teacher supply and demand in the West. *Phi Delta Kappan, 63,* 566–567.

Dewey, J. (1916). *Democracy and education.* New York: Free Press (MacMillan).

Dewey, J. (1933). *How we think.* Boston: D. C. Heath.

Dewey, J. (1897). *My pedagogic creed.* New York: Kellogg.

Dewey, J. (1964). The way out of educational confusion. In R. D. Archambault (Ed.), *John Dewey on education* (pp. 422–426). New York: Random House. (Original pamphlet published by Harvard University Press in 1931.)

The digest of public school finance in Indiana: 1981–83 Biennium. (1981). Indianapolis: Indiana Department of Public Instruction, Division of School Finance.

Dixon, M. (1978). *Women in class struggle.* San Francisco: Synthesis Publications.

Doll, R. C. (1978). *Curriculum improvement.* Boston: Allyn and Bacon.

Donley, M. O. (1976). *Power to the teacher.* Bloomington: Indiana University Press.

Donmoyer, R. (1980). Educators and the legislative process. *Educational Leadership, 38,* 128–129.

Doyle, D. P. (1982). Your meager slice of New Federalism could contain delicious options for schools. *The American School Board Journal, 169,* 23–25.

Due, J. (1982). Shifting sources of financing education and the taxpayer revolt. In

W. W. McMahon & T. G. Geske (Eds.), *Financing education: Overcoming inefficiency and inequity* (pp. 267–286). Urbana: University of Illinois Press.

Dupuis, A. M. (1966). *Philosophy of education in historical perspective.* Chicago: Rand McNally.

Durkheim, E. (1897). *Suicide.* New York: Macmillan.

Eaton, W. E. (1975). *The American Federation of Teachers, 1916–1961: A history of the movement.* Carbondale and Edwardsville: Southern Illinois University Press. London and Amsterdam: Feffer and Simons.

Eby, F. (1952). *The development of modern education.* New York: Prentice-Hall.

Edelman, M. W. (1983). 1982 elections—Their implications for families and children in 1983. *Young Child, 38,* 25.

Educational Research Service, Inc. (1985). *Fringe benefits for teachers in public schools, 1984–85.*

Educational Research Service, Inc. (1985). *Scheduled salaries for professional personnel in public schools, 1984–85:* Part 1, *National survey of salaries and wages in public schools.*

Elam, S. M. (1981). The National Education Association: Political powerhouse or paper tiger? *Phi Delta Kappan, 63* 169–174.

Elementary and Secondary Education Act of 1965, 20 U.S.C. 2701.

Erikson, E. (1968). *Identity: Youth and crisis.* New York: Norton.

Fantini, M. D. (1982). Toward a national public policy for urban education. *Phi Delta Kappan, 63,* 545.

Farnham, J. F. (1983). Ethical ambiguity and the teaching of the holocaust. *English Journal, 72,* 67.

Flygare, T. J. (1977). *Collective bargaining in the public schools.* Fastback No. 99. Bloomington, IN: Phi Delta Kappa.

Foxley, C. H. (1979). *Nonsexist counseling: Helping women and men re-define their roles.* Dubuque, IA: Kendall/Hunt.

Fraser, B. G. (1977). *The educator and child abuse.* Chicago: National Committee for Prevention of Child Abuse.

Friedman, M. S. (1953). *Martin Buber, the life of dialogue.* Chicago: University of Chicago Press.

Friedman, M. (1955). The role of government in education. In R. A. Solo (Ed.), *Economics and the public interest* (pp. 127–128). New Brunswick: Rutgers University Press.

Fuhrman, S. (1980). School finance reform in the 1980's. *Educational Leadership, 38,* 122–124.

Garms, W. I., Guthrie, J. W., & Pierce, L. C. (1978). *School finance: The economics and politics of public education.* Englewood Cliffs, NJ: Prentice-Hall.

Geschwind, N. (1982). Why Orton was right. *Annals of Dyslexia, 32,* 13–30.

Gibson, J. T. (1981). *Financing education: An administrative approach.* Washington, DC: University Press of America.

Gil, D. G. (1969). What schools can do about child abuse. *American Education, 5,* 3.

Glasser, W. (1969). *Schools without failure.* New York: Harper & Row.

Global perspective for teacher education. (1983). Washington, DC: American Association of Colleges for Teacher Preparation.

Good, H. S., & Terrer, J. D. (1973). *A history of American education.* New York: Macmillan.

Goodlad, J. I. (1984). *A place called school.* New York: McGraw-Hill.

Gorman, S. F. (1982). Crackdown on drunk driving. *Senior Scholastic, 115,* 8.

Gough, P. (1976). *Sexism: New issue in American education.* Fastback No. 81. Bloomington, IN: Phi Delta Kappa Educational Foundation.

Grady, J. B. (1980). Peer counseling in the middle school: A model program. *Phi Delta Kappan, 61,* 710.

Grant, M. A. (1983). How to desegregate and like it. *Phi Delta Kappan, 63,* 539.

Greuling, J. W., DeBlassie, R. R. (1980). Adolescent suicide. *Adolescence, 15*(Fall), 589–601.

Gruber, F. C. (1973). *Historical and contemporary philosophies of education.* New York: Thomas Y. Crowell.

Gutek, G. L. (1981). *Basic education: A historical perspective.* Bloomington, IN: Phi Delta Kappa Educational Foundation.

Hamberg, B. V. (1980). Peer counseling can identify and help troubled youngsters. *Phi Delta Kappan, 61,* 562.

Harmin, M. (1977). *What I've learned about values education.* Fastback No. 91. Bloomington, IN: Phi Delta Kappa Educational Foundation.

Harmon, S. B. (1983). Teaming: A concept that works. *Phi Delta Kappan, 64,* 366–367.

Harrison School Township v. *Conrad,* 26 IND 337 (1866).

Hartley, H. J. (1981). 1980's education scenario: From tax revolt to governance reform. *Music Educators Journal, 67,* 35–39.

Hass, G. (1983). *Curriculum planning.* Boston: Allyn and Bacon.

Havighurst, R. J. (1948). *Developmental tasks and education.* New York: Longman's, Green.

Hawley, W. D. (1983). Achieving quality integrated education—With or without federal help. *Phi Delta Kappan, 64,* 335–336.

Hedin, D., & Conrad, D. (1980). Changes in children and youth over two decades: The perceptions of teachers. *Phi Delta Kappan, 61,* 703.

Herman, J. J. (1977). *Administrator's practical guide to school finance.* West Nyack, NJ: Parker Publishing.

Hicks, J. D. (1957). *The federal union.* (3rd ed.). Cambridge, MA: Riverside Press.

Hook, S. (1966). John Dewey: His philosophy of education. In R. D. Archambault (Ed.), *Dewey on education: Appraisals* (pp. 127–159). New York: Random House.

How should schools be ruled? (1980). *Educational Leadership, 38,* 102–105.

Hutchins, R. M. (1936). *The higher learning in America.* New Haven, CT: Yale University Press.

Indiana Department of Public Instruction, Division of School Finance. (1981). *Digest of Public School Finance in Indiana: 1981–83 Biennium.* Indianapolis: Indiana Department of Public Instruction.

Inlow, G. (1966). *The emergent in curriculum.* New York: Wiley.

Jacques, M. J. (1982). The Metropolitan Youth Education Center: A Colorado solution to the problem of high school dropouts. *Phi Delta Kappan, 64,* 136–137.

James, W. (1890). *The principles of psychology.* New York: Holt.

James, W. (1898). *Talks to teachers.* New York: Holt.

Jencks, C. (1972). *Inequality.* New York: Basic Books.

Johns, R. L., & Morphet, E. L. (1975). *The economics and financing of education: A systems approach,* (3rd ed.). Englewood Cliffs, NJ: Prentice-Hall.

Johnson, C. (1963). *Old-time schools and school books.* New York: Dover.

Johnson, J., & Benegar, J. (1981). *Global issues in the curriculum grades 5–8.* Boulder, CO: Social Science Education Consortium, Inc., IRIC Clearing House for Social Studies/Social Science Education, Global Perspective in Education.

Kammann, R. (1972). The case for making each school in your district different—and letting parents choose the one that's best for their child. *American School Board Journal 159*, 37–38.

Katz, M. S. (1976). *A history of compulsory education laws.* Bloomington, IN: Phi Delta Kappa Educational Foundation.

Keeshan, B. (1983). Families and television. *Young Child, 38,* 55.

Kemp, J. E. (1977). *Instructional design.* Belmont, CA: Fearon-Pitman Publishers.

Keppel, F., & Messerli, J. (1975). Horace Mann's client. *American Education, 11,* 18–21.

Kilpatrick, W. H. (1925). *Foundations of method.* New York: Macmillan.

Kilpatrick, W. H. (1918). *The project method.* New York: Teachers' College, Columbia University.

Kirst, M. W. (1982). Why there's a financial squeeze on schools and what to do about it. *Learning, 10,* 70–72.

Kirst, M. W., & Garms, W. I. (1980). Public school finance in 1980's. *The Education Digest, 46,* 5–8.

Kneller, G. F. (1971). *Introduction to the philosophy of education.* New York: Wiley.

Kohlberg, L. (1973). The claim to moral adequacy of a highest stage of moral judgment. *Journal of Philosophy, 70,* 630, 646.

Kraushaar, O. F. (1976). *Private schools: From the Puritans to the present.* Bloomington, IN: Phi Delta Kappa Educational Foundation.

Krohne, P. W. (1982). *An analysis of the State Board of Education in Indiana—Its composition, organization, and operation, and areas of jurisdiction.* Unpublished doctoral dissertation, Indiana University, Bloomington.

Lasley, T. J. (1980). Preservice teacher beliefs about teaching. *Journal of Teacher Education, 31,* 38–41.

Lauderdale, W. B. (1981). *Progressive education: Lessons from three schools.* Bloomington, IN: Phi Delta Kappa Educational Foundation.

Leonard, M. (1982). Reaganomics and K–12 education: Some responses from the private sector. *Phi Delta Kappan, 63,* 600–602.

Lindsey, P., & Lindsey, O. (1974). *Breaking the bonds of racism.* Homewood, IL: ETC Publications.

Magnuson, E. (1983). Child abuse: The ultimate betrayal. *Time, 122* (Sept. 5), pp. 20–22.

Maslow, A. H. (1954). *Motivation and personality.* New York: Harper & Row.

Mason, K. (1979). Responsibility for what's on the tube. *Business Week,* No. 2598 (Aug. 13).

McDonald v. *Santa Fe Trail Transportation Co.,* 427 U.S. 273 (1976).

McGrail v. *Detroit Federation of Teachers.*

McIntire, R. G., Hughes, L. W., Say, M. W. (1982). Houston's successful desegregation plan. *Phi Delta Kappan, 63,* 538.

McKenry, P. C., Tishler, C. L., Christman, K. L. (1980). Adolescent suicide and the classroom teacher. *Education Digest, 46,* 43–45.

McLeon v. *State ex rd. Colmer,* 154 Miss. 468 (1929).

McMahon, W. W., & Geske, T. G. (Eds.). (1982). *Financing education: Overcoming inefficiency and inequity.* Urbana: University of Illinois Press.

Meyer, A. E. (1967). *An educational history of the American people,* (2nd ed.). New York: McGraw-Hill.

Meyer, A. E. (1975). *Grandmasters of educational thought.* New York: McGraw-Hill.

Miel, A. & Kiester Jr., E. (1967). *The shortchanged children of suburbia*. New York: American Jewish Committee.

Monroe, P. (1940). *Founding of the American public school system*. New York: Macmillan.

Montagu, A. (1983). My idea of education. In G. Hass (Ed.), *Curriculum planning: A new approach* (pp. 121–123). Boston: Allyn and Bacon.

Moore, M. (1982, March 13). How I killed someone. *Washington Post*, p. 10.

Moorefield, S. (1972). One woman's fight. *American Education, 10*, 30–31.

Mosier v. *Barren County Board of Health*, 215 S.W.2d 967 (1948).

Murphy, E. M. (1983). *The environment to come: A global summary*. Washington, DC: Population Reference Bureau.

Myers, P. E. (1981). The principal and the beginning teacher, *National Association of Secondary School Principals Bulletin, 65,*(444), 70–75.

A Nation at Risk. (1983). Washington, DC: U.S. Department of Education, Superintendent of Documents, U.S. Government Printing Office.

National Center for Education Statistics and Bureau of Labor Statistics. (1980–1981). *Occupational outlook handbook: Teaching occupations*. Washington, DC: U.S. Government Printing Office.

National Center for Education Statistics (1982). *Digest of Education Statistics 1982*. Washington, DC: U.S. Department of Education.

National Education Association. (1970). *Estimates of school statistics, 1970–71*. Washington, DC.

National Education Association. (1979). *Estimates of school statistics, 1979–80*. Washington, DC.

National Education Association. (1983). *Rankings of the states, 1982*. National Education Association Research Memo. Washington, DC.

NEA Handbook. 1984–1985. Washington, DC: National Education Association.

New Jersey, Petitioner v. *T.L.O.*, U.S. Sup. Ct. (1985).

Nunn, G. D. & Parish, T. S. (1982). Personal and familial adjustment as a function of family type. *Phi Delta Kappan, 64*, 141.

Odden, A., & Augenblick, J. (1981). State policy makers view school finance in the 1980's. *The Education Digest, 46*, 13–15.

O'Reilly, J. (1983). New insight into alcoholism. *Time, 121*(Apr. 25), p. 25.

Ornstein, A. C. (1980). Teacher salaries, past, present, future. *Phi Delta Kappan, 61*, 677–679.

Ovando, C. J. (1983). Bilingual/bicultural education: Its legacy and its future. *Phi Delta Kappan, 64*, 564–568.

Overton, B. (1979). The abused or neglected child: How can we help? Speech given to various professional gatherings, Fort Benjamin Harrison Help Center, Indianapolis, IN.

Ozmon, H., & Craver, S. (1972). *Busing: A moral issue*. Fastback No. 7. Bloomington, IN: Phi Delta Kappa Educational Foundation.

Pearson, J. B., & Fuller, E. (Eds.). (1969). *Education in the states: Historical development and outlook*. Washington, DC: National Education Association.

Pestalozzi, J. H. (1894). *How Gertrude teaches her children*. (L. E. Holland, Trans.). Syracuse, NY: George Allen & Unwin. (Original work published 1801.)

Pfeffer, C. R. (1981). Suicidal behavior of children. *Exceptional Children, 48*, 170–172.

Piaget, J. (1957). *John Amos Comenius*. Paris: United Nations Educational, Scientific, and Cultural Organization.

Piaget, J. (1952). Jean Piaget. In C. A. Murchison (Ed.), *A history of psychology in autobiography* (Vol. 4). Worcester, MA: Clark University Press.

Piaget, J. & Inhelder, B. (1969). *The psychology of the child.* New York: Basic Books.

Pinkney, H. B. (1980). American dilemma: Financing public education. *National Association of Secondary School Principals Bulletin, 64*(439) 68–73.

Pipho, C. (1980). State legislatures and the schools. *Educational Leadership, 38,* 125–27.

Pipho, C. (1981). Rich states, poor states. *Phi Delta Kappan, 62,* 722–723.

Plato. (1929). *The republic* (A. D. Lindsay, Trans.). London: J.M. Dent. (Original work written circa 350 B.C.)

Plessy v. *Ferguson,* 163 U.S. 537 (1896).

Preston, D. J. (1980). *Young Frederick Douglass, The Maryland years.* Baltimore: Johns Hopkins University Press.

Progressive education: Lessons from three schools. (1981). Fastback No. 166. Bloomington, IN: Phi Delta Kappa Educational Foundation.

Pursell, W. M. (1976). *A conservative school: The A+ school in Cupertino.* Fastback No. 67. Bloomington, IN: Phi Delta Kappa Educational Foundation.

Quattlebaum, C. A. (1951). *Federal educational activities and educational issues before congress, 3 vols.* Washington, DC: Government Printing Office.

The Random House College Dictionary (rev. ed.). (1980). New York: Random House.

Raths, L., Harmin, M., & Simon, S. (1966). *Values and teaching.* Columbus, OH: Charles E. Merrill.

Raywid, M. A. (1981). The first decade of public school alternatives. *Phi Delta Kappan. 62,* 551–554.

Robertson, N. L., & Robertson, B. T. (1977). *Education in South Africa.* Fastback No. 90. Bloomington, IN: Phi Delta Kappa Educational Foundation.

Rodriquez v. *San Antonio,* Independent School District 337 F. Supp. 280 (1971). (Reversed 411 U.S. 1 [1973].)

Roland, T., & McGuire, C. (1968). The development of intelligent behavior: Jean Piaget. *Psychology in the Schools, 5,* 47–52.

Rosen, F. B. (1968). *Philosophic systems and education.* Columbus: Charles E. Merrill.

Rossi, A. S. (1971). Equality between the sexes: An immodest proposal. In M. H. Garskof (Ed.), *Roles women play: Readings toward women's liberation.* Belmont, CA: Brooks/Cole.

Rousseau, J-J. (1911). *Émile* (B. Foxley, Trans.). London: J. M. Dent. (Original work published 1762.)

Rousseau, J-J. (1913). *The Social Contract* (G.D.H. Cole, Trans.). London: J. M. Dent. (Original work published 1762.)

Rugg, H. O. (1931). *Culture and Education in America.* New York: Harcourt Brace.

Savage, D. G. (1980). Education of a new department. *Educational Leadership, 38,* 117–118.

Scheffler, I. (1966). Educational liberalism and Dewey's philosophy. In R. D. Archambault (Ed.), *Dewey on education: Appraisals* (pp. 96–110). New York: Random House.

Schlemmer, P. (1981). The zoo school. Evolution of an alternative. *Phi Delta Kappan, 62,* 558–560.

School District of Abington Township, PA. v. *Schempp.* 374 U.S. 203 (1963).

The school's role in community life. *Contemporary Education, 53*(3), 123–125. (Reprinted from *School and Community,* October 1964.)

Selden, H. L. (1975). Kalamazoo and high school too. *American Education, 11,* 22–24.

Selden, J. (1975). Learning by the numbers. *American Education, 11,* 25–27.

Serrano v. *Priest,* 5 Cal. 3d 584 (1971).

Shane, H. (1981). Significant writings that have influenced the curriculum: 1906–81. *Phi Delta Kappan, 62,* 311–314.

Smith, A. D., & Reid, W. J. (1982). Family role revolution. *Journal of Educational Social Work, 18,* 51–57.

Smith, E. J. (1981). Adolescent suicide: A growing problem for the school and family. *Urban Education, 16,* 279–296.

Snitzer, H. (1983). A. S. Neill remembered. *Educational Leadership, 41,* 56.

Spencer, H. (1861). *Education: Intellectual, moral, and physical.* New York: Appleton.

Spencer, S. (1979). Childhood's end. *Harper's Magazine, 259,* 16–19.

Steeves, F. L., & English, F. W. (1978). *Secondary curriculum for a changing world.* Columbus: Charles E. Merrill Company.

Strong, G. (1983). It's time to get tough on alcohol and drug abuse in schools. *American School Board Journal, 170,* 23–24.

Subcommittee on Juvenile Justice of the Committee on the Constitution, U.S. Senate, Oversight Hearing to Fashion Programs to Remove the Juvenile from a Crime Cycle, October 22, 1981, Serial No. j-97-70.

Summers, A. (1979). Angels in purgatory: Los Angeles awaits two decisions on mandatory busing for desegregation. *Phi Delta Kappan, 60,* 718–723.

The Supreme Court, the limits that create liberty and the liberty that creates limits. (1964). *Time* (Oct. 9), 48–58.

The teacher and the drug scene. (1973). Fastback No. 26. Bloomington, IN: Phi Delta Kappa Educational Foundation.

Teeter, R. (1983). *The opening up of American education.* Lanham, MD: University Press of America.

Television and behavior: Ten years of scientific progress and implications for the eighties, (1982) Vol. 1. Summary Report, U.S. Department of Health and Human Services, Public Health Service, Alcohol, Drug Abuse, and Mental Health Administration. Washington, DC: Superintendent of Documents, U.S. Government Printing Office.

Terman, L. M., and Childs, H. G. (1912). A tentative revision and extension of the Binet-Simon measuring scale of intelligence. *Journal of Educational Psychology, 3,* 61–74, 133–143, 198–208, 277–289.

Toffler, A. (1970). *Future shock.* New York: Random House.

Toffler, A. (1980). *The third wave.* New York: Morrow.

Trump, J. L. (1968). *Secondary school curriculum improvement.* Boston: Allyn and Bacon.

Tyack, D. B. (1974). *The One Best System.* Cambridge, MA: Harvard University Press.

Tyler, R. W. (1949). *Basic principles of curriculum and instruction.* Chicago: University of Chicago Press.

Tyler, R. W. (1981). The U.S. vs. the world: A comparison of educational performance. *Phi Delta Kappan, 62,* 207–310.

U.S. Bureau of the Census. (1971). *Residential finance survey, 1970.* Washington, DC: U.S. Government Printing Office.

U.S. Bureau of the Census. (1980). *State government tax collections in 1980.* Washington, DC: U.S. Government Printing Office.

U.S. Department of Commerce, Bureau of the Census. (1984). *Statistical Abstract of the United States.* Washington, DC: U.S. Government Printing Office.

U.S. Department of Commerce, Bureau of the Census. (1985). *Statistical Abstract of the United States.* Washington, DC: U.S. Government Printing Office.

U.S. Public Health Service. (1972). *Television and growing up: The impact of televised violence.* Washington, DC: U.S. Government Printing Office.

Valverde, L. A. (1978). *Bilingual education for Latinos.* Washington, DC: Association for Supervision and Curriculum Development.

Violence in schools: Causes and remedies. (1974). Fastback No. 46. Bloomington, IN: Phi Delta Kappa Educational Foundation.

Watson, G. (1961). *What psychology can we trust?* New York: Teacher College Press.

Wesley, E. B. (1957). *NEA: The first hundred years.* New York: Harper and Brothers.

West, A. M. (1980). *The National Education Association: The power base for education.* New York: Free Press (Macmillan).

Whitehead, A. N. (1929). *The aims of education.* New York: Macmillan.

Wiles, J., & Bondi, J. C. (1984). *Curriculum development: A guide to practice.* Columbus: Charles E. Merrill.

Wise, A. E. (1965). Is denial of equal educational opportunity constitutional? *Administrator's Notebook, 13,* 1–4.

Wise, A. E. (1981). School finance reform: A personal statement. *The Educational Forum, 45,* 485–492.

Yankelovich, D. & Kaagan, L. (1979). Two views on Proposition 13: One year later—What it is and what it isn't. *Social Policy, 10,* 19–23.

Appendix

- Dates of Key Educational Events in America
- Code of Ethics of the National Education Association
- Bill of Rights of the American Federation of Teachers
- Special Professional Organizations

Dates of Key Educational Events in America

1607	Jamestown colony founded.
1620	Plymouth colony founded.
1635	Boston Latin Grammar School opened.
1636	Harvard founded.
1642	Massachusetts passed a law requiring compulsory education (not necessarily in schools).
1647	"Old Deluder Satan Act" of Massachusetts called for schools in every town with more than fifty households.
1648	First property tax for support of schools passed in Dedham, Massachusetts.
1690	*New England Primer* first published in Boston, used until 1802.
1693	William and Mary College founded.
1701	Society for the Propagation of the Gospel in Foreign Parts founded to educate slaves and Indians.
1746	Princeton University founded.
1751	Benjamin Franklin's Philadelphia Academy established (private secondary education).
1776	Phi Beta Kappa founded at William and Mary College.
1779	Thomas Jefferson wrote the Bill for More General Diffusion of Knowledge, a plan for free public education for residents of Virginia (not including slaves).
1780	Sunday school movement began in England.
1785	Land Ordinance—Set aside one section of each township to support education in western areas of the country.
1787	Northwest Ordinance—Set aside one section for schools and two townships for a university.
1789	U.S. Constitution adopted.
1794	The first teacher association established—Society of Associated Teachers of New York City.
1797	Monitorial school started in England by Andrew Bell.
1800–1850	Academy movement dominated secondary education.
1805	The New York Free Society formed by DeWitt Clinton.
1818	Monitorial school begun in America.
1819	The *Dartmouth College* case—Established the rights of private schools.
1820s	Infant school societies begun in England were formed in major U.S. cities.
1821	First American high school established in Boston (English Classical School).
1821	Troy Female Seminary opened by Emma Willard to provide secondary education to women.

1825   University of Virginia founded.

1827   Massachusetts required establishment of high schools in cities.

1828   Hartford Seminary opened by Catherine Beecher to educate girls.

1831   *The Cousin Report*—Frenchman Victor Cousin's report on Prussian education.

1834   Pennsylvania passes the Free School Act doing away with pauper schools.

1836   First *McGuffey Reader* printed.

1837   *The Stowe Report*—American report on Prussian education.

1837   Mount Holyoke College for women established by Mary Lyon.

1837   Horace Mann made secretary of the State Board of Education in Massachusetts.

1840   First child labor law enacted in Rhode Island.

1840s–   Horace Mann, "father of public education," reformed the public
1850s   education system of Massachusetts.

1852   Massachusetts passed the first law requiring compulsory school attendance.

1853   New York Free School Society turned over its "schools for the poor" to the city of New York as public schools.

1855   First kindergarten in the United States opened by Mrs. Carl Schurz, conducted in German.

1856   First coeducational high school opened.

1857   National Education Association formed.

1860   First English-speaking kindergarten opened in Boston by Elizabeth Peabody.

1862   Morrill Land-Grant Act endowed land-grant colleges in each state.

1867   Henry Barnard, public school reformer for Connecticut, became first U.S. Commissioner of Education.

1868   Hampton Institute founded by Samuel Chapman Armstrong to educate blacks.

1874   The *Kalamazoo* case established the public high school as a legitimate part of the public school system.

1875   Progressive education movement in the United States begun by Francis Wayland Parker.

1880   Tuskegee Institute founded by Booker T. Washington for education for blacks.

1892   The Committee of Ten of the National Education Association proposed the first organized secondary-school curriculum.

1896   *Plessy* v. *Ferguson*—U.S. Supreme Court upheld the right of railroads to segregate passengers by race—"Separate but equal" doctrine.

1896   University of Chicago laboratory school begun by John Dewey.

1897   First teachers' union formed—Chicago Teachers Federation.

1909   First junior high schools created in Columbus, Ohio, and Berkeley, California.

1914 Smith-Lever Cooperative Agriculture Extension Act—National aid in distribution of information about agriculture and home economics.

1916 American Federation of Teachers formed.

1917 Smith-Hughes Act provided vocational education in schools below the college level.

1919 Progressive Education Association formed in Washington, DC.

1944 G.I. Bill of Rights—Free education for World War II veterans.

1946 National School Lunch Act.

1948 McCollum case—U.S. Supreme Court ruled religious instruction in the public schools to be unconstitutional.

1952 G.I. Bill of Rights extended to veterans of Korea.

1954 *Brown* v. *Board of Education of Topeka*—U.S. Supreme Court ruled that segregated schools are unequal and must be abandoned.

1958 National Defense Education Act provided scholarships for college and graduate students.

1962 U.S. Supreme Court ruled prayer and Bible reading in the public schools to be unconstitutional.

1964 Economic Opportunity Act (EOA)—Set up the Job Corps and Head Start programs.

1964 Civil Rights Act of 1964—gave the U.S. Justice Department powers to enforce desegregation of schools.

1965 The Elementary and Secondary Education Act (ESEA)—Provided federal aid to elementary- and secondary-education programs, especially aimed at aid to poor and minorities.

1966 G.I. Bill of Rights extended to veterans of Vietnam.

1972 Title IX of the Education Amendments made discrimination on the basis of sex illegal.

1974 Family Educational Rights and Privacy Act—Confidentiality of student records.

1975 Education for All Handicapped Children Act—On "mainstreaming" of handicapped children.

1978 *Bakke* case—U.S. Supreme Court ruled against reverse discrimination.

1982 U.S. Supreme Court ruled that the state of Texas must provide public education for children of illegal aliens.

1983 *A Nation at Risk 1983*—Report of the National Commission on Excellence in Education (created in 1981) on the quality of education in the United States.

CODE OF ETHICS
of the Education Profession

ADOPTED BY THE 1975 NEA REPRESENTATIVE ASSEMBLY

Preamble

The educator, believing in the worth and dignity of each human being, recognizes the supreme importance of the pursuit of truth, devotion to excellence, and the nurture of democratic principles. Essential to these goals is the protection of freedom to learn and to teach and the guarantee of equal educational opportunity for all. The educator accepts the responsibility to adhere to the highest ethical standards.

The educator recognizes the magnitude of the responsibility inherent in the teaching process. The desire for the respect and confidence of one's colleagues, of students, of parents, and of the members of the community provides the incentive to attain and maintain the highest possible degree of ethical conduct. The Code of Ethics of the Education Profession indicates the aspiration of all educators and provides standards by which to judge conduct.

The remedies specified by the NEA and/or its affiliates for the violation of any provision of this Code shall be exclusive and no such provision shall be enforceable in any form other than one specifically designated by the NEA or its affiliates.

Principle I—Commitment to the Student

The educator strives to help each student realize his or her potential as a worthy and effective member of society. The educator therefore works to stimulate the spirit of inquiry, the acquisition of knowledge and understanding, and the thoughtful formulation of worthy goals.

In fulfillment of the obligation to the student, the educator—

1. Shall not unreasonably restrain the student from independent action in the pursuit of learning.
2. Shall not unreasonably deny the student access to varying points of view.
3. Shall not deliberately suppress or distort subject matter relevant to the student's progress.
4. Shall make reasonable effort to protect the student from conditions harmful to learning or to health and safety.
5. Shall not intentionally expose the student to embarrassment or disparagement.
6. Shall not on the basis of race, color, creed, sex, national origin, marital status, political or religious beliefs, family, social or cultural background, or sexual orientation, unfairly:
   a. Exclude any student from participation in any program;
   b. Deny benefits to any student;
   c. Grant any advantage to any student.
7. Shall not use professional relationships with students for private advantage.
8. Shall not disclose information about students obtained in the course of professional service, unless disclosure serves a compelling professional purpose or is required by law.

Principle II—Commitment to the Profession

The education profession is vested by the public with a trust and responsibility requiring the highest ideals of professional service.

In the belief that the quality of the services of the education profession directly influences the nation and its citizens, the educator shall exert every effort to raise professional standards, to promote a climate that encourages the exercise of professional judgment, to achieve conditions which attract persons worthy of the trust to careers in education, and to assist in preventing the practice of the profession by unqualified persons.

In fulfillment of the obligation to the profession, the educator—

1. Shall not in an application for a professional position deliberately make a false statement or fail to disclose a material fact related to competency and qualifications.
2. Shall not misrepresent his/her professional qualifications.
3. Shall not assist entry into the profession of a person known to be unqualified in respect to character, education, or other relevant attribute.
4. Shall not knowingly make a false statement concerning the qualifications of a candidate for a professional position.
5. Shall not assist a noneducator in the unauthorized practice of teaching.
6. Shall not disclose information about colleagues obtained in the course of professional service unless disclosure serves a compelling professional purpose or is required by law.
7. Shall not knowingly make false or malicious statements about a colleague.
8. Shall not accept any gratuity, gift, or favor that might impair or appear to influence professional decisions or actions.

American Federation of Teachers
BILL OF RIGHTS

THE TEACHER IS ENTITLED TO A LIFE OF DIGNITY EQUAL TO THE HIGH STANDARD OF SERVICE THAT IS JUSTLY DEMANDED OF THAT PROFESSION. THEREFORE, WE HOLD THESE TRUTHS TO BE SELF-EVIDENT:

I

TEACHERS have the right to think freely and to express themselves openly and without fear. This includes the right to hold views contrary to the majority.

II

THEY SHALL be entitled to the free exercise of their religion. No restraint shall be put upon them in the manner, time or place of their worship.

III

THEY SHALL have the right to take part in social, civil, and political affairs. They shall have the right, outside the classroom, to participate in political campaigns and to hold office. They may assemble peaceably and may petition any government agency, including their employers, for a redress of grievances. They shall have the same freedom in all things as other citizens.

IV

THE RIGHT of teachers to live in places of their own choosing, to be free of restraints in their mode of living and the use of their leisure time shall not be abridged.

V

TEACHING is a profession, the right to practice which is not subject to the surrender of other human rights. No one shall be deprived of professional status, or the right to practice it, or the practice thereof in any particular position, without due process of law.

VI

THE RIGHT of teachers to be secure in their jobs, free from political influence or public clamor, shall be established by law. The right to teach after qualification in the manner prescribed by law, is a property right, based upon the inalienable rights to life, liberty, and the pursuit of happiness.

VII

IN ALL cases affecting the teacher's employment or professional status a full hearing by an impartial tribunal shall be afforded with the right to full judicial review. No teacher shall be deprived of employment or professional status but for specific causes established by law having a clear relation to the competence or qualification to teach, proved by the weight of the evidence. In all such cases the teacher shall enjoy the right to a speedy and public trial, to be informed of the nature and cause of the accusation; to be confronted with the accusing witnesses, to subpoena witnesses and papers, and to the assistance of counsel. No teacher shall be called upon to answer any charge affecting his employment or professional status but upon probable cause, supported by oath or affirmation.

VIII

IT SHALL be the duty of the employer to provide culturally adequate salaries, security in illness and adequate retirement income. The teacher has the right to such a salary as will: a) Afford a family standard of living comparable to that enjoyed by other professional people in the community; b) To make possible freely chosen professional study; c) Afford the opportunity for leisure and recreation common to our heritage.

IX

TEACHERS shall not be required under penalty of reduction of salary to pursue studies beyond those required to obtain professional status. After serving a reasonable probationary period a teacher shall be entitled to permanent tenure terminable only for just cause. They shall be free as in other professions in the use of their own time. They shall not be required to perform extracurricular work against their will or without added compensation.

X

TO EQUIP people for modern life requires the most advanced educational methods. Therefore, the teacher is entitled to good classrooms, adequate teaching materials, teachable class size and administrative protection and assistance in maintaining discipline.

XI

THESE rights are based upon the proposition that the culture of a people can rise only as its teachers improve. A teaching force accorded the highest possible professional dignity is the surest guarantee that blessings of liberty will be preserved. Therefore, the possession of these rights impose the challenge to be worthy of their enjoyment.

XII

SINCE teachers must be free in order to teach freedom, the right to be members of organizations of their own choosing, without coercion or intimidation must be guaranteed. In all matters pertaining to their salaries, fringe benefits, working conditions and other terms and conditions of employment, they shall be entitled to bargain collectively through representatives of their own choosing with their officially designated employers, such negotiations to culminate in a written legal contract.

Special Professional Organizations

The listing of these organizations is arranged by areas of special interest. The two principal general teacher's organizations, the American Federation of Teachers and the National Education Association, are listed at the end.

Curriculum

ASSOCIATION FOR SUPERVISION AND CURRICULUM DEVELOPMENT (ASCD)
225 N. Washington Street   Phone: (703) 549–9110
Alexandria, VA 22314   Gordon Cawelti, Exec. Dir.
Founded: 1921. **Members:** 35,000. **Staff:** 30. **Affiliated Units:** 52. Professional organization supervisors, curriculum coordinators, directors of curriculum, consultants, professors of education, classroom teachers, principals, superintendents, parents, and others interested in school improvement at any level of education: elementary, secondary, college, or adult. **Publications:** (1) *Educational Leadership*, 8/year; (2) *Yearbook*; also publishes *Update* and booklets.

Elementary Education

ASSOCIATION FOR CHILDHOOD EDUCATION INTERNATIONAL (ACEI)
3615 Wisconsin Ave., N.W.   Phone: (202) 363–6963
Washington, DC 20016   James S. Packer, Exec. Dir.
Founded: 1892. **Members:** 11,000. **Staff:** 11. **State Groups:** 36. **Local Groups:** 350. Teachers, parents, and other adults interested in promoting good educational practices for children from infancy through early adolescence. **Publications:** *Childhood Education*, 5/year; also publishes bulletins, *Bibliography of Books for Children*, and portfolio on nursery school and kindergarten.

English

NATIONAL COUNCIL OF TEACHERS OF ENGLISH (NCTE)
1111 Kenyon Road   Phone: (217) 328–3870
Urbana, IL 61801   John C. Maxwell, Exec. Dir.
Founded: 1911. **Members:** 100,000. **Staff:** 100. **State Groups:** 51. **Local Groups:** 89. Teachers of English at all school levels: elementary, secondary, and college. **Publications:** (1) *English Journal*, 9/year; (2) *Language Arts*, 9/year; (3) *College English*, 8/year; (4) *Council-Grams*, 5/year; (5) *College Composition and Communication*, quarterly; (6) *English Education*, quarterly; (7) *Research in the*

Teaching of English, quarterly; (8) *Directory,* annual; also publishes books and pamphlets, issues cassettes and "literary maps."

French

AMERICAN ASSOCIATION OF TEACHERS OF FRENCH (AATF)
57 E. Armory   Phone: (217) 333–2842
Champaign, IL 61820   Fred M. Jenkins, Exec. Sec.
Founded: 1927. **Members:** 10,100. **Local Groups:** 76. Teachers of French in public and private elementary and secondary schools, colleges, and universities. **Publications:** (1) *French Review,* bimonthly (directory included in May issue); (2) *National Bulletin;* (3) *Directory,* annual.

German

AMERICAN ASSOCIATION OF TEACHERS OF GERMAN (AATG)
523 Bldg., Suite 201   Phone: (609) 663–5264
Rt. 38
Cherry Hill, NJ 08034   Robert A. Govier, Exec. Dir.
Founded: 1926. **Members:** 7,600. **Staff:** 5. **Local Groups:** 60. Professional and educational society of teachers of German at all levels. **Publications:** (1) *German Quarterly;* (2) *Newsletter,* quarterly; (3) *Unterrichtspraxis,* semiannual.

Home Economics

AMERICAN HOME ECONOMICS ASSOCIATION (AHEA)
2010 Massachusetts Ave., N.W.   Phone: (202) 862–8300
Washington, DC 20036   Kinsey B. Green, Exec. Dir.
Founded: 1909. **Members:** 40,000. **Staff:** 40. **State Groups:** 52. Professional organization of home economists. **Publications:** (1) *Washington Dateline,* monthly; (2) *Home Economics Research Journal,* quarterly; (3) *Action,* bimonthly; (4) *Journal of Home Economics,* quarterly; (5) *Publications List,* semiannual; also publishes pamphlets, leaflets, reports, and audiovisual materials.

Honorary

PHI DELTA KAPPA
Eighth St. and Union Ave.   Phone: (812) 339–1156
Bloomington, IN 47401   Dr. Lowell C. Rose, Exec. Sec.
Founded: 1906. **Members:** 116,000. **Chapters:** 550. Professional, honorary, and recognition fraternity, education. **Publications:** (1) *Phi Delta Kappan,* monthly; (2) *CEDR Quarterly;* (3) *News, Notes, and Quotes,* quarterly; also publishes *PAR* (Practical Applications of Research) and monographs.

Library

AMERICAN LIBRARY ASSOCIATION (ALA)
50 E. Huron St.   Phone: (312) 944–6780
Chicago, IL 60611   Robert Wedgeworth, Exec. Dir.
Founded: 1876. **Members:** 37,000. **Staff:** 220. **Regional Groups:** 56. Librarians, libraries, trustees, friends of libraries, and others interested in the responsibilities of libraries in the educational, social, and cultural needs of society. Publications: (1) *Booklist,* semimonthly (except August, monthly); (2) *American Libraries,* monthly (except July/August); (3) *Choice,* 11/year; also publishes books and pamphlets.

Mathematics

NATIONAL COUNCIL OF TEACHERS OF MATHEMATICS (NCTM)
1906 Association Dr.   Phone: (703) 620–9840
Reston, VA 22091   Dr. James D. Gates, Exec. Dir.
Founded: 1920. **Members:** 40,000. **Staff:** 45. **State and Local Groups:** 190. Teachers of mathematics in grades K–12, two-year colleges, and teacher education personnel on college campuses. **Publications:** (1) *Arithmetic Teacher,* 9/year; (2) *Mathematics Teacher,* 9/year; (3) *Journal for Research in Mathematics,* 5/year; (4) *News Bulletin,* 5/year; (5) *Yearbook;* also publishes booklets, pamphlets, reprints, and teaching aids.

Music

MUSIC TEACHERS NATIONAL ASSOCIATION (MTNA)
2113 Carew Tower   Phone: (513) 421–1420
Cincinnati, OH 45202   Mariann H. Clinton, Exec. Dir.
Founded: 1876. **Members:** 19,750. **Staff:** 5. **State Groups:** 51. Professional society of music teachers in studios, conservatories, music schools, public and private schools, colleges, universities, and undergraduate and graduate music students. **Publications:** (1) *American Music Teacher Magazine,* 6/year; (2) *Directory of Nationally Certified Teachers,* annual; also publishes national courses of study and books.

Physical Education

AMERICAN ALLIANCE FOR HEALTH, PHYSICAL EDUCATION, RECREATION AND DANCE (AAHPERD)
1900 Association Dr.   Phone: (703) 476–3400
Reston, VA 22091   Robert K. Windsor, Exec. V. Pres.
Founded: 1885. **Members:** 50,000. **Staff:** 54. **State Groups:** 54. **Regional Groups:** 6. Students and educators in physical education, dance, health, athletics, safety education, recreation, and outdoor education. **Publications:** (1)

Journal of Physical Education and Recreation, 9/year; (2) *Update*, 9/year; (3) *Health Education*, 6/year; (4) *Research Quarterly*; (5) *News Kit on Programs for the Aging* (feature of *Update*), semiannual; (6) *Leisure Today*, 2/year; also publishes manuals and handbooks through their Sports Library for Girls and Women.

Reading

INTERNATIONAL READING ASSOCIATION (IRA)
P.O. Box 8139   Phone: (302) 731–1600
800 Barksdale Rd.
Newark, DE 19711   Ralph C. Staiger, Exec. Dir.
Founded: 1956. **Members:** 61,000. **Staff:** 80. **Local Groups:** 1,100. Individuals engaged in the teaching or supervising of reading at any school level. **Publications:** (1) *Journal of Reading*, 8/year; (2) *Reading Teacher*, 8/year; (3) *Reading Today*, 8/year; (4) *Lectura y Vida*, quarterly; (5) *Reading Research*, quarterly; also publishes books and monographs (10–20/year).

Science

NATIONAL ASSOCIATION OF BIOLOGY TEACHERS (NABT)
11250 Roger Bacon Dr.   Phone: (703) 471–1134
Reston, VA 22090   Dr. Wayne A. Moyer, Exec. Dir.
Founded: 1938. **Members:** 6,000. **Staff:** 7. Professional society of biology teachers and others interested in teaching of biology at secondary and college levels. **Publications:** (1) *American Biology Teacher*, 9/year; (2) *News & Views*, bimonthly.

NATIONAL SCIENCE TEACHERS ASSOCIATION (NSTA)
1742 Connecticut Ave., N.W.   Phone: (202) 328–5800
Washington, DC 20009   Bill G. Aldredge, Exec. Dir.
Founded: 1895. **Members:** 42,000. **Staff:** 40. Teachers "seeking to foster excellence in the whole of science teaching." **Publications:** (1) *The Science Teacher*, 9/year; (2) *Science and Children*, 8/year; (3) *Energy and Education Newsletter*, bimonthly; (4) *Journal of College Science Teaching*, 6/year; (5) Bulletin, 3/year; also publishes curriculum development and professional materials, teaching aids, career booklets, and audiovisual aids.

Social Studies

NATIONAL COUNCIL FOR THE SOCIAL STUDIES (NCSS)
3615 Wisconsin Ave., N.W.   Phone: (202) 966–7840
Washington, DC 20016   Elizabeth Scott, Acting Dir.
Founded: 1921. **Members:** 17,000. **Staff:** 12. **State Groups:** 46. **Local Groups:** 109. Teachers of social studies, including civics, geography, history, and political science. **Publications:** (1) *Social Education*, 7/year; (2) *newsletter*, 5/year; (3) *Bulletins*, 3/year.

Spanish

AMERICAN ASSOCIATION OF TEACHERS OF SPANISH AND PORTU-
GUESE (AATSP)
Holy Cross College   Phone: (617) 832–3779
Worcester, MA 01610   Richard B. Klein, Exec. Dir.
Founded: 1917. **Members:** 14,500. **Local Groups:** 71. Teachers of Spanish and
Portuguese languages and literature and others interested in Hispanic cul-
ture. **Publications:** (1) *Hispania,* quarterly; (2) *Directory,* annual.

Special Education

AMERICAN ASSOCIATION OF MENTAL DEFICIENCY (Mental Retardation) (AAMD)
5101 Wisconsin Ave., N.W.   Phone: (202) 686–5400
Washington, DC 20016   Dr. Albert J. Berkowitz, Exec. Dir.
Founded: 1876. **Members:** 13,000. **Staff:** 17. **Regional Groups:** 10. Physicians,
educators, administrators, social workers, psychologists, psychiatrists, students, and others interested in the general welfare of mentally retarded persons and the study of causes, treatment, and prevention of mental retardation. **Publications:** (1) *American Journal of Mental Deficiency,* bimonthly; (2)
Mental Retardation, bimonthly; also publishes a manual on terminology and
classification in mental retardation, a monograph series, and testing materials.

COUNCIL FOR EXCEPTIONAL CHILDREN (Special Education) (CEC)
1920 Association Dr.   Phone: (703) 620–3660
Reston, VA 22091   Jeptha V. Greer, Exec. Dir.
Founded: 1922. **Members:** 62,000. **Staff:** 89. **State and Provincial Groups:** 55.
Local Groups: 1,000. Teachers, school administrators, teacher educators, and
others with a direct or indirect concern in the education of handicapped and
gifted, defined as "those children and youth whose instructional needs differ
sufficiently from the average to require special services and teachers with
specialized qualifications." **Publications:** (1) *Update,* 8/year; (2) *Exceptional
Children,* 6/year; (4) *Exceptional Child Education Resources,* quarterly; also publishes reprints, produces microfilms, films, books, and other material relevant
to teaching exceptional children.

General Teacher's Organizations

AMERICAN FEDERATION OF TEACHERS (AFT)
11 Dupont Circle, N.W.   Phone: (202) 797–4400
Washington, DC 20036   Albert Shanker, Pres.
Founded: 1916. **Members:** 580,000. **Locals:** 2,100. AFL-CIO. Promotes collective bargaining for teachers and other educational employees. **Publications:**

(1) *American Teacher*, monthly (September–May); (2) *American Educator*, quarterly.

NATIONAL EDUCATION ASSOCIATION (Teachers) (NEA)
1201 16th St., N.W.   Phone: (202) 833–4000
Washington, DC 20036   Don Cameron, Exec. Dir.
Founded: 1857. **Members:** 1,600,800. **Staff:** 600. **State Groups:** 53. **Local Groups:** 10,000. Professional organization and union of elementary- and secondary-school teachers, college and university professors, administrators, principals, counselors, and others concerned with education. **Publications:** (1) *Reporter*, 8/year; (2) *Today's Education*, quarterly; (3) *Handbook*, annual.

Source: Denise S. Akey (Ed.), *Encyclopedia of Associations.* (Detroit: Gale Research Company, 1983).

Index